Reason's Tribunal

Exposing God's Word to End the Nightmare of Religion

Kevin Vincent Kelly

Copyright © 2023 Kevin Vincent Kelly

All rights reserved. No part of this book may be reproduced or transmitted in any form or by any means, electronic or mechanical, including photocopying, recording or by any information storage and retrieval system without permission in writing from the publisher.

Title: *Reason's Tribunal: Exposing God's Word to End the Nightmare of Religion*
Author: Kevin Vincent Kelly
Digital distribution | 2023
Paperback | 2023

Due to widespread religious imposition, I am obliged to give the completion date of this book, *Reason's Tribunal,* as 2023 A.D. ("After the Deception")! The starting date of our present calendar is based solely upon the imposture of two perjurers (*Matthew, Luke*) telling us that a Jewish girl had given birth to God, aka Jesus Christ, after she was spiritually impregnated by another God-pretender, 2023 years ago----events that, surprisingly, the Jews of "Judeo-Christian" fame totally reject and refuse to accept as the starting point of their calendar because it is their claim that their God, Jehovah, like Allah, never fathered a child---Jews and Muslims consider Jesus to be a God-imposter. According to the "inerrant" and "infallible" *Old Testament* chronology of everything Jewish, the world was created in 3761 B.C. (on April 1st no doubt)! It would be scripturally accurate, therefore, to state that this book, *Reason's Tribunal,* was completed in the year 5784 A.B.C. ("After the Bogus Creation") ---(3761 + 2023 = 5784)! I contend, however, that the world was created sometime closer to 3800 B.C. ("Before the Conniving") give or take a few years which is certainly enough *Bible*-time to account for the coming and going of dinosaurs! If you, today's educated folks, don't believe the world is 5784 years old, or thereabouts---if you don't believe the Word of God in this matter, what the hell does that make you?

Epigraph

-IN REASON WE TRUST-

Fix reason firmly in her seat, and call to her tribunal every fact, every opinion. Question with boldness even the existence of a god; because if there be one, he must more approve of the homage of reason, than that of blindfolded fear.

—Thomas Jefferson

-IN TRUTH WE PREVAIL-

Soon after I had published the pamphlet "Common Sense," in America, I saw the exceeding probability that a revolution in the system of government would be followed by a revolution in the system of religion . . . certain, as I am, that when opinions are free, either in matters of government or religion, truth will finally and powerfully prevail.

—Thomas Paine

A Tribute to
the Caretakers of Liberty

CHERISH AMERICA
AND HER HARD-WON FREEDOMS

--- THEY CAME AT A HIGH PRICE ---

CHERISH THE NOBLE PATRIOTS
WHO STRUGGLED AND SACRIFICED
TO ACQUIRE THEM

--- THEY PAID A HIGH PRICE ---

CHERISH OUR BRAVE MILITARY
AND ALL OTHERS
WHO PROTECT AND DEFEND
"LIFE, LIBERTY AND THE PURSUIT OF HAPPINESS"

--- THEY ARE PRICELESS ---

. . . . . .

A Secular
Pledge of Allegiance

I will uphold and defend America's cherished ideals and her hard-won freedoms. I will support her valiant efforts to establish justice, equality, and the peaceful pursuit of happiness in the name of reason, truth, and fairness. I will pay tribute to her noble Patriots who have given us this day to enjoy our daily bread. I will fulfill these, my honorable duties as an American, with utmost gratitude. I pledge my allegiance to America and to her Caretakers of Liberty.

A Thought to Consider

If, one assumes, that American journalism aspires to be fair and balanced in its reporting, why do televised and printed news media, in a nation that honors and protects free-speech, not allow for any fact-based criticism to be made against the *Bible* and *Bible*-based religions (Judaism, Christianity, Islam) when every other topic is fair game for media-scrutiny? Why is the *Bible* placed on a pedestal and considered off-limits to investigation and allowed to get a free-pass on any bold questioning of its parts? Why do America's news media allow time and space to be given (free-of-charge at times) to promote religion and only "certain" parts of the *Bible* but not other parts that would reveal the *Bible's* lack of authority, its malevolence, its divisiveness that separates people into "us" and "them," ---its role in establishing slavery, terrorism, and civil unrest, etc.?---why do they never allow for the rest of the story to be told about this less-than-sacred book? ---sounds very un-American to me!

As there are always two sides to a story, everyone needs to hear them both especially because of the impact the *Bible* has over our lives and our affairs of State. ***"We the people"*** have a right to know and to express our thoughts about why American journalism is so one-sided on this matter? Therefore, for God's sake, <u>DO NOT READ THIS BOOK</u> if you want to continue to believe in the existence of Semitic Deities---if you want to continue to believe that the *Bible* and the *Koran* are sacred books containing nothing but the truth---if you want to continue to believe that the God they reveal to us is a loving, compassionate, and merciful God---if you want to continue to believe in the kindergarten tales about a talking snake and magic fruit, a talking ass and magic wands---if you want to continue to believe. . . .

---Kevin Vincent Kelly

Nothing has been left undone by the enemies of freedom. Every art and artifice, every cruelty and outrage has been practiced and perpetrated to destroy the rights of man. In this great struggle every crime has been rewarded and every virtue has been punished. Reading, writing, thinking, and investigating have all been crimes. Every science has been an outcast . . . Let us thank every good and noble man who stood so grandly, so proudly, in spite of opposition, of hatred and death, for what he believed to be the truth . . . If there is no God, certainly we should not bow and cringe and crawl. If there is a God, there should be no slaves.

---Robert G. Ingersoll, *The Liberty of Man, Woman, and Child*

Religion shackles the mind more securely than did the iron chains used to keep people in physical bondage. Because those who possess religious beliefs become slaves to them, the imperceptible chains that hold people in mental servitude to the *Bible* have yet to be recognized, condemned, broken, and done away with in a freedom-loving land. Sadly, only the *Bible*-sanctioned practice of physical enslavement has been abolished in America. It is only when body and mind have been liberated will anyone be able to experience what it is to be *"free at last"*! ---kvk

To help prevent stumbling around in darkness, light a candle. For greater effect, light a torch! ---kvk

Note To Reader

Bold lettering has been used in this book for the page headings, for intros, and to designate the **bold words** of the tyranny-opposing founders of America, (Jefferson, Paine, John Adams, Washington, Franklin, Madison, Ethan Allen) who knew well the evils of Judeo-Christianity and who had the courage to denounce them. Some, like the author of *The Age of Reason,* Thomas Paine, much moreso than others. All of these men aided America in her struggle to achieve her liberty and her independence from England, some, like the author of *Common Sense, The Rights of Man,* and *The Crisis* papers, Thomas Paine, much moreso than others. They all, however, regardless of any shameful, not-so-enlightened, personal shortcomings several of these founders possessed in regards to their involvement in the *Bible*-sanctioned, Christian-controlled practice of human bondage---deserve recognition, none the less, for their noble achievements---some much moreso than others.

Slave-owners could point to the *Bible* and its God for their justification of slavery---the very same *Bible,* the very same God that slaves and their descendants, for some bewildering reason, have always relied upon to find their salvation from this egregious God-sponsored practice and its enduring racial bigotries---*"Praise the Lord"*! ---really? ---praise someone who caused your ancestors" enslavement and many of the continuing troubles people of color face on a daily basis! Obviously, it helps to be selective in choosing which words written in the *Bible* are to be believed, which words are not to be believed, and which words should be overlooked or abandoned altogether!

The fair and balanced scrutiny and bold questioning of Reason's Tribunal (the process) will reveal the ***"facts and evidence"*** that will prove, beyond any doubt, that the *Bible* and the *Koran*, both of which have been imposed upon the world as being the "inspired" Word of God by their advocates, are entirely fictional works written by anonymous "script-writers" and are based upon more ancient works of fiction known as mythology.

If it is assumed that the *Bible*-writers tell us only the "truth" about their experiences with God, what need had they for "inspiration" to reveal it? If, however, they tell us "lies" and pass along "hearsay" evidence to us, the need for inspiration becomes quite obvious---the need for lubricant a necessity! The factual, truthful "revelations" of Reason's Tribunal when brought to the world's attention, will begin to expose the fraudulence and the deception of all "revealed" Semitic scriptures, even to those folks in the Middle East who because of "inspired" intimidation are still unable to harbor or to voice any doubts about their Islamic religion or to free themselves from its many stifling impositions.

Reason's Tribunal is the only sane way to neutralize the destructive potential of all Semitic scriptures and the smug supremacist-mindedness that their words (the *Bible* and the *Koran*) instill in their billions of beguiled, mindless believers---you can confirm this by simply asking a Jew, a Christian, or a Muslim if their religion differs from the others and if their religion is better than the others——both questions would obviously be answered in the affirmative---which, obviously, results in each one thinking that they and their religious beliefs are better than everyone else's religious beliefs---which, obviously, results in smug and supremacist attitudes on everyone's part who call themselves a Jew, a Christian, a Muslim!

Surely, it is because of their blind devotion to Semitic scripture that generates and proliferates the "us" and "them" mentality that continually manifests itself in racist, homophobic, xenophobic behavior, civil unrest, civil rights violations, and foreign/domestic terrorism—a devotion that tears at the heart of America and constantly retards advancement in the human condition around the globe—a devotion that now threatens to destroy civilization in the name of God. Such supremacist attitudes (fostered by clergy and promoted by family, friends, TV, internet, etc.) also play a significant role in influencing and inspiring the mentally disturbed to target certain peoples and commit acts of atrocity against "them"!

It is important to remember that religious beliefs persist only because so many folks want to believe that after their death and the death of their loved ones, they will be magically reconnected with all of them in a heavenly wonderland and together they will all live on happily ever after and religion provides the magical means and, hence, the consoling comfort that comes from such wishful thinking---and Semitic religions' script-writers knew well how to profit from imposing upon and taking advantage of human weaknesses and human longings---how to profit from imposing upon and taking advantage of vulnerable hearts and minds!

Since "reason" and "truth" have the wonderful and amazing potential to uncover the ***"errors"*** of religion and thus set us free from them, we must begin to utilize their enlightening gifts where they are most urgently needed and most useful. The pandemic disease of religion, of which 9/11 is just a symptom, is totally preventable---thankfully, a vanquishing vaccine has finally been made available!

As I am a carpenter by trade and not a writer, I apologize for this book's many literary long and short-comings which include, but are not limited to beginning *Reason's Tribunal* (the book) with a long introduction and chapter-less pages, with its numerous digressions, with its many redundancies, its many alliterations, its lack of footnotes, its occasional disjointed accounts, its long sentences, and its many many exclamation points! —bear with me—it's not an ordinary book in style but it's worth the read---besides, I had good reason to write it in this way.

I did consider doing a total rehab of *RT* to make needed improvements, but time and circumstance won't allow for it to be done. Besides, (and more importantly) since it was God who inspired me (like He had done to so many others in the long-ago past) to write the words in this book in the exact way He "revealed" them to me, it would surely be a sin to change any part of this work for who am I to defy and deny God and write down something that He didn't actually say to me? ---or write down something He didn't want me to mention or write down something without utilizing the exact punctuation He insisted I use? ---do you think I want to incur God's eternal wrath? ---Hell no! ---for, surely, God knows what He's doing and I, like so much of the world, just blindly follow His instructions!

As you read this book, you'll become aware that God has some annoying mental-issues and tends to zone-out and/or have senior moments. If you've had an intra-cranial chat with Him recently, you'll know what the hell I'm talking about. He is experiencing problems with recall and tends to repeat Himself constantly and I, not wanting to piss Him off, was obliged to record His words the way He had inspired me to write them down. The only thing you can do on your part is to be kind and understanding and for that, we both thank you!

It should become apparent as you continue to read this book that God has made several changes (some drastic!) to the old literary style that He used in the *Old Testament* and the *New Testament* of long ago! It is hoped, therefore, that you, the reader of this divinely inspired book, *Reason's Tribunal*, will accept its God-given, literary changes in the way that He purposely "revealed" His "Latest Word" to me and forgive us our, seemingly, many trespasses in this regard. However, unlike the revered *Bible* and the *Koran*, this book, *Reason's Tribunal*, does not call for the death of anyone---nor does it call for the committing of atrocity---nor does it call for brutal acts of violence to be carried out against certain folks---

behaviors that are highly approved and proudly promoted in blessed Semitic scripture!

It should be apparent, too, to everyone who has tried to read the *Bible* and the *Koran,* that God lacks the proficiency to communicate His "Word" in a perfect, easy to understand, consistent, unchanging manner to all of His various fan clubs for the Semitic *Bible* and the Semitic *Koran* contain quite different messages for Semites and Semites only---sorry, Big Guy, but the truth is the truth after all! Surely, for the reason stated above, I needn't have to constantly remind you of this book's inerrancy and infallibility---just like the *Bible's* inerrancy and infallibility---just like the *Koran's* inerrancy and infallibility! It is further hoped that this "as is" book will enlighten you, entertain you, and, unlike the doomy, gloomy, cheerless nature of Semitic scripture that is cause for so much misery, suffering, and violence in the world---put an occasional smile on your face and/or make you LOL or SIS (snicker in silence).

I do not apologize, however, for the irreverence shown to Semitic scripture in this book, for the *Bible* and the *Koran* are the most uber-irreverent books ever written, for what could be more irreverent than their "anonymous" writers telling us that their God, whom everyone is supposed to love, worship, adore, and praise, is, in so many words, a blood-loving, maniacal mass-murderer, a despiser of non-Jews, a sinister purveyor of plagues and pestilence, a slavery-establisher/slavery-promoter, a shameful, insentient animal abuser, and an encourager and condoner of child-rape---just to name a few of His many less-than-sacred activities and holy hobbies.

The "scripted" words of the many "unknown" authors that fill the *Bible* and the *Koran* have been imposed upon us to swallow whole without question and without having any doubt whatsoever about all of the unbelievable claims contained in both books---imposed upon us to believe that their fabricated words spoken by their fabricated God are the only guiding light, the only beacon of hope for all of the oppressed peoples of the world when, in reality, they so often guide and inspire their oppressed, imposed-upon believers, to further "oppress" and "impose" upon others and to commit deadly atrocities in God's name---sick stuff, folks!

Working lifelong as a carpenter, however, I know the importance of using the right tool for the job and in keeping things on the level and square. Reason's Tribunal is the right tool for the job of "revealing" Semitic scriptures in an effort to improve the lives of everyone, now and in the future. It is not a job, however, that one person can accomplish---I'll need to hire several helpers to work overtime, weekends and holidays, to complete this most important of projects---just kidding!

May this book inspire you enough to want to scrutinize your own indoctrinated, entrenched religious beliefs (surely, you have them---surely, you have "some" questions about them, too!) and enable you to enjoy your ***"Life,"*** your ***"Liberty"*** and your ***"pursuit of Happiness"*** the way America's freedom-loving founders intended—in defiance of those who would impose their tyrannies and their pious pathologies on everyone— pathological endeavors that are deceivingly disguised as being decreed from Almighty God, but which are nothing more than devious deceptions designed by master-minded despots to control our entire lives from birth to death and even beyond.

It is hoped, therefore, that you "will" be tempted to take a bite of the enlightening fruit of "the tree of reason and truth" and, as a result, treasure always the priceless freedoms we enjoy as Americans and never take them for granted or allow any *Bible* or *Koran*-inspired, religious mindset to diminish or destroy them in any way. ***"Life, Liberty and the pursuit of Happiness"*** are the strived-for ideals that make America a great nation--- we will make America a "good" nation, too, when we stop depriving some of our neighbors (whom Jews and Christians are under contract to love!) of these ideals we hold so dear---ideals that are cherished enough by Americans to live and to die for.

Begin your own personal version of Reason's Tribunal---let "reason" and "truth" work their incredible magic to set you free from your mindless devotion to bogus Semitic scriptures and their bogus Semitic deity---let "reason" and "truth" allow you to realize how your revered, long-held, Judeo-Christian religious beliefs are tied to the unspeakable horrors of our times---let "reason" and "truth" enlighten you and, in doing so, inspire you to become a Caretaker of Liberty.

Our religious beliefs should never, in any way, shape, or form, be adding to the miseries of this world---they should never, in any way, shape or form, be a nano-part of any endeavors that cause blood to be shed in the name of God or in His defense which, much much too often, they are responsible for doing. As you read this book and, perhaps, recognize the need to question your own long-held, religious beliefs in order to improve living conditions on our planet, remember that you may not have the power to change the world in a profound way, but you do have the power to change yourself, your thinking, and your God-beliefs, which is how profound change begins, evolves, and becomes manifest in the world---one drop of water, obviously, cannot fill a tall glass---that requires several drops---but each drop is of consequence---each drop is necessary to fill it. The Grand Canyon is a grand example of what can happen when one drop of water goes viral!

Reason's Tribunal (the book) will not attempt to establish or try to convince you of the existence or non-existence of a God or attempt to describe to you what he, she, or it is, or what he, she, or it might be---it will establish, however, what God is "not"---it will establish and, it is hoped, convince you of the non-existence of Jehovah, Jesus, and Allah, the man-created Gods of Semitic scriptures---it will establish and, it is hoped, convince you that all Semitic religions and their "Word" of God are bogus---that the *Bible* and the *Koran,* along with their scripted God(s), are completely lacking in decency and spiritual dimension---that they and their "sacred revelations" should be exposed as the frauds they are---that they should be held accountable for their imposed mental tyrannies and their never-ending inspiration for Jews, Christians, and Muslims to commit atrocities in the name of God.

---Kevin Vincent Kelly

PS: No doubt, this book will be viewed as the work of a racist-minded bigot---a Jew-hater, a Muslim-hater, and a Christian-hater---because I have the God-damned audacity to ***"question with boldness"*** the *Bible* and the *Koran* which are the revered, hands-off, holy books of Semites and Christians. It is neither the Jewish people, the Muslim people, nor the Christian people that I take issue with, nor do I, in any way, shape, or form condone acts of violence, harm, or harassment being taken against anyone because of their religion or their ethnicity---it is only the wickedness and the malevolence contained in their "sacred" scriptures that I abhor because their words promote and inspire their devout readers to believe that they are better than others because of their "us" and "them" religious beliefs---beliefs that naturally result in supremacist-thinking on the part of the holder of them---beliefs that constantly hinder racial and gender harmonies to exist in America and beyond---beliefs that much too often cause otherwise good people to indulge in brutal works of atrocity in order to please their blood-loving, vengeful God.

Surely, these things are reason enough for subjecting both books to the fair and balanced scrutiny of all who desire to make the world a safer and saner place for everyone. Jews, Christians, and Muslims should never be opposed to a thorough investigation of their sacred scriptures unless, of course, they have something to hide---they should never be opposed to a thorough investigation of their scriptures that is conducted with fairness—an investigation where reason and truth are allowed to present their findings.

(A NOTE TO READER: If the *Bible's* facts and evidence I've presented in this book should prove to be different than what others have read and deduced, then apparently, I or they have misinterpreted the facts and the evidence the *Bible* has provided. Obviously then, the *Bible* was not written in a perfect way to be perfectly understood in the very same perfect way by its every reader. No one, I repeat, "no one" should read a "perfectly-written" book and come away having a different understanding than what others have concluded from reading the same *Bible*-texts---no one! ---kvk)

I Dedicate this Book to Thomas Paine

Without the pen of Paine, the sword of Washington would have been wielded in vain.

     ---Joel Barlow, diplomat and friend of Thomas Paine

Thomas Paine's Common Sense, more than any other single piece of writing, set Americans to thinking of the possibility and desirability of an independent place among the nations.

     ---Evarts B. Greene, *The Revolutionary Generation*

"These are the times that try men's souls," rang out like a bugle and heartened the little band of patriots left with Washington. The soldiers who heard the words of Paine's great document—Washington ordered it read to his men—were inspired to face the floes, a blizzard and the swift current of the Delaware River on Christmas Eve and achieve the victory at Trenton which gave the Americans new courage.

     ---Philip S. Foner in his introduction to *The Age of Reason*

The most detestable wickedness, the most horrid cruelties, and the greatest miseries that have afflicted the human race have had their origin in this thing called revelation, or revealed religion. ...Of all the tyrannies that affect mankind, tyranny in religion is the worst; every other species of tyranny is limited to the world we live in; but this attempts to stride beyond the grave, and seeks to pursue us into eternity.

     ---Thomas Paine, *The Age of Reason*

Reason's Tribunal, the book, and Reason's Tribunal, the process, are a clarion call for folks everywhere to engage in a personal and/or a public, bold scrutinization of the *"facts and evidence"* dealing with Semitic religions. This book is dedicated to all Lovers and Defenders of Liberty throughout the ages, especially Thomas Paine, America's long-forgotten, long-disregarded founding father. His eloquent, inspired and inspiring words rallied an imposed-upon nation and General Washington's demoralized and retreating Patriot army during their darkest hour to overcome their seemingly hopeless situation and inevitable defeat by a seemingly invincible enemy. For this and many other exemplary efforts pitted against tyranny and injustice such as his early-on condemnation of slavery, his denouncement of the less-than-equal treatment of women, and his criticism of animal cruelty, Mr. Paine received little grateful recognition from his countrymen and from his country which, to this day, has denied him the credit and the tribute he had so nobly and rightfully earned—a man who never enriched himself by his patriotism or his by political activities— a man who gave generously of the little wealth he had accumulated to aid the cause of Liberty.

Instead of receiving acclaim for his accomplishments, he was slandered and vilified simply because of his efforts to reveal in his liberating book, *The Age of Reason*, the self-evident truths that exposed the fraudulence and the lack of authority of Semitic religions founded upon the deceptive invention of so-called "revealed" scriptures. For his courageous endeavors meant to enlighten us and to enable us to remove the mental shackles of the imposed, uncontested beliefs of Judaism and Christianity—from which Islam is rooted—he was ostracized and denounced as being a despicable social outcast. Sadly, Mr. Paine, because your words fell mostly on ears deafened by centuries of religious indoctrination, the present times, too, have again become times *"that try men's souls"* —the result of malicious, scripture-generated events waged in the name of God that have continued to occur since biblical times to shock and imperil the world with their brutality and utter disregard for the sanctity of mankind's *"unalienable rights."*

Perhaps, Mr. Paine, because the malevolence inherent in Semitic religions is presently engaged in crippling our nation from within---by xenophobic advocates of Judeo-Christianity who foment racial hatred, social inequality, and injustice against others (mostly people of color) by advocates of Judeo-Christianity who promote sexual inequality against women and homosexuals---by advocates of Judeo-Christianity who inspire and encourage the bigotries inherent in the mindset of white-supremacists—and from without---by advocates of Islam who are attempting to eradicate every trace of human progress in the world.

Americans may now want to listen to your ***"facts and evidence"*** and begin to read and heed the reasonable words you've written in *The Age of Reason*—words intended to educate and enlighten us about the cold-blooded realities and the non-sacred ramifications of belief in scripted religions—words intended by Thomas Paine to free mankind from the greatest tyranny that has ever existed.

Perhaps, Mr. Paine, with the liberating tools you have provided us upon your penned pages, freedom-loving people everywhere will rally once again to your liberty-inspired genius and attempt ***"to begin the world over"*** without the ever-present threat of scripture-inspired madness. Perhaps, Mr. Paine, they will begin to pay you the respect, the gratitude, and the honor you abundantly deserve and make amends for your final years having been spent in poverty and for the disgrace of having your tombstone desecrated and your grave plundered. Perhaps, Mr. Paine, a grateful nation will, at last, thank you and honor you with an enduring memorial or a day on the calendar dedicated to your memory---a tribute befitting a Valiant Veteran and Noble Patriot—a Generous Benefactor and Emancipator—a Savior of America and Liberator of the Oppressed—an Honorable World-Changer and above all else—an Exemplary Caretaker of Liberty!

> *Paine's writings inspired men of his day in America, in England and in France to live and die for freedom, and left behind in these countries a vision of a world of men free in body and mind. At a time when men and women are seeking to realize that type of world it would be well to read again the words of Thomas Paine who wrote so much and so well to build the heritage of freedom.*

> ---Philip S. Foner in his introduction to *The Age of Reason*

An Earnest Request or Two

The Bible is a book that has been read more and examined less than any book that ever existed.

---Thomas Paine

Religious beliefs are ideas like any other, though they are defended more fervently and can often seem immune to reasoned argument. ...Christian nationalism has succeeded in part because of Americans' ingrained unwillingness to offend religious sensibilities. ...criticism of religion is the true beginning of freedom. ...True religious freedom comes only when state and church are completely separate, when the government has no power over the human mind at all, neither to prohibit nor to allow thought.

---Andrew Seidel, *The Founding Myth*

With or without it (religion) *you would have good people doing good things and evil people doing evil things. But for good people to do evil things, that takes religion.*

---Steven Weinberg

It's not as if religion hasn't been given every chance, throughout the ages, to improve the world---how's that been workin' out? ---kvk

Since the treasured (un-American!) Judeo-Christian tradition and principle that punishes the innocent for another person's "sin" is not yet deemed "despicable" in a land of *"liberty and justice for all"* ---since it is still considered a worship-worthy practice (in America and elsewhere) to promote the death of Jesus as an honorable, sacred "atonement" for the "disobedience" of Adam---since every man, woman, child, and animal on the planet stands wrongly accused and accursed by a so-called "loving" and "just" God for a mythical man's mythical transgression of eating the mythical fruit of the mythical *"tree of knowledge of good and evil,"* then we, the non-mythical scapegoats who are being punished for something we didn't do---(sounds very un-American to me!)---should, at least, begin to make some "liberating lemonade" from the bitter-tasting fruit we've been beguilingly tempted to consume from the low-hanging branches of the tree of Semitic scripture!

Let us, therefore, put that God-damned *"knowledge of good and evil"* to very "good" use by examining, in Reason's Tribunal, all Semitic religions, their Gods, and their "holy" scriptures to reveal all that is good, all that is evil, all that is true, and all that is untrue about them. To this end, I earnestly encourage every American claiming to be a Christian to read and examine the *Bible,* Part One and Part Two, from the beginning of imposition to the end of reason—that is, to read this supposed Word of God in its entirety from cover to cover or, at least, the first five books of Part One, the *Old Testament,* along with the *New Testament* Gospels of Part Two, (the new but not much improved version of Part One) ---that is if my request is possible to do at all. I say this because it is especially difficult to read and to comprehend a long-winded book written, obviously, in the unique style of language in common use during the times in which it was fabricated by the self-serving minds and hands of men in an unfamiliar, archaic manner of expression to "today's" readers.

The *Bible* is a book of disordered chronology—its unknown authors tell us tales of people, places, and events of long ago—some of them being implausible, disjointed, and contradictory accounts—several of them gleaned from the pre-literate lore and miracle-abounding, storybook mythologies of more ancient "Pagan" cultures and re-formulated, not to educate, but to deceive—a book that has been translated and re-translated, revised and edited time and again into several differing versions. Likewise, many of the people, places, and events given are unknown or unfamiliar to us and, as is often the case, uncorroborated by historical evidence such as the *Bible*-tale about a couple of Jews having *"Once upon a time"* nearly destroyed Egypt with a magic wand.

More importantly—because many of the *Bible's* accounts are lacking in common sense and common decency—because many of the accounts are filled with evil, violence, savagery, vengeance, and injustice, they should never be passed along or taught to anyone, especially children, as the "sacred" scripture of a religious enterprise seeking to improve the "good" conduct and the "good" moral character of mankind---save for the justice-seeking maxim which attempts to convince us that *"as we sow, so shall we reap,"* ---a maxim which should help to assure everyone on the planet that even religion shall reap the terrible harvest it has sown! One thing is for certain concerning the reading of the *Bible* and/or the *Koran*, you, the reader of them, will not find a "good," a "respectable," or a "decent" God portrayed anywhere on their "hallowed" pages.

One would do well to keep the following in mind when reading the above-mentioned Semitic scriptures that have been imposed upon the world as being the "Word of God": ---a "perfect" book of God's truth supposedly written with absolute authority should never contain a single falsehood, a single word written by an unknown author, a single syllable of amended text, a single contradiction, a single discrepancy, or a single statement that can be misconstrued with having a different meaning. A perfect book of God's truth should be easy to understand by all of its readers and never require explanation by others---a perfect book of God's truth should never contain a single word that would cause a drop of blood to be shed---a single word about a loving God indulging in wicked and unjust practices---a single word that favors one people over another---a single word that encourages cruelty and barbarity, bloodshed and vengeance, and punishing the innocent instead of the guilty. A perfect book of God's truth should not contain any screw-ups such as in the case of the last two verses of *II Chronicles* being repeated word for word in the first three verses of the *Book of Ezra.*

> **The last verse in Chronicles is broken abruptly, and ends in the middle of the phrase, with the word "up," without signifying to what place. This abrupt break, and the appearance of the same verses, in different books, show, as I already said, the disorder and ignorance in which the Bible has been put together, and that the compilers of it had no authority for what they were doing, nor we any authority for believing what they have done.**

> ---Thomas Paine

God's Word as given in the *OT* should never conflict with God's Word as given in the *NT* and neither of them should conflict with God's Word as given in the *Koran* if consistency is considered a characteristic of immutable Divinity. If the truth be told, God's undoubted, perfect Word and its "revealing" to the world should be the unsullied product of a perfect God's effort "alone" and not the result of anyone other than God writing it and transmitting it to everyone on the planet in a perfect manner—for God must surely possess the power and means to accomplish such a feat all by Himself without the assistance of others who are not as "infallible" as He. Certainly, it is beyond ridiculous to believe that what is or what isn't to be considered the Word of God can be a matter decided by someone's "vote"!

Because of the problems that attend having absolute belief in God's Word, it is vitally important that we ascertain whether Semitic scriptures can be trusted with being completely truthful and capable of being taken at face value or whether they cannot be relied upon at all. This is especially so because our nation's leaders, oftentimes, allow unchallenged and uncontested statements from the *Bible* to influence their decision-making in matters of crucial, foreign policy being unaware that the *Bible* was written to glorify Israel, its inhabitants, and their doings only. As the God of the *Bible's* "singular" concern has always been for the welfare and promotion of Jewry and no others, I think a more fitting name for this race promoting, self-aggrandizing book would be to call it the Jewish "Chutzpah Chronicles" because of the Jew's "exclusivity" with God and their astounding military exploits and other unbelievable claims boastfully told on its pages and only on its pages.

The *Bible*-Jews were a power-lacking, nomadic people who lacked a homeland and a mighty army but they, obviously, knew the "power" of instilling widespread belief in a vengeful, Semitic God and in the "power" of using words to impress, to impose, and to intimidate others in order to get what they desired---something which they could not have achieved otherwise because of the weakness of their position which, as the *Bible* tells us, was that of their being an enslaved people. How clever! They obviously knew that mere words on a page, if believed, could bring about the same results as if they had been gained through the use of force which the Jews, obviously, were unable to employ at least to the degree boasted about in their Chutzpah Chronicles such as their unbelievable claims about annihilating entire nations of people, separating a body of water into two parts, and being entitled by God to be inheritors of a "Promised Land" stolen from others, etc., etc. And it all began with folks "believing" the words written in the Chutzpah Chronicles of the Jews that tell of their being the only folks on the planet ever to be "chosen" by God to gain His favor and His total attention. How clever, again! And, oh, how those words, to this very day, continue to be believed---the fictional Chutzpah Chronicles rightly deserving credit as truly being a work of genius bent on ***"power and profit"***!

No archaeological records of the exodus exist, even on Egyptian monuments, probably because the Egyptian Hebrews numbered at most a few thousand and probably less than that. Their flight caused, evidently, no great concern in Egypt. In Jewish history, however, the exodus assumed major proportions.

---Funk & Wagnalls, *New Encyclopedia, Vol. 15*

And who but the slick, anonymous God-makers and script-writers of the Chutzpah Chronicles would have the audacity to tell us, in effect, that the Creator of the entire Universe is a "Jewish" man, a walking, talking, meat-eatin', wine-drinkin', belching, farting, sleeping, nose-picking, ball-scratching, crap-takin', piss-takin', ass-wiping, human being---Jesus Christ! Imagine, the Mighty Maker of Everything in the Cosmos having to duck behind a bush to relieve Himself! ---what a heavenly sight that must have been! ---imagine the Mighty Maker of Everything in the Cosmos not being able, in His younger days, to control His own bowel movements and, for years, needed someone to change His divinely-filled diaper---OMG! And, if you don't think that is a load, continue reading the script-written Chutzpah Chronicles, especially *John* 3:16 that tells of a God who *"so loved the world"* that He cursed it, drowned it, and prepared a Hell for the majority of its hapless occupants---a loving God who lovingly said in *Genesis*:

I will destroy man whom I have created from the face of the earth; both man, and beast, and the creeping thing, and the fowls of the air; for it repenteth me that I have made them . . . I will destroy them with the earth.

What a world-loving Guy! And should you ever wonder what a God-fart smells like, be assured, it would have a heavenly aroma and be worthy of praise by His admirers! Every American should ask themselves why it is so that we seek to remove the worst of the worst of criminals from our midst, isolate them from society in prison cells for the rest of their lives and, in some cases, seek to execute them for their dastardly deeds---that is what, I presume, nearly every Jew and Christian in the world would label as "justice"! Yet, when God's evil *Bible*-doings exceeds that of a legion of Hitlers, a legion of bin Ladens, and a legion of serial-killers, we build extravagant cathedrals, churches, schools, and more in order to honor and worship Him and His less-than-sacred history---in order to keep this SOB "alive" in our hearts while seeking (with aiding and abetting journalism) to impose His "Word," as given in the Jewish Chutzpah Chronicles, upon the rest of the world through indoctrination---what the hell is wrong with this picture? What the hell is right with it?

> ***These Books, beginning with Genesis and ending with Revelation [which, by the bye, is a book of riddles that requires a revelation to explain it], are, we are told, the Word of God. It is, therefore, proper for us to know who told us so, that we may know what credit to give to the report. The answer to this question is that nobody can tell, except that we tell one another so. The case, however, historically appears to be as follows: When the Church Mythologists established their system, they collected all the writings they could find and managed them as they pleased. It is a matter altogether of uncertainty to us whether such of the writings as now appear under the name of the Old and New Testaments are in the same state in which those collectors say they found them, or whether they added, altered, abridged or dressed them up. Be this as it may, they decided by vote which of the books out of the collection they had made should be the Word of God, and which should not. They rejected several; they voted others to be doubtful, such as the books called the Apocrypha; and those books which had a majority of votes were voted to be the Word of God. Had they voted otherwise, all the people calling themselves Christians, had believed otherwise—for the belief of the one comes from the vote of the other. Who the people were that did all this, we know nothing of; they called themselves by the general name of the Church, and this is all we know of the matter. As we have no other external evidence or authority for believing these books to be the Word of God than what I have mentioned, which is no evidence or authority at all. . . .***

---Thomas Paine

It is my opinion, after a lifetime of observation of Christian behavior, that because of the above mentioned problems and hindrances to obtaining clear understanding of the modified, voted-upon texts contained in the *Bible*—something that destroys the claim of its having perfect, divine origins! — few believers in the Christian faith ever care to read it in its entirety—fewer still care to examine its ***"errors"*** or its "evil" content—an encouragement, of course, to the aspirations and designs of *Bible*-thumping, *Bible*-

promoters. Most Jesus-believers prefer, instead, to listen to clergy and pampered evangelicals telling them what to believe when it comes to *Bible*-stories—the cherry-picked, embellished accounts they prefer you to hear extolling the "sacredness" of the wonderful and loving Almighty gleaned from "selected" *Bible*-passages for obvious reasons. The same can be said about *Koran*-advocates and their preference to promote only certain *Koran*-passages.

They, the above *Bible*-babblers, prefer that you don't know much about the *OT* books that abound in numerous accounts of God's "chosen" indulging in bloody, barbaric, ritual sacrifice: the slaughter, butchery, and roasting of sentient animals in order to make Jehovah over-the-moon ecstatic by filling His nostrils with the *"sweet savor"* of their barbecued remains. They prefer that you don't know much about the numerous, atrocious accounts of the God of Judeo-Christianity commanding His favorite folks to massacre entire nations of innocent, unoffending beings (men, women, children, infants, and even animals) whom He, the God of the Jews, had deemed to be unfit for coexistence with His sacred, Semitic tribes—unoffending neighbors who were perceived by Jews (and their Almighty God!) to be an obstacle standing in the way to the establishment of a Jews-only, "God-Promised" Land (it's in the contract!) —a supremacist tradition that continues to this very day by another God-favored people, with another holy contract, intent on establishing an Allah-Land for the exclusive benefit of Islamic Semites! Hmm!

Why wasn't it possible for God to accomplish His above Master-Plan for the benefit of the Jews, and only Jews---with just a mere whispered word or a "VOILA," finger-snap Promised Land and avoid all the drama and the wanton bloodshed? Keep in mind that we are to believe that God created the entire Universe in a few days with just a few "spoken" words! Keep in mind that it is only God's self-serving script-writers, not historians, who tell us about the above "divine" activities---activities that God supposedly carried out for the exclusive benefit of His homies! They, the *Bible*-babblers, prefer that you don't know anything about the anonymous, Jewish script-writers of the *OT* who cleverly made their manufactured God promise, in His manufactured Word, to give to the Jews whatever it was they wanted by using the ruse: *"Thus sayeth the Lord"* —how deceptively slick! Who then, under penalty of pain or death, would dare to question the "will" of God and His spoken "Word"?

Even America, because of her indoctrination by the *Bible*-babblers and her intoxication with Judeo-Christianity, has been sucked in by the deception to the point of actually abetting the ambitions of the "God-favored" by assisting them in bringing their contrived, "God-promised" claims to fruition while defending their bogus religious schemings—incredible and outrageous! Man help us!

> ***Could we permit ourselves to suppose that the Almighty would distinguish any nation of people by the name of His chosen people, we must suppose that people to have been an example to all the rest of the world of the purest piety and humanity, and not such a nation of ruffians and cut-throats as the ancient Jews were; a people who, corrupted by and copying after such monsters and imposters as Moses and Aaron, Joshua, Samuel and David, had distinguished above all others on the face of the known earth for barbarity and wickedness.***
>
> ---Thomas Paine

The *Bible*-babblers prefer that you don't know much about the nearly total extermination of the Midianites (and many others!) by the hands of evil and murderous, Jewish terrorists, and the taking of their virgin daughters into captivity by the tens of thousands for a good ol' Jehovah-pleasing rape-fest---*Num.* 31:17,18,35! These babbling spin-meisters and other pious-shysters prefer that you only hear sermons crafted to promote a heart-warming, scriptural "spin" on the subjects of love, kindness, and mercy—not about the actual hate-crimes, malevolence, injustice, bloodshed, and barbarity that fills so many of the pages of their beloved *Bible*! They prefer that you don't know much about the sins of the God of Judeo-Christianity or about the sins of the Catholic Church and its degenerate clergy—they prefer that you don't ask any questions at all about such matters and that you always continue doing your dutiful part in filling the collection plate with your divine dollars!

If, however, you happen to be someone who would enjoy reading what is little more than the concocted diary of a malevolent, genocidal psychopath who, for some reason, favored only the Jews and had constant dealings and conversations with them via Moses, seemingly, on a daily basis when He, God, was not hiding-out behind a cloud and keeping hush-hush as He does today leaving present day Jews without the much-needed, reliable support of their Almighty *Bible*-promoter, *Bible*-protector, and *Bible*-enabler! ---a malevolent, genocidal psychopath who is unworthy of being labeled a loving and decent God---you'll be over-the-moon, too, reading the *OT* Chutzpah Chronicles that glorify this misery-making miscreant and His less-than-sacred doings! ---(NOW HEAR THIS: it is a matter of interest to me to learn the means God used to communicate to the Jews via Moses? Did He "speaketh unto" Moses inside Moses' head---in which case no one else would have been able to hear His mighty words and record them? ---did he speak to him in a thundering sky-voice---in which case everyone would have heard God's commands to Mr. Moe-says---even the Canaanites! ---in which case the Canaanites would have been given a heads-up as to what was to become of their kind and, therefore, they would have had an opportunity to escape their fate---very, very interesting! ---have you heard enough?)

The making of the *OT* God in the carnal image of a lusting meat-connoisseur who revels in killing, bloodshed, butchery, and smelling the vapors of roasted flesh should be a clear tip-off to anyone with an uncorrupted mind as to His bogus, less-than-spiritual existence—an existence brought to life by unknown, insentient script-writers with their own obvious penchant for the *"sweet savor"* of the "heavenly" aroma of barbecued meat, for surely, only a meat-eater would be over-the-moon about detecting the smell of roasted flesh---and, who was it that God "revealed" His intense longings for such *"sweet"* savory smells? It had to be a real close friend for sure---someone on a first name basis---someone who would know God's personal likes and dislikes---His favorite color, (which just happens to be red---blood red!), etc. ---"Hey, Mo, have Aarie throw another fatted calf on the grill for me as I haven't enjoyed an olfactory orgasm in days! ---sniff, sniff, sniff---mmmmm!---thanks, pal! ---how 'bout lighting up a cigarette now and blowing the smoke skyward—aaah!" ---LOL!

One wonders if the fires of barbeque pits are constantly kept ablaze in Heaven to keep God in a happy mood there and, one wonders, too, who will be sacrificed and thrown into the flames up there in order to produce the heavenly scent that tantalizes and pleases God so much? ---"Hi! ---Welcome to Heaven! ---My name is Peter, and I will be leading you through these pearly gates---er---as soon as I can find the key to unlock them---ah, here it is! ---This way, folks! ---'Hey, Pete, what's that smell?' ---CLUNK!" ---LOL!

Imagine God, the Creator of the Universe, a non-physical entity, being aroused by the vapors of animal-cremation arising to His nostrils---really? Imagine, too, such a carnally-stimulated God never having a desire to eat the roasted flesh that smells so wonderful to Him---really? I think I know why a scripted God never made the attempt, in the *Bible,* to eat the meat He so loves to "smell" roasting on an altar-grill---if God had placed an order for some barbecue-take-out to be sent His way, His script-writers, not knowing His address, would certainly not be able to make good on the delivery! In spite of this shortcoming, it seems the *Bible's* script writers had missed a great opportunity to prove that their God is a real person---if only they had thought to leave a plate of *"fatted"* calf-burgers (fries and a soft drink!) on the altar overnight (like the plate of cookies and glass of milk one leaves out for Santa) ---the empty plate and beverage container being witnessed in the morning would certainly be absolute *Bible*-proof of God's existence!

It is interesting to note here that God, whom we are to believe, exists everywhere, in everything, in every atom of every speck of dust at every moment in time, would enjoy having some parts of Himself being hacked to pieces and burned on an altar-grill in order for Him to savor the smell of His own cremation! Hmm! *"Yes, Virginia, God definitely has a nose to detect odors with, and, since man is supposedly made in His image, He, like us, must surely have all the other body parts we have, such as a mouth and vocal cords to speak with, teeth to chew His food with, a stomach, an anus, and the occasional need, like us, of a bowel movement---wonder no more, my dear, about the cause of thunder!"*

It was such script-writers, as described above, who were the "creators" of a Semitic God and the authors of His "infallible" Word—such were they who made their God to be similarly aroused and similarly encumbered with the carnal desires they themselves possessed—such were they who were compelled to make their God a non-physical, spiritual being who, for obvious good reason, could never be seen, yet, in their ignorant paleo-reckonings---a God who would be subject to all the pettiness, vanities, and vices such as anger, vengeance, jealousy, etc., etc. that they, the script-writers of the *Bible* surely possessed, for surely, only human existence is subject to the weaknesses and frailties of "living in the flesh."

The immaculateness of spiritual, non-physical, existence, we're supposed to believe, is incorruptible and not subject to any temptation or sensual pleasure. Thus, the *OT* God has been made entirely in man's image and not the other way around as we are imposed upon to believe! It is my opinion that those of fair and mature mind who can endure reading about the horrific acts proudly performed, proudly proclaimed, and proudly promoted in the *Bible* will be more likely to reject its so-called "sacred" nature rather than accept it as being the "revealed" Word of God—more likely to reject any good that the *Bible* may inspire because of all the wickedness contained therein.

How much better it would have been for mankind if only a pure, simple, and benign "Word of Man" had been "revealed" to us and impressed upon our hearts and minds to follow rather than the corrupting and deceiving, brutal and bloody "Word of God" we were given and imposed upon to believe in. If only the merits of following the benevolent Golden Rule—an enlightened, "heathen" principle in use centuries before Christ—had been instilled in mankind millennia ago there would not have been a record of vengeance and bloodshed, oppression and supremacism, slavery and injustice associated with the "spiritual" endeavors of Judaism, Christianity, and Islam. The less-than-honorable histories and activities of Semitic religions have continued their divisive disruptions into the Space Age no less, with their firmly rooted "us" and "them" mindset that begets racial and gender prejudices, and the superior-mindedness of their adherents yet to be reckoned with and resolved—the result, obviously, of Semitic religions "not" doing the right thing *unto others* throughout the ages---throughout their violent and vengeful pasts.

It is unfortunate that *"E Pluribus Unum"* (out of many, one) has been replaced with the obvious falsehood: *"In God We Trust"* as the official motto of the United States. Sadly, the divisive "us" and "them" mindset that is firmly rooted in Semitic theism is well represented on the streets of America where the race and gender biases of such thinking often manifests itself in violent encounters and clashes that much too often end in needless death and destruction. How is it possible that a supposed "Christian" nation should be troubled so often with wanton, mass-casualty shootings---with uniformed, public servants engaging in unjustifiable homicides? Aren't such acts, to a great measure, the result of the "us" and "them" mentality which is one of the hallmarks of religion---one of the hallmarks of "religious" folks who, because of their certainty of having religious superiority over others, prefer to dress and behave in a certain manner and isolate themselves in enclaves all over our nation rather than integrate, assimilate, or be any part of "the melting pot" endeavors of a multi-racial, multi-ethnic America?

I'm certain that the perpetrators of such insentient acts as stated in the above paragraph, if asked, would not shy away from admitting to being a Christian, a Jew, or a Muslim. I'm certain, too, that the perpetrators of such insentient acts will rarely ever be found to be atheists---for it is a fact that America's prisons are teeming with believers! *"Yes, Virginia, atheism, apparently, is the least of the least of America's concerns, in fact, non-belief in the Gods of religion should be seen as a good thing, a blessing upon our nation---and you thought you had to be religious to be good! Based upon prison population statistics, atheists make up a miniscule percentage of the incarcerated convicts, lagging far far behind law-breaking Judeo-Christian inmates. Atheists will have to step up their criminal activities if they want to level the playing field to be on a par with those inmates who are believers in the Word of God! Yes, Virginia, you'll have to look elsewhere for the 'cause' of the civil unrest and the criminal activity that plagues this Judeo-Christian nation that, supposedly, 'trusts in God' and lives 'under' His spiritual direction!"*

Sadly, rather than focusing our nation's energies on disabling and defeating the religious disease that spawns all of the above abominations with the use of Reason's Tribunal, we, out of ignorance, boast of what else---having *"TRUST"* in God---the source of our very woes to end them—incredible! Incidentally, folks, it should be made quite clear to all that it is only from Jewish scriptures that proudly promote the "us" and "them" mindset, that Gentiles are always regarded upon their pages as "heathens"!

Those men, whom Jewish and Christian idolaters have abusively called heathens, had much better and clearer ideas of justice and morality than are to be found in the Old Testament, so far as it is Jewish; or in the New.

---Thomas Paine

Do for others what you want them to do for you: for this is the Law of Moses and the teaching of the prophets.

---Jesus, *"according to" Matt.* 7:12, *Luke* 6:31

But, much to the shame of Judeo-Christianity, *"the Law of Moses and the teaching of the prophets,"* that supposedly touted the morality and justice of the Golden Rule (of non-Jewish origin), would, obviously, not serve the parasitic ambitions of the script-writers of Semitic religions to do unfairly *"unto others"* for less-than-divine purpose. It is a certainty that the Jews of the *Bible* would not have wanted to be treated in the way they were pleased to treat the Canaanites whom they wantonly exterminated—they would not have wanted to be treated in the way they were pleased to treat their scapegoat victims whom they caused to pay for the sins of others with their innocent lives—they would not have wanted to be treated in the way their holy heroes treated the pre-*Exodus* Egyptians---they would not have wanted to be treated in the way they treated the slaves "they" owned! Had

Christians truly believed and followed the Golden Rule, it is a certainty that they would not have wanted to be treated in the way they were pleased to imprison, torture, and burn *"others"* to death for centuries on the mere suspicion of their having made "deals" with the Devil---just another Judeo-Christian example of: "Do unto others what you don't want done unto you"!

The Golden Rule being a powerful moral deterrent to "doing" malevolence unto others was, sadly, not a favored feature of *"the Law of Moses and the teaching of the prophets"* ---Jesus' words to the contrary. There is "no" evidence of the Golden Rule ever having been a preferred practice in Jewish or Christian traditions or Jewish and Christian principles. There is ample evidence, however, of the time-honored Jewish tradition of blaming and punishing the innocent for the sins and crimes of others— Jesus being a perfect example of this revered yet uncivilized, un-American practice. His death was the ultimate expression of a ritual of barbarians that demanded a *"clean,"* unblemished animal's blood having to be shed and its life having to be sacrificed in order to appease their God, the God of the Israelites, aka the God of Judeo-Christianity, aka the God of Muslims.

The symbolic eating of Jesus' flesh and the symbolic drinking of His blood are evidence that this ritual of barbarians is still being carried out today in a slightly "altared" way. Because promoting and preaching the Golden Rule did not serve the priestly purposes of ***"power and profit,"*** we, the victims of religion, were given instead, the threatening, bellicose words of the *Bible* and the *Koran* because, as Thomas Paine explains, they are but ***"human inventions, set up to terrify and enslave mankind, and monopolize power and profit."*** —even though the Golden Rule, for a time, was a household saying amongst the Jews before the time of Christ.

Would any member of America's legal system or any member of America's Judeo-Christian faithful who is over-the-moon proud to proclaim *"In God We Trust"* ever admit that their trust in God gives, in effect, a seal of approval to a ritual of barbarians whereby the innocent are punished as scapegoats in order to absolve the sinful deeds of the guilty? Would any of the above-mentioned folks ever admit that their trust in God, in effect, sanctions the death of an innocent person, Jesus, as a fair and square atonement for the supposed misdeeds of Adam, regardless of the thousands of years that supposedly separated them? Would such a disgraceful miscarriage of justice ever be considered an example of doing the right thing anywhere in America, especially in her honored legal system? Never! Why then is America's motto: *"In God We Trust"* when her actions reveal it isn't so—reveal that such a maxim about our nation's conduct is obviously an outright lie?

13

America, thankfully, does not, in reality, trust in the God of the *Bible* to set the example of fairness in her system of jurisprudence, she relies, instead, on a justice-seeking, multi-level, legal system to deliver impartiality in her courts of law. America, thankfully, does not trust in God for her security, she relies on a strong military to deal with her enemies. America, thankfully, does not trust in God to feed and clothe her needy citizens and to care for her sick and dying because she has humane programs set in place by Man for dealing with and alleviating such conditions, etc., etc.

Much to the shame of our otherwise noble nation, we still allow ourselves to be imposed upon by those who view the sacrificial death of Jesus as something to be proud of even to the point of celebrating His birth and death as joyous holidays even though their exact dates are unknown— we still allow and honor this offensive and unjust Judeo-Christian tradition, a despicable ritual of *Bible*-barbarians, to sully our nation's achievements and aspirations to instill justice and fairness in our civil laws. According to this treasured tradition, all of the human and animal Garden of Eden inhabitants along with all of their descendants including you and I "deserved" to be punished, made to suffer and die, and suffer yet again in Hell (except for Jesus and His twelve tribes of course) all because of Adam's naive disobedience—a mythological sin that never took place, committed by a mythological person who never existed, in a mythological place that never was, for where, oh where, is the *"flaming sword"* today that was left behind by God *"east of the garden of Eden"* to be used as a deterrent along with, of all things, *"cherubs,"* to *"guard"* the way to the *"tree of life"* ---*Gen.* 3:24?

Imagine for a moment if you will, defenseless, rosy-cheeked, little angels (not intimidating Navy Seal types!) being tasked (unto this day), I repeat, "being tasked" (unto this day) with guarding anything, never mind the supposed one and only, precious *"tree of life"*! Imagine God instructing small, innocent children: "Now kiddies, don't let anyone come near this priceless tree or eat its priceless fruit—use the big flaming sword if you have to but don't burn yourselves or cut your little fingers!" Reason's Tribunal will finally bring this cherub abuser—Adam and Eve abuser— mankind abuser and animal abuser—to American-style justice in order to hold Him accountable, at last, for the egregious acts of injustice and inhumanity He dispensed in Eden and beyond!

If you are a Christian who believes the words of the *Bible's* Eden-tale to be a true account of things, then your God is "revealed" as a mean-spirited, despicable character and Satan-enabler who is unworthy of receiving anyone's respectful attention and worship. Imagine if you will, a responsible parent placing their innocent child, (or any child-minded person), in a room with a bowl of candy and then telling that innocent child, (or child-minded person), never to eat any of the bowl's contents in his or her absence. What would a knowledgeable, mature parent expect would happen as a result? Would you then expect this loving, responsible parent to figuratively or literally kick the crap out of their child-minded candy-eater? Wouldn't you consider such unjust doings as a blatant example of child abuse orchestrated by an irresponsible parent? Of course you would if you were a decent person, but when it comes to being an example of God's divine behavior---oh my! If, however, you are one of those rare Christians who believes the written words of the *Bible's* Eden-tale to be a fictional account, then Jesus' "atonement" (for Adam's "sin") was just another rather cruel hoax played this time upon innocent Gentiles and, therefore, a deed unworthy of receiving anyone's respectful attention and worship.

Regardless of whether you are a person who either believes or disbelieves the veracity of the Eden-tale, either way, the ungodly hand of a conniving script-writer is "revealed," to all. After examining, in Reason's Tribunal, all of the extrapolated ***"facts and evidence"*** of the Eden-tale upon which the Christian religion hinges its entire "sin to salvation" existence, you will know, with certainty, whether it is a true account of things or not!

(NOTE TO THE FAITHFUL BELIEVERS OF *BIBLE*-TALES: do not waste your time and money attempting to locate the Holy Grail, which no one could possibly identify, or remnants of Noah's bogus boat---consider searching, instead, for the above mentioned *"flaming sword"* which, beyond any doubt according to *Bible*-evidence, is still out there somewhere in the Garden where God, Himself, purposely placed it. A flaming sword shouldn't be too difficult to find since we know God never removed it, therefore, it must still be burning bright even after being submerged in Noah's flood, for God's miraculous, *"flaming sword"* is surely not subject to the physical laws of this world, not subject to being extinguished by the physical effects of exposure to wind and water. The *"tree of life"* and its guardian *"cherubs,"* it must be admitted, may have perished in God's world-destroying flood! Seek ye, God's faithful believers, and ye shall find the *"flaming sword"* right where God left it burning and turning all those many years ago! —but I digress . . .)

If we are to believe that Christians, black and white, are proud of their association with the Judeo part of the cherished hyphenated term: "Judeo-Christianity," then they should be proud, too, of all of the "glorious" God-commanded *Bible*-events that occurred on behalf of the Jews in their religious past. They should be very proud, especially evangelical Christians, to declare that the several, unprovoking nations of people who lived in Canaan during biblical times "deserved" to be annihilated (except for certain females!) along with their animals in the name of God for the personal benefit (and sexual interests) of God's "chosen" people. Surely, a loving, merciful God would not have demanded the killing and sexual abuse of folks who didn't deserve such treatment—right?

Christians and Jews, therefore, should be very pleased to declare that it was quite acceptable and pleasing for their shared God---whom they are over-the-moon proud and delighted to tell all the world they worship and adore and have absolute trust in---to demand the killing of homosexuals and unruly children by stoning them to death. Surely, God would not have demanded their deaths by such brutal and cruel means if they didn't deserve such treatment—right? Surely, God would not have approved of the practice of slavery if slaves were not deserving of their fate, too—right? Of course, it must be so---God's actions are always deemed commendable, never deemed condemnable! It follows then that Christians must be uber-proud to declare that America is truly a nation living *"Under God,"* and that every American has unwavering "trust" in Him for their welfare and for His providing 24/7 security for our country! ---really?

If Christians are truly jubilant and proud about the religious heritage they share with the Jews and their greatly-rewarded past associations with God that they supposedly enjoyed because of their "obedience" to Him, as told in their Chutzpah Chronicles, why then the seemingly utter silence about the brutal massacre of innocent folks that occurred time after time in their shared God's name for the exclusive benefit of His "chosen" people throughout their religious history. Shouldn't these "commendable" acts of God, like all the rest of His "commendable" doings for the benefit of Jews only, be praised and promoted from every Christian pulpit too? Of course they should!

Is it possible for any Judeo-Christian to find shame in acknowledging such wicked activities as being a part of their shared God's will? Of course not! Why then is it that we never hear any joyful-noise hymns or Hallelujah songs of praise ever being sung to honor such imposing "commendable" acts of Divinity? Why is there never any righteous Christian outrage over their shared God's establishment and promotion of His "commendable" practice of slavery? In a God-loving, God-praising, God-honoring land, as America is said to be---where obeying God's every Word is deemed so important that it is preached ad nauseum from coast to coast by proud, evangelical, *Bible*-pounding, Zionist-Christian cheerleaders---why are such atrocities and abominations never touted as glorious and honorable acts of God worthy of adulation? Aren't "all" of God's actions worthy of praise? Of course they are! Why oh why then the utter silence from the pulpits concerning these things? Hmm!

It is obviously because such non-sacred endeavors are incapable of being lovingly spun, by His staunchest advocates, into glorious sermons about the supposed love of God for everyone. As proof of their hypocrisy, such advocates are unwilling to admit of them or to admonish them—endeavors that, rightly so, should be embarrassments to every one of His adoring Christian fans. The Chutzpah Chronicle's accounts that proudly boast of the above atrocities are never mentioned, never criticized, never condemned from the many church pulpits of righteousness, from the balcony of the pampered Pope's palace, to the palatial, evangelizing Mega-Churches of posh, parasitic pastors who clearly have a vested interest in avoiding certain "Words" of God and in spinning the remainder of them in order to increase their ***"power and revenue"***!

If America is truly *"one nation under God,"* a nation of believers who truly trusted in Him and His "Word," why is it that we, the citizens of this God-beguiled nation, refuse to obey His "commendable" will that unceasingly calls on His believers to unceasingly stone homosexuals and unruly children to death---why is it that we refuse to continue engaging in the "commendable," God-willed practice of human bondage, that He established forever, etc.? Why is such non-compliance to His "commendable" commands never perceived as a rejection of God and His "Word" in a God-loving land? Reason's Tribunal holds the absolute answers to these annoyingly bold questions about the Almighty for if truth truly prevailed in these matters, we would acknowledge that it is "In Reason We Trust," not in the *Bible*-God of Judeo-Christianity, not in the shysters who pick and choose which chapters and verses of their shared God's Word they can spin for their personal gain and which chapters and verses of their shared God's Word they must spurn and shy away from in their selective sermons that tell us only of God's love for everyone on the planet! ---really?

One would think there would be, at least, one, I repeat, "one" earnest voice raised in protest against the above un-American activities: the atrocities and the abominations that stain so many of the *Bible's* pages with innocent blood---among the journalists at Fox News Channel, an enterprise that supposedly endeavors to vet every story for its source and its accuracy---endeavors to provide "no spin" investigations into corruption and wrongdoing occurring within "all" levels of society. A news agency that is proud to promote what they call "fair and balanced" assessments on every newsworthy subject—a place where journalists, for the sake of evenhandedness in their judgments, would, one assumes, make the attempt to rein-in any religion-conditioned reflex, bias, or default setting they may have on any subject before serving it up to America. Their bias in favor of Judeo-Christianity, however, is often proudly proclaimed and promoted in their reporting while they, too, are curiously silent about the many skeletons found in the Chutzpah Chronicle's many closets such as the *Bible*-commendable, wanton extermination, I repeat, "the *Bible*-commendable, wanton extermination" of the unoffending Canaanites and others coming at the hands of the Jews—they are curiously silent about the "*Bible*-commendable," God-ordered stonings and the "*Bible*-commendable" God-ordered institution of slavery being the commands of a "loving" God!

They are curiously silent, too, in regards to exposing the sordid details about "the rest of the story" on the biggest hoaxes, the biggest scams, and the biggest fraudulent enterprises ever perpetrated on the planet: Semitic theologies! Instead, these proud journalists, who rightfully insist on the necessity of vetting the veracity of the ***"facts and evidence"*** of each and every story before airing their scholarly estimations about them, are also proud to give the advocates of Judeo-Christianity a free-pass with their never having to substantiate any of their religious claims—claims that these news pundits un-journalistically assume to be above criticism and beyond bold scrutiny because of widespread religious indoctrination.

In giving their blind support to Semitic religions in this way, the journalists at FNC (some sporting gold crosses and writing books to confirm their religious bias) who refuse to investigate or expose the inhumane, supremacist-minded activities reported time and time again in the *Bible,* should be counted among the shameless advocates of Judeo-Christianity---the deceivers and misinformers, not the enlighteners and educators of mankind---FNC is, without doubt, a religious organization that promotes Christianity---an organization whose journalism is, obviously, neither fair nor balanced when the subject involves their cherished religion!

Fox News journalists, I'm certain, would resent being thought of and dismissed as "racists" and "bigots" (and rightly so) just for daring to question and challenge the status quo mindset of today's politically correct newsmakers---a maligning effort by the politically correct to slight FNC and dismiss their claims, yet, they, FNC, for the most part, label as "atheists," all who dare to question and challenge the status quo of the religious mindsets of Judaism and Christianity---a maligning effort by

FNC's defenders of religion to slight such folks in order to dismiss them and prevent them from being heard---sounds very un-American to me! Because of religious brainwashing, atheism is perceived in America as a blight, not a blessing.

Isn't it noteworthy, too, that we never hear about any proud members of Judeo-Christian clergy ever conducting religious services to offer thanks to their loving *Bible*-God for commanding, time and again, the "commendable" annihilation of various non-Jewish peoples (Gentile-genocide) by Jews for the benefit of Jews and for the Christians who, curiously, for the most part, happen to be Gentiles and who now, incredibly, follow along in their Semitic mentors' blood-stained footsteps? Shouldn't *Bible*-advocates, therefore, be proud to proclaim that such abominable *Bible*-acts were necessary in order to make it possible for exceptionally holy Jews and exceptionally holy Christians to show the world what it truly means to have a decent and loving God on your side and in your lives?

Isn't it noteworthy, too, that when multitudes upon multitudes of Jews were murdered and exterminated without cause at the hands of brutal-minded men bent on a mission to subdue the world for the benefit of their own master-race---we, out of decency and respect for their millions of victims, have chosen to build (and rightly so!) memorials to honor them and condemn the evil of their supremacist-minded killers? Yet, when multitudes upon multitudes of Gentiles were murdered and exterminated without cause at the hands of Jews acting on their *Bible*-God's "command," we choose not to build memorials to them, the annihilated, but, instead, we build places of worship to honor this murderous God and, in effect, His supremacist-minded followers who, as Muslims, are still carrying out their own master-race mission! Wouldn't this be the equivalent of building Holocaust Memorials to pay tribute to Hitler and the Nazis? Certainly, it would! Why then do we never hear about any proud members of the Judeo-Christian clergy being on a mission to build memorials, out of decency and respect, for the victims of Jewish atrocities so that their lives and their deaths are never forgotten as well? Why is it so that we never hear any of the "fair and balanced" crowd at Fox News make mention of such "unfair' and "unbalanced" behavior taken against Gentiles in the *Bible*---why is it so?

Shame on every proud Jew and every proud Christian, especially Judeo-Christianity-promoting "journalists" —shame on you for remaining silent on this matter, for refusing to investigate the holy-horrors and the destructive doings that took place in your "glorified," religious histories, and for not seeking to end them or make amends for them. Shame on all of you for imposing your pretended "Word of God" upon others in order to promote the insentient, "us" and "them," self-serving interests of Semitic religions. Shame on you for playing a role in helping to justify the irreparable harm done to gullible hearts and minds and to the human-condition because of the, supposed, "inviolable," "irreproachable" nature of the so-called "sacred" endeavors that are proudly promoted in "commendable" Judeo-Christian scripture. Shame on you for having a hand in the racial and gender divisions that are continuing to destroy everything America stands for. Shame on you for making us believe the Creator of Hell is a God of love, kindness, and mercy. Shame on all who believe that Semitic religions are moral institutions! Shame on the journalists at Fox News Channel who are supposed to "report" the facts about everything and anything so that *"We the people"* can "decide" on the worthiness or unworthiness of Semitic theologies! Shame, shame, shame on you all!

Would any of the *OT* injustices and atrocities have become such an integral part of Semitic theology if the inspired words of the heathen's (Gentile's) "Golden Rule" were being preached, practiced, and promoted at the time instead of a demonic God's "infallible" and "inerrant" Word? Find out why these and many other "over-looked" and "under-reported" *Bible* topics deserving your attention are never proudly mentioned in Sunday sermons and begin your own spiritual journey to learn the truth about the Devil-in-the-Details within the sacred books of Jews and Christians (and Muslims) that are kept hushed and hidden from our suppressed notice of them.

Find out, too, if following the *Bible* with its less-than-divine dogmas, or if following the Golden Rule by treating everyone as you would be treated, truly makes one a better person and the world a better, safer place—after a lifetime of Christian acquaintance and observation, I have found the answer *"in which there is no doubt"*! I have found, too, that the Judeo-Christian *Bible* is a fictional work from cover to cover, a book rooted in Pagan mythology that has been re-composed into Jewish mythology for the purpose of promoting their Semitic, cultural chutzpah in order to better serve the needs of its anonymous, parasitic, script-writing, power-seeking priests and their tribes! If you, however, believe the *Bible* to be an "honorable," "commendable" book of truth worthy of your undying respect and loving devotion, please read on . . .

In *Numbers* 31:17,18, after Moses and his pious tribe had religiously murdered every Midianite man---(31:7) at the express command of Jehovah, God of the Israelites (aka Jesus) —he, Moses, acting under divine supervision, further instructed his dutiful, God-minded officers to *"...kill every male among the little ones,"* and to *"kill"* every Midianite woman that *"...hath known man by lying with him. But all the women children, that have not known a man by lying with him, keep alive for yourselves."* What a guy! What a God! What an incredible number of Jew-murdered men, women, and innocent children! ---for in verse 35 of the above chapter, the number of *"women children* (alone!)*, that have not known a man by lying with him"* is given as thirty-two thousand, I repeat, "thirty-two thousand! What an incredible, I repeat, "incredible" number of Jew-abused, innocent *"women children"* destined for sexual violation! The question arises as to how these holy officers, acting "under" God, were able to determine the virginity of these tens of thousands of *"women children"*? It must be assumed that these most innocent of innocents, shortly after having endured witnessing their entire families being mercilessly and brutally hacked to death before their very eyes by God's divine death squads, were forced, most certainly under lethal threat, to expose their genitalia for inspection by Moses' noble, God-fearing, God-obeying officers for surely, they would not have accepted their "virgin-status" based upon their word alone.

Always remember, folks, that when God is on your side, you can rape, kill, abuse, and impose upon others with impunity and without incurring any consequences or outcries---If you are a Jew (an Israelite) you can annihilate nations of people without regret or remorse and without receiving as much as a hint of condemnation from anyone including the clergy, our nation's leaders, and our nation's journalists---*"Praise the Lord"*! That being said---what a gross and sick spectacle of wickedness and cruelty for God's "chosen" to engage in (the murder and the rape of the Midianites) and to make a part of their "religious" history which, incidentally, is replete with the sowing and the reaping of inhumanity! Tens and tens and tens of thousands of Midianite men, women, and children wantonly murdered in the name of God---tens of thousands of them to be raped with God's permission---*"Praise the Lord"*! ---sick stuff, folks! And, don't forget to instruct your children that the way to prevent their spending an eternity experiencing the torments of Hell is to instruct them to love and to honor always the *Bible's* butchery, bloodshedding, and brutality as being the "sacred" endeavors of their loving God---*"Praise the Lord"*! ---sick, sick stuff, folks!

> ***Among the detestable villains that in any period of the world have disgraced the name of man, it is impossible to find a greater than Moses, if this account be true. Here is an order to butcher the boys, to massacre the mothers and debauch the daughters. Let***

any mother put herself in the situation of those mothers; one child murdered, another destined to violation, and herself in the hands of an executioner; let any daughter put herself in the situation of those daughters, destined as a prey to the murderers of a mother and a brother, and what will be their feelings?

---Thomas Paine

What will be your feelings about these dastardly deeds of Moses, a man adored by Jews and Christians, a man who was "chosen" by God to deliver the Ten Commandments? Wouldn't such a "choice" be the moral equivalent of selecting Hitler to deliver the Nobel Peace prize? ---kvk

And what became of those *"women children,"* those hapless, young female sex slaves and the unwanted children that surely resulted from their less-than-sacred encounters with the "holiest" of peoples? They must either have been stoned to death or kept alive to continue to be used as sex slaves for they, surely, were never allowed to become accepted members of their masters' exclusive, supremacist, racist, sexist tribe. This is just one of many disgraceful and disgusting examples from the *Bible* of the moral depravity we are made to believe is the acceptable conduct and the sacred activities of a God-chosen people whose principles and traditions we should, in reality, be ashamed to mention in the same breath when talking about America's foundation and her sacred efforts to achieve liberty and equal justice for all. Is it any wonder that America is still contending with the effects of the imposed, chutzpah-laden, Judeo-Christian mindset that believes it is superior to all other non-Judeo-Christian mindsets in every way because the *Bible* says it is so—a mindset that believes it has a God directing it---a mindset that believes it has a God-given right and duty (a divine license) to impose its divisive delusions and its destructive deceptions upon all others?

Today, while our nation still struggles with finding answers and remedies to the violence caused by the racist, misogynist, and xenophobic bent of the supremacist mindset of Judeo-Christians and the enduring hatreds caused by such "religious" thinking, we, the imposed upon, have yet to recognize the major role religion plays in their genesis and in their long-standing. For it is from the inviolable pages of the *Bible* that we have "learned" the lesson from God, Himself (aka Jesus), that all men are "not" created equal---Christian people of color take note!---that all lives certainly "don't" matter---Christian people of color take note!---that certain people should "enjoy" more rights than others---Christian people of color take note!---that slavery "is" righteous---Christian people of color take note!---that women "should" live under the rule of men---that homosexuals don't deserve to exist---that children can be brutally killed without compunction and without consequence just for being "stubborn,"---that everyone who is not a member of God's chosen tribe are God's enemies (Gentiles)---all Christians take note!, etc., etc., etc.. The imposing folks who constantly tell us we must believe all that is written in their blessed *Bible* and who constantly tell us that we should all sing praises to its lead character definitely have some explaining to do!

When we, the Caretakers of Liberty, are told time and again by our nation's leaders, politicians, news pundits, coddled clergy, and others, how Judeo-Christian traditions and principles were responsible for shaping the moral character along with the justice system of our land, we should ask them to provide biblical evidence and biblical examples of their claims. For the "inspired" *Bible*, in its boastful portrayal of everything Jewish, tells only of the immorality and the injustice prevalent in the shameful, evil history of Judeo-traditions and Judeo-principles. Its pages, which proudly recount each and every atrocity the Jews carried out in the name of God, never contain as much as a syllable about the Jews ever having treated anyone they had dealings with in a civil and equitable manner—the way in which America strives to achieve liberty and justice for all of its citizens. Besides, who amongst us aspires to behave in the malevolent ways the Jews of the *Old Testament* behaved?

We should ask the above brain-washed Americans to provide one example, I repeat, "one example" from the *Old Testament* of a time when fairness and equal justice for all was a concern of the *Bible*-Jews—one example! The wanton, disgraceful actions of the "chosen" people, as told in their Chutzpah Chronicles, is not a history for any decent American to be proud of—shameful traditions and shameful principles that, thankfully, are not, I repeat, "are not" the foundation stones of our freedom-loving, tyranny-opposing nation. According to evidence obtained from the *Bible* that reveals the murder and mayhem the "chosen people" repeatedly engaged in, no Jew should be proud to defend their massacre and extermination of the Canaanites—no Gentile American should be proud to worship and promote the malevolent, pathological God of the Jews (aka Jesus) that ordered it to be done—no one should be proud to accept the *Bible* as being the "Word" of God or any part of its abounding accounts that tell, in a boastful way, of Jewish involvement in bloodshed and wickedness as being the "will" of God being carried out by His faithful followers!

If an avowed anti-Semite had ever set about to write a book to deliberately discredit and malign Jews, he or she would not be able to surpass the slanderous statements made about them and their vicious villainy as reported, incredibly, by Jew-favoring authors in the *Old Testament*! ---slanderous statements that Jews are unashamedly proud to tell us about! The *OT* is a book that proudly boasts of the Jews exclusivity with God and the atrocities they committed in service to Him. If *Bible*-evidence is to be believed in regards to Jewish history, then it is the pages of the *Bible* that provide the greatest indictment of Jewish traditions and principles. If, however, *Bible*-evidence is not to be believed---as I contend and Reason's Tribunal will prove---then Judaism and Christianity will be "revealed" as the bogus, fraudulent enterprises they truly are and not the sacred institutions they pretend to be.

Am I, therefore, to be counted among the slanderous, libelous, hateful anti-Semites of this world who set about to discredit all Jews, or, am I to be counted among their deliverers, as one who prefers, instead, to dismiss the biblical accounts of their diabolical doings by denying and disproving they ever occurred—the result of Reason's Tribunal's revealing the ***"facts and evidence"*** and the "common sense" that confirms it?

Should any American be proud of shameful traditions and shameful principles that nearly destroyed our nation in a war which had Americans killing other Americans because of the highly esteemed, Judeo-Christian tradition of slavery and its attendant racism?—a history that continues well beyond the Civil War to wreak havoc upon our nation—a history that still continues to have Americans despising and killing one another because of its divisive "us and them," supremacist mentality and the many racial and gender injustices, inequalities, and indecencies that have resulted from belief in uncivilized, blood-spilling, Judeo-Christian ritual customs and practices.

When God ordered the Jews to murder outsiders, (their non-Jewish, Canaanite neighbors), surely their thoughts had to be of "us" and "them" --- when the Jew, Jesus, ordered His Jewish disciples to avoid the non-Jewish Gentiles and their territories, surely their thoughts had to be of "us" and "them"! The combined history of the Jewish and Christian religion of "us" and "them," as "revealed" in the *Bible,* and well beyond its bloody pages, is a history of human degradation and wickedness that continues to undermine, century after century, all of the noble ideals that our freedom-loving nation and its Caretakers of Liberty have endeavored to achieve for the betterment of "all." Every American should be proud of the fact that our nation's Constitution was not written to promote the divisive "us" and "them" mentality that religion imparts and imposes; it was written to ensure the welfare of *"We the People,"* a concept that is alien to all God-addicts—a concept that must be honored and cultivated, however, if racial equality, gender equality, and living in harmony amongst all others are ever to become a "welcome" and "honored" part of the American Dream!

When we, the Caretakers of Liberty, are told, time and again, by our nation's leaders, politicians, news pundits, coddled clergy, (and others who have been *Bible*-brainwashed), that the Judeo-Christian God is a God of "love," we should, again, ask them to provide one example, I repeat, "one example" from the *Bible* that proves their claim—one example! —for the *Bible* only tells us otherwise.

Today's Christians who condemn abortion as the wanton murder of the un-born, as they have the right to do---they, however, should be ashamed to proclaim their abhorrence to the practice with a *Bible*-in-hand, a book which proudly promotes God's wanton, commanded murder of babies and children along with His involvement in life-destroying activities and atrocities undertaken against the most innocent and most vulnerable among us—a book that, as we know, encouraged the raping of children which, sadly, has become a "tradition" of Catholic priests and other "exalted" Christian clergy!

Americans, especially those who are proud of the decency inherent in our nation's ideals, should be ashamed, too, to credit the founding of our nation upon despicable Judeo-Christian traditions and principles—the ones proudly touted on the pages of the *Bible*. Be sure to read them—the chilling, abominable, evil *OT* accounts of a contemptible God's indulgence in injustice, in supremacist, (un-American) activity including murder and genocide, rape, misogyny, slavery, racism, xenophobia, hatred, brutality, vengeance, the punishing of the innocent, etc., etc., and then decide for yourself if such evil, malevolent, Semitic traditions and principles should be credited with and honored for the establishment of a freedom-loving, equality-endeavoring, justice-aspiring land. Decide for yourselves, also, after reading the *OT* accounts of the abominable God of Judeo-Christianity, if "IN GOD WE TRUST" is a fitting motto for our nation---a nation that is supposed to honor *"Life, Liberty and the pursuit of Happiness"* or is it a more fitting motto for those who would destroy our *"unalienable rights"*?

When we are told, too, that Islam is "the light of the world," we should remind ourselves that its "Holy" Prophet, Muhammad, married a 6-year-old child, I repeat, "married" a 6-year-old child without so much as a word of protest from high above—incredible! Had Muhammad lusted instead to marry a younger, perhaps diaper-clad female, I'm certain that Allah would have obliged him also---for surely, if it is okay with God that a 6-year-old child can become someone's wife, what possible reason would He have not to allow a toddler to enter into "holy" matrimony?

Only Reason's Tribunal can turn off this sickening, "blinding" light shed by all Semitic religions and allow us to "see" more clearly—allow us ***"to begin the world over again"*** without the abominable abuses that are always honorably allowed under God's direct orders and carried out in His holy name. Abominations that are established and justified by malevolent, immoral religions, their malevolent, immoral Gods, and their malevolent, immoral prophets—for it is obvious that the pursuits of a civilized world and the pursuits of evil Semitic theologies pretending to be good institutions cannot coexist. It is obvious that all of them must decline and go away in order for civilization to survive and thrive! We should, therefore, begin to make good use of our God-damned *"knowledge of good and evil"* by sipping the refreshing, liberating lemonade made from the extracts of reason and truth rather than continue gulping-down religion's poisoned Kool-Aid dogmas!

The *Bible*-babblers and Jesus-jabberers also do not want you to know, with any degree of certainty, that "Jehovah" and "Jesus" are merely different names given to the very one and the very same inseparable, immutable God no matter how convoluted or confusing the deceiving clergy endeavor to make the connection or the separation between them. They, the clergy, will usually resort to "speaking-in-tongues" when delivering their evasive gibberish on the matter such as their telling us that Jesus "is" Jehovah, but not really! ---that God was a man, but not really! ---that Jesus, being God, "created" the Universe, but not really!---that God had actually "died" on a cross, but not really! ---that God's death was a "total atonement," a fully paid debt, for our banishment from Eden, but not really!---really?

The pious "phenomenon" of literally speaking-in-tongues should be deemed a symptom of insanity to those of sound mind who witness it and not as a "special gift" from the Holy Ghost—a gift that, curiously, no Holy Ghost-selected Pope or Catholic priest, to my knowledge, has ever possessed or performed in public—a gift that is completely useless unless mesmerization serves a useful purpose for a mind-controlling religion based upon deception and miraculous VOILA events! Seemingly, I, too, must have received this "blessed gift" from the Holy Ghost for I have been "inspired" and "gifted" to perform what I call "writing-in-tongues," an example of which follows: @!!>?00^##!!UU***)))&?//#-#--#aS/sHo/Le#--#-#! No doubt, many of God's faithful will immediately recognize the divine origin of the gibberish written in the previous sentence! If you are among them, I would recommend that you seek medical attention, the sooner the better, for your mental illness! —but I digress . . .

Christians should never forget the fact that in their worshiping of Jesus Christ, they are, in fact, worshiping none other than Jehovah, the criminal-minded, terrorist God of the Israelites—they should never forget who it is that they are honoring and adoring as proud "mono" theists—do the math! It is very important for Christians to remember this fact when reading the "Inspired Loser's Manual"—the *New Testament*! It is also very important for them to remember this fact when they assemble to *"Praise the Lord"* and give their financial support to those with a vested interest in perpetrating the con job: the deception that would have us believe this *Bible*-God is always good, always there for us, and always ready to pour out His love to everyone regardless of His *OT* doings to the contrary. If that doesn't strike you as being humorous enough, I've created a most interesting game that *Bible*-believers can play that involves their use of the *Bible*---I call the game: "MY WORD"!

This game is played by substituting the God "revealed" in the *Old Testament* for the same God "revealed" in the *New Testament.* So instead of a monstrous Lord/God/Jehovah decreeing the murder of the Canaanites, we have a merciful Jesus giving the order for their extermination. Instead of a monstrous Lord/God/Jehovah giving His "chosen" the license to kill babies, to enslave their captives, to rape their virgin daughters, and to stone unruly children and homosexuals to death, we have a merciful Jesus giving His authority and His blessing for carrying-out such atrocities! Instead of a monstrous Lord/God/Jehovah ordering the mutilations of animals to be sacrificed in His honor, we have a merciful Jesus demanding they be torn limb from limb so that their blood can be sprinkled around His sacred altars while their roasting parts fill His nostrils with *"sweet savor"*! This exchange of speaking roles from the *OT* God to the *NT* God is really quite a lot of fun and quite enlightening, as well---give it a try!

The petulant, capricious, vengeful, *Old Testament* God is surely made in man's less-than-perfect image yet, we are imposed upon to believe that God is steadfast and immutable in His behaviors---a God who because of His omniscient nature is not, one assumes, supposed to be accustomed to changing His mind, His demeanor, or His career plans from one chapter and verse to the next. Understandably, such a flawed, tyrannical deity became a candidate for an extreme make-over. Some slight changes in the *Bible*-God's persona was eventually deemed a necessity by His ever-clever script-writers who realized that as people became slightly more civilized, honey would attract more flies than does vinegar! ---it is evident by the writings of the unknown authors of the *Bible* that they had also realized that excrement works best of all!

Jehovah's own miraculous, "resurrection," from a dark and despicable, genocidal tyrant in the *Old Testament* into a seemingly kinder and gentler (slightly more improved!) tyrant, was brought to life in technicolor on the pages of the *New Testament*. The imposing God-makers had eventually learned to recognize the advantage in substituting everyone's dreadful fear of God with a tender-hearted love for Him. And so it eventually became a matter of utmost importance for His parasitic, script-writing priests to begin using all of their proficient skills at deception and their knowledge of eliciting empathy to modify and morph their intolerant, malevolent God into a squeaky-clean, immaculately-conceived Savior—His new disguise being nothing more than an attempt to transform this chip off the old block into a less-intimidating deity.

The horrible, inhumane treatment God received while sporting His new look as meek and mild Jesus—the horrible treatment He received while performing His many "sacred" endeavors to save certain folks who, as it turned out, totally rejected Him—only helped to serve the script-writers' purpose of evoking and deepening our sympathies, tugging at our heart-strings, and securing our undying love for Him, our pitifully abused, beaten, crucified, and spit-upon "Savior." The pathos and camouflage they employed to keep the evil old block hidden behind the new block's clever disguise was so successful that few folks became the wiser and many more folks were sucked in by the subterfuge—the extreme make-over of scary ol' Jehovah into a squeaky-clean Jesus, the new, but not much improved, version of God—a modification of an un-modifiable deity that only "inspired" and "masterful" script-writers would dare to pull-off. Sadly, their efforts to deceive the world with guilt and guile went viral and virulent!

Wouldn't it have been more *Bible*-believable to think that Jesus, the Son of Jehovah, would have chosen to carry on the joyous and cherished family tradition of slaughtering and dismembering animals---a practice that dear ol' Dad was so fond of and renowned for establishing---and become a butcher (like Father, like Son!) or, at least, a barbecue chef in order to continue in the production of the heavenly, God-pleasing aroma of burning flesh as a means to honor His Father who art in Heaven but who still enjoys and indulges His carnal nature from time to time. Doesn't it make more sense that the Son of a meat-loving God, would have chosen to feed the multitudes with His Father's favorite food-choice: barbecue, instead of with stinkin' ol' fish and bread? But after giving careful consideration to His career-choices: a butcher, a baker, a candle-stick maker, it was decided, by His script-writers, to have Jesus choose to become a carpenter, which He supposedly did---a choice that was okay with Dad as long as He didn't build anything too high above the earth such as any God-detested Tower of Babel-like structures, (such as cathedrals and high steepled churches!), which might tend to push His mentally unstable, single parent over the edge because of His OCD issues! Thankfully, the Gospel script-writers thought it best to make carpentry, not butchery, the "chosen" trade for Jesus whom they were trying to present to *"the lost sheep of the house of Israel,"* not as someone made in the image of a throat-slitting Godzilla wielding a meat-cleaver, but as a meek and mild Guy wielding a hammer and a saw! It surely is a bit of a stretch to believe that God and Jesus are the one and the same deity!

One wonders why Jesus left "Presto Builders," His thriving, lucrative, carpentry business behind to venture-off into the much less prosperous vocation of sheep-saving? I bet He often regretted making that decision knowing how things worked out with His forsaking flock who demanded He be crucified to death! Can you imagine the money this bad-choice-making Guy and His hand-picked crew must have made with each work project taking no longer than 6 days to complete? . . . *"Presto! ---Here's your new house, lady---that'll be 7000 shekels, Roman tax included, and it comes with a never-ending warranty on labor and materials."* ---(God, evidently, doesn't build crap)!

It is quite interesting and amusing to think that Jesus may have gotten a call-back to correct some shoddy work? ---for a door, perhaps, that didn't close quite right or for an ill-fitting window that wouldn't open or close, etc.! Or, on the other hand, can you even imagine something that God, the Carpenter, built with His own hands not being in existence today? ---now that would be really hard to believe, wouldn't it? Something tells me that Jesus must have preferred being paid in cash, too, as He kinda knew His days were numbered! --- but I digress . . .

Sadly, as a result of the viral and virulent nature of religion (and many other diseases), it is Jehovah, God of the Israelites, to whom America chooses to pay tribute to in her Pledge of Allegiance and upon her currency! Americans should begin to realize and never forget the fact that the God of Judaism "is" the God of Christianity! Jehovah/Jesus "is" the one and the only, I repeat, "the one and the only" God of Judeo-Christianity—shocking isn't it? Trust me, their DNA profiles, their fingerprints, and their vengeful mindsets (which always favor the Jews!) are exact matches! Both the *OT* and the *NT* confirm the fact that Jehovah/Jesus did not want peace on this earth—He, Jehovah/Jesus, wants bloodshed and division to exist throughout the world---*Matt.* 10:34, *Luke* 12:49,51. Exact matches, folks! If a tree is known by its fruit, so too is the Mono-God of the Israelites and the Christianites. Man help us!

Thank goodness, Semitic religions and their "created" gods are now in decline in various parts of the world—they are fated like the thundering gods that came before them, to lose their power, their influence, and their moral standing either by evolution or by revolution which both bring about needed changes over time—the latter, of course, usually does it much sooner rather than later! ---Viva la Reason's Tribunal!

I earnestly request, also, that everyone who has been cursed by God for having their eyes opened, for possessing the *"knowledge of good and evil,"* will now begin to use this, understandably, God-prohibited/God-damned gift wisely and purposefully when reading Semitic scriptures. When encountering parts of the *Bible* and the *Koran* that prove difficult to swallow and consume, it is hoped that you, the reader, will remember to wash them down with some of the liberating lemonade made from the *Bible's* lousy lemons mentioned earlier that have been made palatable by the delectable, delicious extracts of reason and truth. This common-sense, rational procedure will enable the body to excrete the toxins embedded in both of the above Chutzpah Chronicles before they have a chance to infect their readers and to cause harm to others. The pandemic of Semitic religion has raged unchecked far too long---please read this irreverent, *Bible*-blasting book in its entirety and don't forget to drink plenty of its life-saving refreshment along the way---the lemonade is on the house, folks! *"Bottoms up"*!

---Kevin Vincent Kelly

Disciples of Dishonor and Disgrace

All of these twelve men were "chosen" (hand-picked!) by Jesus. They left their families, their friends, and their occupations to serve Him and to share their lives with Him. They were amazed and awestruck by His authority in the things He taught them. They traveled about on foot with their "Teacher" listening to His every "Word" that He spoke about things to come while learning the importance of their role in the saving of (Jewish) souls. They willingly gave up everything they were previously accustomed to and enjoyed doing in their former lives to be in the presence of a man they all considered and proclaimed to be the "Son of God."

They witnessed their "Master" perform wondrous miracles: turning water into wine, healing the sick and diseased, curing the blind, deaf, dumb, lame, crippled, paralyzed, epileptic, and the insane. They, too, performed healing miracles through the power that Jesus bestowed upon them. They witnessed Jesus instantly restore a severed ear and return the dead to life. They watched Him calm the wind and waves and walk on water---Peter, who performed this awesome miracle for a moment or two in His presence, even found a coin, amazingly enough, in a fish's mouth as Jesus had predicted he would! ---where would Semitic religions be without their fish stories?

They assisted Jesus when He fed thousands not once, but twice, with only a few loaves of bread and even fewer fishes---ending up with more food than when they had begun---another fish-tale for sure! Peter, John, and James saw Jesus become as bright as the sun and, somehow, in that blinded state, they were able to know with certainty that Jesus was actually talking to the long-dead Moses and the long-dead Elijah! ---they also knew with certainty that in their blinded state, they were hearing a voice that emanated from "within a cloud" telling them, *This is my Son . . . hear ye Him.*

After all of these incredible, unbelievable fish-tale events---after personally witnessing and believing the astounding miracles Jesus performed in their presence---after declaring they would all rather face death than deny Him, each of these twelve, divinely-chosen men ran away (*Exodus II!*) and deserted their "Messiah" while He was being arrested-Peter of rock foundation fame, denying he knew Jesus at all, not once, not twice, but three times! ---methinks something is fishy about this whole story!

While the dead body of their beloved Savior hung on a cross, these faithless disciples, fearing for their own lives, never returned to Jesus, not even to administer to His corpse or to assist in His burial. Even after hearing that Jesus had risen from death, they would not believe it---some still disbelieved in His resurrection after seeing a living Jesus stand before them. If these guys didn't believe what their own ears heard and their own eyes beheld, why should you or I believe it to be true? Why should anyone be convinced now about the certainty of Jesus' divine nature when His own disciples harbored doubts about it?

These twelve deserters were hand-picked by God (who really knows how to pick 'em!) to be His missionaries, to spread His Gospel, to establish His church, and to judge His *"lost sheep"* in Heaven. How interesting! ---when one considers what Jesus stated in *Matt.* 10:33, *"But whosoever shall deny me before men, him will I also deny before my Father which is in Heaven,"* and what He stated in *Luke* 9:24, *"For whosoever will save his life shall lose it."* Even after "denying" Jesus by their words and by their deeds, they still remained His chosen twelve, chosen, one assumes for their cowardice, for their ability to lie and betray, forsake and flee in order to "save" their own sorry asses and abandon His. If Peter wept bitterly out of remorse for denying Jesus in His time of need, he certainly should have dropped dead out of guilt after meeting a risen Christ! The first question, one would think, a resurrected Christ should have asked His disciples---"Where the hell did you guys go when I was being arrested?" ---methinks they went fishing!

Are we now to find only truth in the God-inspired, Gospel words supposedly "revealed" "according to" perjurers and betrayers: *Matthew, Mark, Luke,* and *John*---men who looked into the eyes of Jesus as they lied to Him---men who turned their backs on Him---men who, for some odd reason, are now regarded as saints? If they could willfully lie to someone they considered to be the Son of Almighty God, why are we supposed to believe that what they tell us is nothing but the truth?

In bearing witness to the events surrounding the life and death of Jesus, the Gospel-tale tellers include accounts of their own lying and desertion without offering, anywhere on the pages of the *Bible*, the slightest apology to Him, their Lord Jesus Christ, for having engaged in such shameful and dishonorable acts even though these were guys who knew well, the power of asking for forgiveness and making contrition for their sins. Judas Iscariot, Jesus' betrayer, at least, out of his unbearable remorse, had the integrity of character to repent and return the thirty pieces of silver, then, understandably, hang himself for his dastardly deed---*Matthew* 27:3-5!

It is beyond belief that not one of these twelve men who loved Jesus beyond measure and dedicated their lives to Him, had the courage to stand by their Savior, that day in Gethsemane, as He was being led away. Beyond all doubt, these are twelve disciples of dishonor and disgrace!

· · · · · · ·

The Gospels of *Matthew, Mark, Luke,* and *John* are said to be the "infallible, inspired Word of God," and as such, form the very foundation upon which the Christian religion is raised. Few of Christendom's faithful are aware, however, that the Gospels were written by unknown and contradictory authors, and that they come to us as the author of *Supernatural Religion* states:

> *...unsupported by facts, uncorroborated by evidence, unaccompanied by proof of investigation, and unprovided with material for examination.*

Few of them are aware that:

> **The authenticity of the books of the New Testament was denied, and the books treated as tales, forgeries, and lies, at the time they were voted to be the Word of God.**

> ---Thomas Paine, *The Age of Reason*

No one knows where or when the Gospels were written; no one can locate or produce an original copy of them. Nevertheless, the religious beliefs of Christianity, which are based upon such dubious, unverifiable writings, are considered to be above suspicion and beyond reproach---incredible!

Are the Gospels the product of truthful men? Are we to believe their "sacred" words recount personal and intimate knowledge about Jesus Christ, His life and death, His resurrection and ascension? If so, why do their eventful recollections concerning the life and times of Jesus that, supposedly, took place in their presence, abound in contradictions and inconsistencies? Why do so many of their tales lack not only reason, but reasonableness?

A simple study and comparison of their texts as found in the *New Testament* is all that is necessary to separate the believable from the unbelievable, the wheat from the chaff. What remains, however, is seldom palatable and seldom digestible, hence the need for life-saving, life-liberating lemonade!

These four "inspired" men, we are led to believe, were the eyes that saw the miracles Jesus performed and the ears that heard the words Jesus spoke. As eye-witnesses and ear-witnesses, their testimonies are often beyond belief. Truth, after all, is the product of observation, not inspiration! If, however, they did not see, or hear, or partake in the events they describe, then what they tell us has to be either based on outright lies or on unreliable hearsay alone and, therefore, would be lacking in authority and believability. The absence of their mutual agreement in recounting what they have, supposedly, witnessed together reveals a lack of personal involvement and personal knowledge of the events described in their supposed "first-hand" accounts. Missing, also, is the factual certainty that should proceed from their having lived the same experience---disagreements over time, place, and circumstance expose the fraudulent nature of the Gospel-tales and their authors.

Compare the Gospel words they offer, not with blinded eyes, but with opened eyes freed from the constraints and impositions of religious indoctrination. Imagine yourself being in the company of the disciples and being involved personally in the stories and situations they relate---do this mental exercise for "all" of the *OT* and *NT Bible*-tales you care to read about. Consider the circumstances of the *Bible*-tale you have thus figuratively placed yourself in and try to envision and evaluate all of the untold aspects that your make-believe, re-living of *Bible*-events elicits, then listen to the counsel of your own heart and mind when you draw your own conclusions about them and not just accept conclusions made by others.

It is most important, however, that you examine the often overlooked, smallest detail given in the *Bible's* chapters and verses for there truly are no small details, I repeat, "no small details" to be found in God's "Word" for it is there that the fabrications of evil, deceiving men (the Devil!) are often "revealed" in the extrapolations of seemingly insignificant utterances---you may be surprised by the results of your "detailed" examinations!

Thankfully, in America, it is considered unfair and unjust to present only the defendant's claims and testimony in a trial---a trial that would prevent the prosecution from challenging and cross-examining the defendant's statements and evidence. Our justice-system aspires to fairness because it allows for "both" sides of a case to be heard by a judge and a jury. The religious "defense" side in this matter has long been heard and rests its case, therefore, in fairness, let the other side be heard, too---let the long-overdue scrutiny and prosecution of Semitic religions and their supporting scriptures begin . . .

Welcome, folks, to Reason's Tribunal (the process) and *Reason's Tribunal* (the book) ---may either one or both enlighten you and set you free from your imposed mental bondage to Semitic religious beliefs.

---Kevin Vincent Kelly

Introduction

The following is a list of writers who lived and wrote during the time, or within a century after the time that Christ is said to have lived and performed his wonderful works:

Josephus	*Persius*
Pompon Mela	*Philo-Judaeus*
Plutarch	*Quintius Curtius*
Seneca	*Justus of Tiberia*
Lucian	*Pliny the Elder*
Apollonius	*Pausanius*
Suetonius	*Pliny the Younger*
Valerius Flaccus	*Juvenal*
Tacitus	*Florus Lucias*
Martial	*Quintilian*
Favorinus	*Arrian*
Lucanus	*Phaedrus*
Petronius	*Epictetus*
Damis	*Dion Pruseus*
Silius Italicus	*Aulus Gellius*
Paterculus	*Statius*
Columella	*Appian*
Ptolemy	*Dio Chrysostom*
Theon of Smyrna	*Hermogenes*
Lysias	*Phlegon*
Valerius Maximus	*Appion of Alexandria*

Enough of the writings of the authors named in the foregoing list remains to form a library. Yet in the mass of Jewish and Pagan literature, aside from two forged passages in the works of a Jewish author, and two disputed passages in the works of Roman writers, there is to be found no mention of Jesus Christ.

---John E. Remsberg, *The Christ*

To talk of immaterial existences is to talk of nothings. To say that the human soul, angels, god, are immaterial, is to say they are nothings, or that there is no god, no angels, no soul. I cannot reason otherwise . . . without plunging into the fathomless abyss of dreams and phantasms. I am satisfied, and sufficiently occupied with the things which are, without tormenting or troubling myself about those which may indeed be, but of which I have no evidence.

---Thomas Jefferson

What evidence does anyone have of the existence of God? ---a boundless, complex, mysterious, awe-inspiring Universe is only proof of the existence of a boundless, complex, mysterious, awe-inspiring Universe!

---kvk

I almost shudder at the thought of alluding to the most fatal example of the abuses of grief which the history of mankind has preserved—the Cross. Consider the calamities that engine of grief has produced! ...Facts are stubborn things; and whatever may be our wishes, our inclination, or the dictates of our passions, they cannot alter the state of facts and evidence. . .

---John Adams

If we are made to believe that the *Bible* is a "divinely-inspired" work, then shouldn't we also believe that God was, truly, its one and only author? Surely, God would not have "inspired" anyone to write something about Himself that He did not want written, or inspire someone to write something that He, God, did not intend to convey, therefore, it was God who, by proxy, wrote the entire *Bible*---every word of it! Deducing, from common-sense, that God, Himself, was the *Bible's* ultimate author, why would He have His "inspired" proxies write one thing upon its pages and have it mean something other than what was literally written?

Certainly, God wouldn't have intended for His "inspired" words to be confusing, misleading, or deceiving---that's the Devil's job---right? So, when God's "inspired" words have been written in a manner that is difficult to comprehend or believe, or when His "inspired" words are subject to various meanings and differing interpretations, they, obviously, should never be considered as an example of divine communication---never!

If the *Bible,* as well as the *Koran,* cannot be believed literally as written, they should be completely dismissed as having been "divinely" authored or having a divine component for how is it possible to determine which words are to be taken literally, which figuratively, and which should be disregarded altogether? Why should any *Bible*-believer who is able to read, ever have any need for spiritual-spin-doctors to tell them which of God's words are to be believed as written and which are not? Doesn't that speak of incompetency of the part of the "inspired" writer of them? It is especially so when their status as being the "Word of God" has been decided by someone's vote as in the case of the books of the *Bible*, or has been accomplished by the accumulation of dubious chapter (sura) and verse (ayat) hearsay recollections of various individuals, as in the case of the *Koran.*

Shouldn't every one of the *Bible's* devout believers, therefore, have absolute faith in the fact that God always says what He means and always means what He says? Of course they should! Why, therefore, when God's literal "Word" informs, not once, but twice, that man has *"dominion"* over animals---*Gen.* 1:26,28, why do Jews and Christians never believe it to be literally so? Why do the *Bible*-spinners always make excuses for the Almighty by telling us what it was that God really meant to convey in His use of His "inspired" word *"dominion,"* a word He used to clearly tell His readers that man has absolute control "*over every living thing that moveth upon the earth*" ---no exceptions?

Likewise, when Jesus informs His believers in *John* 14:12 that they not only have the ability to perform the miracles that He supposedly performed, they will be able to accomplish *"even greater ones"*! Does anyone really need convincing that Jesus "lied" when He, God, caused these "inspired" words to be written down in "His" Gospels? If He didn't lie, why does His "Greater Works Society" still lack a single member? ---"liar, liar, pants on fire"! ---why, therefore, is every Christian, I repeat, "every Christian" (2 billion faithful believers in Christ) unable to perform the miracles that Jesus had said each and every one of them would be able to perform? ---Reason's Tribunal holds the truthful answer!

Surely, if God did not intend to have us believe what He had caused to be "literally" stated in the *Bible*, He certainly would have found a better way to convey His personal "idea" of what "having dominion over animals" or "doing greater works" really meant to Him and, in doing so, avoid having always to rely on others to "spin" His words into "more believable" terms.

Unlike God's adoring preachers, I (of all people!) totally accept at face value every "literal" Word that God had caused to be written in the *Bible*! There is a valid reason, however, for God's adoring advocates to have "selective" belief in the words written by the hand of "God-inspired" men in the *Bible* and in the *Koran* especially when they reveal the Almighty to be a criminal psychopath. Otherwise, having belief in scriptural-literalisms demands that we must believe, with certainty, in absurdities---that we must accept and promote the injustice and malevolence of God's actions---that all who "believe" in the words of the *Bible* or the *Koran* must indulge in the committing of atrocities in the sacred name of God---something that all the faithful are compelled to "believe" and "commanded" to carry-out!

This book, *Reason's Tribunal,* will expose to its fair-minded readers much of the insanity and the evils of having "belief" in ungodly Semitic religions, their not-so-sacred scriptures, and their not so sacred deities; it will give us the means, the only means, to sanely end the terror-minded madness of their insane-minded, "Word of God" believers! Trust me with all of your heart and mind when I tell you that "all" of the words written in this "holy" book: *Reason's Tribunal,* were "revealed" by God directly and exclusively to me (in an unwitnessed manner of course) —the contents of which He wants communicated only to those who will greatly benefit from "believing" its every syllable. All of the words contained herein, voiced by the Almighty only to me in secret should never be doubted, neither should anyone seek proof of the claims they tell of for God doesn't lie and, of course, neither do I!

Never question why God always needs the help of others to get His "Word" out—that's just His way of doing things. Go now, after reading this book, and inform certain folks only about what God has told me to have you tell them. Impose upon them to "believe" every God-given word He has "revealed" only to me without error in this "sacred" work and then have them impose what it instructs upon the rest of the world even if it involves killing, in His Holy Name of course, all who stand in the way. For God, whom we don't wish to anger in the least, has promised that those who "receive" and "believe" His Word will soon be living the hedonistic lifestyle of the rich and famous in Forever-Land but only after you die, of course--- isn't such an arrangement the equivalent of someone saying: "I'd be happy to pay you all of the money I owe you but only after you pass away" --- such a deal! ---does anyone really think that a Jew, a Christian, or a Muslim exists who would be willing to accept payment "after death" for their services? (I know that my telling you what God had told me to relay to you will not be believed, and rightly so, but why then accept the words contained in the *Bible* and the *Koran* as being truthful and credible when they, too, are entirely based merely upon an unknown, someone's saying it is so? ---at least in the case of *Reason's Tribunal,* the author is known!)

All one has to do to deserve a pleasure-filled eternity after you have died is to devote your living days to imposing His Word with zeal upon all of mankind by any means possible. Otherwise, merely calling out Jesus' name with your dying breath will suffice (*Luke* 23:42,43) —who then can deny God's mercy, God's greatness, and God's generosity? May peace be upon you every day you are among the living and pleasure be upon you every day you are among the dead!

(NOTE TO READER: Assuming that Jesus has the miraculous ability to hear, with His own ears, every sound generated every moment all across the world, will He, therefore, give everyone the opportunity and the ability to call out the name of Jesus with their dying breath? ---of course not! Some folks leave this world in a non-verbal coma---some folks die instantly---some folks die who never had the ability to speak in their entire lives, etc., ---so what becomes of their sorry asses?

Does merciful Jesus wake these deceased folks momentarily in order to give them voice so that He can inquire of them if they prefer to say *"Jesus forgive me"* at that very moment or if they prefer instead to go to Hell to be roasted in the eternal flames? Is there really a spiritual dimension to any of this BS-*Bible*-babble that would, in effect, allow the likes of Adolf Hitler, Adolf bin Laden, Adolf Putin to be granted amnesty just for calling out to God with their last breath?)

Why would anyone believe that the God of the *Bible* is merciful? ---a Guy who, like the above human excrement, enjoys adding to the miseries of this world and even beyond? ---come on folks, start putting your gift of "the knowledge of good and evil" to "good" use! (A FURTHER NOTE: Because the *Bible* has "revealed" that God's first attempt to share His blissful, heavenly paradise with every living thing in Eden had ended in complete failure, He has confided in me that He has made all the necessary adjustments to His infallible Word, (the scripted plans for our heavenly, pie-in-the-sky future) —in order to prevent a deceiving Devil, in the guise of a talking snake, and someone's naivete and lack of street-smarts, from screwing things up for everyone again. God's deceased followers can now rest assured that He and His script-writers have gotten it right this time! However, those who are planning to book a permanent room at the Paradise Inn should keep in mind that Heaven, for all of its many perfections, is not immune from evil for that is the exact location where the Devil learned his trade and began his missssion, nevertheless, enjoy the blissssssssss! — sounds serpent-like doesn't it?)

You should laugh when you read the above words in the preceding paragraphs for they truly are ridiculous but you should cry knowing that Semitic religions with their "revealed" Word of God scriptures, the *Bible* and the *Koran*, were similarly fabricated and imposingly disseminated, and that billions believe in them and their "after-death" promises—billions continue to live and to act under their not-so-spiritual spell—billions continue to eagerly anticipate, some with pins and needles, being bodily lifted into the air by the welcoming arms of Jesus' to begin experiencing the eternal glories of their "after-life" existence in a "much-improved" Eden where Happy-Hour never ends. While the world has slowly progressed since these "Word" of God scriptures made their civilization-hindering, destructive and deceiving debuts---scriptures whose sacrosanct words were responsible for demanding the extermination of entire nations of innocent people in order to rob their lands and to rape their virgin daughters—for stoning certain people to death---for inspiring the Crusades (short for <u>cru</u>el and <u>sad</u>istic!), the Inquisition, the burning of witches and heretics, the slaying of infidels, and the horrors of 9/11—scriptures whose sacrosanct words are still on the books waiting to convince others to commit murder and atrocity in the name of God.

Still on the books are God's inspiring words that sanction slavery "forever" —still on the books are God's inspiring words that demand the murder of homosexuals, unruly children, and non-believers "forever" — still on the books are God's inspiring words that justify terrorism and *"Death to America."* Such words and such deeds---because they happen to be expressed (or hinted at), on the pages of the "inerrant" *Bible* and the "undoubted" *Koran*—are deemed, like the books that contain them, to be honorable and worthy of unquestioned respect because they are believed to be God's "revealed" will—they are believed even today, in this more enlightened age, by our leaders tasked with upholding and preserving our liberties—even by those whose descendants were victims of slavery—even by those whose lives were stricken by acts of terror that were inspired by words written on the hallowed pages of the *Koran*—incredible! Refusing to question the authority and the sacredness of these Word of God scriptures—refusing to denounce the malevolent, murderous God who is glorified on their pages for His crimes against humanity is but the mindless continuation of our tacit acceptance, compliance, and servitude to Semitic religious dogma! Sadly, for the most part, our knowledge of things relating to belief in God and "spiritual behavior" comes to us from just these two bogus books written by the hand of man for the obvious purposes of ***"power and revenue"***!

It is little doubted or disputed that we, as innocent-minded, knowledge-lacking children, received and accepted our first lessons about the existence of a "Semitic" God and "religion" from our well-meaning parents who, in turn, received and accepted, without question, the things they were instructed about their God and their religion from their well-meaning parents. With little ability to reason things out, children have no way to disprove or investigate the religious claims they received from the lips of Mom and Dad and others who got their information from their parents as well, and later from clerics—priests, preachers, teachers, rabbis, imams, mullahs, and other spin-doctors, etc., —who got their information in the same way or from books written by those with a vested interest in promoting belief in Semitic religions.

As naive children, who are obviously vulnerable to the impositions of their nurturers, vulnerable to genital mutilation being undertaken at eight days of age, we are never taught to question or seek proof of the religious claims that are imposed upon our innocent hearts, gullible minds, and easily violated bodies---we are educated, instructed, indoctrinated, and conditioned "only" to believe them. Thus, the unchallenged religious mindset of the parents is passed along unaltered, for the most part, generation after generation and it all begins with the indoctrination of naive children. The religious habits now begun and imposed in childhood, within well-meaning family settings, will continue for a lifetime, reinforced by culture and tradition, seldom, if ever, to be suspect.

> *If you are religious at all it is overwhelmingly probable that your religion is that of your parents. If you were born in Arkansas and you think Christianity is true and Islam false, knowing full well that you would think the opposite if you had been born in Afghanistan, you are the victim of childhood indoctrination.*
>
> --- Richard Dawkins, *The God Delusion*

> *We have names for people who have many beliefs for which there is no rational justification. When their beliefs are extremely common we call them 'religious'; otherwise, they are likely to be called 'mad', 'psychotic' or 'delusional' . . . Clearly there is sanity in numbers. And yet, it is merely an accident of history that it is considered*

---Sam Harris, *The End of Faith*

The children of Jews are thus programmed to believe, without any doubt whatsoever, the teachings of the Jewish religion—for the sole interest of God, they are told, is to "favor" only the Jews and no others—the children of Christians are thus programmed to believe, without any doubt whatsoever, the teachings of the Christian religion—for the sole interest of God, they are told, is to "favor" only the Christians and no others—the children of Muslims are thus programmed to believe, without any doubt whatsoever, the teachings of the Muslim religion—for the sole interest of God, they are told, is to "favor" only the Muslims and no others. And the same can be said for the children of the various divisions and offshoots of the above Semitic religions. It should be obvious to anyone with a functioning brain that Jews, Christians, Muslims, et al., cannot all be correct about their exclusivity with God—their differing religions cannot all be the one and only Semitic religion "favored" by the one and only Semitic God, but which one? Is there truly a "correct" one or are they all bogus religions concocted in the ungodly heart and ungodly mind of parasites who wrote their "sacred" scripts with ungodly hands for the self-interests of a "favored," ungodly few?

Do the Gods of Semitic religions truly exist or are they, too, the creation of script-writing priests and their less-than-godly self-interests? Are we to believe that all the differing Semitic religions and the divisions within them are the result of a "perfect" God's doing? Are we to believe it is the desire of Divinity to promote discord among all who believe in Him or is it, perhaps, the desire of His scriptural script-writers to promote such "us" and "them" dissensions in order to benefit from them? Reason's Tribunal will help you determine the correct answers to these questions—help you determine why Semitic religions must always maintain their control of the faithful ("us") by attempting to denigrate and/or destroy everyone whom their religion considers to be an outsider ("them") —everyone whom their religion considers to be disobedient or disrespectful to their God by not worshiping and adoring Him and not following His orders. The "God-favoring" indoctrination visited upon the gullible, innocent children mentioned above

43

would be tolerable if the religious teachings being "instilled" in them resulted in improving the planet and the human-condition, however, when such divisive, supremacist-minded, cultural chutzpah is responsible, time and again throughout the ages, for the intentional commission of acts of violence, bloody atrocities, mass-casualty suicide missions, etc., etc., carried out in God's name, as well as the religion-generated, racial discrimination and dehumanizing incidents that too often end in violence and/or death on our nation's streets, there must come a time of reckoning, a time when a revolution in that *"system of religion"* can no longer be denied, dismissed, or delayed!

Because of an innate concern and desire for the survival of our species, we, as adults, are tasked with the responsibility of striving to create a better world not only for ourselves, but for the generations that, it is hoped, will follow. The time has come, therefore, to begin to openly question all aspects of the religious beliefs that, for the most part, were lovingly transferred to us for our blind, naive acceptance. It is time now for those of mature age to demand to see valid proof of their veracity. It is time for Jewish males of mature age to make the decision whether or not they want to be circumcised. It is time now for us of mature age to boldly investigate the fabulous claims made in all Semitic scriptures by means of a fair and balanced scrutiny of their texts without fearing the consequences of honest and reasonable inquiry. It is time now for Reason's Tribunal to begin to uncover the fraudulence of these so-called "Word of God" writings that continue to inspire and encourage the dealing-out of death and destruction—writings that remain inviolable and publicly unchallenged to this very day. It is time now for Reason's Tribunal to begin the de-programming and the de-bunking that will set us free at last from the deceiving dogmas and death-dealing impositions of Semitic religions---just think of your participation in Reason's Tribunal as if you are taking *"One small step for Man, one giant leap for mankind!"* ---(Neil Armstrong, stepping foot on the moon.)

> *If each child were allowed to wait until of mature age before investigating religions and was then required to study all religions and all opposition to religions, few persons would be believers.*

> ---James Hervey Johnson, *Superior Men*

Even fewer persons, would be inspired to become suicide bombers and terrorists! ---kvk

(NOTE TO READER: A "Deist" is . . . (A) —someone who believes that God exists only as the Creator of the Universe but takes no part in its daily operation nor interferes in the lives of human beings . . . (B) —someone who doesn't believe in "revealed" religion and its Ruler . . . (C) —someone who believes the way to understand God is by studying the works of nature and by using one's intelligence—a "Unitarian" is . . . (A) —someone who accepts only the moral teachings of Jesus but rejects His divinity and the doctrine of the Trinity . . . (B) —someone who rejects the orthodox beliefs of Christianity . . . (C) —someone who encourages freedom in religious thought—a "Theist" is . . . (A) —someone who believes in a personal God (Jehovah, Jesus, Allah) who created and rules the Universe . . . (B) —someone who believes that God rewards or punishes us for our behavior and who continually intervenes in our daily personal lives . . . (C) —someone who believes in the existence of devils, demons, eternal perdition, and miracles . . . (D) —someone who believes that God has "revealed" Himself and His plans for us via His "infallible" and "inerrant" Semitic scriptures . . . (E) —someone who believes that prayers and rituals make God compliant with our whims and our wishes—an "Atheist" is . . . (A) —someone who rejects all the Gods of religion along with their "revealed" scriptures. . . (B) —someone who doesn't believe in the existence of devils, demons, eternal perdition, and miracles—an "Agnostic" is someone who contends that nothing is known or can be known about the existence of God or about things outside of human experience—a "Secularist" is someone whose interest and concerns are only for the world we exist in and not for the interest and concerns of any religion and its afterlife offerings.)

America's founding fathers: Jefferson, Paine, John Adams, Washington, Franklin, and Madison were "not" Christians as is commonly proclaimed. They were Deists or Unitarians, men who may have admired certain aspects about the biblical Jesus but who were not advocates of the "cruel and unusual" dogmas of Judeo-Christianity. Slavery, which Jesus, in His Jehovah disguise, instituted forever in the *OT* and, obviously, never condemned nor spoke against in the *NT,* was not deemed, for the most part, to be "cruel and unusual" by "Christian" Colonials who recognized it as being an important part of God's will and wisdom since it was "revealed" as such in His holy Word: the *Bible.* All of the above-named men who were, for the most part, considered enlightened for the times in which they lived, rejected the orthodoxy of the Christian Church and the divinity of Jesus Christ/Jehovah. This fact alone would classify all of the above founding fathers of America as being "atheists"! All of these men rejected belief in a capricious and petulant, mean-spirited and personally interested deity who, as the *Bible* informs, had "chosen" a few certain folks to be His one and only favored people, a decision God later regretted and, thankfully, for their sake, *"repented of the evil which He thought to do unto His people"* ---*Ex.* 32:14!

One wonders if God ever *"repented of the evil"* He did *"do unto"* non-Jews as reported, time and again, in the *Bible*? Did He ever "repent" of His decision to destroy the world and nearly all of its inhabitants who, seemingly on day 1 of their existence, resorted so readily to sinfulness and violence? ---did He ever "repent" of preparing a Hell to eternally punish nearly every one of the world's inhabitants? Hmm! Imagine a perfect God regretting or repenting of anything He did and, in effect, admit of His incompetence---really? Hmm! Hmm! Doesn't the *Bible* reveal to us that its imperfect God was, in reality, made exactly in man's imperfect image? It is my opinion that it was during one of God's weaker moments when He had made the decision to favor Jews only---a time when He had thought it was a good idea to establish a Hebrew fan club in order to bestow His glorious blessings upon them exclusively—a time when they weren't pissing Him off by bowing to a golden calf---a time when He wasn't planning to kill every last one of them for their choosing to worship such an idol over His "golden bull" —incredible, incredible! —but, I digress . . .

The religion-condoned enslavement of black men, black women, and black children was an established practice of the times in which America's founders lived and which, to their credit, they all spoke against and desired to see abolished. Slavery was a practice that was powered by economic concerns and sanctioned, no doubt, by earnest Judeo-Christian indoctrination which justified human bondage without exception or interruption until the end of time in its shared scripture---*Gen.* 9:25,26, *Lev.* 25:44-46, *Col.* 3:22.

> *In all the ages the Roman Church has owned slaves, bought and sold slaves, authorized and encouraged her children to trade in them. Long after some Christian peoples had freed their slaves the Church still held on to hers. If any could know, to absolute certainty, that all this was right, and according to God's will and desire, surely it was she, since she was God's specially appointed representative in the earth and sole authorized and infallible expounder of his Bible. There were the texts; there was no mistaking their meaning; she was right, she was doing in this thing what the Bible had mapped out for her to do. So unassailable was*

her position that in all the centuries she had no word to say against human slavery. Yet now at last, in our immediate day, we hear a Pope saying slave trading is wrong, and we see him sending an expedition to Africa to stop it. The texts remain: it is the practice that has changed Why? Because the world (and Reason's Tribunal ---kvk) has corrected the Bible. The Church never corrects it; and also never fails to drop in at the tail of the procession—and take the credit for the correction. As she will probably do in this instance.

---Mark Twain

Christian Colonials, for the most part, were convinced, by the words written in the *Bible,* that God, having sanctioned slavery had, therefore, given His stamp of approval to its practice. Few Christian Colonials, therefore, regarded this practice as either "sinful" or an "abomination" as a result of their Christian education, their *Bible*-learning, and their *Bible*-indoctrination---the few who thought otherwise were mostly unwilling to stand in open opposition to it, and even fewer still were willing to risk their good standing in a *Bible*-beguiled nation of ***"Christianized people"*** —but the times were beginning to change. Thomas Paine who was never a slave owner, had begun to raise his earnest voice and to take earnest action against this Judeo-Christian tradition and principle that had been passed down through the ages to his generation. Just a few weeks after his arrival in America, Mr. Paine wrote an article entitled, *African Slavery in America,* upon witnessing the inhumanity of a slave market operating in Philadelphia. In this article that was printed on March 8, 1775, he had this to say:

That some desperate wretches should be willing to steal and enslave men by violence and murder for gain, is rather lamentable than strange. But that many civilized, nay, Christianized people should approve, and be concerned in the savage practice, is surprising.

Thomas Paine denounced those who quoted ***"sacred scriptures"*** to defend what he deemed a ***"wicked practice"*** placing the enslavement of the Negro people on a par with ***"murder, robbery, lewdness, and barbarity,"*** and called upon Americans to immediately ***"discontinue and renounce it, with grief and abhorrence."*** Later that year, in an article entitled *"A Serious Thought"* published October 18, 1775, he stated:

...may our first gratitude be shown by an act of continental legislation, which shall put a stop to the importation of Negroes for sale, soften the hard fate of those already here, and in time procure their freedom.

A short time later, after penning the above, he became a founding member of Benjamin Franklin's Anti-Slavery Society, the first of its kind in America. As Clerk of the Pennsylvania Assembly, Mr. Paine wrote the Preamble to the Act passed by the Pennsylvania Assembly March 1, 1780, which provided for the gradual emancipation of Negro slaves in the state. It was the very first legislative measure passed in America for the emancipation of slaves! Sadly, as I approach my 76th year of existence, I have yet to hear any black person in this nation so much as mention the name of Thomas Paine or credit him for his efforts to abolish slavery so early on in our nation's history—incredible! The founding fathers, however, who were involved in this *"wicked practice"* of slavery were beginning to recognize the error of their ways—George Washington, in a letter written to Robert Morris in 1786 stated:

...there is not a man living who wishes more sincerely than I do, to see a plan adopted for the abolition of slavery.

Benjamin Franklin had divested himself of his slaves by 1781—Washington, in his Last Will and Testament, freed his personal slave, William Lee, and left instructions for the emancipation of his remaining slaves upon Martha's death. John Adams and Thomas Paine, never owned slaves. Thomas Jefferson and James Madison, however, much to their shame and discredit, never freed their slaves. To see other examples of the persistence of certain religious customs being passed down through the generations, one has only to look to the Muslim world today to bear witness to the "cruel and unusual" traditions and accepted behaviors of long ago still being condoned, practiced, and seldom given a second thought by Muslims because of their Islamic education, their *Koran*-learning, and their *Koran*-indoctrination---traditions such as the cutting-off of hands and other body-part mutilations, and stonings for disobedience to Allah's "Word."

In regards to the persistence of these religious customs, one should be made aware that any attempts, past and present, to raise an earnest voice against them in Allah-Land are soon squelched—not unlike the stifling, brutal history of Judeo-Christianity to silence its critics or to eliminate them. It should be acknowledged, too, that our founding fathers were far from being perfect men, but thankfully, to their credit and to our good fortune, they raised their insurrectionist voices and risked their "white-privileged" lives to give us a nation where grievances and injustices could be resolved in fair and even-handed ways even for people of color who, unfortunately and to America's shame, still remain victims of racism and inequality in a freedom-loving land that strives to promote and provide fairness and justice to all of its citizens. These secular-minded founders struggled, sacrificed, and risked their lives and their fortunes to give *"Life, Liberty and the pursuit of Happiness"* a worthy homeland for the benefit of "all" of its citizens—a worthy homeland which has become the envy of the world—not bad for the fruits of non-perfect, non-Christianized men—not bad for a nation of people who have yet to live up to the righteous standards we preach to others and pretend to uphold. Not bad for men whose imperfections certainly do not exceed those of today's newsmakers of all skin colors: world leaders, clergy, and the politically-correct, morality police who have yet to fix their critical gaze upon the sins of Semitic religions, their God(s), and the shameful actions and pursuits of their zealous advocates and followers that, in great measure, are responsible for so much misery on our planet and so much of the world's societal problems!

We should, therefore, be grateful for the efforts of our nation's flawed founders and all of the countless other patriots at the time (including women and people of color) whose noble efforts pitted against tyranny and oppression, while mostly forgotten and/or overlooked by historians, have resulted in providing us, the citizens of this imperfectly-begotten land, with many but not all of the freedoms we yearn for and should enjoy as human beings—the freedoms needed to live our lives to the fullest—the freedoms that, one day, will be shared in full by every American. We should never forget them, the above-mentioned Caretakers of Liberty who have given us this day to enjoy our daily bread! To give credit and honor to the clergy in this regard, knowing of their religion's role in opposing our nation's ideals, would be a disgraceful disservice to our nation's founders/patriots and their noble efforts. We should honor and respect, with pride—all who have opposed the oppressors of mankind throughout the centuries—all who have raised the torch of Liberty in the past and all who continue to protect and defend its sacred light with a hats-off "Thank You!" —a grateful-hearted "Salute" from a freedom-loving people to all the Caretakers of Liberty, past and present, for their honorable service to "all" of mankind!

Our secular-minded founders understood well the horror and terror that the Semitic theologies of Judaism, Christianity, and Islam had imposed upon the Old World and sought to prevent them from happening in the New

World by keeping the interests of an oppressive Church and a progressive State separated. As diplomats dealing with the problem of Islamic, Barbary pirates who were molesting American shipping and enslaving American sailors shortly after the American Revolution, John Adams and Thomas Jefferson were aware that these terrifying, maritime marauders were acting under Allah's direct orders as stated in the *Koran*. However, because they could not "envision" the horror that future, terrifying Islamic pirates and their incorrigible religious mindset would inflict upon America on September 11, 2001, it is for us, the beneficiaries of our nation's founders' Legacy of Liberty, to locate and neutralize the source of all religion-generated offenses and fanaticisms carried out in the name of God—offenses and fanaticisms that result only from the unquestioned, religious indoctrination that seeks to impose its scriptural beliefs—offenses and fanaticisms that continue to threaten the entire world with bloodshed and mass destruction merely because of some words written in a book.

"We the People,": freedom-loving Americans and Caretakers of Liberty, must *"hold these truths,"* too, *"to be self-evident,"* that terror and tribulation are rooted in the "revealed" "Word of God" of Semitic religions—that the *Bible* and the *Koran*, despite their undeserved adoration and reputation as "sacred" texts, are but instruction manuals for tyrants, terrorists, and supremacist-minded racists! In these present day, religion-troubled times that *"try men's souls,"* our secular-minded founding fathers have given us the only intelligent means to prevail against the unchallenged, impious impositions and deadly designs inherent in these so-called "Word of God" scriptures written with diabolical intention by the ungodly hand of man. Let us heed their wisdom, their warnings, and their advice on recognizing and dealing with the evils of Semitic religion---let us heed the words of Thomas Paine which assured his struggling, independence-seeking countrymen, *"We have it in our power to begin the world over again"* —and, amazingly, they did! Thanks to our founders' noble and successful endeavors, we have it in our power today to sanely end scripture-inspired madness once and for all so that we can *"begin the world over again"* without its ever-present threat—and we will!

The seeds of religious terrorism are sown and grown in the Semitic scriptures known as the *Bible* and the *Koran*---scriptures that Jews, Christians, and Muslims are indoctrinated to believe in their entirety for we, the above brainwashed folks, are never educated or instructed to disbelieve, doubt, or question any part of them. Such imposed scriptural belief proudly accepts as worship-worthy a God who commanded His followers to involve themselves in inexcusable wickedness, wanton cruelty, and blatant injustice—someone who, as "revealed" on the pages of the *Bible*, was content to indulge in carnage with His commanded annihilations—the wiping-out of entire nations of unoffending men, women, children, and animals by His supremacist-minded followers which, with the inclusion of supremacist-minded Christians and supremacist-minded Muslims, number in the billions today---a God who attempted to destroy *"every living thing"* —someone who sanctioned belief in the prejudicial "us" and "them," mindset---someone who sanctioned slavery and its attendant racial evils--- someone who sanctioned male domination over women---someone who sanctioned ethnic cleansing and eternal torment—someone who lacks not only divinity in His doings, but, obviously, humanity as well—someone who, quite frankly, we should have expected much much much better, "spiritual" behavior from!

Such imposed belief proudly accepts as praise-worthy an extremist, tyrannical Madman—a God whom the ***"facts and evidence"*** produced from Semitic scriptures alone proclaim to be utterly undeserving of our respect and our reverence—someone undeserving of our bowed heads, our bent knees, our blind allegiance, and our beneficial financial support. It is time, though long-overdue, for the scrutiny and justice of Reason's Tribunal to fairly and squarely set things right—it is finally time for "revealed" religions themselves to be "revealed"! It is time to expose "holy" scripture to the light of reason and truth without any reservations. It is time for "holy" scriptures to be investigated, as if conducted in a court of law, to uncover their fraudulence—their constant threat to world peace demands it be done. Only then will we, the religion indoctrinated masses, become enlightened enough to attempt to free ourselves from the inherent and enduring malevolence of Semitic fictions pretending to be revelations from God!

As long as the *Bible* and the *Koran* continue through unopposed preaching and teaching to be regarded as the not-to-be-doubted Word of God, we, the freedom-loving people of the civilized world, will remain at the mercy of these scriptures which sustain and support the supremacist attitudes of their incorrigible followers and their level of devotion to the diabolical dogmas of criminal God-impostors (Jehovah, Jesus, Allah) —we will remain at the mercy of ("us" and "them"-minded) religious zealots who are motivated to kill "us" because their pretended Word of God has instructed or inspired "them" to do so and given "them" the justification and the authorization for indulging in bloodshed and atrocity against "us."

Without Reason's Tribunal, we will remain at the mercy of Semitic theologies whose deluded followers believe with certainty in an after-life existence spent either enjoying the eternal pleasures of a blissful Heaven just for pleasing God or suffering the never-ending torment of a blistering Hell just for not pleasing Him, (the carrot and stick of Abrahamic theologies!). They, the deluded dedicated followers mentioned above, act predictably by obeying, without question, the imposing orders of their Semitic Divinity—even to oblivion-seeking extremes such as the horrors unleashed on 9/11 by those who were willing to commit suicide in order to please a bogus Semitic deity—all in anticipation of receiving a bigger piece of His bogus sky-pie and all the virgin, sexual partners one can "overshadow" every minute of every day in Paradise—incredible! *"Yes, Virginia, God is Great, ("Allahu Akbar") but only when His "spiritual" abilities are focused on murder, mayhem, malevolence, and molestation, however, He is not so great when it comes to improving or removing life's miseries: the poverty, the hunger, and the diseases, etc. that plague so many of His devoted followers and their children—for, it is obvious, that any and all improvement and relief in these areas comes not from God, but from Man!"*

The horrendous, terrifying events unleashed on September 11, 2001, were not only attacks meant to destroy the lives of Americans and their major buildings and institutions---they were among the initial assaults by *Koran*-inspired fanatics who seek, ultimately, the annihilation of America, her honored ideals and freedoms, and all that the ***"Blessings of Liberty"*** have bestowed upon civilization. More than twenty years have passed since that day when the words, "Allahu Akbar!" rang out in the cockpits of those 4 doomed airliners flying over our nation. Sadly, we have yet to deliver a weakening blow or to retaliate in any meaningful or productive manner against the singular, motivational source of our religion-minded enemies' Holy Terror now directed continually against freedom-loving people everywhere—an enemy whose mindset has been programmed to never doubt or dispute the religious "fare" it ingests and pays allegiance to 5 or more times a day. Since it is obvious, too, that we are most vulnerable to attacks when we least expect them to occur, months and years, even several years, may pass between their occurrences, but any lull, especially a prolonged one, in the violence should never be perceived as an end to the violence or the hostilities---more 9/11's are yet to come!

The "sacred" words of Semitic scripture that inspired the 9/11 attacks are still on the books, still being taught, still being preached, still being imposed upon the innocent minds of gullible children. The ticking time-bomb of scripture-generated terrorism will never be completely defused, I repeat, "will never be completely defused," until we employ an intelligent, non-violent means to permanently neutralize their sources: the *Koran* and its inspiring parent, the *Bible*. Both of which, unfortunately, have remained undiminished in their power and potential to incite and energize people to engage in bloodshed and atrocity thinking it as part of their sacred duty— undiminished in their power and potential to instill prejudicial thinking and to promote destruction and devastation century after bloody, religion-dominated century in the name of God. Without employing Reason's Tribunal, the *Koran* and the *Bible* will remain undiminished in their power and undiminished in their potential to inspire their followers, who would otherwise be a threat to no one, to become race-denouncing, gender-hating folks, and martyr-minded, holy terrors!

Sadly, there is seldom any lull in the iniquities committed by the "us" and "them," default mindset of many white Americans against Americans of color, especially those of African descent who haven't a clue about the role their beloved Judeo-Christian religion continues to play in their subjugation, in their being discriminated against, in their being viewed as inferior people. It was supremacist-minded, *Bible*-inspired, Judeo-Christian Caucasians who, with God's blessing, enslaved the black race. It was because of supremacist-minded, *Bible*-inspired, Judeo-Christian Caucasians that black people were ever perceived in the first place as not deserving of the dignities and decencies afforded to Caucasian human beings and thus racial disdain of blacks, racial discrimination against them, and racial intimidation used to control them in the form of burning crosses, lynchings, Jim Crow laws, red-lining their neighborhoods, etc., etc., came to be because of the Christian religion and its proud, parasitic Judeo-tradition of *Bible*-promoted, human bondage—a Judeo-principle that nearly destroyed America with an internal war. Since "us" and "them"-minded Judeo-Christians would never seek to enslave anyone they considered their equal, the black slave, therefore, was regarded as something less than human and something undeserving of decent, humane, and equitable treatment. America, unfortunately, will never free herself from these insentient, religion-generated abominations which have continued for centuries to plague her moral progress as a freedom-inspired, freedom-loving nation until her racially biased, white inhabitants realize the source of their intolerant, anti-black sentiment and anti-black prejudice lies in a less-than-sacred, Judeo-Christian scripture, a scripture they have been conditioned to believe without question.

When that long-awaited realization has been "revealed" and established, an intelligent, non-violent means to permanently neutralize the authority of the slavery-endorsing, race-condemning *Bible* can then be brought to bear against this malevolent book---a book which, as stated above, has remained undiminished in its power to inspire and to incite racial hatred and racial discrimination which, too often, ends in violence against certain Americans solely because of their ethnicity. No one should ever forget the fate of the unoffending Canaanites who were wiped from the face of the earth because of the racial and spiritual superiority of the Jews, a supposed master race of people who, because of their religious indoctrination believed they had a right and a "command" given them by God to take whatever they wanted, whenever they wanted, even if it required the extermination of peaceful neighbors! Wake up, America---a similar condition exists in our Judeo-Christian-beguiled nation, the supremacist thinking of the supposed superior-mindedness of white-privileged Christians who, like the Jews, are religiously indoctrinated to believe that only they, the *Bible*-believing, white race, have the ability to please God and that whatever they decide to do unto others is righteous and okay with Heaven's Hitler, following the example, of course, of God's superior-minded, "chosen people" --- Christians' spiritual kin!

It should be remembered here, also, that it was America's white European settlers who, proud of their Judeo-Christian heritage, were the ones engaged in nearly wiping-out America's indigenous population, the Native Americans, who were perceived in a similar fashion to the biblical Canaanites. They, the native peoples of America were regarded as folks who stood in the way of the ambitions of white, God-pleasing people---as folks who needed to be eliminated by another master-race bent on grabbing their lands away from them. It is for the most part, the present-day descendants of these *Bible*-believing settlers who retain and maintain their ancestral biblical-mindset and its inherent, racial prejudices that, sadly and continually, make the headlines? Man help us! Let us begin the tribunal that will set us free, for all time, from the mental-conditioning of Judeo-Christianity, its non-sacred traditions and its non-sacred principles that always benefit the few (us) at the expense of the many (them)! Sadly, there is still widespread belief around the world that without God being in everyone's' lives, the world will collapse into chaos, curiously however, when God "is" in everyone's' lives, chaos always ensues!

For America to prevail against the racial discord that darkens her efforts to excel at being an enlightened, progressive nation, she must begin to deal effectively with the religion-imposed, racist mentality of her inhabitants that, if left unchecked and un-challenged, could eventually result in the utter demise of everyone's ***"unalienable rights"*** of ***"Life, Liberty and the pursuit of Happiness."*** It is incumbent, therefore, that all Americans, concerned with making the world a better place, initiate the long-overdue *"revolution in the system of religion"* that Thomas Paine envisioned and Thomas Jefferson endorsed in his written advice to a nephew (Peter Carr) to *"Question with boldness even the existence of a god"* in a *"tribunal"* presided over by *"reason."* The emancipation of the black race in this country will truly become a reality the day when most Americans (black and white) are able to emancipate themselves from the mental shackles imposed by the *Bible*-pushers, the *Bible*-promoting, *Bible*-pounding fanatics whose fervor for Judeo-Christian traditions and principles hinder the advancement of America's sacred endeavor to insure that *"liberty and justice for all"* are not just words spoken in a Jehovah-honoring Pledge of Allegiance! It is only when the doors that separate "us" from "them" are opened wide, will *"We the People"* replace "In God We Trust" ---(by the way, how's that working out for America?) as the motto of:

> *A new nation conceived in Liberty, and dedicated to the proposition that all men are created equal.* ---(a proposition that cannot be found in any Semitic scripture---you can "trust" me on that! ---kvk)

> ---Abraham Lincoln

> *The further the spiritual evolution of mankind advances, the more certain it seems to me that the path to genuine religiosity does not lie through the fear of life, and the fear of death, and blind faith, but through striving after rational knowledge.*

> ---Albert Einstein, *Science, Philosophy, and Religion*

Enlightened, progressive Americans must begin to examine and expose the fraudulent and fabricated "Word of God" foundations of Semitic religions that justify, encourage, and inspire their devotees to commit crimes against humanity, to engage in despicable conduct that they consider God-pleasing because of their blind obedience to a fraudulent and fabricated God whether He is called Jehovah, Jesus, or Allah. We must begin to understand the importance of why Jehovah/Jesus, the God of Judeo-Christianity is never, I repeat, "never" mentioned by name in the founding documents of a supposed "Judeo-Christian" America. We must begin to challenge the primacy, the literary legitimacy, and the divine authority of all Semitic scripture, determine who their real authors were, where they got their plagiarized source material, and reveal their self-serving, ungodly endeavors. We must begin to challenge and investigate the veracity of all deeply-held, uncontested scriptural dogmas if we are earnest in ridding the world of the never-ending threats to everyone's ***"unalienable rights"*** that are embedded, embraced, and employed in the self-serving, divisive, and deadly designs of Semitic Theism as "revealed" in their DIY manuals: the *Bible* and the *Koran*. The destructive, parasitic belief-systems being promoted on their pages have been imposed upon the world as "God's Word," a slick trick used to prevent folks from harboring any doubts or questions about their "infallible" authority and, therefore, their "inerrant" veracity.

The *Bible* and the *Koran* have never, in any meaningful way, been subjected to a rigorous, criminal background-check---as is commonly done today by so many American institutions wanting to protect themselves---to bring past transgressions and past transgressors to light and to uncover, for all to see with cleansing clarity, the wolves who lurk in our midst in pious sheep's clothing and designer togs. Americans must begin this noble quest by acknowledging the blessings of the Legacy of Liberty bestowed upon us by our nation's founding fathers, and by proclaiming the righteous reasons that justify another Declaration of Independence and another American Revolution to be fought against another formidable enemy whose tyranny is focused on destroying our way of life. May the shots fired in this book be heard 'round the world, too—may their only casualty, however, be the demise of bogus religions.

> *Every day around the world Islamist fanatics are plotting ways to kill us. They do so under the banner of a supremacist ideology that pits Islam against the rest of the world and commands the murder of those who do not willingly submit.*
>
> ---Glenn Beck, *It Is About Islam*

Thanks for warning us, Mr. Beck. Unfortunately, it is a bit too late to attempt to warn the Canaanites about Jewish fanatics and their annihilating, supremacist ideology! ---kvk

"We shall overcome" the impositions and the oppressions of all Semitic religions that aid and abet criminal activity because we are not afraid to confront the religion-indoctrinated enemies of freedom and the despisers of civilization with the only weapon capable of vanquishing their scripture-authorized, scripture-generated, supremacist mindset of terror. In Thomas Jefferson's words, ***"We are not afraid to follow truth*** (in matters of religion)

wherever it may lead, nor to tolerate any error so long as reason is left free to combat it" —we are not afraid to wage the bold investigations of Reason's Tribunal!

> *I know that this bold investigation* (*The Age of Reason*) *will alarm many, but it would be paying too great a compliment to their credulity to forbear it upon this account; the times and the subject demand it to be done. The suspicion that the theory of what is called the Christian Church is fabulous* (not believable) *is becoming very extensive in all countries; and it will be a consolation to men staggering under that suspicion, and doubting what to believe and what to disbelieve, to see the subject freely investigated.*

> ---Thomas Paine

I know, too, that this bold investigation, (*Reason's Tribunal*) will alarm many, but it would be paying too great a compliment to their credulity to forbear it upon this account; the times and the subject demand it to be done—to see the subject (of religion) freely investigated. ---kvk

Introduction
continued . . .

<u>From the Declaration of Independence</u>

"We hold these truths to be self-evident, that all men are created equal, that they are endowed by their Creator with certain unalienable Rights, that among these are Life, Liberty and the pursuit of Happiness."

<u>Preamble to the Constitution of the United States</u>

"We the People of the United States, in Order to form a more perfect Union, establish Justice, insure domestic Tranquility, provide for the common defence, promote the general Welfare, and secure the Blessings of Liberty to ourselves and our Posterity, do ordain and establish this Constitution for the United States of America."

<u>From the *Bible*</u>

"That which is highly esteemed among men is abomination in the sight of God." ---Jesus, *Luke* 16:15 (Therefore, the Declaration of Independence and the Constitution of the United States are both an *"abomination in the sight of God,"* but don't take my word for it! ---kvk)

<u>From the *Koran*</u>

"This is the book in which there is no doubt." ---Allah, *Koran* 2:2 *"...Slay the idolators wherever you find them."* ---Allah, *Koran* 9:5

<u>From the author</u>

There is no doubt---after reading, (as much as one can tolerate), about the cruelty---the belligerent, malevolent words of the *Bible* and the *Koran*--- that among the things being touted as *"highly esteemed"* by Semitic religions, (as "revealed" in their "Word of God" scriptures), are the following: the racial superiority of their believers, the sacred superiority of their supremacist mindset, and their being deserving of a blissful eternity in Heaven simply because of their superior qualities while the never-ending torments of Hell await all non-believers. Also *"highly esteemed"* by Semitic religions are the institution of slavery and the slaying of idolators (unbelievers, infidels) both of which happen to be an *"abomination in the sight"* of reasonable, decent men. Man help us!

Inspired to run

Run like a Canaanite, a homosexual, a stubborn child, or a fatted calf attempting to flee from Jews inspired by God's Word as given in the *Old Testament*—run like a heretic or a scientific thinker attempting to flee from Christians inspired by God's Word as given in the *Bible*—run like an infidel attempting to flee from Muslims inspired by Allah's Word as given in the *Koran*—run like hell when you hear others claim that their beliefs are inspired by God—run! —run! —run!

The Chutzpah Chronicles of Semites

The *Bible*, we're told, is beyond error and the *Koran*, we're told, is beyond doubt, yet both perfections are truly beyond belief. The "infallibility" and "inerrancy" of the Semitic *Bible* and the "flawless" certainty of the Semitic *Koran* would have us presume that man's hand can create what a Semitic God's hand could not: "PERFECTION"! A flawed angel and an imperfect Eden reveal the best efforts of a flawed, imperfect God (made in man's image!) who could not create a better world even with a second attempt—a flawed, imperfect God (made in man's image) whose intellect proved no match for the superior wisdom and intelligence of a cunning Semite named Moses who was able to stop this Almighty God in His tracks as told in *Ex.* 32:11-14—and you want to bow down to whom?

What a Guy

Incredibly, many "educated" folks today still credit the "grace of God" and His merciful heart as the reason for their survival after being the hapless victim of an illness, an accident, a natural or man-made disaster, etc. "Thank you, sweet Lord Jesus, for the miracle you have bestowed upon me that has allowed me to continue living---thank you, merciful God, for choosing to save my sorry ass and for allowing others to suffer and succumb instead. *"Praise the Lord"! "Praise the Lord"!* Imagine a person crediting the grace of God for being the lone survivor of a vehicle crash that killed all of that person's family members! God surely does act in mysterious ways! I wonder how many such miraculously blessed folks are truly proud to worship such a God---someone who uses His loving God-powers to pick and choose who lives, who dies, who suffers, who loses a child or a family member, who loses a limb, etc., etc., etc., --what a Guy! Obviously, there aren't enough temples, churches, and mosques in the world to honor and glorify this Glorious Guy, His spiritual endeavors, and His many tremendous mercies!

We should all know who is responsible

The defenders of religion like to instruct us that the existence of a watch (which, obviously, is incapable of creating itself) is certain proof of the existence of a watchmaker. Certainly, if so, it must follow then, that the existence of a God is certain proof of the existence of a God-maker! It must follow, also, that if a watch fails to operate properly by not keeping the correct time because of a manufacturing defect, we should all know beyond a doubt that it is the manufacturer of the watch who is to blame. Beyond a doubt, we should all know, too, who is to blame for creating the defects found in God's "Creation" —for it could not have been anyone who lacks the ability to create themselves and that would include the likes of the Devil whom God created and could destroy, if He wanted to in a nano-second if He truly *"so loved the world"*! Incidentally, according to *Bible*-evidence, the Devil is not the only deity who enjoys adding to the miseries of this world! Man help us!

Belief in one or belief in none, that is the question

Know that to accept belief in the "exclusive," God-given authority of one Semitic religion's inviolable Word of God is to reject belief in the "exclusive," God-given authority of the inviolable Word of God of the other Semitic religions. And so it remains that the vested interests of the advocates of the one will always be in opposition and contention with the vested interests of the advocates of the others. Know that there can never be peace in a world where God's inviolable Word, the *Bible*, promotes only the sacred beliefs held by Jews and Christians but rejects the sacred beliefs held by Muslims. There can never be peace in a world where God's inviolable

Word, the *Koran*, promotes only the sacred beliefs held by Muslims but rejects the sacred beliefs held by Jews and Christians. All three Semitic religions constantly reject and offend each other's sacred beliefs with constant devotion to their own inviolable Word of God which constantly rejects and offends the inviolable, religious beliefs of the other Semitic religions. Man help us!

What else don't you know

Who is it that was a divine incarnation whose "miraculous conception" was announced before his birth? Who is it that led a blameless life, had the childhood wisdom of a sage and whose moral teachings were declared the best the world had known? Who is it that was averse to riches, remained a celibate, and purified the religious temples? Who is it that predicted future events, performed miracles, cast out devils, healed the sick, and restored the dead to life? Who is it that rose from the grave, ascended to Heaven, and was worshiped as a god? —Appolonius of Tyana, that's who! Were you thinking of someone else? Appolonius of Tyana was a contemporary of the Galilean and, according to John E Remsburg in his book titled *The Christ*, the biographers of Appolonius are as worthy of credence as the evangelists! If such a disclosure comes as a shock to the Christian mind so will a study of the lives of Krishna and Buddha who both lived hundreds of years before the Christian era and which prove that the Christ story is not an original. The parallels existing between them are too numerous and too exact to be accidental. Reason's Tribunal demands the "truth" be told about Semitic religions and their plagiarized Pagan origins. For the ancient myths of the so-called "heathen" world contained the accumulated wisdom of the ages told figuratively in story form—wisdom that, because of religion, was lost, forgotten, purposely destroyed, or purposely re-told in such a way as to serve Semitic religions' need for *"power and profit"*!

Made to believe in make-believe

Have you ever wondered why the *Old Testament* God of the Israelites, whom we are made to believe could accomplish any task imaginable, was incapable, I repeat, "was incapable" of revealing Himself to others? Surely, if this God, the God of Judeo-Christianity and of Islam also, had the ability to communicate personally with impeccable precision and clarity "directly" with each and every person whom He desired to communicate with, there would, of course, be no need ever on His part of always having to resort to

the efforts of anonymous, "inspired" script-writers to get His message out---
script-writers with whom He must constantly rely on to "reveal" His
perfect "Word" which, at first He wanted only to be given to a certain
"chosen" Semitic people, the Jews, *the lost sheep of the house of Israel,"* in
order to have them receive all of the pertinent and profound instructions
designed for their exclusive benefit along with all the perks and privileges
that naturally come with their being "chosen of God" and that's according to
book #1, the *Old Testament*. Hmm! Surprisingly, later on, God, for some
strange reason, decided to reveal His perfect "Word" a second time, with
the assistance of His script-writers of course---only to the Jews once again
via book #2, the *New Testament*---a book which ended, for some strange
reason, with God's allowing (after His death coming at the hand of the Jews)
the losers known as Gentiles, to "share" in the special privileges that
previously were only supposed to be granted to the *"lost sheep"* ---a book
which sported several script-changes from book #1 including a glorious tale
about the extreme make-over of scary ol' Jehovah into a, supposedly, loving,
caring, less-intimidating Jesus. Hmm! Hmm! More surprisingly, God then
decided, for some strange reason, to reveal His perfect "Word" again for a
third time via the anonymously written, multi-authored *Koran* for the
exclusive benefit of another "chosen" Semitic people: the Arabs (Muslims)
---a book which sported several more script-changes designed for their
exclusive benefit only. Hmm! Hmm! Hmm! God, it appears, surely has a
problem deciding who His "favorite" folks really are! Hmm x 4!

Grab your well-worn copy of God's "Word," book #2, folks, and read the
very last "words" spoken by Jesus (after His death!) as given in *Matthew*---
words that would have us believe that it was then, and only then, that He,
Jesus, for some strange reason, had a complete change-of-heart regarding
His lifelong disgust for, and avoidance of, Gentiles and their territories---
Matt. 10:5,6. It was then and only then (after His death!) that He suddenly
stepped out of character during the final moments of His time on earth and
now, post-death, welcomed those He constantly spurned throughout His
lifetime into the fold with His last utterance to His disciples: *"Go ye
therefore, and teach all nations . . . to observe all things whatsoever I have
commanded you..."* Imagine God, during His lifetime as Jesus, having
second thoughts or having uncertainty about anything such as whether He
disliked Gentiles, or not---whether He liked them enough to want to "save"
them, or not---whether His life's mission was to minister only to *"the lost
sheep of the house of Israel,"* or not! Hmm!

The implausible, last-minute inclusion of Gentiles to share in the
exclusive privileges and blessings afforded only to members of the Jewish

race by Jesus, a Jew who went out of His way to speak in parables in order to exclude and deceive Gentiles from sharing in the exclusive privileges and blessings afforded only to His race of people, deserves further explanation and much greater scrutiny in Reason's Tribunal. The inclusion of Gentiles into the fold came about, interestingly enough, not as the "first" thought of a living, breathing Savior who *"so loved the world,"* but as the "last" thought of a deceased and resurrected Redeemer whose "life's mission" was to reject and avoid the detested Gentiles at all costs while seeking to save only God's "chosen" people! Hmm x 5! Reason's Tribunal, however, provides a plausible explanation for this radical and sudden reversal of heart.

Since Jesus, according to the *Bible*, was born to be *"King of the Jews"* ---*Matt.* 2:2 and His lifelong mission was to "save" Israel's *"lost sheep"* --- 15:24, isn't there a rather foul odor arising from the fact that both of these Gospel-certainties came to naught because the Jews rejected Him as their Ruler and as their Messiah? In fact, the Jews cried out for His crucifixion and that "they" wanted: *"His blood be on us, and on our children."* --- 27:23,25—curious choices for God's "chosen" to make, don't you think? It strikes me that the blatant, willful rejection of Jesus by hordes of His favorite flock of people far exceeds any trespasses made by naive, child-minded simpletons in Eden---wouldn't you agree? The *Bible* proudly exhorts "The Parable of the Lost Sheep," but fails to mention in the least "The Parable of the Lost Shepherd" who had lost not just one of His flock's members but all of them, the *"lost sheep of the house of Israel,"* ---who remain to this day, the *"lost sheep of the house of Israel"*! During His ministry, Jesus, obviously, lacked the power to convince Jews of His divinity---the very reason for His existence, yet we are to believe that His only concern now (post-ministry) is for the everlasting, blissful welfare of Gentiles---can you smell it now?

Jesus' final utterance in *Matthew*, which, incidentally, differs from His final utterance given in the other Gospel accounts! ---not only reveals His less-than-divine nature and His hypocrisy---it confirmingly reveals the ungodly hand of the self-serving script-writers who penned the *New Testament.* This Jewish rejection of Jesus and their denial of Him as being the Savior of *"lost sheep"* if continued any further in the scripted *Bible* would, obviously, have resulted in the loss of ***"power and revenue"*** for these parasitic script-writers who realized they and their parasitic religion-promoters would soon find themselves struggling to get by having much fewer sheep to fleece, hence Jesus' last moment's concern and outpouring of love for the much more numerous Gentiles!

This unbelievable, final utterance of Jesus: *"Go ye therefore, and teach all nations, baptizing them in the name of the Father, and of the Son, and of the Holy Ghost: teaching them to observe all things whatsoever I have commanded you..."* was, obviously, a further contrivance inserted into the wholly contrived Gospels in order to prevent any further losses to their "pious" cause from occurring, and all it took was a few strokes of the pen---slick! With Jesus' obvious failure to achieve His previous, script-written goals and ambitions for the exclusive benefit of the Jews, the ever-clever script-writers of the *NT* realized that it would be in their best interest to begin permitting the "losers," (Gentile dogs), to enter where previously only Jewish sheep were allowed admission. And thus "The Greatest Story Ever Told" was brought to life by the anticlimactic death, resurrection, and ascension of a rejected Ruler and Savior of untold numbers of sheep who, it is obvious, continue to go astray, remaining lost and irredeemable to this very day unless, as further stated in *Matthew*, they acquiesce to being baptized in the name of the Father, and of the Son, and of the Holy Ghost and obey all of Jesus' teachings! Oy vey! It is quite interesting to note here that the "Judeo" part of Judeo-Christianity disbelieves and rejects the Christian part of it as do the atheists! The term, Judeo-Christianity, therefore, is not something that Christians should be proud to promote unless sharing their cherished hyphenated title with non-believers in Christ is just another example of God working in mysterious ways!

> **They** (the Jews) **are regularly descended from the people who lived in the times this resurrection and ascension** (of Jesus) **is said to have happened, and they say, it is not true.**

> ---Thomas Paine

Every Christian who is proud of their Judeo-affiliations should ponder the above words of Mr. Paine! ---kvk

Isn't it interesting that we are imposed upon to believe that the most important message of all time, (from God's lips to the supposed "entirety" of mankind's ears---a message that Jesus wanted preached to *"all nations"*) ---should only be "revealed" at the outset to an insignificant number of certain, idol-worshiping, nomadic, Semitic folks who only numbered a few thousand at best during the supposed time of the supposed Exodus. One wonders why God didn't think to reveal His all-important "Word" to the Chinese, the most numerous people on earth! Hmm! Isn't it interesting that when the Jews wrote their God-inspired Chutzpah Chronicles and told us that God *"so loved the world,"* they revealed their ignorance of that "world" that existed beyond the borders of their known environs and hence God's ignorance, too, of the world He supposedly created for how would it be possible that a man-made God could have greater knowledge than that of His male fabricators. Hmm! Evidently, their personal, Jews-only-favoring-God didn't give a crap about the welfare of Asians who at the time probably numbered in the billions. Hmm!

We are made to believe, too, that God would consider the delivery of such an all-important, vital communication to mankind to be a job perfectly suited for someone other than Himself to accomplish! Hmm, again! We are made to believe that God, in all of His wisdom, would have no problem allowing "imperfect" others to reveal His "perfect" Word to everyone on the planet by having it conveyed in at least four contradictory, written versions—the *OT*, the *NT*, the *Koran*, and the *Book of Mormon* (*BM* for short!) —which their advocates are forced to admit---all came into existence the result of indirect, second-hand, hearsay-reporting messengers—individuals about whom we know very little or nothing at all except what they have supposedly written or caused to be written in the *Bible*, the *Koran*, and the *BM*. God surely must have had a lot of vital spiritual knowledge to convey to the world judging by the hundreds of thousands of words these books contain in combination and yet, none of the spiritual lessons expressed and promoted in any of them exceeds the morality and decency inherent in the few words that comprise the Golden Rule formulated and "revealed" by people whom the Jews regarded as "heathens"! Hmm! Hmm! Hmm!

Where is the solid evidence contained in the first five books of the *Old Testament* that proves Moses was the author of them? Not a shred can be found! If Moses had authored them, how was he able to disclose the location of the place where he was buried? ---*Deut.* 34:5,6. Hmm! Where is the solid evidence contained in the anonymous Gospels which proves they were written *"according to"* Matthew, Mark, Luke, and John? Not a shred can be found! They may as well have been written *"according to"* Tom, Dick, Harry, and Larry! Where is the solid evidence contained in the *Koran* that proves it was an angel of God who "revealed" its contents to Muhammad? Not a shred can be found! Where is the solid evidence contained in the *BM* which proves that another angel (aptly named Moroni!) "revealed" its contents to Joe Smith? Not a shred can be found! On whose authority are we to believe that the *Bible*, the *Koran*, or the *BM* are truly the Word of God? On whose authority are we to believe "all" of them are?

Who but mindless, religion-programmed robots would allow the unsubstantiated pretense found on the pages of these books to pass as the absolute truth without any solid evidence to back up their claims when it is known that other unvetted dossiers of deception have sometimes surfaced and been disseminated to deliberately dupe us from time to time! Apparently, most politicians allow such rubbish to pass as the absolute truth—along with every news commentator/media pundit in America who consider themselves to be "fair and balanced," "no spin" journalists! Thankfully, however, every "fair and balanced" court of justice in America will never accept the words and deeds given in the *Bible*-tales, which the *Koran* and the *BM* are rooted in, as being truthful accounts—as being reliable proof or evidence of anything—yet, incredibly, they use the placing of a hand on the *Bible*, a book of lies, deception, and injustice, to solicit oaths from folks to provide only truthful testimony in their court proceedings! Such a tradition belies the separation of Church and State and should be discontinued if it is justice and fairness that are being honored and sought in this ridiculous ritual which, in effect, gives sanction and legitimacy to the *Bible's* every word.

What could possibly have prevented God from having direct communication with each and every person on the planet if His intent, according to the *Bible,* was to inform and save everyone? ---the answer is "nothing"! If every person on the planet received God's Word from God Himself, it would, of course, result in an unanimity of belief occurring throughout the entire world in matters of religion. It would have eliminated the rejecting of His Word from ever taking place by preventing the possibility of any disagreement occurring in the minds of every one of His personally informed folks from one part of the globe to all the other parts of it. Jews, as a result, would hold the same exact beliefs about God as Christians do—Christians, as a result, would hold the same exact beliefs about God as Muslims do---Muslims would hold the same exact beliefs as the Chinese do and so on and so forth. There would, of course, be but one religion, not dozens and dozens more with each attempting to reveal a different deity to us as the one and only God with each religion revealing a dramatically different message from Him for His believers to abide by!

If only God had "revealed" Himself and His will to everyone in an incorruptible manner, there would, of course, be no possibility for any uncertainty to accompany any part of His message. With God being the one and only messenger spreading "His" message, there would, of course, be no possibility of a single word being misconstrued or of anyone being deceived, manipulated, or misled by the ulterior motives of pious frauds.

The same cannot be said about the writings of the power-hungry, parasitic priests of all Semitic religions who tell us that they "are" the ones, the only ones, who have the ability to reveal God and His will to us with perfection---what chutzpah! The scripted, hearsay-at-best, texts of their bogus "Word of God" scriptures written by various, unknown authors who, by the way, differ dramatically in various details from one bogus Semitic religion to the next---unknown authors who have the bogus, *Old Testament* God acting contrary to His teachings in the bogus *New Testament* which, in turn, has Him acting contrary to His teachings in the bogus *Koran* which, in turn, has Him acting contrary to His teachings in the bogus *Book of Mormon*! Haven't we been made to believe, also, by these very same bogus writers of religions' Chutzpah Chronicles that God's will and God's message are immutable? ---another example of religion having it both ways! Bogus in, bogus out!

Due to God's shortcomings at making personal appearances to get His message across, we must assume that He does not possess the ability to reveal Himself in an undoubted, irreproachable way to everyone even though we're made to believe that He can do anything, including the impossible, with ease, such as His "knowing" every second of every day, what everyone on the planet is thinking and doing---an amazing ability for certain! However, as the story goes, Satan, who happens to be invisible, too, just like God, is represented to us as a "lesser" deity, yet, he possesses the ability, unlike God, to transform himself into a non-intimidating, viewable entity who could make himself visible in order to convey his most important message via a personal, face to face conversation with Eve. Satan, it appears, not only has the power, just like God, to "know" what everyone on the planet is thinking and doing at all times—he, it appears, also "has" the power to influence and control much of the actions and thoughts of nearly everyone on the planet to do "his" bidding!

If Satan is capable of communicating his "will" all by himself without the assistance of agents to act on His behalf---if he is capable of making himself visible in a non-threatening way to others—why not God? It makes one wonder what else the Devil can do that an ability-lacking, less-talented God cannot? It makes one wonder why the *Bible* never gives us an example of God's "love" for His enemy, Satan, (hell no!) or an example of God having "punished" the Devil for any of "his" sins and wickedness? It makes one wonder, too, why the *Bible* would have us believe that this very same God wants "us" to "love" our enemies and to "forgive" all of the trespasses they make against us---*Matt.* 5:44, 6:14, while He, quite contrarily, makes arrangements to roast His opposers, (those who have trespassed against

Him), in the fires of a forever-Hell that "He" has *"prepared for the Devil and his angels"* ---25:41,46? Did you ***"fools and hypocrites"*** of Christendumb get that? He, a vengeful, unmerciful SOB wants "us," to love our enemies and forgive them—what the hell? Why would God instruct us to behave in ways that He in His perfection is opposed to doing? Shame on Him for His "do as I say, not as I do" hypocrisy and shame on you for believing in Him and in His bountiful "love" for everyone---another example of religion having it both ways. Garbage in, garbage out!

Isn't it quite remarkable that for all of His mighty power to do the impossible, God, even to this day, apparently lacks the proficiencies of Satan to morph into a non-threatening, viewable entity such as a talking snake or a talking ass---the existence of both being *OT* certainties! Incredibly, both vocal, *OT* lifeforms have been able to survive the ages and can still be seen and heard every time a *Bible*-preacher opens his/her mouth to speak! Isn't it quite remarkable that the Creator of countless gazillions of galaxies and innumerable black holes, etc., etc., cannot, I repeat, "cannot" make Himself into a visible, non-threatening being in order to speak to others in order to convey His essential, consequential, and personal, first-hand message to the entirety of mankind or, at least, to each and every one of His favored folks---really?

One would think that an Almighty God would, somehow, be able to find a more direct, inerrant, and infallible means to achieve getting His Word out to the masses without the possibility of error or inaccuracy occurring in its transfer. Due to this lack of ability, God is of necessity resigned always to rely on the questionable divinity and non-authority of several unknown script-writers and a skulking angel appearing in murky dream-visions as in the case of Muhammad and Joe Smith, to communicate His Word and to accomplish His goals! In confirming this lack of ability in Semitic Gods, even the *Koran* (42:51) tellingly reveals to us: *"It is not fitting for a man that Allah should speak to him except by inspiration, or from behind a veil, or by the sending of a messenger to reveal, with Allah's permission, what Allah wills: for He is Most High, Most Wise."* And, I might add, His creators are Most Cunning to always keep their God hidden *"behind a veil"* and His Muhammad-messenger, Gabriel, hiding out in a cave unseen by others because their non-existence obviously precludes the possibility of their physical forms ever being seen! Reason's Tribunal will, thankfully, "reveal" for all to see clearly and in great detail, the scams and shams of bogus, less-than-sacred Semitic theologies!

Because of the inability of the script-writers of Semitic theologies to describe their God's appearance, for obvious reasons, it is of necessity for them to always employ concealment whenever they have God speak or arrive on scene—the need for such a ruse being quite apparent. Therefore, it is quite "fitting," after all, for God's script-writers to always have *"inspiration"* be an "infallible" substitute for direct communication with Him, and it is *"Most Wise"* of them to always have His visage obscured (ala the Wizard of Oz) lest the "veil" be removed and the fraud detected. It is also *"Most Wise,"* I repeat, *"Most Wise"* of them to create a God who *"cannot be questioned concerning what He does"* ---*Koran* 21:23—(ain't that the truth! ---kvk)

Since I consider this book, *Reason's Tribunal,* a work of "inspiration," is more proof needed to convince everyone that it was He who is *"Most High, Most Wise"* telling me in an inspired way, of course, what to convey in it and, therefore, He alone should be given credit for its authorship? According to the "inspired" words of the *Koran,* I am just *"a messenger,"* too, whom the *"Most High"* has given *"permission"* to write *Reason's Tribunal* and, as the story goes, nothing happens unless Allah "wills" it to happen! I'm, therefore, over-the-moon delighted that Allah has "willed" me to co-write this book with Him! Thanks Al!

(NOTE TO READER: Protect yourself at all times especially while asleep, high on drugs, or buzzed by alcohol and, therefore, vulnerable to experiencing altered states of reality—never accept anyone's "inspired" words to be the absolute truth without questioning what is being said especially when they are spoken to you in your vivid, intra-cranial dream-visions, for if it is only the truth that is being told, what need is there for inspiration on the part of the speaker or the listener?

Do yourself a favor and demand to see proof of the speaker's identity and proof of the claims being made in your altered, sleep-state of mind (in your dreams). In my case, I'm fairly certain that it was God, disguised as a dancing circus clown of all things, who spoke to me in my slumber-vision---thankfully, I had the presence of mind and wherewithal in this dream-state to ask to see some ID and He reluctantly showed me His recently expired membership card in the *"Most High, Most Wise"* Club—hey, you just can't take any chances these days! —it is especially so when so many folks believe that what takes place in their night-visions, lucid sleep-states, and intra-cranial chats are direct communications between God and themselves!)

Why are we always made to believe by the script-writers of Semitic theologies that, unlike the easily viewable Satan, it was always necessary for God to be hidden by clouds, by smoke, by fire, by a veil, etc.? Can you come up with a plausible answer for such a cover-up? Why are we made to believe that His presence was such a traumatic experience that even the earth trembled when He spoke always in thunderous tones or that everyone should always be fearful of Him for *"thou shalt fear thy God"* ---*Lev.* 25:17? Why are we made to believe that no one can ever approach God's whereabouts without being struck down *"for no man shall see me, and live"* ---*Ex.* 33:20 (except for Moses who was able to speak face to face with God *"as a man speaketh unto his friend."*) ---*Ex.* 33:11!---evidently, as a man wearing blazing pants! Can you come up with a plausible answer why the script-writers of the Chutzpah Chronicles would need to intimidate and threaten everyone with death for attempting to get up close and personal with their bogus God or for attempting to investigate His physical existence or lack of?

"Once upon a time," when some *"men of Bethshemesh"* tried to take a look inside the curious, ornate, wooden God-box known as the *"ark of the Lord,"* which, according to various sources, contained Moses and Aaron's "magic wand," a pot of moldering manna, and the two stone tablets of the Ten Commandments that God handed to Moses and quite possibly, the ship's bell from Noah's Ark! (Thankfully for believers, the ark's whereabouts remains unknown to this very day! ---imagine that!) For their terribly foolish attempt to take a peek inside this box, God in His divine manner of meting out Semitic-style justice, *"smote of the people fifty thousand and threescore and ten men"* ---now what could be fairer than that! Because of the innocuous curiosity of a few men, God murdered tens of thousands of innocent men---Wow! ---not exactly an eye for an eye justice here! ---*I Samuel* 6:19.

Did the God-loving disciples of Osama bin Hiden do a worse thing on 9/11? ---not quite! How is it possible for any member of God's fan club--- Jew or Christian---to be okay with God's wanton massacre of 50,070 blameless men? Really, how is that possible? If there is any pulpit promoter of Judeo-Christianity who cares to defend the unjustified killing of tens of thousands because of the mere curiosity of a few fellas, please let me know of your location---I will gladly attend your church services, with my boots on of course, just to bear witness to the steaming pile of spiritual "spin" needed to sanctify this *Bible-"abomination"*!

Surely, folks, the message intended to be conveyed here is, of course, to frighten away, under penalty of death, anyone so inclined as to investigate the religious claims of the Jews and their religious artifacts for only they have exclusive rights to anything relating to God (it's in the contract!) and anyone curious enough to want to check further into things---will be killed on the spot! The *Bible's* script-writers, obviously, had good reason to try to prevent anyone from looking too deeply into their lucrative treasure chest!

To give you, the reader, some scale of God's indiscriminate slaughter of exactly 50,070 Bethshemites, the entire population of the City of Kingston, New York (2020 census) would have to be "doubled" to approximate this number!

Who was it that was tasked with carrying out the precise body-count of so many God-murdered victims? Who was it that was tasked with burying the tens of thousands of innocent guys that God *"smote"* that day merely because a few fellas tried to peek into a box? Think about it folks, how did such a vile deity come to be honored on America's currency and in her Pledge of Allegiance? Where is the Judeo-Christian outrage over such an atrocity being performed by their beloved Mono-God, their Hebrew Hitler? There is none—there is only adulation and admiration for this monster whom they spare no expense to build extravagant places of worship to praise and to honor Him—incredible! If 50,070 puppies and kittens had been wantonly killed anywhere in the world today because a few of them had misbehaved, I can only imagine the outrage, the outcry, and the outpouring of sympathy that would ensue from "devout" Jews and "devout" Christians everywhere. I can only imagine the punishment they would choose for the perpetrator(s) of such an insentient, brutal deed, but, when it comes to the insentient, brutal deeds carried out by their "beloved" God, they choose to look the other way and to remain in denial about the wicked nature of their *Bible*-God—incredible!

"Once upon another time," another Wow! -moment occurred as told in the 13th chapter of *II Chronicles,* when, in one day, "exactly" 500,000 "chosen" men of Israel were slain by Commander Smotely while fighting on the battlefield simply because they had transgressed against their Mono-Monster by worshiping a golden calf! The message intended to be conveyed here, folks, is obvious, too, ---obedience to God is all that matters especially so for His "chosen"! If God could do such a thing to His favorite followers, what the hell would He have done to His not-so-favored (Gentile Christians) had they acted in a similar way? Let us not forget that God, Himself, had come very close to exterminating every *"lost sheep of the house of Israel"* on the planet because of their persistence in the worship of golden idols as told in Chapter 32 and 33 of *Exodus.* Ironically, however, it was God, Himself who later lost His own life in His failed attempt to save these very same sheep—Wow! again.

Evidently, God had "chosen" the wrong people to be His "chosen" ---He surely knows how to pick 'em! And once again, referring to the above half-million, God-slaughtered "Jews," it should be asked, who was it that was tasked to do the phenomenal and always precise "even-numbered" body-count of the dead whose remains were, surely, haphazardly strewn about a battlefield? Who was it that was tasked with the monumental act of burying half a million decomposing bodies? Hey, what's that smell? And yet again, "once upon another time" as relayed in *II Chronicles* 14:9-13, we are informed that Cmdr. Smotely, doing what He does best, caused the deaths of "exactly" 1,000,000 Ethiopians, I repeat, "exactly" 1,000,000 Ethiopians! ---probably because someone had left the toilet-seat up! Keep in mind that a million murdered folks, according to the 2020 census, would amount to killing every resident of the following cities in upstate New York: Albany, Schenectady, Troy, Buffalo, Rochester, Elmira, Corning, Ithaca, Syracuse, Malone, Kingston, Beacon, and Poughkeepsie---how believable is that? Keep in mind that the non-Jewish historians of the time failed to take note of the slaughter of a *"thousand thousand"* Ethiopians! ---how believable is that?! Keep in mind that such an abominable million-man holocaust resulted from the pleadings of just one Jew, Asa, to his Jew-favoring God for His help---14:11---a Jew-favoring God who, curiously, no longer answers Jewish pleas for assistance---how believable is that!

It must be asked how anyone was able to know the exact Ethiopian head-count? ---it must be asked, who was it that was tasked to undertake the ghastly and gruesome, "even-numbered" body-count especially with the absolute certainty needed to be "proudly" mentioned in an inerrant and infallible book of God's truth which is never off in its tallies by even one body? Was it one counting man? Was it ten? Or, was it one hundred men who were to count, without error, ten thousand dead bodies each? Imagine yourself trying to count just a thousand of any objects without making a mistake—now imagine counting that many objects ten or a thousand times over and doing it perfectly! Hmm! ---do you smell it now?

Once again, who was it that was tasked with the monumental burden of burying a million rotting bodies---why doesn't history record the massacre and burial (or non-burial) of so many, many people? I'm certain that the supremacist mindset of God's "chosen" would not have allowed them to stoop so low as to work up an undignified sweat with a pick and a shovel in order to bury the reeking bodies of their "enemies," besides, that would take time away from their God-pleasing efforts to impose themselves upon others. In giving some perspective to these astounding numbers which, by the way, lack a shred of historical evidence to support them, the greatest single day loss of America's Caretakers of Liberty during WWII occurred on D-Day and amounted to about 3,000 killed—now you'll begin to understand why I call the *Bible*: the Chutzpah Chronicles! If one wishes to believe as true every word (every Jew-praising, Jew glorifying word) given in the *Bible*, you have the right to do so, just as I have the right to ridicule and boldly question your absurd beliefs about God that exist only as words on a page in a boastful book—beliefs that because of their rotten nature continue to stink to high Heaven!

Because Jehovah, God of the Israelites, was responsible for the above outrageous atrocities, and many more, shouldn't the present-day Jews of Israel, at least, out of decency and respect for the multitude of unoffending folks their *Bible*-kin slaughtered, be endeavoring to make amends by, at least, building a monument or two in Jerusalem in memory of their unjust demise? Shouldn't they be endeavoring to build a memorial or two to the untold number of innocent Gentile men, women, children, and animals who were wiped out by the hundreds of thousands or more by their *Bible*-ancestors as part of the ethnic cleansings that their God supposedly "demanded" of them? Had the annihilated Canaanite population totaled in the thousands or in the millions, or even beyond a billion, the *Bible*, I'm certain, would still have revealed how proud and delighted God's chosen people were to boast, in their Chutzpah Chronicles, about their participation in the Canaanite holocaust! In the least, shouldn't Israelites be endeavoring to build a memorial to the above mentioned half-million Jews, their *Bible*-brothers, who were unjustly slain by their God, Jehovah, merely because they bowed to a golden calf---Holy Cow! (NOTE TO JEWS: be very careful not to devote your lives and livelihoods to worshiping anything in this world that might appear to your jealous God as idolatry!)

As to God's "chosen" folks building memorials to their "supposed" *Bible*-victims---it will never happen because too many Jews know mythology when they see, read, and hear it. Besides, there is ***"power and profit"*** to be found in promoting their own bogus mythology—their own Chutzpah Chronicles that contain their contrived history of fellowship with their personal and partisan God. This scam has been so well accepted and supported by the gullible (every Gentile Christian in the world!) and so lucrative, too, why end this deception of epic proportions and, in effect, kill the golden goose that provides so much benefit for the Jews and the Jewish State of Israel at, seemingly, so little a price—a price that amounts to nothing more than words written on the pages of a book that is believed, by the gullible (the imposed upon), to be the "Word of God." After all, Jehovah never did give a damn about Gentiles, so why not exploit them for the benefit of Jewry? Such a deal! Or is it "such a deal" knowing of the Jews' tragic and sorrowful history of bondage and extermination by the millions—a "cruel and unusual" history, indeed, for a "God-favored" people to experience? It is my opinion, which, thankfully, I have a right to express---that the Jews would do well to disown the entire fraudulent enterprise known as Judaism and its bogus, insentient, scripted scriptures.

The world isn't endeared by a racial and religious résumé that begins early on with a history of the murder and annihilation of all of their non-Jewish (Gentile) neighbors and the stealing of their lands, their punishing of the innocent instead of the guilty, their cruel and unusual, God-pleasing "remedy" for homosexual behavior and for stubbornness in children, their supremacist mindset and smugness that comes from their bogus claim of being God's "chosen" people—a claim that supposedly gave them license to kill all who got in their way, rob them of their lands and possessions, and enslave their virgin females for the sexual gratification they would provide to their masters, and the list goes on. It is my claim, supported by a lack of corroborating historical evidence, that the *Bible's* accounts of the Jews annihilating people by the hundreds of thousands (or more) never occurred including their boastful account of their having nearly destroyed Egypt—that they are merely fictional tales written on the pages of a self-glorifying book of Jewish mythology, the *OT* Chutzpah Chronicles—fictional tales that the Jews have yet to distance themselves from—fictional tales that no decent people anywhere on earth should be proud to support or associate themselves with whether they actually occurred or not! —but I digress . . .

Why was it impossible for this so-called Almighty God to transform Himself, even momentarily (ala Satan), into a kinder, gentler, viewable being who could communicate His "SHALT" and "SHALT NOT" directives in person without all of the *OT* drama, without all the *OT* bloodshed, and without all of the *OT* bullying on His part—did He really lack the ability, the dignity, or the decency to do so? Why, too, was it always necessary for Him to delegate "His" responsibilities and enlist the services of others to relay His messages or to do His bidding—there is a plausible answer for such skulking, furtive behavior, absenteeism, and the need always for a stand-in or a cover-up when God decides to make contact or a personal "appearance"? We are made to believe *"no man shall see me and live"* because the art and craft of scriptural script-writing involves utilizing the most powerful means to grab and hold peoples' attention in order to divert it away from their malevolent maneuverings---even the *Koran* makes this clear: *"He that fears God shall be forgiven his sins and richly recompensed"* ---*Koran* 65:5. And, as for those koranic sinners, *"God has prepared a grievous scourge for them. Have fear of God, you that have sense and faith."* ---*Koran* 65:9. By the way, where else have you heard the word "scourge" being used so often except in "religious" texts!

They, the script-writers of the Semitic Chutzpah Chronicles (the *Bible* and the *Koran*) knew well how to take full advantage of the fear of physical punishment and the losing of one's life in this world and/or the threat of suffering eternal torment in the next when both result, they assure us, from not believing and not following their manufactured "Word" of God. Semitic religions, after all, according to Thomas Paine, are but ***"human inventions set up to terrify and enslave mankind, and monopolize power and profit."*** The proof of which is that billions of people, who incorrectly assume that the Chutzpah Chronicles were written for the benefit of "everyone," have been made vulnerable to manipulation by power-hungry, pious parasites and their far-from-impoverished, clerical and evangelical proselytizers who know well, too, how to ***"profit"*** from religious imposition.

They, the script-writers of Semitic religions knew, as do their modern minions know, how to take advantage of having folks believe that the terrifying, tormenting fires of Hell await all who disobey their "sacred" script-ures. They, the script-writers knew, too, that for the most part, people are disinclined to seek out or investigate, to any degree, any sacred, Semitic object that when viewed up close would result in their sudden death—where would Semitic religions be without the constant use of fear, terror, and threats of death—where would they be without our enslavement to their spiritual inventions and deceptions—where would they be without the ***"power and profit"*** we provide them for deceiving us?

For things to be seen, obviously, requires their having a physical existence—the God of the Israelites, for plausible, obvious reasons, could not be seen because He, like Zeus, Jupiter, and Apollo before Him, never physically existed for they are nothing more than the leading men of mythology's fictional tales, and if, perchance, the God of the Israelites did exist and could be seen by others, He should be ashamed to show His ugly, miserable face and continue to remain in hiding, like most criminals, for His shameful deeds, but where is the ***"power and profit"*** in having belief in an amiable, viewable God who is decent, humane, and approachable—a God who doesn't require the services of script-writers to establish His bogus existence and to make frightening excuses for His "inability" to be physically seen—a God who doesn't require the services of "pious" agents to constantly act on His behalf or to wash away our sins in order to prevent our eternal torment, or to tell us what is currently on God's mind. That is why the *OT* God of the Israelites was created as someone incapable of existing as a good God, a meek and mild Guy---that is, until a more-conniving religious mindset sought a change in the script that would transform this invisible, inhumane, intolerant God-zilla, Jehovah, into a completely physical, more endearing, visible entity and a somewhat less-intimidating character—Jesus Christ!

And, as always, the anonymous God-makers and script-writers of the Chutzpah Chronicles were eager and ready to oblige and indulge in chutzpah-laden make-believe once again in the *NT* in their attempt to re-create God in the image of man---imagine that! —as long as ***"power and profit"*** remained in the metamorphosis—as long as fear and terror, in the form of the eternal agony and the *"gnashing of teeth"* of Gnashville's teeming residents, could continue to be utilized to their advantage—as long as the *NT*'s message they were about to invent for Jesus to speak in the Gospels benefitted the Jews, *"the lost sheep of the house of Israel,"* and not the Gentiles whom Jesus avoided, detested, and regarded as *"dogs"* His entire lifetime, but don't take my word for it---*Matt.* 10:5,6; 15:24-26!

In fairness to Commander Smotely, the God of the *OT* who inspires Taliban type mentalities---His smoting of others was, it appears, the ultimate and final end of story—the means He used to forever obliterate, (not forever punish in Hell), the sentient, physical lives of those who displeased Him as is evidenced in his destroying, by flood, of all of the evil-minded beings He had created and who were filling the earth *"with violence"* ---*Gen.* 6:13. This same guy disguised as the God of the *NT*, however, wants everyone who displeases Him to not only suffer in this life but, post-death also---to be bodily resurrected and given "eternal" life in order for them to be physically tormented for ever and ever in the Hell He *"prepared for the devil"* ---*Matt.* 25:41—what a Guy, what a Glorious Guy who *"so loved the world"*! I'd prefer being zapped into oblivion on the spot by Cmdr. Smotely than being re-animated after death by Jesus bin Laden in order to have Him enjoy listening to the sounds of the incessant *"gnashing"* of my teeth---wouldn't you? I am curious, however, about what sounds a toothless person makes in Hell! ---but I digress . . .

In the make-believe world of Semitic religion, who do you believe is the real Monster now---Jehovah or Jesus? This is a trick question because for Jews, Christians, Muslims, and for other God-addicts there is really only one God to worship and adore and He was and still remains, no matter what disguise He wears, a malevolent and malicious monster! In fairness to idol worship, have you ever heard of a golden calf commanding its "heathen" followers to kill folks and steal their lands---have you ever heard of a golden calf being charged with the spiteful, vengeful, race-loathing behaviors assigned to Jehovah, Jesus, and Allah? *"Oh come let us adore Him"* ---really?

<u>Anti-Semitism or anti-Semitic Theism</u>

(NOTE TO READER: Those who are prejudiced against Semitic peoples are rightly labelled as "anti-Semites"—those who are prejudiced against Jews, a Semitic people, are "anti-Semites"—those who are prejudiced against Arabs, a Semitic people, are certainly anti-Semites, as well! ---right? How strange, indeed, that anti-Semitism should exist between Semitic peoples! Imagine a Jew being labelled as an anti-Semite!)

Thanks to the hard-won freedoms bestowed upon Americans by our nation's Caretakers of Liberty who struggled and sacrificed to acquire them, I am able—without the fear of being tortured, maimed, burned alive, or stoned to death (paleo-minded actions that are still being imposed upon "sinners" in certain parts of the world that aspire to live "under God" and His "Word") —to express my observations and opinions upon "Semitic Theism" which I oppose and challenge on many levels.

It does not make me a bigot, a hater, a racist, or an "anti-Semite" to oppose, to challenge, to criticize, or to ridicule Semitic religious beliefs and Semitic religious dogmas imposed upon so much of the world while denouncing the wickedness that results from them—it makes me a freedom-loving person who cherishes having the right to free-expression--- a freedom-loving person who strives to exercise this right whenever and wherever injustice and imposition are encountered. Unfortunately, this "natural right" to free-expression does not exist in many parts of the modern world where basic human freedoms are still verboten by religion-controlled, tyrannical governments commandeered by a Semitic theology continuing its enforced stiflings upon any advancements in the human-condition.

Unfortunately, too, this Constitutional right to free expression is being threatened today in the Land of the Free by political and religious appeasers who would prefer to silence the freedom-loving rebels and boat-rockers as their counterparts did with less success in Colonial America. These political and religious appeasers would prefer to silence anyone who dares to *"question with boldness"* the very existence of a Semitic God and the inviolable, sacrosanct status of the Semitic *Bible* and the Semitic *Koran*. These things, in my opinion, are but the necessary first steps to be taken for the gradual improvement of the welfare of all—especially Americans of African descent and other people of color—through the enlightenment that comes from gaining knowledge and understanding. These things are necessary if homosexuality is ever to be recognized, no longer as a *Bible-"abomination,"* but as a mere inconsequential fact of life.

And let us never forget the plight of Native Americans, (Nativites) a terribly mistreated and forgotten people, who were perceived in ways similar to the ways the *Bible*-Jews perceived the Canaanites. Unfortunately, many of these Semitic perceptions still persist today. Early on in our nation's history, the Nativites were regarded by supremacist-minded, white Christian settlers who, blinded by their *Bible*-indoctrination, were unable to see the evil involved in eradicating Native American culture---taking away their lands, and destroying their lives almost to the point of annihilation. It pains me to recount the following events that took place on American soil, but, sadly, the "us and them" remnants of the mindset of those who took part in these long-ago events is still with us---still affecting our lives in a negative way. The following account comes from *The American Heritage Book of Indians*---it tells of a farmer who killed a female Indian who was stealing peaches---her relatives and friends wantonly killed the farmer and refused to turn the murderers over to the Dutch authorities:

> *In 1643 (17 years after the purchase of Manhattan Island) the Dutch governor ...ordered the massacre of a number of Wappinger people* (Native Americans) *who had run to the Dutch for protection from raiding Mohawks. The Indian refugees were lulled by friendly Dutch treatment for several days, and then were attacked by the Dutch while they slept (in a village on the Jersey side of the Hudson), and 80 heads of men, women, and children were brought back to Manhattan, to Fort Amsterdam, where a New Amsterdam dowager played kickball with them in the street. A captive Hackensack Indian was publicly tortured ...by being skinned in strips and fed with his own flesh while the "poor, naked, simple creature" stubbornly tried to keep up his death song, until at last, flayed from his fingers to his knees, castrated, dragged through the streets, but still alive, he was placed on a mill stone and his head beaten off by the soldiers. The Dutch governor looked on throughout and "laughed right heartily."*

This heartless, nauseating account is not, I repeat, "is not" describing the sick doings of Afghanistan's Taliban who revel in performing similar atrocities, but rather, it describes the sick doings of Americans who were fond to call themselves "Christians"! Nearly 300 years later, in like fashion, a supremacist-minded mob of "us and them" white Christians, bent on revenge, was responsible for massacring hundreds of blacks in cold blood and burning down their homes in Tulsa, Oklahoma in 1921---both horrible events being wiped clean (or almost so) from the pages of America's proud Judeo-Christian heritage and history! In either case, I'm willing to bet that not one member of those despicable "mobs-on-a-murder-mission" was an "abominable" atheist or an "ungodly" heathen! Fast-Forward a hundred years and I'm willing to bet that every member of the mob that raided and desecrated The Capitol Building in Washington, DC would be proud to identify themselves as Christians! I'm also willing to bet that even Derek Chauvin would identify himself as a believer in Jesus and as someone who, at the time, perceived his actions in the killing of George Floyd as "public service" ---I could be wrong on these assessments, but I don't think so!

Since it should be obvious that "greatness" cannot exist without "goodness," we need to begin making our "great" nation into a "good" nation, too---by addressing and attempting to right the wrongs of our past and present times---by determining the uber-reasons that gave cause and sanction to them in the first place---by determining the uber-reasons behind the chaos, the bloodshed, and the killings that continue to happen on a daily basis, time and time again across America---by cultivating a more enlightened mindset amongst all of our fellow citizens—a mindset capable of creating a peaceful and prosperous future that will inspire the entire world to do better than before---a mindset that no longer allows unknown, self-serving, Chutzpah Chronicle script-writers to put, in the name of God, their twisted thoughts into our minds---or their contrived words into our mouths---or their insentient beliefs into our hearts---a mindset that no longer allows the fraudulent scriptures of fraudulent Semitic religions to have any further control over our lives and our destinies.

Thanks to America's hard-won freedoms that were acquired and bestowed upon us by America's Caretakers of Liberty, her noble Patriots, past and present—because of their efforts to secure and defend our nation's precious ideals against all who would tread upon our lives, our liberties, and our pursuits of happiness, I have not only the right but the duty to voice my earnest opposition against the blinded believers of Semitic religions, their bogus books, and their bogus Gods---believers who, knowingly or unknowingly, become, in effect, the enemies of civilization. It took an armed revolution carried out by the Sons and Daughters of Liberty that secured America's freedom in the past; it will take, this time, a peaceful revolution (Reason's Tribunal) to enable us, their enlightened heirs, to use that gift of freedom as it was intended—for the betterment of "all" in the days ahead!

I oppose and challenge the thinking of Jews, Christians, and Muslims who are programmed to believe that they are doing God's "work" regardless of whether it begets loving, benevolent actions or hateful, brutal ones for, curiously, "both" activities result from "obeying" God's Word, as written in the *Bible* and in the *Koran*---just another example of religion having it both ways! This contradiction in sentiment alone makes these scriptures worthy of condemnation and derision for their preaching and promotion of both love and hate—warranting our bold scrutiny and even bolder criticism of them for in the words of Thomas Jefferson: ***"Ridicule is the only weapon which can be used against unintelligible propositions."*** From God's "Word" the justification for indulging in merciful as well as indulging in malevolent activities are given—this fact alone should command the attention and concern of every freedom-loving, peace-enjoying person to take measures to safeguard ourselves and future generations from the chapter and verse, "sura" and "ayat" enemies of progress and civilization disguised as being beneficial guides to all of mankind.

My opposition to Semitic Theism: Judaism, Christianity, and Islam is exceedingly justified because of the lack of authority, I repeat, "the lack of authority" in their "never-to-be-doubted" scriptures whose uncontested dogmas continually give inspiration and direction, sanction and support to ***"the most detestable wickedness, the most horrid cruelties, and the greatest miseries that have afflicted the human race."*** The critical observations and opinions that I and many of America's founding fathers, and others, have unflinchingly expressed on the following pages dealing with Semitic religions are based upon facts and fairness, not prejudicial thinking---they result not from a loathing for Jews, a loathing for Christians, or a loathing for Muslims. They result not from bigotry, hatred, racism, or anti-Semitism as many religious supporters will certainly claim—they result from a loathing for wickedness, cruelty, and injustice carried out in the name of God—they result from the ***"facts and evidence"*** gleaned, in great measure, from Semitic scriptures themselves utilizing bold questioning and common-sense-reasoning along with a reliance on truth and fairness—a process called Reason's Tribunal—a process that was honed in America, but has yet to be fully utilized here—a process of honest and impartial treatment that has never played a part in any Judeo-Christian-Islamic supremacist-minded traditions or principles—a process that, until now, has yet to focus its attention in any profound way upon Semitic religions and their supporting scriptures! All Jews, Christians, and Muslims, therefore, are encouraged to take a break from clutching their holy books and place them in a safe location out of the reach of innocent minded, vulnerable children and partake of Reason's Tribunal's sane, sober, and solemn revelations . . .

The Call to Reason

Fix reason firmly in her seat, and call to her tribunal every fact, every opinion. Question with boldness even the existence of a god; because, if there be one, he must more approve of the homage of reason, than that of blindfolded fear. ...Do not be frightened from this inquiry by any fear of its consequences. ...we are not afraid to follow truth wherever it may lead, nor to tolerate any error so long as reason is left free to combat it. ...Reason and free enquiry are the only effectual agents against error. Give a loose to them, they will support the true religion, by bringing every false one to their tribunal, to the test of their investigation. They are the natural enemies of error, and of error only. ...Millions of innocent men, women and children, since the introduction of Christianity, have been burnt, tortured, fined, imprisoned; yet we have not advanced an inch towards uniformity. What has been the effect of coercion? To make one half the world fools, and the other half hypocrites; to support roguery and error all over the earth.

---Thomas Jefferson

We have abundant reason to rejoice that in this Land the light of truth and reason has triumphed over the power of bigotry and superstition.

---George Washington

All national institutions of churches, whether Jewish, Christian or Turkish, appear to me no other than human inventions, set up to terrify and enslave mankind, and monopolize power and profit. ...The most formidable weapon against errors of every kind is reason. ...when opinions are free, either in matters of government or religion, truth will finally and powerfully prevail.

---Thomas Paine

This would be the best of all possible worlds, if there were no religion in it!

---John Adams

82

Reason's Tribunal
Exposing God's Word To End
The Nightmare Of Religion

"*When in the course of human events,*" difficult times beset our nation or threaten our free existence, we often look to our nation's freedom-seeking, founding fathers for guidance that will inspire and direct us in ways that will honor their Legacy of Liberty. Because the scripture-inspired, supremacist mindset that manifests itself in racial discord and acts of terror is a major source of America's ongoing troubles at home and around the world, we should seek the wisdom of those founders who had the courage to seek a walled separation between sanity and insanity---founders who, thankfully, were well versed upon the subject of Semitic religions, their non-sacred dogmas, and their continuous, menacing effects upon society. Let us, therefore, pay homage to their secular-minded insights and warnings by heeding the timely advice and knowledge they have bequeathed to us on such matters. Let us, a freedom-loving people, become rebels once again in defiance of our Liberty-destroying oppressors and make, once again, another Declaration of Independence from their imposing endeavors. Let us begin to wage the long overdue *"revolution in the system of religion."*

Let us honor Thomas Jefferson's courageous request and begin to *"Question with boldness"* even the very existence of God (Jehovah, Jesus, and Allah) in a tribunal presided over by reason to better understand their respective, "revealed" religions and their inherent propensities for producing infamy and terror. Such a personal inquisition or public court of examination will provide the *"facts and evidence"* that will enable us to overcome our religious indoctrination---enable us to rise up from our subservient and mindless kneeling positions---enable us to remove our rose-colored eyeglasses, and begin to see, clearly, the destructive and deadly dynamics embedded in the uncontested scriptural dogmas of Semitic religions: Judaism, Christianity, and Islam—dynamics that have remained undiminished in their potential to inspire folks to harm and to kill—dynamics that are still eagerly embraced enough at times to be employed by eager devotees to the obvious detriment of others. Let us, therefore, *"give a loose"* to *"reason and free enquiry"* in our scrutiny of the *Bible* and the *Koran* in order to find a way to neutralize their deadly potentials and their less-than-sacred pursuits.

We need to begin to see, clearly, the malevolence authorized and endorsed in the Judeo-Christian *Bible* and in the Islamic *Koran* which grew from its very roots—malevolence that is, once again, being indulged in as prescribed, in no uncertain terms, on the pages of the *Koran*---malevolence that is meant to utterly destroy America, the *"Blessings of Liberty,"* and all of the human progress acquired through the religion-stifled advancements of civilization. In our sane and reasonable attempt to end the evils of Abrahamic religions---(Jews and Arabs both claim Abraham (Ibrahim) as their common ancestor) ---the "First Duty" of a freedom-loving people is to see, clearly, that the benevolence of humanity's spiritual and ethical behavior is "not" in any way dependent upon Semitic religious beliefs. Our "Second Duty" is to determine if such religious beliefs are free from deception and deserving of our respect, our devotion, our nation's Constitutional protection, and our financial support. Our "Third Duty" is to learn where to direct our earnest, rational, and critical energies against all scripture-inspired madness without *"any fear of its consequences."*

Since Abraham is the "revered" founding father of Judaism, Christianity, and Islam, it is important to note here the type of person that God "picked" to be the patriarch of Semitic religions and in whose *"seed shall all the nations of the earth be blessed."* God's choice for this coveted position was Abraham, a slave-owning, despicable human being, reprobate, and pimp, I repeat, "a slave-owning, despicable human being, reprobate, and pimp"! Abraham married his half-sister and, in essence, pimped her off to the Pharaoh of Egypt and to Abimilech, the King of Gerar, in order to avoid receiving any harm to himself. Later, with knife in hand, this shining light of the Semitic world, and inspiration to Taliban types, was preparing, without giving it a second thought of course, to murder his own son, his only son, Isaac, and burn his body as a sacred sacrifice to please his God as told in Chapter 22 of *Genesis*—a God who savors the heavenly scent of burnt flesh arising to his nostrils---a God who disgraced Himself and His holy name for His "tempting" of Abraham to kill his child even though He called off the heinous execution and holocaust at the last moment. What a glorious, wonderful Guy---*"Praise the Lord"*! Sick stuff, folks—really sick stuff!

Had God decided not to call-off this sick-minded homicide and holocaust, would He still be honored and worshiped around the globe? Yes, of course He would, for it is not a matter of concern for Jews and for

Christians, (the eager supporters of everything dealing with Judaism and the State of Israel), that their shared, beloved God is a murderer. According to their shared, beloved *Bible,* it was Jehovah, God of Jews and Christians, who was responsible for the brutal deaths of millions of unoffending men, women, children, and animals—a fact that, shockingly, has never resulted in a notable decrease in the membership of His Jewish and Christian fan clubs! For Abraham's devotion to God to commit the heartless, mindless murder of his son without question, God, (who can really pick 'em!), "blessed" Abraham with "Father-of-the-Year" status for all time—telling this murderous-minded miscreant that He would multiply his seed *"exceedingly"* while assuring him, *"in thy seed shall all the nations of the earth be blessed."* Really? How *"exceedingly"* disgusting and disgraceful! The message intended to be conveyed here, folks, is obvious: Never Disobey God, I repeat, "Never Disobey God" even if it involves murdering members of your own family, and you, the unjust and undeserving, with evil intent in your heart and mind, will be *"blessed"* greatly, as well as all the rest of the world!

Sadly, it continues to be preached in America, that our nation has been *"blessed,"* too, by the criminal behavior and wickedness of this evil, sick-minded monster and, if this be so, how so? Isn't it time to investigate this claim made by all Jews, all Christians, and, one assumes, even Taliban members who, being of the seed of Abraham, must surely rejoice in knowing that they are following the example set by their heartless, murder-minded, Semitic ancestor who, with knife in hand, spreads God's blessing upon *"all the nations of the earth"*! Surely, they too, with knife in hand, will be greatly rewarded for their devotion to God---*"Allahu Akbar"*!

> *All three monotheisms, just to take the most salient example, praise Abraham for being willing to hear voices and then to take his son Isaac for a long and rather mad and gloomy walk. And then the caprice by which his murderous hand is finally stayed is written down as divine mercy.*
>
> ---Christopher Hitchens, *God Is Not Great*

Committing, or attempting to commit, without any second thoughts whatsoever, heinous acts of atrocity in God's "holy" name is, seemingly, the honorable way to please this Semitic deity and His "loving" heart—9/11 being a perfect example of religious devotion by the "seed" of Abraham/Ibrahim which now "blesses" all the world with its divine fruits served up from the pages of a Semitic scripture known as the *Koran*! It is interesting to note here that God, like the founding father of His murder-minded fan club in the Semitic world, was willing to sacrifice His "only" son, too, but preferred, this time, not to call off the sickening execution at the very last second. Thankfully, for all of the joy it now brings to members of His expanded fan club, God had willed the brutal crucifixion and murder of His own seed, Jesus, as recompense---as an atonement---for someone else's long-ago, naive disobedience---a revered tradition of "that old time religion" ---Judaism! What a Guy—what a Great and Glorious Guy! This was done, we are made to believe, so that God's fatuous, *New Testament* followers would, somehow, be *"blessed,"* too, by indulgence, once again, in this paleo-minded Judeo-ritual that all Christians seem to admire, a ritual that required an innocent "scapegoat" (Jesus) to be punished instead of the guilty party---in this instance, the sacrifice of God's "unblemished" Son, in order to make right a supposed wrong committed thousands of years earlier by the child-minded, mythological Adam---a wrong Jesus had no part in but, nevertheless, must die for---a wonderful example of the Judeo-justice that is credited with being the cornerstone of the foundation that America's legal system was built upon---really?

How *"exceedingly"* repugnant and un-American is this disgusting and disgraceful Semitic tradition of "vicarious atonement," yet we praise *"Our Father who art in Heaven, hallowed be thy name . . ."* Hallowed for what? . . . for His wickedness in having His innocent Son murdered so that all the nations of the earth will be rewarded and *"blessed"* as a result of this horrendous *"abomination"*? Really? ---think about that, pilgrims! Thankfully, in America, any father who attempted to murder his son for any reason would be treated, not as a hero or a blessed religious icon, but as a mentally-deranged criminal and rightly so, yet Christian-Americans, blinded by the insentient nature of their Semitic religion, choose to worship such a malefactor for the "blessings" born of His brutality—unbelievable, truly unbelievable!

As "humane" beings, we should never feel *"blessed"* by the death of anyone, especially a wanton death. We should feel repulsion instead of admiration when the death of Jesus is equated with the death of a "sacrificial lamb" whose demise, supposedly, washes away another's sins. We should feel repulsion instead of admiration, especially in America, over our condoning of a religious ritual, a heartless practice from an age of ignorance that punishes the innocent for someone else's doings! We should feel repulsion instead of admiration, especially in America, for a Semitic religious endeavor which, if the truth be told, is but a ritual of barbarians that decent-minded folks should be ashamed to acknowledge as "sacred" activity. We should feel repulsion instead of admiration for the Judeo-tradition of slaughtering, dismembering animals, sprinkling their blood upon "sacred" altars and roasting their remains in order to please God with the aroma of their barbecued flesh---we should feel repulsion instead of admiration for the Judeo-tradition of believing that indulging in such activities will result in ones receiving God's blessings and forgiveness. Yet, the mindset that finds sacredness in such uncivilized paleo-traditions flourishes to this day in America and many elsewheres—for the crucifixion and death of an "innocent" Son undertaken by His "loving" Father to erase and atone for another's transgression had its origins in this brutal pastime of savages. And for this abominable act of injustice rooted in human and animal sacrifice, we thank and adore this monster God to whom we continue to bow our heads, bend our knees, and fill the collection plate for the benefit of His proud promoters! Does a more detestable, pathological *"system of religion"* exist?

For Jews and Christians who have been *"blessed"* by the *"seed"* of Abraham, the committing of atrocity in the name of God is a justified activity as long as it results from a reading of God's perfect Word as "revealed" without error in the inerrant and infallible *Bible*. For Muslims who have been *"blessed"* by the "seed" of Ibrahim, the committing of atrocity in the name of Allah is justified as long as it results from a reading of Allah's Word as "revealed" without error in the undoubted *Koran*. The *Bible* and the *Koran*, therefore, must be the focus of our attention if we are to begin to understand why acts of terror are indulged in by those who claim they personally take God's "written" interests to heart. Having absolute faith in the veracity of Semitic scripture, however, is not proof of their truthfulness for it is obvious that those who have absolute faith in God's Word as expressed in the *Bible* disagree with those who have absolute faith in God's Word as expressed in the *Koran*. How is it possible to disagree over God's truth? To be fair, however, in any serious scrutiny of these two Semitic scriptures, we must not only examine the evidence of those who tell us the above Word of God texts are infallible, inerrant, and beyond doubt---we must also examine all evidence to the contrary. How would it be possible, otherwise, to determine whether believers in these man-made manuals have been imposed upon especially by those who have an impious interest in preaching, teaching, and promoting them for their livelihood—those who have an overriding, impious interest in *"power and profit"*?

Religiously justified violence is first and foremost a problem of 'sacred' texts and not a problem of misinterpretation of texts.

---Jack Nelson-Pallmeyer

We must begin to educate and enlighten ourselves about the irreligious, bogus foundations of Judaism, Christianity, and Islam. We must begin to tell "the rest of the story" to those exposed only to the one-sided indoctrination delivered in their synagogues, churches, mosques, and beyond by the multitude of radio, television, and internet programs devoted to promoting the self-interests of fraudulent, fabricated religions based upon, of all things, Pagan mythology! We must level the playing field and begin to balance the Hallelujah airwaves with opposing effect. We must begin to analyze the ***"facts and evidence"*** that not only supports the case for having belief in Semitic religions but also the ***"facts and evidence"*** that supports the worthy case for not having belief in them—the worthy case that belies the claim of America being a nation UNDER GOD—the worthy case that belies the claim of America having been established upon Judeo-Christian traditions and principles. We must begin to allow the case made against Semitic religions by secularist plaintiffs to finally be heard loud and clear. We must begin to allow secularist plaintiffs to have their opportunity to present their verifiable claims made against religion in a venue where, until now, we have only ever heard from the defendants of religion—fair and balanced justice demands it be done. It is time for our nation's hotels and motels to stop their tacit preaching and end their mindless promotion of Semitic religion by the placing of *Bibles* and, perhaps, *Korans* in their rented rooms---a custom that should not be viewed as a "WELCOME" mat for all of their guests, especially those who happen to be non-believers---unless the promotion of Semitic religion is part of their business endeavors. It is time for all the world to hear, at last, the long-overdue case made against religion with a fervor not to exceed that extolled in its constant promotion. It is time for Gideon *Bibles* to be replaced with copies of *The Age of Reason.*

To help achieve this end, Thomas Paine, focused his genius to ***"Fix reason firmly in her seat"*** on the subject of religion in his above-named book. In it, the rigorous critical and logical analysis he employed against the *Bible*, using its very own chapter and verse ***"facts and evidence,"*** I repeat, "using its very own chapter and verse ***"facts and evidence""*** to reveal the *Bible's* fraudulence were the only tools Mr. Paine utilized to enable us, his readers, to remove the mental shackles imposed by the coerced and uncontested religious beliefs of Judaism and Christianity. His efforts, in effect, have provided us the means to overcome their "pious" mental tyrannies by exposing the contriving, power-hungry minds, the outright lies, and the brutal, fisted hands that were involved in the making and marketing of their shared *Bible*—a book Mr. Paine has shown to be replete with contradictions and impossibilities—a book devoid of solid literary credentials and authority—a book written by deceiving, ungodly script-writers—a book imposed upon billions through the centuries by insentient, bloodthirsty, power-seeking, lying, anonymous, pious-pretending impostors as being the "Word of God"!

The bible's reputation was imposed and propagated for millennia with the sword, fire, and mandatory reinforcements sessions held weekly—church.

Andrew L. Seidel, *The Founding Myth*

Some Christians pretend that Christianity was not established by the sword; but of what period of time do they speak? It was impossible that twelve men could begin with the sword; they had not the power; but no sooner were the professors of Christianity sufficiently powerful to employ the sword than they did so, and the stake and fagot, too; and Mahomet could not do it sooner. By the same spirit that Peter cut off the ear of the high priest's servant [if the story be true], he would have cut off his head, and the head of his master, had he been able.

---Thomas Paine, *The Age of Reason*

By the same spirit mentioned above, Osama bin Laden would have used weapons of mass destruction on 9/11 had he been able to acquire them! ---kvk

...Christianity founds itself originally upon the Bible, and the Bible was established altogether by the sword, and that in the worst use of it—not to terrify, but to extirpate. The Jews made no converts; they butchered all. The Bible is the sire of the Testament, and both are called the Word of God. The Christians read both books; the ministers preach from both books; and this thing called Christianity is made up of both. It is then false to say that

Christianity was not established by the sword. (Note: when Paine refers to the *"Bible,"* he is referring to the *Old Testament*---kvk)

---Thomas Paine

The courageous scrutiny and common-sense reasoning utilized by Thomas Paine in *The Age of Reason* were all that was required for him to reveal the bogus authority of the *Bible* and its imposing script-writers. Such fearless scrutiny and reasoning applied to the *Bible's* offshoot, the *Koran*, which Muslims regard as being "immune-from-error," will likewise reveal its bogus authority and that of its imposing script-writers. Exposing the *Koran's* "errors" will give us the most effective weapon that has a chance to succeed against a religion-oppressed people unable, at this time, to harbor any doubts or to voice any free opinions about their imposed and uncontested "Word of Allah" because Islam forbids its followers to question its religious authority without risking, of course, their very existence to do so. The "cruel and unusual" penalties for one's infidelity to the dogmas promoted on the pages of the *Koran* include beatings and burnings, numerous physical and mental tortures, body mutilation, amputation of hands, feet, and entire limbs, stonings and hangings—all of which have proved quite effective in silencing the critics of Islam---imagine that! Imagine any religion having to resort to such tactics for the advancement of spiritual behavior! ---really? Where would Semitic religions be without their threats to life and limb for disbelief or for perceived infidelity to God and His "Word"? Thankfully, the persuasive power of Mr. Paine's "inspired" words and rationale proved indispensable in our nation's initial struggle against tyranny—thankfully, they are indispensable, if used wisely, in her present struggle, too.

Slowly and painfully, but surely and clearly, men are becoming convinced that there are no divine beings and no supernatural religions—that all the gods, including Christ, are myths, and all the religions, including Christianity, human productions.

---John E. Remsburg, *The Christ*

Like Thomas Paine before him, the above author, John E. Remsburg (1848-1919), using the tools of textual criticism and applying rigorous logical analysis, carefully examined the *New Testament* scriptures and the writings of well-known Pagan authors

90

from the time of Jesus, along with the works of later Christian apologists. His conclusion is that the divine, miracle-working Christ of traditional Christianity is a myth, which was developed over many centuries by a community of believers and was heavily influenced by mythic elements of Greek, Roman, and eastern religions. ---kvk

We can no longer allow the perceptions and practices of cruel, *"human productions,"* their fearful, punishing doctrines, and their perverse rationalizations to continue to go unchallenged—perverse rationalizations such as believing that the Creator of the never-ending torments of a Hell is a "loving" and a "merciful" God. Really folks? ---this is a no-brainer—no one deserves to suffer "eternally"—no one! Those who believe there is a spiritual dimension to the above *"abomination"* of everlasting agony should seek professional help right away for their mental illness! We can no longer allow the boasts and exaggerations of the Chutzpah Chronicles of Semitic religions to go unchallenged, too, such as the previously mentioned, precise claim made about the exact number (50,070) of Bethshemesh men who died from the effects of smoting! In Chapter 20 of *I Kings,* the claim is made of "exactly" 7000 Jews having killed "exactly" 100,000 Syrians in a single day while "exactly" 27,000 Syrians who were fortunate enough to have survived the slaughter were later killed by a wall falling upon each of them, I repeat, "by a wall falling upon each of them" —a mighty, mighty, mighty big wall! How many thousands of Syrians were seriously "injured" that day by this very same falling wall is anyone's guess!

A glance at the highest number of deaths that occurred in a single day during our nation's armed conflicts from the Revolutionary War to the Vietnam War reveals, beyond a doubt, that the total of "exactly" 127,000 dead Syrians amounts to precisely 127,000 steaming piles being delivered to us in the above *Bible*-tale—an attempt by its script-writers to convince the gullible that this unbelievable tale is a factual part of Jewish history—a factual part of their inerrant, infallible Word of God! If the Jews of the *Bible* were truly racially-favored by God, as we're supposed to believe, and they had truly possessed such legendary, military might, history would have noted it somewhere. Instead, it is only upon the pages of their Chutzpah Chronicles that make mention of, and memorialize, such glorious, God-assisted, unstoppable conquests and self-aggrandizing, racial claims. The "recorded" history of the Jews, however, is a sad, inglorious history of dispersion, persecution, and extermination—rather strange predicaments, in my opinion, for God's "chosen" folks to experience! ---my condolences to a race of people whom God, supposedly, found favor with and then, seemingly, abandoned. I consider myself fortunate not to be counted among God's favorites---phwhew! I consider myself fortunate, too, for the decent-minded men who had the courage to "outlaw" many of the "cruel and unusual" Judeo-punishments that are such an integral part of the Semitic justice- system that is so unashamedly "revealed" in the *Bible.*

We can no longer allow the perceptions, practices, and chutzpah-laden, criminal histories, begotten in an age of stifling ignorance, superstition, and religious domination, to continue to go unchecked—an age that was convinced the earth was flat and the center of the visible Universe—an age that forbid scientific inquiry while demanding strict obedience to paleo-minded rituals under penalty of torture and death---strict obedience to the Church and its morbid teachings under penalty of torture and death. The Semitic *Bible* is a product of that ignorant age, so, too, is its God, a product of that ignorant age—a God who some call Jehovah—a God who some call Jesus—a God who some call Allah, even though we're made to believe that they are the very one and the very same God. A God who curiously allowed His "chosen people" to break His "THOU SHALT NOT KILL" Commandment without cause, concern, or consequence because the Ten Commandments were not written for anyone but the Jews to abide by, I repeat, "the Ten Commandments were not written for anyone but the Jews to abide by" and when the Decalogue is understood in its original context, the above Commandment is understood to mean: "THOU SHALT NOT KILL MEMBERS OF YOUR TRIBE" —meaning in effect: THOU MAYEST KILL OTHERS!

That's why the "us and them-minded" Jews considered the lives of every non-Jew to be worthless and quite expendable—that's why the Jews could exterminate the Canaanites without compunction—the permission to do so is written into their God-given laws, laws that were meant to favor Jews only and to sanction all of their doings! (Read Andrew Seidel's book, *The Founding Myth,* where he boldly examines the *Bible's* four differing accounts of the Ten Commandments and convincingly sets the record straight on their original texts, their original meanings and their tribal intent! He also sets the record straight about the "Ten Laws for Members Only" being un-American and, therefore, unworthy of receiving credit as the basis of America's criminal justice system).

Amazingly, it is the supposed author of these laws, a child-murdering God, whom Americans teach their children to love, respect, and have belief in (how's that workin' out?) —a God whom America declares her trust in and pledges allegiance to (how's that workin' out?) —a God who watches over America and guides her every action (how's that workin' out?) ---a God whom we are imposed upon to believe is a God of love even though He expressly "commanded" the following activities be carried out in His hallowed name because they are the "right" thing to do (and we all should know how a righteous God does His sacred work---His best work):

It is right, in the most holy name of Jehovah-Jesus, to stone blasphemers to death---*Lev.* 24:10-16—it is right, in the most holy name of Jehovah-Jesus to stone homosexuals to death---*Lev.* 20:13—it is right, in the most holy name of Jehovah-Jesus, to stone stubborn children to death---*Deut.* 21:1—it is right, in the most holy name of Jehovah-Jesus, to stone to death all who, of all things, have the audacity to gather wood (or otherwise work) on the Sabbath day-—*Num.* 15:32-36, (imagine someone in America sitting on death-row awaiting execution for merely stacking firewood or mowing their lawn on a weekend! —it is right, in the most holy name of Jehovah-Jesus to stone fortunetellers (future-tellers) to death---*Lev.* 20:27--- evangelical Christian oracles and Jehovah Witness prognosticators BEWARE! —incidentally, a "witness" is someone who has seen a certain thing or event with their own eyes---someone who is able to give firsthand evidence because of what they had seen---who then can say they have been a witness to anything associated with Jehovah when no one has seen Him or heard Him (except for some mentally-deranged folks!)? ---does reading His scripted words in the *Bible* constitute absolute proof of His existence?-- -absolutely not! If, on the other hand, reading His scripted *Bible*-words is, somehow, considered proof of Jehovah's existence, then He is revealed, not as a world-loving Guy, but as a malevolent psychopath---at least to this witness of *Bible*-fact! Now back to where I left off:

It is right, in the most holy name of Jehovah-Jesus, when under the duress of hunger, to kill your children and eat their flesh---*Deut.* 28:53—it is right, in the most holy name of Jehovah-Jesus, for a father to sell his daughter into slavery---*Exodus* 21:7—it is right, in the most holy name of Jehovah-Jesus, to murder, rape, and enslave non-Jews (Gentiles), plunder their cities, and steal their lands---*Deut.* 20:10-18---it is right to punish children for the iniquity of their parents---*Exodus* 20:5! Surely, it isn't "right," however, that such malevolent actions be condoned, tolerated, or deemed acceptable by any freedom-loving person or any freedom-loving nation as being part of a loving God's designs for the moral improvement of man, woman, child, or country! Such actions should never be condoned, tolerated, or deemed acceptable just because we're told by ignoramuses and morally-corrupt clergy that they are part of God's most sacred "will." No ethnic group should benefit or be rewarded for their history of such ungodly behavior especially when it results in atrocities being committed upon innocent others. Yet, the perpetrators of these and other wicked abominations promoted in Judeo-theology are never denounced for their despicable actions, instead, the *Bible,* and all that is contained therein, is revered and, curiously, held in high regard for the death-dealing dogmas and criminal injustices that its faithful continue to impose upon others. How well the wickedness of religion is reflected in the mirror of world events and world history! It is "right," therefore, that we now strive, via Reason's Tribunal, to end the *Bible's* unhindered ability to impose its vile aberrations upon us in the guise of "spiritual" activity—ditto for the *Koran*!

> *The God of the Old Testament is arguably the most unpleasant character in all fiction: jealous and proud of it; a petty, unjust, unforgiving control-freak; a vindictive, bloodthirsty, ethnic cleanser; a misogynistic, homophobic, racist, infanticidal, genocidal, filicidal, pestilential, megalomaniacal, sado-masochistic, capriciously malevolent bully...psychotic delinquent.*

---Richard Dawkins

We can no longer allow the abuse and threats of abuse (the fear-factor), and corporal punishments—the imposed mental and physical tyranny of doctrinal religions---to have boundless freedom in conducting their dreadful pursuits. We can no longer allow doctrinal religions to be practiced, protected, and promoted without question, without any counterbalance measures being taken, without a thorough background-check to reveal their past corruptions and criminal offenses—the risk of religion re-offending has become too great for the civilized world to bear. It is "right," therefore, in the name of fairness and decency to conduct Reason's Tribunal against such *"human productions."* It is "right" that America and her freedom-loving citizens denounce the God of the *Bible* who, incidentally, is "not" the ***"Creator"*** mentioned in the Declaration of Independence!

Only by employing Reason's Tribunal will it be possible to reveal to one and all that the *Koran* and its progenitor, the Judeo-Christian *Bible*, were written by cruel, selfish, power-hungry men, not by the hand of any infallible and inerrant possessor of divinity. Who but power-hungry tyrants would demand absolute compliance to the decrees of a vengeful, malicious God, a carnivorous, bloodthirsty, slavery-promoting criminal who spreads His message through fear and intimidation, cruelty, murder, and moral injustice: death by stonings, the plundering and extermination of entire nations, blood sacrifices and burnt offerings, the rape of enslaved women by their Semitic masters, eternal torment for doubters, and, in the case of the *Koran*, carnal rewards for all Heaven-bound, male martyrs? These wanton, vengeful pursuits, perverse practices, and carnal obsessions alone should reveal, to the uncorrupted mind, the contrived, parasitic, ungodly, and less-than-sacred nature of Semitic scriptures, their less-than-sacred male authors, and their less-than-sacred Gods.

In every religion, priests alone have a right to decide what is pleasing or displeasing to their God; we are certain they will always decide that it is what pleases or displeases themselves.

---Paul Henri Thiry, *Natural Ideas Opposed to Supernatural*

Those who can make you believe absurdities can make you commit atrocities.

---Voltaire

It doesn't matter what men believe; it's what they do that matters. Yet what they do is but the outer expression of their beliefs.

---Lloyd M. Graham, *Deceptions and Myths of the Bible*

We can no longer allow Semitic religions to have free-rein in imposing their scripture-inspired madness, their theological tyrannies upon the masses, upon politics and world events. It is time for Reason's Tribunal to pull the plug on religious doctrines that pose a threat, not only to the survival of our freedom-loving nation and her founding principles, but to the survival of civilization---religious practices that are continually allowed to exist and operate without any structured opposition which would protect the secular interests of all non-believers. We, Americans, can no longer continue fooling ourselves with the belief that our nation conducts all of it affairs under God's protection, guidance, and supervision---Vietnam and Afghanistan should be convincing proof of that!

The continuing contagion we face today for allowing destructive, religious dogmas to survive unscathed throughout the ages has now reached critical-mass. Thankfully, due to the civilizing effects of the enlightened, progressive pursuits of secularism occurring throughout the same religion-dominated ages of Western civilization such as the Magna Carta's successful challenge to the "divine rights" of kings---Judeo-Christianity is no longer the dire threat to ***"Life, Liberty and the pursuit of Happiness"*** that it posed in the past. Being alienated, however, from such reforming secular achievements, a younger sibling religion, Islam, has now become the greatest threat to America's freedoms. Islam has taken over the supremacist endeavors promoted in Jewish theology to mercilessly destroy all non-believers---an act of compliance and devotion to its bogus scripture---the *Koran*---an act of compliance and devotion to its bogus deity—Allah. We may have entered the scientific Space Age of the 21st century A.D., but we are still being hindered by the paleo-mindset of B.C. Stone-Age, Semitic religions. In these more enlightened times, we are forced now to deal with the Muslim version of Jew versus Canaanite—and we all know how that turned out!

The *Koran* is the "beating" heart of Islam; it is a book which makes Muslim terrorists believe that the evil they do unto others is noble and done solely to please Allah; it is a book whose "undoubted" words and praise for Allah exited the lips of devout believers as they carried out their religion-inspired, plans for 9/11 and every other atrocity they've undertaken in the name of their God. Undoubted words are always the singular source of every Semitic religion's murderous undertakings. Therefore, in order to benefit from Mr. Paine's sane and sage legacy, we must acquire the Jeffersonian courage to examine, in Reason's Tribunal, ***"every fact, every opinion"*** dealing with the undoubted words upon which believers in Judaism, Christianity, and Islam justify their terrorist activities as sacred, God-pleasing services. We must expose the diabolical deceptions woven into the "sacrosanct" words of all Semitic scriptures—words that, otherwise, will continue to inspire future believers as they have inspired past and present believers to commit mindless barbarities in the name of God whether He is called Jehovah, Jesus, or Allah. We must begin to ***"Question with boldness even the existence"*** of the God "revealed" in the *Bible* and the *Koran*.

It is error only, and not truth, that shrinks from inquiry.

---Thomas Paine

The critical, rational tools Mr. Paine employed in *The Age of Reason* against the fabricated texts of the *Bible* are useful, also, to lay bare the fabricated texts of the *Koran*—for no religion should fear inquiry into its foundational literature unless, of course, it has something to hide! As I have stated (and re-re-stated!) in this book, the *Bible* and the *Koran* must be held responsible for their underlying roles in the crimes committed against humanity by their past and present devotees who, too, must be held accountable for their vile actions. We must begin to subject the ***"facts and evidence"*** that these written works provide, about their purported God's existence and His purported endeavors, to the same rigorous and impartial standards employed in America's legal system to determine truth or falsehood, guilt or innocence. We must begin to determine the worthiness or the unworthiness of the testimonies given in these so-called "Word of God" texts—the worthiness or the unworthiness of our having unconditional belief in them.

Reason's Tribunal will reveal that the *Bible* and the *Koran* are neither sacred nor divinely inspired books—that the wickedness portrayed and promoted on their blood-stained pages is not worthy of anyone's reverence, respect, or acceptance as being the "Word" of God. The *Bible* and the *Koran's* hateful incitements which, time and again, have resulted in cruel and deadly pursuits by their adoring fans should be condemned the world over along with their sanctioning of slavery, their continuing promotion of racial and sexual discrimination and their hideous Hell of eternal torments that awaits all who have "sinned." Shouldn't we, a freedom-loving nation of decent-minded human beings, condemn rather than condone the "divine" intentions and the "divine" directives that justify and encourage vengeful, malevolent activities? Shouldn't divinely-inspired religions be opposed to aiding and abetting the suffering and demise of others?

How is anyone to know with any degree of certainty that the *Bible* is truly the work of authors who were "inspired" by God? How is anyone to know with any degree of certainty that the *Koran* was truly "revealed" to Muhammad by an angel in the darkened recesses of a cave? Would anyone believe me if I were to say and even swear to it that this book, *Reason's Tribunal*, was dictated by God, word for word, to me—of course not! Would anyone believe me even if it actually happened? —of course not! The same standards of credibility apply to Semitic scripture. It should certainly take much more than my telling you that it was God who spoke to me in order to convince you of the truthfulness of my statements, and rightly so. It should take much more than someone's telling us that the *Bible* is the "Word" of God in order to convince us it is so. Because such convincing evidence does not exist, the *Bible* and the *Koran* are both lacking in the authority that their script-writers, whom we don't know the identity of, want us to believe they have. Because of the *Bible* and the *Koran's* lack of fairness and lack of decency, because of the intolerance and injustice they proudly promote, they should be regarded as irreconcilably hostile to ***"Life, Liberty and the pursuit of Happiness,"*** —hostile to the positive, healthy development of the innocent hearts and the innocent minds of gullible, impressionable children.

> *More generally (and this applies to Christianity no less than to Islam), what is really pernicious is the practice of teaching children that faith itself is a virtue. Faith is an evil precisely because it requires no justification and brooks no argument. Teaching children that unquestioned faith is a virtue primes them—given certain other ingredients that are not hard to come by—to grow up into potentially lethal weapons for future jihads or crusades. Immunized against fear by the promise of a martyr's paradise, the authentic faith-head deserves a high place in the history of armaments, alongside the longbow, the warhorse, the tank and the cluster bomb. If children were taught to question and think through their beliefs, instead of being taught the superior virtue of faith without question, it is a good bet that there would be no suicide bombers. Suicide bombers do what they do because they really believe what they were taught in their religious schools: that duty to God exceeds all other priorities, and that martyrdom in his service will be rewarded in the gardens of Paradise. And they were taught that lesson not necessarily by extremist fanatics but by decent, gentle, mainstream religious instructors, who lined them up in their madrasas, sitting in rows, rhythmically nodding their innocent little heads up and down while they learned every word of the holy book like demented parrots. Faith can be very very dangerous, and deliberately to implant it into the vulnerable mind of an innocent child is a grievous wrong.*

---Richard Dawkins

Because of the unquestioned, privileged status of Semitic scriptures, their potential for generating malevolent actions continues virtually unimpeded into the 21st century to endanger the entire planet seemingly on a daily basis. Today, it is America's young Sons and Daughters of Liberty who, in service to our nation, suffer loss of life and limb because of it. Daily, they along with countless innocent civilians around the world, are targeted for torture, injury, and death in an unceasing war of extirpation directed against all infidels: non-believers in the Islamic faith. It is wholly a "Holy War" (Jihad)!

It is a war in which we have not yet delivered an effective, weakening blow against an enemy who, because of imposed religious indoctrination, believes it is their sacred duty to honor their God, Allah, by inflicting, through whatever means necessary, His cruel and unusual punishments upon everyone even if it involves the sacrificing of one's life in order to carry it out—submit to Islamic rule and the supposed "will" of Allah, or be tortured, and/or killed, and tortured again forever in Hell! Adding to the miseries of this world is what the sick business of Semitic religions have always been about!

With bombs, bullets, and billions upon billions upon billions of dollars (involving the death, traumatic injury, and long-suffering of American and Afghan Forces along with countless, innocent civilians), we have tried in vain, to defeat the unwavering insanity of Islamic terrorists (the Taliban, Isis, Al Queda, etc.) through military endeavors---the reason is because these folks are devout believers in the *Koran*---their jihadi-hearts are filled with rapturous joy and their jihadi-mindsets are uber-inspired to fight and die in defense of their God and His written Word which exhorts them to *"slay the idolators."* What could be more noble for a *Koranimal* than to die a martyr! Eviscerate the *Koran* and its sacred words that are responsible for causing the desire to die by martyrdom in the name of Allah, and the War on Terror will begin to wane! It should be obvious to every American that twenty years of bomb-dropping in Iraq and Afghanistan has not resulted in any devastating effect being incurred upon Talibanimals---their ever-increasing numbers and their ever-continuing, brutal behaviors? Wouldn't twenty years of effort spent debunking and neutralizing the *Koran* have achieved better results than having our nation experience a bitter defeat which only strengthened our enemies and which further imperils our future? America has to develop a weapon that can effectively deal with religious insanity---a weapon that will eventually lay siege to the terrorist mindset, rooted in scripture, and utterly destroy it---a weapon to be used only to improve the lives of people not destroy them---that weapon is Reason's Tribunal and it deployment begins when we begin to ***"Question with boldness"*** the very source of religious terrorism!

Isn't it considered "insanity" to engage in the same activities time and again and expect there to be different outcomes each time? Why haven't Americans learned that religious fanaticism cannot be defeated on the battlefield? ---how many more Afghanistans will we have to involve ourselves with before we finally get it? Why haven't Americans learned, from our uber-disgraceful defeats in Vietnam and Afghanistan, that carrying a "big stick" is not the answer to everything? Why haven't Americans learned that it is a Semitic scripture (the *Koran*) that is our nation's greatest adversary rather than constantly believe it is only some "radical" Islamists who are misunderstanding the words written on its pages? ---rather than constantly be in denial about this Semitic scripture's role in so many of the world's problems? ---rather than accept the reality of this Semitic scripture's role in inspiring *Koranimals* to establish a world-wide Islamic caliphate at all costs in order to please Allah and impose His Sharia law on all of the earth's inhabitants? Isn't it time that Americans be told what is written upon Taliban and Isis flags so we can know, beyond any doubt, what America's enemies are fighting for. Isn't it time we learned what it is that every member of the above terror-groups lives and dies for---my guess is, as I said before, it has something to do with Allah and His "words" that are written on the pages of the *Koran*! For Man's sake, "Wake up, America! ---Wake up!"

Just imagine for a moment, the possible outcome of spending 20 years of our nation's might undermining, via Reason's Tribunal, the Semitic scriptures that are "totally" responsible for creating such seemingly incorrigible, terrorist mindsets---and do so without having to fire a shot! Would we not have been able to change the thinking of at least a few *Koranimals* via exposing them to the enlightening ***"facts and evidence"*** that challenges their previously unchallenged religious thinking? Would we not have been able to change the thinking of, possibly, many many more? Wouldn't such a small victory have been better than America having to experience yet another humiliating defeat in war with nothing to show for her years and years of incredible and uber-expensive military effort that resulted only in the injury, death, and misery of so many decent folks and the strengthening of our nation's enemies? Would it not have been worth the effort on our part to send a reason-guided, smart missile into the very source of Islamic terrorism: the *Koran*? Isn't it time for a freedom-loving people to finally determine who the real enemies of civilization are---where they get their inspiration to do what they do---where they get the resolve to die in order to carry out attacks like that on 9/11? We must begin studying, in earnest, the histories of all Semitic religions and inform ourselves of their oppressive, malevolent, and vengeful natures. In doing so, we will learn that God's "Word" as "revealed" in the *Old* and *New Testaments* and the *Koran,* is not the answer to any of our problems; it is the cause of them. The sooner we become aware of where so many of the world's troubles begin, the sooner we can develop strategies to defeat and vanquish the real threat to our ***"Life, Liberty and the pursuit of Happiness"***!

Why, after carrying-out such intense military endeavors in Afghanistan, is there no end in sight to the bloodshed and chaos that proceeds from the Taliban's entrenched, death-seeking, Jihad-Warrior mindset? The answer is because their fervor for committing atrocity: shooting, stabbing, torturing, mutilating, beheading, and bombing others, etc., etc., is thoroughly rooted in the unquestioned, inviolable nature of the *Koran* and its hallowed status as the "perfect" Word of Allah—a fervor increased by the Islamic yearning to please Allah by attempting to obey His every written "Word." It is a fervor that only fools believe can be bombed into submission (unless one is referring to Option II—more on this later) —something that actually would require killing every Muslim in order to end their religious devotion to Allah's Word—a tactic that only another mindset-of-terror would give consideration to.

All past and present violent activity undertaken in the name of God, whether *Bible* or *Koran*-endorsed, is, in essence, the highest form of worship of a Semitic deity and His "Word" by His zealous, devoted fans—a form of worship encouraged by fanatical, dogmatic scriptures that remain off-limits to rigorous investigation, rational criticism, and doubtful consideration. Because of our reluctance to contest such scriptures, we, the freedom-loving people of the world, are, in part, responsible for the ravages caused by them. Because of such reluctance, Islamic terrorists are perceived in the Muslim world as noble Crusaders bent on establishing a world-wide Holy Land: an Islamic Caliphate operating under Sharia law to honor Allah by whatever brutal means necessary. It is a certainty that the unchallenged Muslim-mania that would exist in such an exclusive Allah-Land would not tolerate any coexistence with blasphemers---Infidel-Land's unbelievers— it's Allah or nothing! This explains why the Muslim, Allah-worshiping world is averse to denouncing the gruesome, homicidal activities of "Islamic" terrorists. Their silence speaks volumes about their religious beliefs and their religious endeavors—a silence that results from their absolute confidence in "the indubitable truth" of the *Koran* (69:51), a book which, like Muhammad, Muslims consider to be immune-from-error and, therefore, "free from any flaw" ---*Koran* 39:28. Hmm!

Remember the following words when someone tells you that Islam is a peaceful religion—read them until you can begin to hear the faint sounds of razor-sharp, box-cutters being made at the ready in jet planes miles above your head—read the following words until you are convinced of the need for Reason's Tribunal:

Muslims, and especially the learned among them, should spread Shari'a law to the world—that and nothing else. Not laws under the 'umbrella of justice, morality, and rights' as understood by the masses. No, the Shari'a of Islam is the foundation. . . . In fact, Muslims are obligated to raid the lands of the infidels, occupy them, and exchange their system of governance for an Islamic system, barring any practice that contradicts Shari'a from being publicly voiced among the people, as was the case in the dawn of Islam. . . . They say that our Shari'a does not impose our particular beliefs upon others; this is a false assertion. For it is, in fact, part of our religion to impose our particular beliefs upon others. . . . Thus whoever refuses the principle of terror against the enemy also refuses the commandment of Allah the Exalted, the Most High, and His Shari'a. . . . And we also stress to honest Muslims that, in the midst of such momentous events and in this heated atmosphere, they must move, incite, and mobilize the Muslim umma (Islamic community) *to liberate itself from being enthralled to these unjust and apostate ruling regimes, who themselves are enslaved to America, and to establish the Shari'a of Allah on earth.*

---Osama bin Laden

Such is the mindset of an Islamic "warrior" who, fortunately, is no longer amongst the living—yet his threatening words live on and on and on—so, too, the threatening words of the Islamic scripture that inspired him and countless others to follow their religion of terror—may Americans find the courage to face our real enemy—the words of Semitic scripture that inspire atrocity!

God hath preferred those who fight for the faith above those who stay at home.

---script-writer, *Koran* 4:9

Headin' out the door to kill others is much *"preferred"* over *"staying at home"* and minding your own stinkin' business---you got that? ---kvk

Besides being a handbook for terrorists and the above mentioned *"honest Muslims"* who strive, by means of atrocity, to establish Muslim supremacy throughout the world—the *Koran* is a book replete with rules on the correct behavior and sinless conduct for Muslims to abide by—a book whose sole

102

purpose was meant only to bring the Arab-speaking, "spiritual" descendants of Abraham (Ibrahim) back to the right path that Adam's terrible "sin" had caused mankind to stray from. The *Koran* is also a book that Muslims believe, with certainty, has been in existence forever---has been in existence even before Allah created the Creation! ---lemonade, anyone?

Muslims are convinced beyond any doubt and beyond any evidence whatsoever, that the *Koran* has existed as long as God has existed because, they tell us, it was physically spoken and written by God Himself in Forever-Land (with, I assume, some sort of writing instrument: a pen, pencil, or my guess: a magic marker!) on an "imperishable tablet" (whatever that is!) ---*Koran* 85:22. The *Koran* which is supposedly comprised "entirely" of Allah's direct words that He physically vocalized, one assumes, in His native tongue, (which, surprisingly, for a former Hebrew-speaking, *Bible*-God, is Arabic!) ---the very first of His unwitnessed utterances spoken to no one because the Universe and the existence of other beings capable of hearing and understanding God's first words had yet to be fabricated. That's at least according to the timeline provided by Allah's script-writers who want us to believe, with absolute certainty, in their knowledge of things they had no possible way of knowing—(Chutzpah Chronicles always contain imposing, implausible claims and outright lies!). The date when this bogus (unheard by human ears!) speech occurred is anyone's guess for God is said to be forever-existing. It is anyone's guess, therefore, as to which came first: a talking God, the imperishable *Koran*, the writing instrument, or the deceiving script-writers who have attempted to convince us about the forever-existence of an "imperishable" book and its "imperishable" author. It is only by believing in their impossible claims, however, that makes one "imperishable," too, —doubt them and you risk becoming quite "perishable"! I believe, therefore, that the first chapter of the *Koran* which goes under the mysterious heading of "The Cow," should be changed to "The Bull" which, it seems apparent to me, would make a much more-fitting title!

Muslims are certain, beyond any doubt and beyond any evidence whatsoever, that their God's very first task was accomplished in His uttering and writing down every word in the *Koran*! This took place prior to His creating the entire Cosmos with nothing but another utterance to no one because, as noted above, the Universe and the existence of beings capable of understanding the Arabic language had yet to be fabricated, at least according to the script-writers of the *Bible* who want us to believe, with absolute certainty, in their knowledge of things they had no possible way of knowing! All of this we are to believe, according to the Chutzpah Chronicles of Muslims, was done entirely for the welfare of Arabs only, even though they, along with the heavens and the earth, didn't even exist according to the timeline established in the *Koran* by Allah's script-writers. What incredible nonsense! —what cultural chutzpah! —Muslims believing without any proof whatsoever that their bogus God's very first concern was for them, His "chosen" people—Jewish claims to the contrary.

Muslims are convinced, too, that those who would express any doubts about the certainty of what God initially said and what He physically did in Forever-Land, even when there were no eyewitnesses or earwitnesses to confirm these events had actually taken place---are to be religiously put to death in Allah-land—seems fair to me! ---that's why believers, beyond any doubt, outnumber non-believers there! That's why Reason's Tribunal should be among the very top priorities of a liberty-loving people to insure that we don't lose our lives, our freedoms, and our country because of the bogus claims made in uncontested Semitic scripture—for the horrors of 9/11 are just one example of Islamic devotion to Allah and His "Word" — undertaken not by any capable Muslim state, but by mere nomadic novices inspired by nothing more than mere words written in a book that is imposed upon untold millions to have unquestioned belief in---words that were written by intolerant, ignorant, and unenlightened men---words that have remained unchallenged for fourteen centuries!

The *Koran*, if one believes the impositions of Semitic theology, was created before there was a Heaven and a Hell, before there were planets or people—before there was ever a sin committed—before any justification existed for a book to be written about mercy and redemption. Surely, Muslims are being imposed upon because they must believe things about the Almighty and His Word that defy logic, common-sense, and common-decency especially when they give acknowledgement to similar accounts "revealed" in the *Old Testament*. The *"Once upon a time"* Garden of Eden-tale being found in the *Koran* is a prime example of this. The *Bible's* version of events in an idyllic Eden is not a Hebrew original---it was "borrowed" from older, Pagan mythology and embellished for priestly purpose. Because the *Bible's* mythology-derived, kindergarten-minded story-line about Adam and Eve is the basis and underlying theme of the madness, mayhem, and make-believe of all three Semitic religions, it deserves a much closer and impartial look at its parts and pieces---its injustices, indecencies, inconsistencies, and insanities that we are imposed upon to believe actually took place and have such profound spiritual consequence for everyone and everything on the planet.

We deserve to know with much greater clarity *"every fact, every opinion"* about a naive Adam and his innocent descendants' damnation by a God of love and about man's salvation and his being spared from the torments of an eternal Hell (by sin-absolving clergy!) via belief in Jesus, the scapegoat, who was caused to suffer and die for someone else's disobedience. Beyond a doubt, from the standpoint of scriptural script-writers, human beings are most susceptible to manipulation when they are experiencing intense, heartfelt emotions such as empathy, compassion, sorrow, and guilt for the sufferings of others as in the case of Jesus whose sufferings we are made to believe we are totally responsible for. It is especially so when we are told that Jesus was intentionally crucified to death for "our" sinful deeds. It is important, therefore, that we take heed and be on guard against being emotionally exploited when our hearts and minds are most vulnerable— when our hearts and minds are being intentionally imposed upon to believe the *Bible*-tale about a pitiable, Jewish fella, Jesus, (aka God!) who was betrayed by one of His dearest, Jewish disciples and then abandoned by all twelve of them---a Jewish fella who was mocked, beaten, and caused to suffer a brutal, agonizing death to "atone" for something He didn't do. *"Yes, Virginia, God had to die for someone else's naive doings in order to bless us---O-M-G! ---how uber-terrible! ---it's called Semitic justice!*

The reason, we are imposed upon to believe that it became necessary for God to end His life to "wipe clean" Adam's "sin" was that God decided, after thousands of years had passed since Adam had "apple-ed," that He would finally make an atonement for Adam's gullibility and, in doing so, make things 'right' for all the world. And, after giving centuries, I repeat, "centuries" of thought and consideration to this pathological idea, Almighty God, who, of course, is incapable of experiencing death, hatched a plan to be born, not in the entirety of His Universe-filling entity, but within the confines of the flesh of a mere man who, obviously, was lacking in all of his God-parts yet completely subject to the effects of death if only for a very short time! Jesus did not choose, however, to become an instantly created (VOILA!) man, like His instantly created Adam, as that, obviously, would not generate the eye-welling empathy of His choosing to be born as an innocent man-child in, of all places, an animal's feed trough! He, in all of His wisdom, decided that the only right thing for Him to do was to commit suicide and that He should do it, not as Himself in His own humongous, infinite, God body but in the much much much smaller-sized body of someone else, His earthly stand-in, aka Jesus, who, we're told, was not God in His entirety but only in part!

This was all done in order for Jesus, an expendable part of God, to suffer and to die in order to make a 'vicarious' atonement for something He didn't do and had no part in---just as God is punishing all of mankind for something we never did or had any part in either---it's called 'divine Semitic justice'---are you taking notes, Virginia? ---don't try to figure this out, my dear---your eyes will bleed and you'll probably experience spasms of the cerebral cortex! Unbelievably, after God had physically 'died,' in part, on the cross, He was, nonetheless, 'born again' as 'Mr. Rise 'n' Shine, an extraordinary, comic-book superhero-type character whose resume included the ability to defy death and leap tall buildings in a single bound, walk on water and through walls, move a mountain whenever it should get in His way, fly on a cloud to Heaven above and make dead people not be dead anymore, etc., etc., in fact, He can even make folks who have died continue to live forever and ever in order to be able to punish the many and reward the few---our own oblivion, (our physical deaths), evidentially, is not retribution enough to please this Guy, yet the short-lived physical death of Jesus was, somehow, enough payment to balance the unbalanced scales of Semitic justice!

God's life and death, we're told, was nothing more than an effort to wipe clean the slate dirtied by Adam's sin and, one assumes, restore the planet to its former, glorious, Edenic state which, obviously, like His efforts to destroy the entire earth and to save the "lost sheep" of Israel, didn't quite work out according to the script! The only thing 'Mr. Rise 'n' Shine' seemingly can't do, is to be successful in achieving any of His best-laid-plans and His earnest endeavors! The tragic tale about the death of God---about an innocent man whose blood was purposely shed and whose life was purposely ended (at least momentarily!) for a 'sin' He never committed—a tale intentionally made up and intentionally told so as to tug at our hearts. The death of God (Jesus) was a necessary part of a barbaric, Jewish 'ritual sacrifice'---a sacrifice where the un-blemished innocent are made to pay with their blood and their lives to make amends for the transgressions of others---"I didn't know, my dear, Virginia, that you enjoyed drinking lemonade so much!"

This woeful tale about Jesus becomes even more compelling and interesting when we are told by its script-writers that this fella had the ability to prevent all of the punishments heaped upon Him from ever happening because, after all, He is God! Instead, this betrayed, beaten-down fella "chose" to suffer and to die in a sacrificial, bloodshedding manner, of course---it's always about the blood, the stinkin', blessed blood! ---but without the traditional *"sweet savor"* barbecue ending. This was done in order to give God's *"lost sheep"* the ability to gain His favor once again by His atoning for Adam's apple-eating *"abomination"* and, as an added bonus, all the sins of the world to boot. Wow! ---such a deal! What a Guy!, what a glorious Guy! —what an incredible sacred sacrifice! —what a bunch of crapola!

As it turned out, we learn with more saddened hearts, that for all of His tormented sufferings and death on the cross, the *"lost sheep"* rejected Jesus as their Savior and His sacred mission to save them only—they rejected His resurrection, His ascension, and His "atonement"! I think it would be safe to say, at this point, that, seemingly, the Jews were no longer God's favorite folks as, apparently, they didn't give a shekel about missing-out on the promised, eternal joys of Hebrew-Heaven—they didn't give a damn either about the prospect of spending eternity in Hell for their non-belief even though Jesus stated in *Mark* 16:16: ...*"he that believeth not shall be damned"*! Imagine, God damning the *"lost sheep"* —that's quite a revealing eye-opener! But, alas, all was not lost for the parasites who feed off of peoples' fears---it only took a few more "inspired" pen strokes at the close of *Matthew, Mark,* and *Luke's* tales to keep this bogus *Bible*-scam continuing, alive and well, without God's "chosen" people receiving any more favored treatment in the exchange of places between the *"lost sheep,"* (the Jews) and the "losers," (the Gentiles). God's astounding, but understandable, last minute, after-death, "sudden" change of heart about His exclusive mission to redeem only the *"lost sheep"* would now allow and welcome, with open arms, the "losers" (Gentiles) into His fold of favorites! Jesus, after being totally rejected by the Jews, suddenly wants now to redeem the "losers," the very folks He despised and avoided during His entire ministry---imagine that! Hmm!

Such a compelling story about the life and death of Jesus deserves much more than a cursory glance at its astounding assertions—it deserves much more than a Sunday sermon searing us about our complicity and guilt in Jesus' demise while assuring us about the merits of His agony, His shedding of blood, His dying, and His defeat of death. To begin at the bogus beginning of this convoluted tale---we deserve to know, with certainty beyond any doubt, the name of the person in the mythological Garden of Eden who was an eye-witness and ear-witness to all of the mythological events that supposedly took place there *"Once upon a time"* about 6000 yrs. ago!—the name of the person whose written accounts of these events are given in *Genesis* of the *OT*—was it God? —was it Adam? —was it Eve? —was it the amazing talking snake? —was it the mythical Moses (who hadn't yet been fabricated)? —or was it an inspired, script-writing liar and deceiver telling us about things he had no possible way of knowing?

Reason's Tribunal will reveal, beyond any doubt, why this mystery person, God's first witness and biographer, never identifies himself and must remain unknown for ever and ever—think about it folks, think about it!

On whose authority should anyone believe the words telling us that A & E heard the voice of God as He was walking around in the Garden (something He evidently enjoyed doing on His day off!) ---*Gen.* 3:8? How did this tell-all person know it to be a fact? Did this unknown tale-teller actually hear God speak with his own ears and observe God walking in the Garden with his own eyes *"in the cool of the day,"* no less? Or, was it A&E who informed this unknown tale-teller about what they thought they had heard and surmised? Surely, these *Bible*-facts deserve a much closer look because every single word in the *Bible* is of utmost importance, I repeat "of utmost importance" ---God, certainly, would never have inspired the authors of the *Bible* to write a word that was of little importance or of little consequence to its readers.

Doesn't the *Bible* and its enforcers impose upon us to believe that no one can see God and that He also exists in every part of the Universe? ---which would make His li'l piggy toe probably the size of Jupiter! Yet, in so many words, the author of *Gen.* 3:8, reveals to us that God is nearer man-size than gargantuan-size because God's creator made Him to be small enough to walk around in the Garden and that would only be possible if God was made the size of a man and in man's exact image, for God, in order to move about, required His having legs and feet to walk around on, just like the writer of this tale had legs and feet to walk around on! Just like His created God has voice (the ability to make sound through His mouth and vocal cords to make that voice heard, but to whom was God using His voice when A&E "overheard" Him speaking? ---who the hell was He talking to? Surely the writer of this tale must have known who it was! Surely, because man enjoys a leisurely stroll, now and then, in the cool of the day, the writer of this tale has God enjoying the same!

How, one wonders, was it possible that Adam and Eve knew, with absolute certainty, the disembodied voice they were hearing was that of God---someone they, obviously, had never seen---someone they knew absolutely nothing about? Couldn't they just as well have been hearing the voice of a talking snake doing what he does best? ---and what did they know about deception and talking snakes? Aren't we to believe with all of our heart and mind that this unknown tale-teller actually observed God fashioning Adam from *"the dust of the ground"* as he stated in *Gen.* 2:7? If this unknown tale-teller didn't actually witness Adam's creation from dust, how did he learn of it and know it to be true? If this tale be true, why didn't

God simply return Adam back into the dust-bunny he was created from after his cursed apple-eating---wouldn't that have been a more humane and more believable way to have settled the matter? ---dust to dust! ---*Gen.* 3:19.

After all, God's "only" reason for creating man in the First Place was just to have someone who could cultivate the "perfect" soil in the Garden of Eden because *"there was not a man* (slave!) *to till the ground." ---Gen.* 2:5---(there was not a man (slave!) around to impose upon is more like it!). One can only further assume (because mythology is, of necessity, always lacking in details!) that Adam would have had to "till" the ground in Eden with his bare hands because the simple tools needed for the job---rakes, shovels, hoes, etc., ---and even the practice of tilling, were completely unknown by one and all, so soon after the earth's "supposed" voice-creation and, certainly, there would be no need of tools, tilling, or toil in such an idyllic place!

Certainly, too, the author of this "tilling" tale was unaware that he had placed the cart before the horse! This little, anachronous slip of the pen tells us a lot more than the script-writer of the Eden-tale ever intended for it reveals that this bogus story and its bogus God were fabricated sometime after "tilling" the ground became a known and common practice among earthlings---sometime after man had learned how to fashion tools for tilling the soil---something the script-writer of the Eden-tale was obviously familiar with and, therefore, made His scripted-God familiar with also.

The physical labors involved in tilling the ground should not have been something a resident of Eden, Paradise #1, would be required to engage in---tilling the ground was a practice that even God had no previous experience with---a practice that came from a later time in mankind's/womankind's history. This seemingly innocuous, scriptural slip-up reveals a lot about God being made in man's fallible image! Come to think of it, why should anyone living in a spiritual Paradise have the need to eat at all? ---have need of a stomach and an anus? --- have need to consume anything? ---have need to live a parasitic existence? Shouldn't living one's life in the presence of God have been sufficient nourishment for man and animal to exist on?

> *Consider the ravens: for they neither sow nor reap; which neither have storehouse or barn; and God feedeth them; how much more are ye better than the fowls?*

> ---Jesus, *Luke* 12:24

It was only "after" Adam and Eve's expulsion from Eden that God commanded them to eat food acquired by their own *"sweat"* (except for clergy!) and, therefore, such a cursed, labor-intensive condition, obviously, did not exist before that time? ---*Gen* 3:19. Surely, during their sweat-free days spent enjoying life in "Paradise #1," Adam and Eve would have been fed and cared for *"better"* than the above *"ravens"* who, we're told by God neither *"sow nor reap"* nor toil, nor *"till"* the ground? ---nor *"sweat,"* I might add! On the other hand, why would an idyllic place like Eden ever need a farm worker to "labor" in its fields! —a place where the *Bible* informs us: *"every tree that is pleasant to the sight, and good for food"* offered their abundant, life-sustaining fruits free for the picking, without any tilling or toiling whatsoever! ---*Gen.* 2:9. Can you imagine a place like Eden needing someone to improve the soil conditions there? Was it possible that Adam could have tilled the ground in Eden without working up a sweat? ---what was the point of having Adam *"till the ground"* in the First Place when fruit trees were so abundant? Is anyone aware of the fact that the fruit-eating residents of Eden had to have had regular bowel movements, too? ---where, oh where, one wonders, did they go to relieve themselves?

My idea of an earthly Paradise would surely have restrooms, toilets, and toilet paper---things that certainly didn't exist in Eden! ---do restrooms exist in Paradise #2 above? ---O-M-G! Can you imagine a resident of Eden walking about in the Garden and stepping in someone's fruit-poops? ---do you think God would have engaged in the "washing of feet" there, in Eden, like He was so eager to do as told in the Gospel tales? What's that smell? Can you imagine a resident of Eden not having running water or flushing toilets? ---what the hell! ---you call this place a five-star resort? ---"Eve-ee!---get the dogs---we're leaving!"

Can you imagine something that was so vitally important to God, I repeat, "so vitally important to God": to have someone in Eden to *"till the ground,"* and yet, nowhere else in the entire *Bible* does God show the slightest interest, or give a flying fig tree, about the cultivation of the earth? Hmm---quite interesting isn't it? It makes one wonder, too, what sort of menial tasks God has in store for the eternal residents (His Gentile believers?) of Paradise #2 who think they're just gonna sit around on their lazy asses all day in Heaven watching TV, drinking beer, and playing video games---they're all in for a big surprise---the gardens up there need tilling, too! ---and, there's only one bathroom for each of the twelve tribes to share---talk about living in Hell! If, however, you are counted among one of the lucky, lottery winners who reach the coveted pearly gates and are greeted in person by St. Peter---*"Yes, Virginia, he's the guy who denied Jesus three times!"* ---you'll be gifted with a "Hallelujah" Shovel along with a *"Praise the Lord"* Rake and a "Cloud Nine" Hoe as soon as you enter Paradise #2 so that you can be in the cherished presence of God, your slaveholding Lord and Master, and begin doing God's unceasing, heavenly work in earnest with few bathroom breaks!

Why would anyone expect things to be different in Upper Paradise than they were in Lower Paradise where there was not a man (until Adam's creation) *"to till the ground"*? Surely, the soil in Upper Eden would be in need of tillers, too, just like the soil in Lower Eden was in need of them! Does any Christian really expect that God would willingly allow Himself to be spit upon, to be mocked, beaten, crucified, and put to death, just to be able to save a few of our sorry asses---that He would have suffered such an agonized ordeal for so little recompense---just to be able to reward Gentile "dogs," with a permanent residence in Heaven---just so that "they," not the *"lost sheep"* can blissfully live forever in the lap of luxury and never-ending splendor? ---really, folks,---really? Did anyone ever consider the possibility that Adam, after learning that he was to be a laboring field-worker and groundskeeper in an amenity-lacking Eden 24/7, 365 days a year for eternity, that he, without the slightest bit of coaxing from a talking snake, ate of the goddammed apple just to be able to pack his bags and get the hell out of town---taking his chances living in the burbs? Hmm! ---but I digress . . .

In short, had a loving and merciful Creator done the right thing in Eden, every life form on the planet would have been spared punishment, some eternally, for a bad decision on the part of an all-knowing God and a child-minded decision on the part of naive Adam, a gullible piece of dust! "Man-up, Big Guy, and admit that you really screwed-up---that you could have handled the situation in Eden in a more decent, pious, and peaceful manner without all of the dreadful drama!" I guess it may be true, after all, that Adam really "was" made in God's image---a dust-man made from a God who was also made from dust! Dust in, dust out! Back to Eden . . .

Think about it, folks---shouldn't we all know, beyond any doubt, who the *Bible's* one and only witness and recorder of events in Paradise #1 was? Had this furtive fibber and unknown observer in Eden been a bit more forthcoming in covering "the rest of the story" there, he could have informed us if God, while tip-toeing through the tulips in the Garden was in His customary cloud disguise and whether or not He was wearing any clothes at all to hide His sacred, naked self which, as in the case of A&E, would certainly have been a sign of His having been a rotten-apple-eater, too! Personally, I'd like to know if God does wear sin-covering clothes or if

He prefers going around in the buff of sinlessness? Personally, I'm certain that the long, white, (sin-revealing, sin-covering) robes and the long, white beard shown in so many of God's "graven" images are contrivances just like the entire Eden-tale. I think it is quite interesting, too, that "images" of God exist at all because no one, except Moses, has ever seen the Big Guy, and, especially, since one of the Ten Commandments forbids the making of them! Is there any doubt that this foundational story of the Chutzpah Chronicles is a bogus, fairy-tale account not worth the papyrus it was written on? Is there any doubt that the deception, the lies, and the common-sense that destroy the credibility of the mythic Eden-tale also destroy the credibility of the redeeming religion built upon it? Contrivances built upon contrivances!

We deserve to know, with certainty beyond any doubt, how much credence should be given to the invented testimony of an unknown witness' account of events in Eden because of their profound importance to the makers of Semitic religions and to us, their gullible, imposed-upon prey. We deserve to know, beyond any doubt, if the death of Jesus was truly an "atonement" for the fictional disobedience of a mythical man? —for in a Hindu book, *The Prophecies,* written around two thousand years before the *Bible* and its Hebrew account of events in Eden, as is given in *Genesis,* is told almost word for word about Adama and Heva—even the Babylonians had an identical story of Creation long before the *Bible* existed. Why is it that when such tales are found in older, Pagan sources, they are always regarded as "unbelievable" mythology—but when such tales are found in the *Bible*, they instantly become the "believable" Word of God? We deserve a believable answer to this question—one that will end the impositions of Semitic religions and their borrowed, re-constructed myths from continuing to be swallowed whole—from continuing to mess with our emotions and our minds—from continuing to threaten our well-being every day of our future existence! (NOTE TO READER: The Eden-tale, having been plagiarized from much older, Pagan source material is a solid fact that, in effect, pulls the plug on all three Semitic religions especially the Christian religion for it was solely upon the fictional account of Adam's naive disobedience that Christianity's fraudulent foundation has been "raised" and subsequently "razed, " like the walls of Jericho, by Reason's Tribunal!)

Continuing, post-mortem, with the bold investigations of the Eden-tale, another "error" found in *Genesis 1* tells us that plants and animals were created "before" the arrival of both Adam and Eve while *Genesis 2* tells us that Adam alone was created "before" plants and animals ever existed and that Eve made her appearance only "after" plants and animals came to be.

Common-sense reveals that one of these accounts must be a falsehood since, obviously, both accounts cannot be true, I repeat, "both accounts cannot be true"! One lie, one contradiction, one word that can be misconstrued, one word of false or invented testimony found anywhere on the pages of the *Bible* is all that is necessary to put an end to its "inerrant," "infallible," and "divine" status—end its reputation as being the "perfect" Word of God.

It is helpful to remember the following when reading the "borrowed" and embellished tales of Pagan mythology that appear in the *Bible*: Firstly—all of its plagiarized tales were "re-written" to promote priestly ambitions by the contriving and imposing hands of its "unknown" writers and their less-than-godly self-interests. Secondly—many important "details" in the *Bible*-tales, as in the Pagan myths they were copied from, are always lacking in specifics---such is the nature of mythology to never be too precise or too informative about the finer points of imposing story lines which, after all, were initially invented to account for something occurring in nature and not to be literally believed---something that helped to explain the unknown in order to understand it in story-form! Thirdly— aside from literally believing everything written in *Genesis* and the rest of the *Bible*-tales, the religious mind will always find a way to compensate for this absence of data and make the needed mental adjustments to detail-lacking, *Bible*-tales by filling in the blanks with spiritual-spin---spiritual-spin that always favors God and absolves Him of any malice or wrongdoing---spiritual-spin that never admits of, or even hints at, the incompetence of the "God-inspired" writers who, supposedly, communicated God's "perfect" Word "perfectly" in the *Bible* without there being any gaps, confusion, or unanswered questions in the stories being told---without there being any chance of misinterpretation of anything stated (or not stated) in its chapter and verse accounts! It is time, therefore, for the bold questioning and bold scrutiny of Reason's Tribunal to extrapolate the correct missing information gleaned entirely from these bogus *Bible*-tales and let the ***"facts and evidence"*** that describe a despicable deity and His fraudulent religion speak for themselves.

Every Jew, every Christian, and every Muslim, is imposed upon to believe that an even-handed sentence was handed-out in the Garden of Eden-tale even though the Almighty acted quite contrarily to His eye-for-an-eye nature by punishing every blameless human being and every blameless animal for the disobedience of a naive, gullible, child-minded individual. This, we are to believe, is Semitic justice at its finest and the supposed model for America's judicial system—outrageous! This "Original

Sin" of injustice deserves to be "revealed" and assigned to its correct "Originator" whose heartless, Garden of Eden's decisions and actions were certainly more egregious than those of its innocent-minded and trusting inhabitants. Since we, all of the human population of earth, have been *Bible*-blamed and *Bible*-punished for Adam's partaking of the fruit of the *"tree of knowledge of good and evil,"* let us all begin to put that enlightening knowledge to *"good"* use by exposing the *"evil"* side of Semitic religions.

How was the instantly-created Adam instantly able to understand and to speak fluently the Hebrew language, instantly able to assign names to *"every living creature"* ---*Gen.* 2:19, for we are told that God was curious (as if God could be curious about anything or that His knowledge was somehow lacking---more evidence of God being made in man's image!) to see what moniker Adam would give to each animal as God paraded each one of them by? I'm fairly certain that "jackass" must surely have been one of names that exited Adam's mouth during this amazing event, perhaps, more than once! One wonders who it was that gave Adam and Eve their names? ---most likely it was some unknown, "inspired" story-telling *Bible*-author who plagiarized ancient mythology!

Considering the vast number of animals that exist on land and in the sea, this naming of *"every living creature"* must have taken many many days to complete—it is my belief that Adam might have also taken a nibble or two of the fruit of the "tree of animal names" to be able to complete this daunting task! On day #5 of the Creation, God miraculously created, by word of mouth alone, *"every living creature that moveth"* as stated in *Gen.* 1:20-25. Somehow, God must have forgotten about this *Bible*-fact when He created animals all over again---this time from *"out of the ground"* ---*Gen* 2:19 and proceeded to bring each and every one of them (including dinosaurs?) before the eyes of Adam to *"see,"* what he would name them. Surely there must have been someone hanging around in the bushes with pen and papyrus, or chisel and stone in hand, in order to make a detailed record of all the countless names of animals that God was so interested to learn---otherwise, the many many many miracles employed by God in order to make this daunting event possible would have all been for naught. The tale about the three little pigs comes to mind as being more believable in its telling!

Imagine the unbelievable, incredible effort made by God to have huge creatures (whales!) emerge from the ground---certainly that would have required a separate miracle being performed for each of the earth's innumerable creatures to suddenly make their cameo appearance above ground---creatures, as in the case of whales, with no legs or any other means to move about on their own, being made to appear on dry land directly in front of Adam who, in naming them, had no idea that such legless animals were destined to live in the sea---for Adam, never having seen a body of water, surely had no idea or knowledge of what a "sea" is or might be! Maybe his witnessing such a humongous, puzzling creature floundering about on land was a factor in Adam's wanting to partake of the fruit of a *"tree of knowledge"* to make sense of it all! In any event, God, having gone through all the trouble to make this colossal event happen---utilizing millions of miracles along the way---must have regarded it as tremendously important: the naming, by Adam, of *"every living creature,"* otherwise, one must assume, that miracle after miracle after miracle after miracle was foolishly wasted by God for trivial purpose---for His mere amusement.

For my mere amusement, I would like to hear a *Bible*-babbler explain why---if all the animals in Eden were created to exist on green herbs as stated in *Gen.* 1:30, why were so many of them made with claws and teeth designed for ripping and tearing flesh? Or, were alligators, grizzly bears, lions, saber-toothed tigers and certain dinosaurs etc., etc., all fangless, cud-chewing critters? ---really! Somebody surely has some "splaining" to do! Surely, too, the naming of *"every living creature"* must have been considered a highly significant event by the *Bible's* script-writers, an event that was, obviously, uber-worthy of mention in the *Bible,* the inerrant and infallible "Word" of God---it must, therefore, have been deemed very consequential as nothing written in the *Bible* is lacking in importance and consequence. Unfortunately, however, no record exists in the *Bible,* or anywhere else, of "any" of these animal names---not one! Not even a tattered fragment of the list of animal names given by Adam was found in the revered Dead Sea Scrolls—a glaring error on the part of the scrupulous, *Old Testament* script-writers to omit any part of God's erstwhile endeavors! It is sad, however, that God never received the recognition He deserved for the millions of mighty works He had to perform in order to pull fully grown animals out of the ground---therefore, I want to give a great big "Shout-Out" to God Almighty and thank Him for His countless, mighty works done in the name of amusement---perhaps one day He will use a few of His amazing miracles to accomplish something truly worthwhile! From one "world-lover" to another, I have a list of such "worthwhile" endeavors and if you're not too busy playing Hide-n-Seek in the clouds, we can get started tomorrow to improve living conditions on the planet---how's 8 a.m. sound? ---in the meantime, get some rest!

Surely, the many, many, many miracles that were required by God in order for Adam to be able to name *"every living creature"* that suddenly appeared from out of the ground before his very eyes doesn't surpass the singular miracle needed to believe this "animal-naming" contest actually happened---doesn't surpass the miracle needed to believe that God gave human beings the *Bible*-guaranteed ability that gives every person on the planet *"dominion"* over great white sharks, grizzly bears, lions, tigers, alligators, and a boatload of other animals that, quite obviously, didn't get the memo about what God had said in *Gen.* 1:28! What do you think about Mr. Blazing Pants now? Has He not proved Himself a liar in the very first *Bible*-chapter by His very own words telling us (in His inerrant and infallible "Word") that man has supremacy, has dominance and control, over every *"fish,"* every *"fowl,"* and *"every living thing that moveth upon the earth"*? Is there any Jew or Christian to be found who is willing to prove the veracity of this God-spoken *Bible*-certainty about man having *"dominion"* over animals? *"Yes, Virginia, God 'is' a liar and His 'Word' in the Bible is not to be believed---but don't take my word for it! ---I'm quite certain that God must have been wearing boots and watching where He stepped during His frequent walks in the Garden which must have become covered quickly with the excrement of every animal on the planet---can you smell it now? ---it's no wonder the talking serpent moved about in the trees! Isn't it interesting, Virginia, that myth and miracle are always revealed to us shrouded in so many mysteries and with so many logical questions left unanswered? Surely, there must be logical reasons for the ever-present silence---maybe someone should start an investigation!"*

Are we not being further imposed upon to believe that Adam and Eve, who were to be lethally punished by a loving God (*"thou shalt surely die"* ---*Gen.* 2:17) for Adam's disobedience in eating an apple---were never granted an opportunity to beseech the Almighty for His divine mercy—were never granted an opportunity to repent of their apple-eating even though God, aka Allah, supposedly wrote a book about redemption on an "imperishable" tablet on the first nano-second of His existence in Forever-Land! A & E were never granted an opportunity to plead their case before Mr. Merciful nor allowed to repent their child-minded naivete for believing the statements that Satan "revealed" to them via a beguiling, talking serpent, a creature they were never warned about. Satan, like A & E, had disobeyed God, too, but, curiously, never received a *"thou shalt surely die"* sentence from his Maker or any punitive restrictions for his disrespectful behavior and infidelity for it is obvious that he continues to live free from any constraint while enjoying increasing prosperity, popularity, and power over the entire Creation. Hmm! Hmm! Hmm! Mythology can be so unbelievable at times especially when it portrays the Almighty as being "Akbar" and "Merciful," ---not to A & E and the animals---but only to His greatest, constant Opposer—incredible

!

> *And the Lord said unto the woman, What is this that thou hast done? And the woman said, the serpent beguiled me, and I did eat. And the Lord said unto the serpent, Because thou hast done this, thou art cursed above all cattle, and above every beast of the field; upon thy belly shalt thou go, and dust shalt thou eat all the days of thy life: And I will put enmity between thee and the woman, and between thy seed and her seed; it shall bruise thy head, and thou shalt bruise his heel.*

--- God, Gen. 3:13-15

The Eden-tale would have us believe that Satan, who made his appearance in Eden as a talking snake, was cursed and punished by God for "beguiling" Eve by sentencing him, the Devil in his reptile disguise, to eat dust and by making him crawl on his belly for his entire life—imagine that! ---imagine punishing a snake by having it crawl around on its belly all the days of its life—incredible! Are we supposed to believe, too, from reading the above *Bible*-quote, that the Devil is actually going to die one day after all the days of his *"entire life"* as a talking reptile have ended? Of course not, that would only spell the end of Semitic religions and their lucrative business of absolving sinners of their Devil-caused sins! The belly-crawling curse of God must have been given only, I repeat, "only" to the talking snake, the one and the only snake ever cursed by the Almighty to be a dust-eater because it is a certainty, that "dust-eating" reptiles do not exist on this planet and never have---God's words to the contrary! —and this, we are to believe, is the absolute truth because, it is so written upon one of the pages of the *Bible*---because it is supposed, and wrongly so, that the God of the *Bible* doesn't lie or inspire His script-writers to do so, either.

Think about it folks---God, the creator of serpents, must have made them with either wings or with legs and feet before the "Fall" or else the crawling-curse He placed upon Satan, who appeared to Eve as a talking snake, was uber-ridiculous and all for naught. Think about it folks—how did this belly-crawling curse of God result in any punitive or negative effect upon an animal who was already a crawling creature? And, how would it impede Satan, who apparently has the ability to easily morph into other

117

creatures, by sentencing one of his morphings to eat dust? It is obvious that the crawling-curse didn't have any dire effect on the life of the Devil or any of his doings? But one should never dismiss these curse-verses as being insignificant, for "everything" that is stated in the *Bible* is there because God intended for it to be there and, therefore, it is of grave consequence to everyone and everything on the planet in one way or another, especially to our sanity, our lives, our liberties, and our pursuits of happiness.

Can any Christian ***"fool"*** or ***"hypocrite,"*** script-writer or script-improver tell us what the "innocent" cattle and beasts of the field, that God had just created, had done in order to receive His scornful, "cursed" consideration as stated in the same *Genesis* quote given above? Of course not! Can any Christian ***"fool"*** or ***"hypocrite"*** tell us if God was correct when He stated that all of Eve's descendants (everyone on the planet) will possess an "enmity," a hatred of snakes? Of course not, again! *"Yes, Virginia, Reason's Tribunal has proven that the God of the Bible is a habitual liar, but that's only if you believe His scripted words in the First Place!"* Surely then, no *Bible*-verse should be spared from receiving bold scrutiny of its every Word! Surely then, it is not biblically correct that every Sunday School indoctrinator depicts Eve's "beguiling" with cartoonish illustrations that show a crawling serpent, without a leg to stand on, coiled around a fruit tree. Shouldn't they, instead, be representing this "talking" reptile as either "standing" alongside the forbidden fruit tree or "perched" upon one of its branches for it couldn't have been a belly-crawling creature at the time of the beguilement without making a cursing God look like a complete idiot! (NOTE TO ALL SUNDAY SCHOOL TEACHERS: please make the necessary improvements, the necessary changes to your cartoon renderings of this most important of *Bible*-events—God forbid that you, too, should be perceived as deceivers of children! My suggestion would be to depict this deceiving snake as having legs and feet—something he would surely have need of since he is constantly kicking God's ass!)

As a justice-seeking, great-grandchild of distant relatives who were treated so unfairly in the Garden of Eden, I am on a mission to clear the names of my great-grandparents, Adam and Eve Finklestein, of any criminal wrongdoing. What? ---you didn't know they were Jewish? If A&E had the opportunity to lawyer-up or seek help from the ACLU, as the accused do today, they, most likely, would have been able to plead guilty to a lesser-charge and, perhaps, gotten a reduced sentence of 5 years' probation and 100 hours of community service for it became an established fact that God was open to argument and negotiation, otherwise, the clever Moses would not have been able to make Him change His "steadfast" mind---*Ex.* 32:9-14—so much for God's omniscient and immutable nature! The Creator of the entire Creation, it appears, had met His intellectual superior in Moses—imagine that! ---isn't this just another example of God having been made in man's imperfect, egocentric image? It was quite fortunate for God that He never played "Rock/Paper/Scissors" with Moses---He would have got His butt kicked for sure! Always remember, folks, the unbelievable amount of "chutzpah" it takes to proclaim (in the Jewish Chutzpah Chronicles!) that it was a Jew who outwitted Almighty God! ---and if a Jew could do that, what could possibly prevent the Jews from endeavoring to make much of the world believe all of their other Chutzpah Chronicle's claims? The lesson to be learned here, folks, is that if God can be made to do the bidding of the Jews, so should you!

In the effort to bring *"every fact, every opinion"* about the God of Judeo-Christianity to the magnifying glass and microscope of Reason's Tribunal, wouldn't it be interesting to hear the opinions of the United States Supreme Court Justices on the very first summary judgment this God handed down in Eden to get their take on the fairness of the sentence that He---the Almighty to whom they credit and honor as being the Founding Father of American law and the American justice system---meted out in the Garden of Eden---especially since so many people are being affected by it---especially since Americans are taught to believe that our nation was founded upon supposed, worship-worthy, Judeo-Christian traditions, principles, and chutzpah-laden *Bible*-tales? Wouldn't it be interesting, after their having reviewed all the known, script-written *Bible*-facts in this case, to learn their judicious thoughts on whether Adam and Eve and all of their descendants, along with all of the animals in Eden and their descendants, as well, got the justice they deserved?

Did Satan, wearing his snake disguise, get the justice he deserved for deceiving Eve and for calling God, in effect, a liar? Wouldn't it be interesting to learn their thoughts on the fairness of Jesus' having to die on the cross in order to physically pay with His life as an atonement for the disobedience of someone else---a naive apple-eater? Wouldn't it be interesting to learn the opinions of the Supreme Court Justices on these matters? ---Justices who are proud to display the Ten Commandments on their chamber's doors along with the words: IN GOD WE TRUST emblazoned on the wall of the room where their legal decisions are supposedly made with complete impartiality!

How can atheists in their appeals to the SCOTUS ever expect to receive fair, balanced and unprejudiced judgments from such religiously indoctrinated magistrates who demonstrate their bias for God-promoting pursuits? Wouldn't it be interesting, too, to learn if any of the Supreme Court Justices would knowingly allow an "innocent" person to sit on death row and await execution in order to pay for someone else's crime? Wouldn't it be interesting---to learn what the Supremes think about the Judeo-tradition and principle that regards the hating of one's brother to be the equivalent of one's committing a capital offense? ---*I John* 3:15---to learn what the Supremes think about the Judeo-tradition and principle that determines one's guilt by the agreement of just two witnesses? ---*John* 8:17---to learn what the Supremes think about the Judeo-tradition and principle that regards the breaking of any "one" of the Ten Commandments to be deemed the equivalent of breaking "all" of them which, in effect, treats coveting a neighbor's goods, committing adultery, or even the making of a graven image of God to be the moral equivalent of having committed murder? ---*Ex.* 20:4, *James* 2:10, but don't take my word for it! If the Supremes are truly over-the-moon about Judeo-traditions and principles, wouldn't it be interesting to learn what their opinions are about the existence of so many graven images of God?

Because the prohibition against creating such graven images is important enough to make the exalted *"THOU SHALT NOT"* list, I wonder what the Supremes would have to say about the immense *"graven image"* of God that is emblazoned upon the ceiling of the Sistine chapel in the Vatican, an image that is strangely "revered" in Christendumb instead of "condemned" as one of God's Top Ten "abominations"? Would any of the Ten Commandment-promoting Supremes have the chutzpah to "condemn" or to criticize the wearing of crucifixes with their *"graven"* images of a crucified Godman that are proudly displayed dangling from the necks of so many "faithful" Christians? Would any of the Supremes have the chutzpah to condemn the graven images of God that are found adorning rosary beads and the altars of Christian worship knowing that God has forbid their use— knowing that the God they honor has demanded that all who disobey His Commandments will be spending an eternity in Hell? Wouldn't it be interesting to learn what their "fair and balanced" thoughts would be about "all," not just "some" of the Ten Commandments that the Supremes are so proud to promote and pay tribute to?

Isn't it quite interesting and remarkable that almost every Christian home displays a "likeness" of God even though no one knows what God or Jesus looks like? Surely, every portrayed image of these Guys is an absolute fraud and invention—another example of God being made in man's image! How is it possible for Christians to sleep at night "knowing" that the fires of Hell await every Commandment-breaker who possesses graven images of God?

Why, one wonders, do Christians allow such God-damned "abominations" of graven images to exist? Hmm! Why are marble and plaster likenesses of God glorified instead of being ground into dust like the God-damned golden calf of the Israelites? Is more proof needed to prove that Christians are "not" all believers in "all" that is written in their Judeo-Christian *Bible*? I hope I have the good fortune to never find myself in a Christian house during a thunderstorm---a house that contains a crucifix or some other graven image of Jesus---that would just be asking for it!

> *Thou shalt not make unto thee any graven image, or any likeness of anything that is in heaven above, or that is in the earth beneath, or that is in the water under the earth.*

> God giving Commandment #2 ---*Ex.* 20:4

No *Bible*-believer ever wants to admit and accept that their loving God could be so cruel, so petty, and so punishing to those who don't heed His words in the above Commandment. No *Bible*-believer wants to believe that their God of love would want to torment anyone for ever and ever for engaging in such innocuous trifles---such as placing a plastic Jesus on the dashboard of their car, or for making a likeness of anything in the heavens above, or in the earth below, or even in the waters of the earth. Who knew that you could go to Hell just for taking a photograph of the moon, a rock, or a fish! Why would God have "commanded" such, seemingly, "innocuous" things if they weren't very, very important to Him---as important as His prohibition against killing? Would Christianity really be able to exist without the use of God's "likeness," a make-believe, fabricated image of Him nailed to a cross, to worship and adore—would Christianity be able to exist without its blatant hypocrisy about having mandatory belief in God's Word but never really following it? Wouldn't it, therefore, be interesting to learn the worthy thoughts of any or all of the Supreme Court Justices about the above Judeo-traditions and principles that Jews and Christians proudly promote as being the foundation of America's legal system. Since it is a system that provides all of these Judges with lucrative, lifelong employment, don't expect to hear any of them offer his or her unbiased opinions on these matters any time soon! I, on the other hand, will offer a couple of my reasonable opinions on the above matters:

The nine individuals who comprise the Supreme Court—the nine individuals who credit the above Judeo-traditions and principles as the model for the establishment of America's evenhanded, criminal justice system should cringe at the thought of giving credit to a Judeo-tradition that determined one's guilt or innocence by the removal of a Urim stone or a Thummin stone from a bag or pouch---they should cringe at the thought of Satan being acquitted of any wrongdoing by God, and, after receiving a meaningless belly-crawling curse for his successful attempt to tempt a child-minded couple, he was, in effect, enriched by God for his deceiving role in the "Fall" of mankind which resulted in the damnation of everyone and everything in Eden and beyond by God—a God who has judged everyone a criminal just for being born! All nine Supreme Court Justices should cringe in shame at the pronouncement of "IN GOD WE TRUST" knowing, as they do, that the God of Judeo-Christianity is a tyrannical, vengeful, criminal-minded miscreant who would be serving multiple life-sentences if ever He had to face American justice for His crimes against humanity! What say you, America's eminent Magistrates, about the Judeo-traditions and principles of "injustice" "revealed" in the *Bible* about God's "Laws" and His "unjust" penalties for breaking them—what say you? Would you, after hearing all the known facts in this case continue to defend and declare with pride that our nation's legal system is based upon the God-given, legal system of Semites that sentences the accused to death (without any ability to appeal their convictions) for merely coveting a neighbor's possessions? ---I don't think so! If Reason's Tribunal v. the "Word of God" were ever to come before the Supreme Court of the United States to decide if America is truly *"one nation under God,"* what do you think that decision would be?

Shame on you, too—the kindergarten-minded, mythology-believing, God-addicts in Allah-Land—who make such a fuss over any voiced opposition to their deity that they are willing to impose lethal punishment on those whom they and their sacred texts deem to be sinners, idolators, blasphemers, and infidels---which seems to be a beloved tradition among Semites. Shouldn't they, out of their deep devotion to please their "borrowed" deity, have declared a "Jihad" against the first Sinner—the first Infidel—the first Blasphemer—the first and constant Opposer of God—Satan? Shouldn't they as devout Muslims bent on defending God's name against all sinners have called for the death of Satan instead of being content with Allah's rewarding him as He did for all of his anti-Allah activities—isn't that more suited to the kind of retaliation and vengeance that believers in Semitic religions aspire to?

If the Supreme Court Justices were ever given the task to name every transgressor in the Eden-tale, it would be incumbent upon them, in their examination of *Bible*-evidence, to make note of the fact that Adam and Eve, whom the *Bible* and its promoters would have us believe were sinful ingrates, didn't start out in life like you or I. They, as the story reveals, were fatherless and motherless children who had no siblings—no parental guidance or parental care—no childhood experiences in which to learn life's lessons, no sense of right and wrong, no idea what a lie is, no idea that the talking snake was not to be believed, no concept of what death is—no education, no street smarts—nothing except an amazing fluency in Hebrew and Adam's incredible ability to name *"every living creature"* on the spot! Eve, in her state of total innocence, was not even surprised in the least to hear a serpent speak! If *Bible*-evidence is to be believed, Adam and Eve didn't know a damned thing about a damned thing in the First Place and who better for malefactors to impose upon but guileless, child-minded individuals? Even Catholic priests continue this shameful, despicable, Semitic tradition, begun in Eden, to take advantage of those who because of their innate innocence are the weakest and most vulnerable among us! *"Bless and forgive me Father for I have sinned"* ---yeahhh right!

Adam didn't even know that the disembodied voice he was hearing and telling him what and what not to eat, was that of God, and what did he, Adam, know about God? Nothing! Adam never saw God with his own eyes and, therefore, never "witnessed" Him create anything, not even the animals that suddenly and inexplicably emerged from the ground apparently without cause---without the presence of a visible creator---animals that he, for no believable reason, gave immediate names to. Adam and Eve did not know what "truth" is or what "lies" are; they didn't even know, therefore, who was telling the truth and who wasn't when Adam was told by a disembodied voice that *"Thou shalt surely die"* or when Eve was told by a visible, talking snake *"Ye shall not surely die"* —for death and deception, truth and lies were experiences that were unknown to them both whom but a moment before their instant, abracadabra creation into fully-grown beings, existed as dust and bone! Adam, who was told by an unseen speaker that he would *"surely die"* for his disobedience, lived on for 9.3 centuries after hearing of his death sentence from that mysterious, disembodied voice. Adam's long long long-delayed, long long long-anticipated death surely occurred, no doubt, on April 1st of his final year! Don't you think so, too? Isn't it a bit strange that we are made to believe God's sentencing of Adam---his expulsion from Eden---was carried out on the very day of Adam's disobedience, yet his sentence of death wasn't fulfilled for nearly a thousand years later! Hmm! It is my impious opinion that if anyone in the Garden of Eden-tale deserved to be condemned and damned for their despicable transgressions, it should not have been Adam and Eve---for they were but innocents abroad, surely!

Because of the naivete and child-like innocence of Adam and Eve, why didn't a merciful Creator offer them clemency and commute His "cruel and unusual" sentence of suffering and death for the eating of an apple from a certain apple tree---a fruit they were commanded to consume for their sustenance in *Gen.* 1:29? Why didn't God settle the matter instantly with their instant death as He had forewarned, or, at least, with their infertility which, as it turns out, would have been the humane thing to do. Why, too, did God find it absolutely necessary and so vitally important to have Himself become a "mortal" man in order to experience a "cruel and unusual" death when the only thing that an "immortal" God can never do is cease to exist---just another example of religion having it both ways!

If God had died on the cross and remained dead for 3 days then, obviously, the Universe can exist and carry-on without Him! If it wasn't God who died on the cross, why should we care about His cloned stand-in? And why should God be so concerned anyway with an apple-eating Adam, a deceived dupe who didn't know any better, when God with His all-knowing, loving and merciful nature caused the indiscriminate slaughter of *Bible*-millions---an *"abomination"* that certainly far surpasses any Edenic offense! The bizarre events that supposedly occurred in the Garden of Eden, and the bizarre damnation that resulted from Adam and Eve's fruit-eating, we're made to believe, were all done in order for a bizarre God, in His Jesus disguise, not the apple-eaters or Satan, to make an atonement for the "disobedience" which resulted from Eve's longing to eat an apple even though God never warned her against eating it—only Adam! Bizarro!

How is it that the Devil's insubordination is never the object of God's eternal wrath directed at "disobedience," and why did a very impatient, petulant God wait nearly 4000 years, I repeat, "nearly 4000 years" to "settle" the matter with the death of Himself in His innocent man disguise: Jesus? Really? Did God content Himself with being full of anger and vengeance for four millennia before He decided to do something about it? This is the kind of chutzpah-laden crap we are spoon-fed to believe is "spiritual," "rational," "decent," and "moral" behavior! Incredibly, all that was necessary on Satan's part to upset the entire apple-cart of the Universe---all that was necessary for Satan to lay waste to the Almighty's plans for Paradise #1 and compel God to kill Himself (by proxy) forty centuries later---was to speak just three sentences as given in chapter #3 of *Genesis.* It only required less than fifty words for Satan to subordinate the All-intelligent Creator of the Universe---his Maker!---and "make" Him his servant---to do his bidding---to make God into a laughable, cursing fool---

to make God suffer and die on the cross---to make God aid and abet his bidding by Having Him "prepare" a Hell so that he, the Devil and his evil minions, could enjoy indulging in their ungodly wickedness for all eternity---and all it took was to speak a few sentences---amazing and quite ridiculous! This is inerrant and infallible *Bible*-evidence, folks! Lemonade, anyone?

> *For God so loved the world, that he gave his only begotten Son, that whosoever believeth in him should not perish, but have everlasting life.*

Jesus---John 3:16

As long as the '*whosoever*' didn't include any Gentiles! ---kvk

Just imagine, if someone in America today (a male parent in this case), were to bring his son before a church altar, during church services, and announce to everyone assembled there that out of his fatherly love and concern for the future welfare of everyone, his son was going to be brutally murdered in order to atone for someone else's "sin" and then proceeded to carry out the execution—what do you think would happen to such a someone? Would anyone witnessing such a spectacle be inspired to drop to their knees in worshipful praise of the perpetrator? I don't think so. Would anyone condone or feel blessed by such an event? I don't think so! We should all be sickened by the thought of it. I can assure you, the reader, that had God waited another 2000 years or so until the present time---where all life now seemingly "matters" to most people in our nation---to attempt to pull off His murder-of-a-scapegoat stunt, Christianity would be immediately recognized as the outrageous and fraudulent, criminal enterprise and scam that it is! And today's black protesters who are intent on removing statued reminders of their ancestors' past enslavement and current oppressions in America should also be motivated to remove cross-adorned steeples and statues of Jesus---they should be motivated to burn every *Bible* at their disposal if they were made aware of the role their beloved Christian religion and its beloved Christian *Bible* played in causing the above past abominations and causing the ongoing injustices heaped upon their race.

Surely, if a poll were to be currently taken in "Christian" America asking folks if they think it is "honorable" that the innocent should be punished instead of the guilty, the answer, in my opinion, surely would be an obvious and unanimous: "No!" If that same poll were to ask if it is "honorable" that

125

an innocent Jesus should be deserving of punishment instead of the guilty, apple-eating Adam, what would you expect the answer to be? Surely it, too, would be, overwhelmingly, another "No!" Someone should consider taking such a poll, in our supposedly Christian nation, to confirm or disprove my opinion and know that, if I am correct in my assertions, it is only a matter of time before all of the oppressors of humanity, past and present, will be identified and reckoned with, and their symbols of oppression removed from public view.

Lacking fairness and decency in every detail, lacking logic and morality in every action, the absurdity of the Garden of Eden-tale could never have ended with Adam and Eve's living "happily ever after," for such a scenario would not have explained the sorrows of life mankind still endures on a daily basis nor would it have served the all-important, selfish purposes of script-writing priests who had the chutzpah to make even their God physically pay with His life in the fulfilling of a primitive-minded, ritual sacrifice where the death of an innocent-being serves as a "vicarious" atonement for the sins of the guilty even though the death of Jesus, the man/God, only lasted, we're told, but a few days. Therefore, out of kindness and respect to ourselves and to our sanity—to our compassionate, sentient nature as human (humane) beings—we should avoid the effort needed to digest the incredible fare given to us in this tale and in the unjust sequel to this tale—the woeful, Gospel accounts about a brutalized scapegoat, an innocent man---a tale crafted to evoke our compassionate empathy and feelings of guilt for "our" supposed part in His cruel and agonized execution. Before taking a bite of the beguiling *Bible* and the beguiling *Koran*, shouldn't we, the gullible Adams and Eves of today, be warned that these books were purposely written for ungodly, less-than-sacred purpose by pious-pretenders—the deceiving, manipulative script-writers and their parasitic minions, the deceiving belly-crawlers known as "clergy" for, it is said, the Devil wears many disguises?

I find it quite interesting that our knowledge about God comes from just two books of Semitic chutzpah: the *Old* and the *New Testament*---two books of Jewish mythology that were written by authority-lacking, anonymous authors---books that always favor their own kind---imagine that! I find it quite interesting, too, that there are no other books existing in the world that can tell us anything with absolute "certainty" ---aside from the bogus *Bible* and the bogus *Koran*---about what God is and what He has done---what He has said to certain others and what He often thinks about--- what His major concerns are and what He feels in His heart---what He regrets having done and what His personal jealousies are---what He doesn't want us to do: *"THOU SHALT NOT KILL"* and what He does want certain folks to do unto certain others: *"THOU SHALT SAVE ALIVE NOTHING THAT BREATHETH"* (evidently, God has some difficulty making up His mind about whether killing is a good thing or a bad thing---just another example of religion having it both ways!) ---what He wants us to eat and when to eat it, what He wants us to wear, what He wants us to do with our hair, what He wants us to do to the genitals of certain male babies, etc., etc., etc.

Think about it folks, isn't it a bit strange that it is only the self-serving script-writers of the Chutzpah Chronicles of Semites who have the audacity to tell us, with absolute certainty beyond any doubt, "everything" there is to know about God, including very intimate details about Him, from A to Z, from Alpha to Omega---incredibly strange isn't it? If we can be made to believe that snakes can talk, what prevents us from believing that they can write Semitic scripture as well? Shouldn't we, too, the present day, easily imposed upon inhabitants of this garden planet, Earth, be warned, like Adam was warned, about the dangers and the consequences of what we are about to consume when we taste of the low-hanging fruits of these Semitic scriptures---scriptures which Reason's Tribunal, (by turning the bitter lemons they serve us into refreshing, liberating lemonade), will prove are but ***human inventions, set up to terrify and enslave mankind, and monopolize power and profit"***?

Based on the Muslim belief of the *Koran's* eternal existence as an "imperishable tablet," written upon by Allah's own hand, (in Arabic, no less!), we must also believe the lunacy that this tablet "existed" before Allah created anything else in the Universe—before He ever had any reason to speak, (in Arabic, no less!), or to write, (in Arabic, no less!) ---for no one else existed who could hear Him or read His writing. Interestingly, God's native tongue in the *Bible* is said to be Hebrew—a language, amazingly enough, the talking snake must have been fluent in also, as well as Adam and Eve—oy vey! *"Yes, Virginia, God has hands that are able to write like you and I, vocal cords to physically voice His concerns even when no one existed who could hear them, and He has most of the other parts of the human body, too. And, 'Once upon a time,' He sported long, flowing white hair and, depending on who you talk to, His foreskin went AWOL, at least according to some folks made exactly in His image!"*

The *Koran*, we are to believe, was in existence even before God had supposedly made the heavens and the earth—before anyone on earth had disobeyed His spoken command to avoid the fruit of a certain tree! We must believe, too, that the *Koran* "existed" before Allah ever made the decision to create human beings---a decision that was merely an afterthought, I repeat, "merely an afterthought" on His part because *there was not a man to till the ground"* in Eden. The *Koran,* we are to believe, "existed" even before Adam exercised his "free will" to be an apple-eater or not, "existed" even before Allah had learned that Adam and Eve had "apple-ed" and only from that point on, I repeat, "only from that point on," would anyone have the (supposed) need for Allah's chapter and verse (sura and ayat) heavenly guidance to regain what was lost in man's (supposed) "Fall" from grace. How nonsensically absurd it is to believe that the *Koran* and its redemptive instructions should be "in existence" before they were ever needed, before Allah could have possibly known the outcome of Adam's decision to eat or not to eat the fruit of *"the tree of the knowledge of good and evil."* The *Koran* obviously existed before "disobedience" had made its debut in the world. Hmm! Hmm! Hmm! Such would be the equivalent of the Declaration of Independence having been written before---long before the existence of England and America—how nonsensically absurd!

We must also believe, based on the above scriptural "evidence," that God, before creating the world, had "foreknowledge" of events in Eden and, with malice aforethought, let them transpire anyway—what a Guy! If redemption was so important to God, why didn't He, Mr. Know-It-All, expel Adam and Eve (and the talking snake!) from Eden with, at least, a copy of His "imperishable tablet"? But, on second thought, since A&E were, presumedly, illiterate, they would not have been able to "read" its merciful words dealing with their "redemption." It would have been possible, however, for God to have sent a literate angel along to read it word for word to them, as He had done for Muhammad such a long, long time after the "Fall." This, in my opinion, would have served greater purpose for a loving "Redeemer" and His uber-important "redeeming" religion!

Oh, what a tangled web we weave. . .when at first we practice to deceive.

---Walter Scott

As beings endowed with the unpredictable, unknowable nature of their free willed, decision-making, Adam and Eve, if we wish to believe the many impositions of the Eden-tale, might just as well have chosen "not" to eat of the apple—what then? The *Koran's* pre-existence in such a case would have served no purpose because it would be lacking any justification for its fabrication—a case where its pre-Garden of Eden existence would make it an absurd and meaningless book because its "effect" would have preceded its "cause." If one allows that God had foreknowledge of Adam and Eve's free willed choice before they even had a chance to make it, (which, obviously, would be impossible as the outcome of free-willed decisions cannot be known before they are made! ---duhhh!), but, assuming God did know beforehand of Adam's decision, He is a despicable character for allowing their apple-eating to have occurred—He is a despicable character for punishing us, their innocent descendants along with all the animals, for something we didn't do, especially for something as innocuous as the naive disobedience of our beguiled and gullible, innocent-minded great-grandparents.

Shouldn't everyone be surprised to learn that the "imperishable" *Koran* was "in existence" long before the necessity of Allah having to create it for the good fortune and salvation of Arabs only, as there have been no reports of Gabriel ever having made an appearance to any Chinese caveman for the good fortune and the "salvation" of the much more numerous Asians? Hmm! Hmm! Hmm! Shouldn't everyone be surprised to learn that God's only concern was for the welfare of Semites and Semites only? ---Hmm! ---how interesting---seems a little racially motivated to me! Shouldn't everyone be surprised to learn that God, lacking any company to hear and record His words (except for His incredible script-writers, of course!), had need for speech so early on in His non-verbal, solo career, had need for a writing instrument and a "tablet" to inscribe His speech upon, (as if His memorization skills were lacking!) had need for agents to deliver and promote His "Word" spoken and written to no one? Shouldn't we be surprised to learn that Allah, apparently, had someone to speak to at all before the "Big Bang" or that He, lacking the company of others, muttered the *Koran* all to Himself and wrote it all down on an "imperishable tablet," one might assume, so that He would not forget what He had said and always have a record of it for future reference? And, who knows, it just might come in so handy one day that He might even decide to publish it? Hmm! Hmm! Hmm! Which came first, the chicken or the egg? —God or the "imperishable tablet"? My guess would be that only scriptural script-writers are capable of answering the latter question, for they, and only they, know, with certainty, "all" that transpires in an "invisible" world---and, they have "revealed" to us, that both God and the "imperishable tablet" were always I repeat, "always" in existence which is proof that God couldn't have been the author of the "imperishable" *Koran* for it could not have been in existence before Allah wrote it---duhhh! ---but try telling that to a Muslim!

Shouldn't everyone be surprised to learn that Allah, who we are supposed to believe wrote the *Koran*, is not the only speaker in the *Koran*—Allah is often referred to in the third person on its pages as doing this thing or that thing—a moronic way for God to speak of Himself and His doings—a moronic way for God to reveal His "undoubted," message to Muslims in an easy to understand, comprehensible way! Besides, how is it possible that an ever-existing tablet could contain knowledge of events that occurred before they even happened---how is it possible that everything talked about in the "ever-existing" *Koran* transpired post-Creation, not pre-Creation when the *Koran* was supposedly written---how is it possible, therefore, to hear mention of idol worship in an ever-existing book written "before" the existence of idols? ---more duhhhs! If Allah/God had an urgent, fundamental "need" to communicate His redemptive measures a second time, (first time to Moses for the exclusive benefit of the Jews) to certain other "chosen" Semites (imagine God being in need of anything and always favoring Semites! ---Hmm!), why did He also have a need to depend on an angelic spokesperson to relay His "perfect" book to Muslims especially knowing that, as the story goes, it was an angel, Satan, who really screwed things up in a "perfect" Heaven and a "perfect" Eden. Imagine God having need to rely on anyone other than Himself to get the job done!

(NOTE TO MUSLIMS: Allah really doesn't need your help! However, many folks in Muslim communities around the world could use a hand-out and/or a helping hand from Merciful Allah—they, in their less-than-heavenly, living conditions here on earth are in need of the basics of life more than they need their religion to churn-out another suicide-bomber---another inspired infidel killer---which seems to be Allah's major concern---Man help us! —but I digress . . .)

Are these things not evidence of an Almighty Divinity and His "forever-existing book" having been created by imperfect human manufacture, a book written by the un-divine hands of script-writers for, as always, the self-serving interests of the few and not the spiritual interests of the many? Who but an imposing, less-than-divine, deception-minded, script-writing priest would find it necessary to tell us upon its very pages that the *Koran* should never be doubted---*Koran* 2:2---that the *Koran* is free from flaw---that anyone who doubts any part of it, in effect, is viewed as having unbelief in God's "Word" and, therefore, is uber-deserving of God's divine wrath?

Would God, the supposed "perfect" author of the entire, "perfect" *Koran*, have need to make such a bolstering endorsement about His "perfection" on the pages of His "perfect" book---have need to vouch for the veracity of His "own" statements in an attempt to eliminate any doubt about the *Koran* being His "perfect" Word? Absolutely not! Would God ever have a need to confirm the truth of His statements? Absolutely not! Only a control-seeking, script-writing God-impostor would have need to insert such words in the *Koran* to make folks believe, without any doubt, its every syllable—or else, in failing this, one of God's joy-filled, Islamic enforcers, will get you and give you a morsel of God's mercy and a full meal of His miseries!

Only a control-seeking God-impostor would demand that every Muslim have absolute faith in the "error-free," "doubt-free," hearsay *Koran*. Only a control-seeking, script-writing God-impostor would demand that all Muslims have absolute faith in the infallible, absolute authority of its every word that was supposedly "revealed" to a caveman who never recorded them---"revealed" via a skulking, non-descript, shadowy figure of an extraterrestrial entity (Gabriel) that nobody besides Muhammad ever saw and then only in strange visions. Such spurious, bogus evidence may suffice for creating the book of hearsay known as the *Koran*, the Muslim Chutzpah Chronicles, but not for anything where reason and truth, decency and fairness, common-sense and sanity are concerned.

Why was God seemingly incapable of speaking directly to Muhammad when we are told in the *Bible* that He spoke directly to Adam, to Noah, to Moses, and to others? Why did God choose to speak directly at times and indirectly at other times? Either way, His communications were always given in a furtive and unwitnessed manner to all of the above just as they are still being given to suicide-bombers, jihadists, and other delusional disciples of Islam, Christianity, and Judaism who hear God speak to them inside their heads without the disrupting thunder and lightning events associated with so many of His past discourses? And, if God's message is meant for the multitudes, why does He always reveal it in secret to only one individual who then reveals it only to a select few? Hmm!

These are the souls that try men's times! ---kvk

Isn't the hearing of a voice, especially an imposing voice in one's mind (or one's dreams), considered by many religious devotees to be convincing proof of direct communication with God? Isn't the hearing of a voice inside one's head, that commands one to commit murder and to engage in atrocity, absolute proof of personal contact with a loving Semitic deity? Wouldn't Muhammad's telling his avid listeners that, instead of being lectured to by an angel, he was hearing God speak to him, firsthand, inside his head---

wouldn't such a direct, heavenly communication have been considered just as worthy of belief as Gabriel's decades-long effort? Or, is it more believable, somehow, that Muhammad was tasked with having to memorize the "hearsay" revelations of God that were relayed, in perplexing visions, from a suddenly appearing---suddenly disappearing---enigmatic stranger from the land of Oz—year after year, after year, after year in the darkened recesses of a cave? (Under penalty of pain, the Chutzpah Chronicles always contain tales of unbelievable, supernatural events meant to beguile and intimidate us in order to stifle investigation and inquiry into their unbelievable claims. They always contain cunning, jaw-dropping, awe-inspiring occurrences meant to paralyze our attention from employing the use of logic and reason against the stupefying, spellbinding fabrications of Semitic theologies and their feared reprisals for unbelief)

"Yes, Virginia, the God of Semitic religions, along with Gabriel, His skulking angel, and Santa Claus certainly do exist, but only in the minds of beguiled believers—only in the minds of naive and gullible children—only in the minds of folks who prefer to accept rather than to question the existence of such entities and their fabled ability to act in miraculous and mysterious ways for their own personal benefit of course in this life and beyond. Why would anyone reject belief in God, belief in angels, and belief in flying reindeer when they bring the world such great comfort, good tidings, and gift packages? Yes, Virginia, it's true---for the joy of toys we deceive our children with tales about Santa Claus and his gift-giving for we believe there is a greater need being served in the happiness that it brings them. We deceive ourselves with tales about God and His heavenly paradise for the same reason. The latter deception persists beyond childhood only because of the hope of receiving bigger and better amusements!"

If you tell a big enough lie and tell it frequently enough, it will be believed.

---Adolph Hitler, *Mein Kampf*

...the world is fast coming to a realization of the fact that this whole theological structure, founded on sleeper's dreams and angel's tales, is but 'The baseless fabric of a vision.'

---John E. Remsburg

The *Koran* is a book that we are imposed upon to believe is of such great importance to Muslims that one would think Allah would have made its unimpeachable delivery to the Muslim world all by Himself. Since that didn't occur (for some strange reason!), we must believe that Allah thought it best to enlist the services of one of His heavenly associates, a flighty, winged fella named Gabriel, to get the job done with impeccability. Since Allah (for some strange reason!), was unable to provide His flying assistant, Gabriel, with a snap-of-His-fingers written copy of the *Koran* to present to Muhammad---Gabriel---who obviously possessed an incredible memory and an enduring patience---memorized the *Koran* in its entirety in order to relay it word for word to Muhammad (in a furtive manner unwitnessed by others, of course!). The cause of Allah's inability to communicate directly with His glorious Prophet of Islam---the cause of His inability to furnish Muhammad with an autographed copy of His "imperishable" book remains a curious mystery for Reason's Tribunal to scrutinize and attempt to solve.

We are further imposed upon to believe that in order to get His Word out to the Muslim world, it appears that it was absolutely necessary for Allah to delegate this top priority undertaking and initiate implausible events that, one assumes, He'd hoped would result in mule-man Muhammad, a cave-dwelling pedophile, committing to memory, every word of the *Koran* spoken to him by Gabriel. Incidentally, it is not "blasphemy" to call Muhammad a mule-man or a cave-dwelling pedophile---it is "biography"! Allah had further hoped, one assumes, that Muhammad would then reveal the puzzling revelations he received from Gabriel only to his gullible Muslim brothers whom, one assumes, Allah had even further hoped, would believe them without question! This, we are to believe, was Allah's "perfect" means of disseminating His hearsay Word, "without error," to the Muslim world but which resulted, strangely enough, in neither Muhammad nor Gabriel making any attempt to memorialize these Allah-revelations in book-form for the spiritual edification of future generations of Muslim "men" to learn and to disseminate Allah's momentous message meant just for them---Muslim males! ---Hmm! This, we are to believe, is a stellar example of the loving Genius at work in Heaven above that runs the incomprehensible complexity of the entire Universe with exacting precision and complete competency—amazing! What an incompetent fool, man has made his created, mirror-image God to be!

If only God had been capable of communicating directly with everyone, there wouldn't be so many differing versions of His "Word" and we would not have to rely on the unconvincing and disputed words of others—we would not have to rely on *"sleeper's dreams and angel's tales"* for His "indubitable" message. If only Allah was capable of expressing Himself in the *Koran* with "indubitable" clarity instead of with indecipherable confusion where He sometimes narrates in the first-person plural, then often changes to the first-person singular or to the third-person singular in the course of the same sentence—a confusing flaw in the text that is more a symptom of fallible authors rather than infallible writing by an infallible author. If only Allah had thought to explain the meaning of the cryptic Arabic letters which head certain chapters of the *Koran* as part of His painstaking effort to "reveal" everything to its readers. If only Muslims didn't have constant need to resort to the Hadith, another set of Chutzpah Chronicles—another set of "inspired," "immune-from-error" writings of various others. The Hadith helps to explain the obvious imperfections of a perfect Allah in His perfect effort to relay, in indisputable detail, His perfect Word to Muslims via His perfect *Koran*. The fact that the *Koran* requires the services of the Hadith to be understood more clearly should inform the uncorrupted mind that the *Koran* is not the work of a perfect, all-knowing author and articulate communicator. However, that being said . . .

This is the book in which there is no doubt.

---script-writer, *Koran* 2:2

(meaning of *Koran* 2:2: "Believe this book, pal, ---or else"!) ---kvk

What *"book"* was being referred to in *Koran* 2:2 and who was the imposing author of its ten words? —was it God attempting to vouch for the veracity of His own "revealed" Word in order to gain the reader's confidence in His being the true "author" of the *Koran*? Think about it— would God, the paragon of virtue and moral perfection—someone who, supposedly, could never tell a lie or deceive—have need to make such an assuring declaration about His "impeccable" revelations? Allah was certainly not the author of *Koran* 2:2! Such a declaration would only be a "necessity" for Allah's less-than-impeccable script-writers to make since they and their minions share a parasitic interest in having folks believe that every word they've written in the "revealed" *Koran* has been placed there by Allah. Such a declaration was especially "needed" for a book that is derived from the "third-hand" recollections of others who supposedly heard it spoken from the lips of Muhammad who received his "second-hand" revelations from the lips of Gabriel who, it is supposed, heard it "first-hand" from the lips of Allah. In my mind, there is no doubt that such a declaration is evidence of "uneven-handedness," for it attempts to have folks believe that every word in the hearsay upon hearsay *Koran* is beyond doubt and beyond scrutiny---Oh, those cunning, script-writing deceivers and coercers!

Muhammad, strangely enough, wasn't gifted with this *"book"* from Gabriel, Allah's angelic, literary agent, and he, the Mighty Muhammad, never produced a copy of this *"book"* and, amazingly, never sought to do so because the *Koran* "did not" exist in book-form on this planet until decades after Muhammad's death. Why Muhammad is considered deserving of honor and adoration as a Prophet of God in the Muslim world remains a mystery to this writer! Muhammad could not have been the author of *Koran* 2:2 because the *"book,"* referred to in its ten words had yet to be written down, at least, here on earth! If one assumes that Allah was the "author" of the words contained in *Koran* 2:2, why would He undermine His credibility and His irreproachable, perfect nature by including such a qualifying statement about His written Word when we are made to believe that "everything" God says is, without question, the absolute truth—that "everything" God says is, without question, stated with impeccability and without dishonesty, without suspicion and without ulterior motive. Wouldn't it, therefore, be uber-ridiculous to be told by a perfect God that His perfect Word should not be doubted? How could anyone in the Muslim world possibly doubt that God is the author of the *Koran* when we are told by a delusional and hallucinating megalomaniac, a cave-dwelling pervert and child-rapist, that we must believe it is so based on the purity of his word alone that "he," Muhammad is a Messenger of God? ---what incredible BS chutzpah! Such credentials may qualify someone to be an Islamic "Prophet," but not someone to be trusted around young, female children for sure!

Would any Muslim ever ever believe for a moment that Allah could possibly have ever done or said anything that might be considered "dubious"? Of course not! ---so why the need for His written caveat about not doubting His "Word"? It is obvious that a perfect Allah was not the perfect author of *Koran* 2:2, it was written by some imperfect, power-tripping script-writer who wants everyone to believe (for some strange reason!), that Allah "is" the *Koran's* one and only author! Why a "perfect" God would choose such an "imperfect" means to get His perfect "Word" out to His homies is anyone's guess!

It is interesting to consider that the "revealed" *Koran* was written and compiled by men who, unlike Muhammad, never experienced the shock and awe and inspiration of encountering Gabriel themselves—men who were never personally encouraged by an angel of God (or, at least, a murky cave-vision of him!) to write and record it—men who, nevertheless, were engaged and energized enough for decades to make a written compilation of Muhammad's every single word that he, not they, supposedly received from this visionary informant? The "revealed" *Koran* is a book in which there "is" much doubt especially since the person that Allah chose to relay His personal message to the Muslim world, Muhammad, never made a copy of *"the book in which there is no doubt."* Allah employed all the powers of Heaven to teach the *Koran's* every word to Muhammad via an imaginary, extraterrestrial, Gabriel, whom we are told, recited each and every word of the *Koran,* over and over and over again, to this "Prophet of Islam" with nothing to show for all the Heavenly effort that had been squandered on him! Muhammad, the one and only man that Allah "chose" to memorize the *Koran* and relay it to the Muslim world, "died" before completing his prophetic work---Allah, the Infallible, for some infallible reason known only to Him, had made the decision to kill His beloved, infallible "Messenger" before he could complete this most sacred of Allah's infallible missions---Wow! Both events, quite curiously, quite tellingly, and quite incredibly were, we're made to believe, the result of Allah's infallible "will." Wow, again!

There's no doubt, however, in my mind, that Allah had finally realized He had "chosen" the wrong guy for the job and that Gabriel, no doubt, had wasted his precious time on earth trying to train a degenerate cave man to be a pious "prophet" worthy of promoting the perfect Word of Allah! Wouldn't Alley and Gabey have had a better handle on the situation if they, instead, focused their attention on the person(s) who actually penned the perfect pages of the *Koran* rather than on someone who was, obviously, unqualified for the job? Since Al and Gabe's intent was to make the *Koran* known to everyone in the Muslim world, why was it so important for them to introduce "the light of the world" ---(LOL!) to a degenerate yokel, making it a private affair conducted furtively in the "darkened" recesses of a cave—an affair that was meant, after all, to make the contents of the "revealed" *Koran* public knowledge that was to be preached everywhere several times a day and made available for every set of Muslim eyes to behold? Hmm, again! Reason's Tribunal, I'm certain, holds the key to understanding why any and all "doubts" about the *Koran* being the absolute "Word of God" must always be "eliminated" so that the Islamic version of God's "Word" can flourish and continue unimpeded to impose its life-threatening, self-serving designs of sicko power-hungry clergy upon others---or else!

In attempting to swallow the unbelievable nonsense surrounding the "revealed" *Koran's* creation without choking on its many impositions---try taking a sip of Reason's Tribunal's refreshing, liberating lemonade to help wash it down. Doing so will help you to remember with clarity that Gabriel's incredible odyssey to relay the entire *Koran* to every Muslim by relaying it word for word to a dysfunctional, cave-dwelling degenerate had ended in complete failure . . . duhhh! One should recall here, with clarity, that it took Allah just 6 days, I repeat, "just 6 days" to create the entire galaxy- teeming Universe all by Himself . . . duh, again! Yet, we are made to believe that this same Guy, even with the assistance of His heavenly helper, Gabriel, invested their precious time and effort into a promotional project with nothing to show for it—incredible! If it weren't for the efforts of Muhammad's detailed-record-keeping associates and their remarkable, "infallible"" and inerrant," verse-recalling memories, the heavenly "revealed" *Koran* would not exist today at all in book-form. The writing of the *Koran* was quite a remarkable accomplishment considering that these incredible, religion-minded chroniclers were not acting under any divine intervention or under any divine mandate from Allah or from Gabriel to commit to and complete their arduous, error-free mission. Thankfully, for believers in Islam, God had chanced upon finding so many "perfect" memorizers of Muhammad's every word who were able to rescue His less-than-perfect plans for publishing the *Koran* that He'd relayed, with great effort, to His one and only, less-than-perfect Prophet of Islam, and they did so with absolute perfection---"with absolute perfection"!

We are further imposed upon to believe that these various individuals were, somehow, deemed worthy enough in all of Allah-Land to "complete" the prophetic job delegated entirely to Muhammad from on high---that these men were, somehow, deemed worthy enough by Al and Gabe to be trusted with remembering and writing down, without any omissions whatsoever, everything that Muhammad had supposedly told them about what was written on Al's *"imperishable tablet."* All of this effort was supposedly accomplished without as much as one error ever being made even though their amazing efforts produced a third-hand account of Allah's Perfect Word! If Muhammad is to be called a "Prophet" for "not" writing down the "revealed" *Koran*, what are we to call these remarkable men, with their remarkable memories, who did write it down? ---are they not "Propheteers" all? Isn't it quite strange, however, that none of these prophetic fellas were ever deemed worthy enough to merit a single meeting with Ol' Gabe, the one and only heavenly agent Allah relied upon to get His "Word" out? For all of their tremendous labors to compile the *Koran*, they were "never" deemed worthy enough to be granted a vision or two, "ala

Muhammad," to meet and greet Allah's *Koran*-revealing emissary at least once, if only to confirm the fact that they had not forgotten any of Muhammad's momentous words that each of them, supposedly, had all committed to memory over the course of their impeccable, decades-long odyssey---an "immune-from-error" odyssey that involved their listening to, memorizing and/or recording, in some fashion, every one of Muhammad's hearsay revelations. Hmm! Hmm! Hmm! "Is the lemonade pitcher leaking?"

It remains for Reason's Tribunal to determine the ultimate limits of Muslim credulity and, it is hoped, give us, at last, a good, unobscured glimpse of gabby Gabriel for all to bear witness to. It remains for Reason's Tribunal to determine, too, if the so-called poetic character of the *Koran* is certain proof of its divine origin as many Muslims claim. Certainly, I am impressed with Allah's poetic talents as expressed in the *Koran* and His incredible serendipity at finding such extraordinary literary agents at the last minute who were competent enough (unlike Muhammad!) to make a perfect record of His every hearsay Word contained in it! I suppose that had the *Koran* been written in the juvenile manner of rhyming verse instead of poetic composition, we would know that Allah could not have been its author for it is my opinion that Allah detests anything consisting of rhyme, which "would" make Him appear foolish---or anything consisting of reason, which "would" prove it beyond a doubt!

What we are imposed upon to believe with certainty is that various individuals among Muhammad's followers were ever-present at the entrance of his solemn sanctuary—his reclusive cave retreat—or at his side whenever he ventured forth, day after day for 8000+ days to bear witness to his every word. They did this, one assumes, in order to either commit to memory or to jot down with "indubitable" accuracy the latest from the Greatest without missing a syllable of what he uttered. What *"book,"* therefore, was being referred to in *Koran* 2:2, when an authorized, "perfect" version of the *Koran* did not exist for more than 20 years after Muhammad's death? —during which time all "unauthorized" versions of the *Koran* were being sought out and destroyed—(I suppose there must have been some *"doubt"* about their "divine" origins!) One thing we can believe with certainty regarding *"this"* book: the fabrication of God's "indubitable" Word and the distribution of it to His chosen Semites has "never" been a simple task for God or His emissaries, His secret agents, or even His unknown script-writers to accomplish---never!

The *Bible*, too, is not a book to be doubted as touted because pain or penalty accompanies unbelief—imagine that! ---such is the imposed physical and mental tyranny of both Semitic scriptures which were successfully designed to stifle inquiry, century after century, into their literary legitimacy by decreeing or dishing-out punishment to doubters in this temporal life and in the eternity that follows it. Therefore, to make the world a safer and saner place where the freedom of conscience along with the freedom to doubt and to disbelieve are regarded as sacraments, not as sacrileges, the *Bible* and the *Koran's* bogus authority and ungodly nature must be exposed for they are books in which there is overwhelming doubt about their God-given origins—there is overwhelming doubt, too, about the very existence of their incompetent and unfit God. We can no longer allow these "Word of God" Semitic scriptures to remain off-limits to critical examination and exposure, off-limits to the disabling ***"facts and evidence"*** that "will" result from employing Reason's Tribunal. We can no longer be silent and complacent about their embedded malevolence which continues to inspire acts of madness and deadly mayhem; we can no longer allow their intimidating, threatening behaviors to silence us or to prevent us from engaging in the necessary, bold investigation of the sanctum sanctorums of Semitic religions and their sanguinary pursuits.

There must be something wrong with religion when its supporters try to suppress all investigation and inquiry into it.

---James Hervey Johnson, *Superior Men*

It will not do to investigate the subject of religion too closely, as it is apt to lead to infidelity.

---Abraham Lincoln

Precisely, Mr. Lincoln, precisely! ---kvk

The beloved *Bible* and the beloved *Koran* share much in common—they both contain Semitic DNA; both have made iniquity (deep breath, folks!) ---war, conquest, vengeance, homicide, genocide, hatred, racism, murder, torture, mutilation, stoning, cruelty, suffering, intolerance, misogyny, xenophobia, slavery, annihilation, supremacism, terror, eternal torment, etc., ---the beloved "will" of the Almighty for it is so expressed or condoned in His biblical and koranic Word. And, of course, what loving worshiper of God/Allah doesn't want to please the Big Guy in the Sky by doing His "will"!

There will, however, never be lasting peace in the world as long as such pedestal-placed, uncontested books remain hands-off to bold investigation while the *"facts and evidence"* of their fraudulent origins are kept hidden from our scrutiny. Without a very inspired reading of their very "inspired" words, there is little to be found in their doom and gloom texts that can be deemed holy or sacred—texts which are better suited appearing on the pages of handbooks written for blood-spilling tyrants rather than appearing on the pages of handbooks written for soul-saving saints.

We will ascertain in Reason's Tribunal why these so-called "Word of God" scriptures are revered instead of rejected and renounced---why they are seemingly granted exemption from close examination and exposure, and why their staunch advocates label all attempts to do so as *"Bible*-bashing" or *"Koran*-kicking." Seemingly, bashing and kicking are activities better suited for helping to carry out God's merciful, loving work! The more I learn about the *Bible* and the *Koran,* and the folks who believe in their words and their Gods, the more thankful I am to be counted among the atheists, heretics, and infidels---someone, unlike Jews, Christians, and Muslims, who chooses to live by the maxim: "Do No Harm Unto Others" ---something is obviously wrong with this picture!

Today's Sons and Daughters of Liberty must summon the will to challenge the persistent source of religious fanaticism—the total mindless acceptance of the validity and veracity of the *Bible* and the *Koran* whose ungodly texts have given sanction to atrocity in every generation since their inceptions.

Could we get some otherwise normal humans and somehow persuade them that they are not going to die as a consequence of flying a plane smack into a skyscraper? . . . The afterlife-obsessed suicidal brain really is a weapon of immense power and danger. It is comparable to a smart missile. . . . Yet . . . it is very very cheap. . . . To fill a world with religion, or religions of the Abrahamic kind, is like littering the streets with loaded guns. Do not be surprised if they are used.

---Richard Dawkins

A sane and safe future for the continuation of *"Life, Liberty and the pursuit of Happiness"* in our nation now hinges upon another American Revolution—this time *"in the system of religion"* (Judeo-Christianity) that still colors and clouds our thinking, our actions, and our politics—a system of religion that is responsible for spawning the Islamic faith---hence, the religious insanity of our times. Because the list of appalling abuses of Semitic theology continues to grow along with the body-count of its victims, we must begin to take remedial action against it.

Time and again, year after year, the world recoils in shock from horrific acts of religion-generated violence and terror, and awaits with dread their certain return. Thankfully, we Americans, as a freedom-loving people with courageous, tyranny-defying experience, have a secret weapon at our disposal with the means to successfully counter these insane, religion-fueled actions without endangering the lives of America's noble warriors (Caretakers of Liberty) or resorting to the use of arms or Treasury funds.

We will begin to stem the tide of Islam's scripture-inspired madness when we fearlessly begin to examine and expose the related, scripture-inspired madness of its Semitic parents—Judaism and Christianity. To put a halt to Islam's imposed, criminal malevolence and reverse its forward march across the planet, we must begin our enlightened, counter-terrorism efforts here at home by revealing not only the fraudulent roots of this *"system of religion"* but, first and foremost, the fraudulent roots of its progenitors. We cannot expect to do unto others what we refuse to do unto ourselves—we must, therefore, set the example for Muslims to follow.

The sane solution for ending their mindset of terror, for ending their Jihad mission to subdue the world, lies in Reason's Tribunal's ability to reveal the lack of authority of the Semitic scriptures that are responsible for producing it. We Americans must be willing to declare our "independence" from the religious indoctrination of Judeo-Christianity, the Semitic theology that not only has direct, past and present ties to the terrorist pursuits of *Koranimals* around the world, but also the religious indoctrination that underlies the hypocritical and righteous arrogance emblazoned on our national banners such as "IN GOD WE TRUST," and the haughty notion about America being a nation "UNDER GOD." We should not be honored to connect the values we hold dear in this country with the vile actions and aspirations of Judeo-Christian Divinity—we should, as decent human beings, be ashamed of the association.

Since Jehovah/Jesus is the one-and-the-same Judeo-Christian deity, Americans, blinded by the delusional belief and the chutzpah of religious indoctrination, proudly declare that we, all of the people of this religion-beguiled, Judeo-Christian nation, "trust" solely in Him—the *Old Testament's* ruthless, mass-murdering, genocidal monster and the *New Testament's* sugar-coated, "Good News" Deliverer and Prince of Wails whose stated intent was not to bring peace to the earth, but rather a "Bad News" sword---*Matt.* 10:34—to have His enemies put to death while He looks on (more Bad News!) ---*Luke* 19:27—to set fire to the earth and cause division within families (even more Bad News!) ---*Luke* 12:49,51— to celebrate listening to the never-ending screams of agonized torment imposed upon 9/10ths of the world: the *"wailing and gnashing of teeth"* coming from His joyful-noise-producing furnace (really really Bad News!) ---*Matt.* 13:41,42. It should be obvious to any fair-minded reader of the *Bible* that this "singular" Duo of Destruction is an imposing psychopath, a Divine Despot severely afflicted with cruel, sadistic tendencies, OCD, anger-management issues, and bipolarity. Because His "example-setting" behavior results in similar acts of violence and destruction being carried out by His exemplary, devoted fans, America has an obligation to a religion-ravaged world to examine His disease in hopes of finding a lasting cure for the chronic disorders of Semitic Theism—by finding a vaccine to end the pandemic of Judeo-Christianity (and Islamic) virulence for once and for all time! Shame on us for honoring and promoting a Semitic God's pathology in our freedom-loving land---let Reason's Tribunal be your shot in the arm that is needed to stem the tide of the pandemic of disease-causing, religious dogma!

> *If a man would follow, today, the teachings of the Old Testament, he would be a criminal. If he would follow strictly the teachings of the New, he would be insane.*

> ---Robert Ingersoll

If a man would follow strictly the teachings of the *Koran,* he, too, would not only be a criminal, he would be insane as well! ---kvk

Somehow, believing that we are either God-loving or God-fearing folks, Americans are not ashamed to bend our knees and bow our heads to a bloodthirsty, criminal terrorist and slavery-condoning tyrant: Jehovah/Jesus. We are all quite proud, in fact, to declare our devotion to this miscreant on our nation's currency and in our nation's Pledge of Allegiance regardless of His wickedness and His malevolence. We are all quite proud to teach our children to believe in Him, to love, respect, and praise Him and His theistic thuggery, and to support, in every way, all of His advocates and their "sanctimonious" doings. We are all quite proud to worship and declare our servitude to a callous, impious God, whether out of affection or out of dread, because it shows the world that our impressive strength and abilities as a civilized nation has resulted entirely from His "indiscernible" efforts alone--

-how's that workin' out? We are all quite proud, too, believing that America receives His "undivided" attention—how's that workin' out? ---what incredible chutzpah and BS! Sadly, to be fair, it does appear at times however, that America is under the direction of such a callous Semitic deity when it comes to the plight of Native Americans, women, homosexuals, and blacks who are often treated worse than abused animals by those in authority. It is not to America's credit that so many of her citizens continue to be regarded and treated, by Judeo-Christians, like the Canaanites of the *Bible* who were regarded, by "God-chosen people," as less-than-equal neighbors and treated with bigotry and brutality just for being who they are. Sound familiar?

Is the mindless devotion and praise we give to this God-impostor truly descriptive of the enlightened beliefs and rational thinking of the freedom-loving people of America? Or is it descriptive of the imposed beliefs and irrational thinking of the millions of gullible, brain-washed members of the American Congregational Assembly For The Promotion Of Semitic Chutzpah? Surely, as any devout member of this beguiled Assembly would be well pleased to announce---they are all quite proud, too, of their Christian "obligation" to dutifully serve and support Jewry with "carnal things," of all things! —as a result of their Christian "indebtedness" to them, as stated in their version of the Chutzpah Chronicles (the *New Testament)* for the "indiscernible" spiritual blessings they have indiscernibly bestowed upon the Gentile world.

> *For if the Gentiles have been made partakers of their spiritual things, their duty is also to minister unto them in carnal things.* (Hmm! ---kvk)

> ---*Romans* 15:2

The Christian Chutzpah Chronicles, known as the Gospels that all Christians profess to believe in, declares that God exists in trinity—three "almost" equal parts? Part #1 being the Know-it-all Father-of-All---#2 being Jesus, the Son of the Know-it-all Father-of-All who is represented as a dying man on a cross---#3 being the Holy Ghost, the spirit of the Know-it-all Father-of-All who is represented by the image of a flying fowl. I said "almost" equal parts because #2 and #3 are not All-Knowing for, we are told, they do not know the hour or the day when "The Judgment" will be occurring (I suppose they couldn't be trusted to keep it a secret!) ---*Mark* 13:32. So much for the omniscient nature of a three-part God! The Holy

Trinity of Judeo-Christianity, therefore, consists of a God who cannot be seen, a Holy Ghost who, likewise, is not visible to anyone, and a Jewish man whom we are to believe, is all of the above—two invisible beings and one visible fraud—the buy-one, get-two-free Gods of Judeo-Christianity—such a deal!

In doing the math, aren't we to believe that #2, Jesus, is really #1, *"our Father who art in Heaven"*? —that He, a Jewish man, in effect, created us and everything else that exists in the entire Universe---oy vey! Is it not another deceiving, belly-crawling, script-writing snake who seeks to beguile us with such a race-glorifying story? In giving credit where credit is due—it was Jesus, the Jew, who was responsible for creating the Devil and who was also responsible for preparing the Hell that awaits the vast majority of the earth's inhabitants including, one assumes, all of His chosen *"lost sheep"* who have rejected Him as their Messiah! I am of the opinion that every animal (every puppy and kitten) that ever existed will also be among Hell's eternally-suffering residents, because, of the inspired *Genesis*-tale that places them among the cursed of God!

Of course, on the other hand, referring back to the previous (before parentheses) sentences that describe a three-part God, it doesn't hurt Jewry to establish a clever genetic association with #1 since, after all, they created every part of Him! It doesn't hurt Jewry to have a third part of Him, Jesus, be their own home-boy whom we must believe in and have faith in if we wish to avoid the travails of His thermally-elevated eternity! Hmm! It certainly does take a lot of belief in #2, I repeat, "a lot of belief in #2" in order to make us believe the entire trinity-thing is not just a steaming pile of God-parts—a steaming pile that includes four Semitic Guys: Jehovah, Holy Ghost, Jesus, and Allah, sharing top billing as the one and only Semitic God! Does it really surprise anyone that the Chutzpah Chronicles of the Jews, in so many words, would reveal that the very first man God created and communicated with was a Jew? ---for the third chapter of *Luke* reveals an unbroken genealogical connection from Jesus, the Jew, all the way back to who else but Adam, the Jew? Does it make me a Jew-loathing "anti-Semite" for merely re-telling what Jews have proudly stated and proudly promoted in their Chutzpah Chronicles, the *Old Testament* of the *Bible*?

If we are to believe authority-lacking scripture, especially the Gospel tales, then behold: —it was a Jew named Jesus who was able to walk on water and raise the dead to life---Wow! Wow! Wow! Therefore, we should never have any doubts about any of this Guy's other purported abilities and words that are "revealed" to us in the *Bible*. Undoubtedly, therefore, we should also believe Jesus when He called the founder of His Church:

144

"Satan"! ---*Matt.* 16:23---Wow! Wow! Wow! ---there may be some truth to be found in the *Bible* after all! By inference alone, we are supposed to believe that because of their intimacy, their *"favor,"* and their shared DNA with the Almighty who declared all Jews to be His "chosen people," that they are to be considered the finest and noblest life-forms on earth even though #2, disguised as #3, "overshadowed" (impregnated!) his own mother, (#4?). Isn't there another more fitting name than "Holy Ghost" for the molesting perpetrator of such an imposing debauchery performed upon the undefiled body of a young naive girl—an innocent who was engaged to be married to a decent Joe—a guy who had no say in the matter—a guy who was, nonetheless, obligated to raise Jesus, the bastard child fathered by someone else! The "immaculate conception" when "revealed" without its spiritual spin should rightly be called: the "immoral deception"!

(NOTE TO READER: had the Gospel tales been written to glorify the comings and goings of a Gentile man rather than those of a Jew, I, being a God-detested Gentile of Irish descent, assure you that my bold opinions and examination of the subject would be, deservedly, just as blistering and even more so! No one, no race of people, should be exempt from the intense scrutiny of Reason's Tribunal! The Catholic Church, through the subjugating efforts of its mind-manipulating priest-enforcers, has long held the Irish people in fear of the Church's power and its vengeful God; it has kept them living in ignorance of their true spiritual nature due to the Church's deceptive manipulations, a "pious" practice that has kept the Irish down on their knees for centuries. Much of that time, England imposed her will upon the religion-weakened Irish whom she has long dominated. It is hoped that one day, the folks who now attempt to "free the Irish" from all of the oppressions imposed upon them by the Catholic Church will be regarded as Caretakers of Liberty like the past patriots who struggled to "free the Irish," from the oppressions imposed upon them by England, are now regarded---especially, since it was a "Catholic" Pope, Adrian IV, who gave Henry II of England the permission and the "right" to enter Ireland for the purpose of enriching the Church with *"St. Peter's Pence"* . . .

> *It is not doubted, ...that Ireland and all those islands which have received the faith, belong to the Church of Rome; if you wish to enter that Island, to drive vice out of it, to cause law to be obeyed and St. Peter's Pence to be paid by every house, it will please us to assign it to you.*

> ---Pope Adrian IV

The above power-tripping Pope of the Catholic Church was "pleased" to place the sovereignty of Ireland under English control—Irish Catholics should remember this every time they genuflect and add their *"Pence"* to the collection plate. Along with England's abuse of the Catholics in Ireland that was sanctioned by the Pope—the black-robed, Church of Rome enforcers---have also added their own trespasses. For generations, they have controlled the religion-oppressed lives of the Irish from birth to death, they have defiled their children, and continue to feed off and impose upon the inherent goodness and spiritual nature of the compassionate, beguiled nature of the Irish. It is time to put these dirty, deceiving dogs and their domineering dogmas on trial—it is time to allow Reason's Tribunal to set the Irish free, truly free, from the oppressors of their hearts and their minds, their lives and their liberties! Thankfully, today, the Catholic Church in Ireland and the worship of its patron saint are now in decline as well they should be—but I digress . . .)

It would not be an overstatement to declare Gabriel's "Annunciation" role in the "immoral deception" as being thought of as little more than an act of pandering as a pimp for #3 in securing Mary's "consent" to "sacred insemination." When the familiar details of this mythology-based tale and many other *Bible* stories are presented in this bold manner, without the pious hype, would they still be deemed "sacred" affairs worthy of our consideration, our belief, and our financial support? Can the Creator of eternal torment, I repeat, "can the Creator of eternal torment," really be considered a "loving" and a "merciful" God---only religion, when preaching such absurdities, can have it both ways and get away with it. Shouldn't we, instead, be questioning in Reason's Tribunal, the fables and claims of Judeo-Christianity rather than accepting them without question--- accepting them without any **"facts and evidence"** that proves they are legit and believable?

Only religion can impose upon us with impunity and receive Constitutional protection to do so---only religion can "overshadow" us and get away with making the debauchery of a young woman appear as a blessed event—a debauchery that we are made to believe resulted in her non-physical, non-sexual impregnation and, therefore, her "divine" de-flowering is supposed to be deemed by the imposed-upon as an "immaculate conception" —a religious "improvement," no doubt, on the sexual intercourse (overshadowing!) that took place so often in Pagan mythology between the gods above and the irresistible daughters of men below where this imposing tale about Jesus being "celestially-begotten" owes its origin---is this not more evidence of God (gods) being created in man's carnal image! Surely it must follow then that all the male gods above have continually lusted after human females, get sexually aroused, and do what comes naturally when being in such a divine state---commence "immaculate penetration"! Why, therefore, does our present male God (according to His script-writers) deem it so detestable (especially to His sterling reputation) for folks to "engage in" the physical, lust-filled, sexual relations that He wants everyone to involve themselves with in order to produce offspring, when He is the Guy responsible for setting up this world, His finest Creation, so that folks will be compelled by their natural, lusting, carnal impulses to follow His command to be fruitful and to multiply--- certainly He didn't intend that the propagation of the human race be done in the "immaculate" overshadowing way preferred by His sexually- dysfunctional script-writers who promote the belief that sex is filthy, sex is sin, and carnal existence is evil when He, God, intended otherwise---that it be done by His preferred method---having sexual intercourse!---shocking isn't it?

Whosoever looketh on a woman to lust after her hath committed adultery with her already in his heart. And if thy right eye offend thee, pluck it out, and cast it from thee: for it is profitable for thee that one of thy members should perish and not that thy whole body should be cast into hell. And if thy right hand offend thee, cut it off, and cast it from thee: for it is profitable for thee that one of thy members should perish, and not that thy whole body should be cast into hell.

---Matthew 5:28-30

And, of course, we all know what lies in store for every adultery- committing, male heart that has lusted even for a nano-second! *"Yes, Virginia, you make a good point: whosoever looketh on a man to lust after him is obviously exempt from this "Shalt Not" Commandment and its horrible, hellish consequences---lusting in your heart, as we all know from reading the inspired Bible, is the moral equivalent of committing murder! ---James 2:10. Yes, Virginia, you were given that name for a damn good reason!"* Surely then, the above plucking/cutting remarks made by the Taliban-minded Jesus, if truly believed and followed, would result in millions upon millions of folks being totally eye-less and handless in our God-loving, God-believing, God-trusting, God-following nation alone---including clergyman (except for Catholic priests who, seemingly, only lust after children) are exempt from performing self-mutilation and that's just fine with the Big Guy! If, however, adultery is committed in one's "heart," why pluck out an eye? ---and since we *"looketh"* with both eyes, shouldn't both eyes be plucked out? Incidentally, how is it possible for a one-handed man to cast away his other offending hand? ---"Hey, buddy, can you lend me a hand?" According to Jesus' script-written words, the way to remove the "sin" of lust from our lives is to remove the sensory organ(s) that perceives it and since carnal desire (lust) can be perceived through all of our five senses, what is one to do when aroused? ---go pluck yourself? Believing and following the body and soul-saving instructions of Jesus, the Good Shepherd, will cause many of His flock's members to end up, if not butchered, then totally blinded and completely plucked-over! ---how true! The only advice I can give to you about this evil, brutal, and sicko plucking tale is the following: if your *Bible "offend thee,"* cast it from thee as far as you pluckin' can---problem solved! ---kvk

If, however, non-sexual procreation is really God's preferred method of doing business, He should have given human beings the means to accomplish it---but since He didn't, He must have found no fault with our enjoyment of sexual relations---the way He obviously intended human procreation to be carried out! Isn't it counter-intuitive (and even blasphemous!) to believe, therefore, that God would "inspire" His script-writing biographers to stigmatize man's natural, sexual desires and behaviors by making them into sinful activities---activities that He, in all of His divine wisdom, purposely designed for man and woman to engage in and actually encouraged in order to populate the world? It doesn't make any sense that God would be displeased with our doing something He wants us to do---right? To believe otherwise, then it was God who intentionally made sinners out of all of us from day one just for following His perfect *Bible*-orders to get out there and start making babies? Isn't it more likely that a script-writer of the *Bible* who harbored puritanical and pathological hang-ups about sexual activity would have a "pious" need to create an "immaculate conception" for his created God? ---is this not more evidence of God being created in the image of messed-up men who believe themselves to be more spiritual-minded than He?

We must overcome the sexual hang-ups that the sexually repressed script-writers of religion have imposed upon us---sexual hang-ups that have screwed-up so many lives, caused so much misery and frustration in the world through their sick, "puritanical" beliefs and their condemnation of sex as a filthy habit! Members of the clergy who sexually molest children or indulge in other deviant sexual behavior should be "revealed" as scriptural scofflaws and the uber-abusers of the *Bible*-words they hypocritically preach to others---for how great is their belief in God when they know with "absolute" certainty the price they will be made to pay for indulging their adulterous, less-than-immaculate, lust-filled, carnal appetites? Isn't the "sexemplary" behavior of such "pious" proselytizers and paragons of Christian-living proof-enough that the *Bible* is, in effect, bogus, harmful, and not to be believed especially when those who love to stick God's Word up our hind parts are counted among the *Bible's* worst defilers? If they, in their superior role as God's top agents, don't abide by the *Bible* and its rules why should we be expected to do so, the less than perfect, sinful flock that keeps these "revered" scam artists living in ease and splendor?

For all of the many incidents of sexual misconduct and sexcesses reported about these anointed, "Come to Jesus," preachers of God's Word, I've yet to see or hear of any one of them eye-plucking and/or cutting-off their hands. Why is that? Why are we reluctant to blame God for the crimes He and His script-written "Word" have created---for, surely, the God who encourages such barbarities---the clawing-out of eyes and the chopping-off of hands---should be deemed a Taliban-type-sicko and psycho-monster instead of a merciful, loving-deity! ---surely, not as someone deserving of adoration---and any *Bible*-thumper who preaches the godliness and sacredness of committing such *Bible*-abominations should be deemed a sicko-psycho as well!

Most God-heads would probably agree that it was their loving God who made man into a carnal, sensual being with the senses necessary to exist and to survive, to reproduce and to replenish our species---that it was their loving God who has given man and woman the sexual organs necessary to create other human beings and the means to stimulate those organs through none other than "LUST" --sexual desire and sexual arousal---and for that we should *"Praise the Lord"*! Then, their loving God commands human beings to populate the world---and that can only happen when folks have "God-designed, God-approved" sex! Then, for some strange reason, their loving, script-written, Semitic God decides to lay a guilt-trip on everyone for doing what He wants us to do---what the hell! What could have caused a loving God to become a pluckin' son of a bitch---a God who equipped us with sexual organs that are activated by lust and then sets about to denounce lust as an abomination---an evil that will send everyone off to hell? Where, oh where would Semitic religions be without the use of guilt and fear, the use of threats and intimidation? Because we are human beings who cannot escape the natural instincts and natural inclinations that God has made our bodies subject to, the "inspired" script-writers of Semitic theology were able to use this innate and inescapable fact of life to their sick, "pious" advantage by turning our natural, God-given desires for sex and procreation into vile, sinful activities in order to be able to pluck us over and over and over again by such a devious deception! Of course, as all devious, deceiving, Semitic religions teach us, it is only through the hocus-pocus rituals of clergy that God's wrath is kept from raining down cats and dogs, eyes and hands upon us and our terrible, lustful lives while helping to keep us on the glorious path, with no missing parts, to taking up residence in one of those many, many rooms in the sky-mansion made just for believers! --- how bountiful are the hearts of Jesus and His exemplary clergy when we are deceased!

The reason the advocates of Semitic religions (who just happen to be well skilled in the art of using of guilt to serve their needs!) are so eager to have every possessor of a human nature believe that they are all guilty of being lustful sinners---despite God's commanding to us to have sex in order to be fruitful and to multiply---is so that there will always be a need for them, the parasitic clergy, to clean-up our dirtied-by-lust slate and put things right with God. In doing so, these scheming bastards---scam artists all---by preaching the imposing, guilt-tripping, script-written words written in their "holy" books by like-minded psychopaths---books that criminalize and stigmatize God's intended-sexual activities for man and woman to engage in---not only gain for themselves tremendous plucking power over others, but they have created a continuous source of income without their having to work to acquire any of it! ---such a deal! ---and all it took was words in a book written by who knows who!

I digress here to take note of some more "pious" pluckings---Jesus, we're told, (because of His weak, less-than-godly, self-interests and human nature!) lived in fear, I repeat, "lived in fear" of His "chosen people" for they, we're told, sought to kick His ass and kill Him---*John* 7:1. *"Yes, Virginia, God Almighty, Creator of the Universe, actually lived in fear of losing His life by the hands of His "chosen people" ---imagine that!"* Yet, we are to believe that a fearful and cowardly Jesus had, somehow, found the fortitude, grit, and courage to face and endure the agonies of His crucifixion---a crucifixion witnessed by none of his forsaking, disciple biographers (*Matthew, Mark, Luke*, and *John*) who had all run off during His arrest but, nonetheless, they were able to inform us, without error of course, about each and every word that was spoken by Pontius Pilate and about all of the other day's many events they hadn't been witness to---really? ---must have been someone with pen in hand, no doubt, hanging around in the bushes again!

I'm certain that no one experiencing the excruciating torments of "crucifixion" would not have ended them ASAP if they could have---and a fearing-for-His-life-Jesus could have and would have if He really had the means to! Jesus, according to His *Bible*-script only had to "die" (which He supposedly was born to do---not be "crucified" to atone for the curse He placed upon Adam for his eating of an apple---for the sentence God placed upon Adam was *"thou shalt surely die"* ---not *"thou shall surely be crucified"* and as we all know, that sentence was carried out---for Adam was long, long dead before Jesus came to life---His suffering on the cross, obviously, was just an added, heart-tugging bonus---a scam artist's way of eliciting more sympathy for this God-turned-man/man-turned-God! "Are you following all of this, Virginia? ---your eyes appear to be bleeding!" On the other hand, Jesus, the immaculately conceived King of the Jews, "deserved" to suffer for all the misery, torment, bloodshed, and death that He and His "Good News" ministry has caused and continues to cause! Besides, how "immaculate" was Jesus' birth when He had to make His divine entrance into this world emerging from a woman's you know what? ---and while on the subject of being "overshadowed" (screwed with and plucked over!) by religious beliefs:

Only religion can make the incoherent, non-sensical rantings (speaking-in-tongues) appear as a divine gift given, curiously, only to certain Christians (for uncertain reasons!) from the Holy Ghost who has a penchant for screwing with folks, (and little else!), as gleaned from the Gospels. Speaking-in-tongues is considered a "divine" gift that, curiously, no Pope has ever been blessed with even though all Christians believe that the Pope is expressly "hand-picked" by the Holy Ghost and "guided" by Him, at least the benevolent ones—the evil ones, the fornicating and murdering Popes, were, obviously, selected and guided by someone or something else! Speaking-in-tongues is, obviously, a totally useless gift that no one could possibly benefit from except by those who have a need to beguile others with the attention-grabbing spectacle of gibberish-speaking morons and maniacs. Even an *OT* script-writer, (speaking in tongue-in-cheek, no doubt,) tells us a tale that tests the limits of religious credulity for it involves our having belief in the antics of a talking jackass (speaking-in-animals)! At least that former dumb-ass had horse-sense enough to speak in a coherent manner in order to get its message across as told in the 22nd chapter of *Numbers.*

The asses of today who speak-in-tongues should, at least, take note of that improvement and step up their game to get their mesmerizing, Holy Ghost-inspired message across to others who don't speak or understand their bizarre rantings. Surely, for the Holy Ghost to involve Himself in creating these theatrical, vocal-seizures, there must be a vitally important, spiritual message behind them—right? Or else, the HG possesses a unique sense of "overshadowing" humor! While on the subject of talking asses, in Muhammad's case, the mule-driving man, a talking mule might have been able to accomplish more with him than a talking angel ever could have because of the Prophet of Islam's intimacy with their kind!

Imagine, if you will, the Holy Ghost---in a world filled with need---finding the time to go through all the trouble and effort to intervene in the affairs of man only to make *Bible*-buffoons babble-on like deranged psychos just for its entertainment value—incredible! If, however, it should turn out that there is no profound message behind such lunacy, then those who perform its antics should, at least, make speaking-in-tongues a more amusing and a more spectacular spectacle by doing it while standing on one leg, balancing a *Bible* on one's head and playing an air-guitar! (I think it is a possibility, from the fanciful stretch of its parts, that some of the *Bible's,* wondrous tales may have been composed in an Irish pub—slainte!) While on the subject of religious wonders, there is the amazing substance known as "Holy Water" which is just plain ol' tap water that has been spiritually enhanced (probably by the HG!) by being blessed by a priest (often by a pedophile priest!). Holy Water has been credited, especially in the past, with the ability to cure every malady known to mankind—if, however, it should fail to perform for believers as touted, they should just return the unused portion for a full refund—no questions asked!

...religion continues to be granted far too much respect and too little critical examination in our culture and mainstream media. We need to change the cultural climate so as to make supernatural, occult, and faith-based claptrap feel unwelcome and to make adults ashamed of the blithe surrender of their otherwise sound minds to idiocy.

---Jack Huberman, *The Quotable Atheist*

That which is highly esteemed among men is abomination in the sight of God.

                                   ---Jesus, *Luke* 16:15

Therefore, the *Bible* and the *Koran* being highly esteemed among men are certainly abominations, too, but don't take my word for it! ---kvk

Everyone must obey the state authorities, because no authority exists without God's permission, and the existing authorities have been put there by God.

                                   ---Romans 13:1

That's right, folks, Hitler operated his Death Camps with God's permission, I repeat, "Hitler operated his Death Camps with God's permission"! —and if you don't believe the above *Bible*-statement, the above *Bible*-fact to be true, what does that make you? ---kvk

Do Americans truly "trust in" and "live under" the likes of Jehovah/Jesus bin Laden, the Semitic deity whose criminal behavior included the destruction of the unalienable rights---the lives, the liberties, and the happy pursuits---of entire nations of non-Jews? Are we truly proud, as a freedom-loving people, to admit that we "trust in" and "live under" a racist, ethnocidal, Hebrew Hitler! If our nation, in truth, had "trusted" in this bigoted, cruel and unusual, murderous Monster, and lived "under" Him by obeying His every infallible and inerrant Word, what need would there have been for the "abominations" of the Declaration of Independence, the American Revolution, and the *"highly esteemed"* Constitution of the United States?

Surely, the trio of the above-listed, American *"abominations"* in the "sight" of God all undeniably proclaim: "IN GOD WE TRUST NOT"! Thankfully, Colonial Americans had placed their "trust" in the secular-minded founding fathers and the secular-minded Sons of Liberty to achieve their hard-won independence from freedom-destroying English rule and to secure their *"highly esteemed,"* God-loathing ***unalienable rights***"! It was solely upon their long-sufferings, their noble sacrifices, and their valiant actions that, clearly, were not in step with God's "Word" as stated above in *Luke* 16:15, that enabled a defiant America to free herself from the oppressions imposed by England, a tyrannical government. Why, therefore, do we bestow credit upon another freedom-destroying tyrant, the God of Judeo-Christianity, for our nation's founders' secular and heretical accomplishments in defying religious authority and securing our freedoms? Thankfully, the God-damned "abominations" of Semitic theology: ***"Life, Liberty and the pursuit of Happiness"*** are still *"highly esteemed"* across this secularly-begotten nation living "UNDER DELUSION"! If one were tasked with finding a suitable motto to explain the moral and intellectual decay---the physical decline of people's lives and living conditions that occurred during the religion-dominated Dark and Middle Ages in Europe, it surely would have been: "IN GOD WE TRUST AND UNDER GOD WE WITHER"!

> *And now that Christianity is firmly established* (referring to the Dark and Middle Ages---kvk) *what do we find? 'The kingdom of heaven upon earth'? On the contrary, a moral and intellectual degradation unparalleled in human history.*

---Lloyd M. Graham

> ***...however unwilling the partisans of the Christian system may be to believe or acknowledge it, it is nevertheless true that the age of ignorance commenced with the Christian system. There was more knowledge in the world before that period than for many centuries afterwards and as to religious knowledge, the Christian system, as already said, was only another species of mythology, and the mythology to which it succeeded was a corruption of an ancient system of theism.***

---Thomas Paine

As a freedom-loving, progressive people, 21st century Americans are, unfortunately, still living in ***"the age of ignorance"*** that ***"commenced with the Christian system."*** We are still believing in the legitimacy and veracity of the biblical accounts of Creation; we are still convinced that God "spoke" the Universe into existence; we are still certain that Adam and Eve, along with Noah and his containment vessel were actual physical entities. We are still believing these things because we were never educated to disbelieve or to doubt them, never shown the ***"facts and evidence"*** that would "reveal" them to be re-worked tales stolen from more-ancient, more knowledgeable Pagan cultures and modified to accommodate the self-serving purposes of

154

Semitic theology and its Semitic interests.

We must begin to wage the long-overdue *"revolution in the system of religion"* against the *"age of ignorance"* that commenced with belief in Semitic theologies—theologies that have continued to operate unimpeded throughout the centuries—theologies that are still proud to declare their love for a Heavenly Hitler who destroyed entire nations of innocent people—theologies that continue to shamelessly promote the "sacredness" of indulging in wickedness as long as it is done in the name of God— parasitic theologies that feed off of our ignorance of their fraudulent foundations. We must begin Reason's Tribunal to gain our freedom, at last, from mankind's ever-present threat to *"Life, Liberty and the pursuit of Happiness."* We must begin to *"Question with boldness"* the scriptural foundations of all Semitic religions and, in doing so, neutralize their malevolence and avoid the dire consequences that lie in wait for us because of their uncontested status. We must begin to recognize that the greatest threat to mankind, from the ancient to the modern world, has always been and continues to be, the so-called "revealed" scriptures of Semitic religions and their ungodly dogmas which we unwittingly accept as being legitimate because of our imposed indoctrinations that forbid anyone from questioning them.

The supposed "God-given," "God-inspired" words of the *Bible* and the *Koran* teach their imposed-upon fan clubs to have contempt for those considered outside the fold of their group of believers, and, in doing so, these books will forever remain a threat to civilization and to world peace because they continually promote division, distrust, racism, sexism, exclusion, intolerance, vengeance, bloodshed, and supremacism against all who don't fit their sacred mold and thus the origin of the "us" and "them" religious mindset was born! The Fourth of July that Americans proudly celebrate is only a "partial" Independence Day because of religion's continuing imposition and interference in our lives and in our nation's affairs—let us make it "whole" by completing the liberating job begun by our nation's secular-minded founders—let us begin making reason, sanity, and knowledge, rather than sentiment, fear, and ignorance, dominate mankind! Let us honor the birthday of our nation by crediting the enlightened nation-builders whose intent and mission was to separate and protect a freedom-loving nation of people from its constant enemy--- freedom-destroying religions---we will truly honor them and their noble efforts when we make the effort to remove religion from the driver's seat and take control over our nation's steering wheel!

It is important to note here that it was not *"Nature's God,"* the endower of *"Life, Liberty and the pursuit of Happiness"* mentioned in America's Declaration of Independence that sought to alienate us from these, our *"unalienable rights"* —it is only the manufactured Gods of religion—the created pious frauds of contrived scriptures—the bogus Gods made in the image of those who would subdue us with guile and guilt—it is they who would deny us our natural instincts and natural rights. Freedom-loving, freedom-defending Americans need to firmly establish that the term *"Nature's God"* and the word *"Creator"* used intentionally in our nation's founding document do not refer to, or correspond to, any Semitic deity as many Jews and Christians would have us believe.

Had the signers of the Declaration truly been devout, thankful, and grateful Christians who deemed America a Christian nation founded upon Judeo-Christian traditions and principles, they would not have failed to credit Jehovah or Jesus Christ for having created all men *"equal"* and for having endowed all men with the *"unalienable rights"* that this famous document is famous for proclaiming? This eye-opening omission was done on purpose because the Infidels who had a hand in drafting and signing this heretical proclamation were of the opinion that there truly was an important distinction to be made between belief in an impersonal God and belief in a personal one. They deliberately chose, instead, to credit *"Nature's God"* as the source of our natural rights. Surprisingly, for a so-called "Christian" nation, the men who signed the Declaration of Independence did not make any mention of Jesus Christ or credit Him for having any part in America's founding—that, in my opinion, was a profoundly telling and completely overlooked decision on their part!

The author of the Declaration of Independence and its many signers were of one mind when they decided to pay tribute to an impersonal and non-scripted *"Creator,"* the generic deity of Deism, for such a deity did not endanger anyone—a benevolent deity whom they believed didn't interfere in the affairs of man. They knew from history that promoting belief in any of the partisan Gods of malevolent Semitic religions, Jehovah, Jesus, Allah, endangered all who dared to stand in their way or denied their existence. Making a distinction between the God of Deism and the God(s) of Theism in our nation's founding document was a revolutionary act in and of itself and a Declaration of Independence, not only from Mother England, but from scripted, Semitic theology, too.

It was our founders' knowledge of the cruel and unusual history of the "old time religion" that gave them pause in assigning a more personal name to America's perceived providential benefactor. Certainly, it was their knowledge of Judeo-Christianity's oppressive and peace-destroying past that prevented the mention of Jehovah or Jesus in their forward-looking document. Fortunately, due to other enlightened, forward-looking, secularist interventions and input occurring throughout the ages of Western civilization, the violence-prone, scripture-inspired mindset of Jewish and Christian jihadists that sought to impose the biased and brutal will of their personal God: Jehovah/Jesus, has been significantly sidelined. Unfortunately, due to an obvious lack of secularist intervention having taken place in the Islamic world, Allah, the personal God of Muslims, has now taken over command of the sacred duties of Semitic Divinity to darken our days! Those who declare that America's foundation is rooted upon Judeo-Christian principles and traditions should explain why George Washington allowed the following declaration to be squarely stated in the 1797 Treaty of Tripoli which was ratified unanimously in the Senate and signed into law by President John Adams who made it known:

> ***...the government of the United States of America is not, in any sense, founded on the Christian religion . . . In the formation of the American government . . . it will never be pretended that any persons employed in that service had interviews with the gods, or were in any degree under the influence of heaven.*** (that bears repeating! ---kvk)

If the list of grievances and abuses outlined in the historical Declaration of Independence were deemed harsh and intolerable to Colonial Americans, they pale in comparison to the list of horrors awaiting us today under the encroaching "Sharia law" of Islam. Taxation without representation seems a mild complaint when compared to public stonings, whippings, beatings, mutilations, cutting off of hands and feet, beheadings, terrorism, etc., etc. The globally-acting mindset of terror of our present time arises solely from the Muslim fervor for Islam's unquestioned religious beliefs which grew from the unquestioned, bloodied, fisted-hand nature of the religious beliefs of Judeo-Christianity. If anyone has need to continue believing in a deity, let it be ***"Nature's God"*** and not any part of the three-headed, Semitic monster known as Jehovah, Jesus, Allah. If anyone has need to continue believing in a religion—let it be the benevolent deism of our nation's founders and not the malevolent "us" and "them" Semitic theisms that continue to inspire and promote deadly atrocity—let it be the benevolent deism that does not require anyone to kill or impose upon one another—that does not require the need of a Devil, a Hell, a parasitic priesthood, or self-serving, anonymous script-writers in order to get the "Word" out!

It has now become a matter of survival for freedom-loving people everywhere that the scripted scriptures of all "revealed" faiths raised upon foundations of fraudulent texts be challenged and exposed—texts that authorize, support, sponsor, and justify the enslavement, brutal punishment, and/or total annihilation of those considered outside the fold—texts that continually inspire and condone, in the names of Jehovah, Jesus, Allah, the commission of unspeakable, bloodshedding atrocities against such folks ("them") time and again by those who believe that they ("us") act "under" divine command and "under" divine blessing. In the name of all the ideals that America stands for and continues to struggle to achieve: freedom, equality, justice, decency, fairness, etc., it remains a top priority of Reason's Tribunal to expose these Semitic Gods as frauds, their blasphemies as victim-less crimes, and their scriptures as *"human productions."*

"UNDER GOD" went the criminal *Bible*-terrorists and *Bible*-jihadist: Crusaders, Inquisitors, Conquistadors, and the criminal *Old Testament* UNDER-lings whose merciless, murderous UNDER-takings plundered and exterminated, time and again, entire nations without cause or second-thought, I repeat, "without cause or second thought"! UNDER GOD's express command and perceived blessing these unoffending nations were put to the sword and utterly destroyed:

...thou shalt save alive nothing that breatheth.

---Jehovah (off His meds! ---kvk)

---*Deut.* 20:13-17

These unprovoked atrocities were carried out upon innocent men, women, children, (and animals) simply because they were perceived, I repeat, "perceived" by Jewish jihadists as an *"abomination"* and a blasphemous profanity to Jehovah, aka Merciful Jesus! Apparently, Jehovah/Jesus is "Akbar," too, and His Reign of Terror---an inspiration and a justification from glorified, Semitic scripture for the Muslim-mania of today's Islamic jihadists and their mindset of madness---an inspiration and justification for murder and mayhem which has its pious precedence in Judaism!

Whenever we read the obscene stories, the voluptuous debaucheries, the cruel and torturous executions, the unrelenting vindictiveness, with which more than half the Bible is filled, it would be more consistent that we called it the word of a demon

than the Word of God. It is a history of wickedness that has served to corrupt and brutalize mankind; and for my part, I sincerely detest it as I detest anything that is cruel.

---Thomas Paine

The modern, Western world is "perceived" by Muslim-maniacs as an *"abomination"* and a blasphemous profanity to Allah and, therefore, they consider it their sacred duty to "reform" the Earth, too, following the example of another Semitic tribe, in order to "purify" it and make it ready for Allah and His divine justice to rule the world. To them, America is today's "Land of Canaan" and all of its inhabitants must likewise be slated for annihilation by who else, but present-day, genocidal, Semitic fanatics to make room for Allah-addicts, *Koranimals*, and prayer-rug-kneeling enthusiasts. And who are these purifying reformers? —none other than suicide-bombers, mutilating torturers, abusers of women, abusers of children, Infidel-beheaders, etc., and of course, last but not least, the cowardly and clever Muslim clerics and bin Laden-types who exhort such activities but who always seem to avoid risking their own lives in the "glorious" battles of Islam's "Holy War"!

Why would any member of Muslim clergy or Osama bin Hiden take the chance of losing life or limb in atrocities like those carried out on 9/11 when they can lurk in the shadows and still perform their parasitic duties by manipulating countless others to carry out the blessed necessities of jihad? —countless other Muslims whom they indoctrinate to consider themselves as being the "chosen-of-God." Does such cultural chutzpah sound familiar? —a cultural chutzpah that causes countless Muslim-maniacs to believe that only they act exclusively on God's behalf (more cultural chutzpah!) — countless others in the Islamic world whom they make capable of committing mindless, remorseless atrocity in God's name—countless others whom they passionately inspire to don suicide-vests or place them on children. Only such indoctrinated folks are capable of contemplating and committing all manner of evil and wickedness under the banner of "sacred" duty—Allah-lujah! Be assured that if greater, more agonizing torture methods are ever discovered, it will be in the name of God that they are employed!

THOU SHALT NOT KILL!

---Jehovah (on His meds! ---kvk)

---*Deut.* 5:17

However, THOU SHALT KILL and do so without compunction when God's "Word" demands KILLING—and, like Jehovah's Word, the *Bible*—Allah's Word, the *Koran*, surely demands it! Under Allah's express command and perceived blessing went the 9/11 perpetrators to become religion's maniacal martyrs and mindless murderers of the Modern Age. The brutality of theologically-begotten terror—from torture and mutilation, to death by stoning, beheading, incineration, etc., —hasn't really changed much over the religion-darkened and religion-dominated centuries---it is only the weapons and tactics that differ. The only justification needed for all of the above scripture-inspired madness to be carried out was simply having belief in mere "words" written on the pages of books believed to be "authored" by the Almighty. The following words written about the *Bible* are from the pages of *The Age of Reason*—they are entirely applicable, as well, to the *Koran*:

> ***People in general do not know what wickedness there is in this pretended Word of God. Brought up in habits of superstition, they take it for granted that the Bible is true, and that it is good; they permit themselves not to doubt of it, and they carry the ideas they form of the benevolence of the Almighty to the book which they have been taught to believe was written by His authority. Good heavens! It is quite another thing; it is a book of lies, wickedness and blasphemy; for what can be of greater blasphemy than to ascribe the wickedness of man to the orders of the Almighty?***

---Thomas Paine

Reason's Tribunal, however, will ***"permit"*** ourselves ***"to doubt of it"*** ---***"this pretended Word of God,"***: Semitic scriptures---and to challenge their demonic words that instruct all Muslims that they are under divine obligation to destroy the entire non-Muslim world—demonic words that had previously, in a similar manner as expressed in the *Bible*, instructed the *OT* Jews to murder anyone whom they perceived as standing in their way.

In the name of Jehovah, Jesus, and Allah, an ocean of innocent blood has been shed and will continue to be shed. Only by educating ourselves and enlightening our deluded enemies about their supremacist-minded, Semitic religious beliefs and religious endeavors, their contrived, "sacred" origins, and their bogus, God-authorized incitements to violence, can we begin to achieve a sane and peaceful world, a secure future for humanity. Because of just one man's courageous efforts, the truth about Christianity's contrived roots has been made known:

> *I here close the subject of the Old Testament and the New. The evidence I have produced to prove them forgeries is extracted from the books themselves, and acts, like a two-edged sword, either way. If the evidence be denied, the authenticity of the scriptures is denied with it, for it is scripture evidence; and if the evidence be admitted, the authenticity of the books is disproved. The contradictory impossibilities contained in the Old Testament and the New put them in the case of a man who swears for and against. Either evidence convicts him of perjury, and equally destroys reputation. Should the Bible and the New Testament hereafter fall, it is not I that have done it. I have done no more than extracted the evidence from the confused mass of matter with which it is mixed, and arranged that evidence in a point of light to be clearly seen and easily comprehended; and, having done this, I leave the reader to judge for himself, as I have judged for myself. ...I have shown in all the foregoing parts of this work* (The Age of Reason) *that the Bible and the Testament are impositions and forgeries; and I leave the evidence I have produced in proof of it to be refuted, if anyone can do it; and I leave the ideas that are suggested in the conclusion of the work to rest on the mind of the reader; certain, as I am, that when opinions are free, either in matters of government or religion, truth will finally and powerfully prevail.* (that bears repeating! --- kvk)*

> ---Thomas Paine

Because the *"authenticity"* of the "undoubted" *Koran* was established upon the *"contradictory impossibilities"* and irrefutable *"proof"* of *"impositions and forgeries"* contained in the *Bible*, surely then, *"when opinions are free ...in matters ...of religion"* the truth about the *Koran* and its corrupt foundation will *"finally and powerfully prevail,"* too! In Reason's Tribunal, the *"facts and evidence"* of a purloined and re-purposed "heathen" mythology adjusted to serve the religionized purposes of *"power and profit"* —the hidden Pagan origins of all Semitic religions—will be brought to light:

We are all aware that Egyptian-Babylonian culture set European civilization going; but few modern people have observed the fact, so important in the history of morals and religion, that Egypto-Babylonian culture also set Hebrew civilization going.

---James H. Breasted

It is curious to observe how the theory of what is called the Christian Church sprung out of the tail of the heathen mythology. A direct incorporation took place in the first instance, by making the reputed founder to be celestially begotten. The trinity of gods that then followed was no other than a reduction of the former plurality, which was about twenty or thirty thousand; the statue of Mary succeeded the statue of Diana of Ephesus; the deification of heroes changed into the canonization of saints; the Mythologists had gods for everything; the Christian Mythologists had saints for everything; the Church became as crowded with the one as the Pantheon had been with the other, and Rome was the place of both. The Christian theory is little else than the idolatry of the ancient Mythologists, accommodated to the purposes of power and revenue; and it yet remains to reason and philosophy (aka Reason's Tribunal! ---kvk) **to abolish the amphibious fraud.**

---Thomas Paine

I have recently been examining all the known superstitions of the world, and do not find in our particular superstition (Christianity) **one redeeming feature. They are all alike, founded upon fables and mythologies. ...The day will come when the mystical generation of Jesus, by the Supreme Being as his father, in the womb of a virgin, will be classed with the fable of the generation of Minerva in the brain of Jupiter.**

---Thomas Jefferson

It is hoped that **"day"** of enlightenment will soon appear on the horizon, Mr. Jefferson---a day when truly wise men, guided by the light of reason and truth, will regard the mystical generation of Jesus as wholly fiction, and not as holy fact! It will, of course, take time for this to occur as so many folks have a vested interest in Christmas and its beguilings! No one, however, should celebrate the birth of a "pious" psychopath---Thomas Jefferson surely didn't!

Apparently, the author of the "historical" Declaration of Independence—as well as the "spiritual" Declaration of Independence given in the quote above—had more in mind than just the removal of a tyrannical government from our shores. Hasten the day when Reason's Tribunal will reveal the truth about fabricated, self-serving, religionized myths—will reveal the truth that will result in abolishing the *"amphibious fraud"* of Christianity and begin the noble mission that will neutralize the scripture-inspired mindset of terror that always accompanies Semitic theologies. Hasten the day, too, when the rationale utilized in *The Age of Reason* will be used to rid the entire world of Islamophobia—not from Muslim appeasement—not from Muslim annihilation—but from Muslim enlightenment.

> ***It has often been said, that anything may be proved from the Bible, but before anything can be admitted as proved by the Bible, the Bible itself must be proved to be true; for if the Bible be not true, or the truth of it be doubtful, it ceases to have authority, and cannot be admitted as proof of anything.*** (ditto for the *Koran*! ---kvk)

---Thomas Paine

Using only the *Bible's* own *"facts and evidence,"* Thomas Paine has proved that the so-called five books of Moses: *Genesis*, *Exodus*, *Leviticus*, *Numbers*, and *Deuteronomy*, are *"spurious, and that Moses is not the author of them."* Using only the *Bible's* own chapter and verse statements, he proved that the author of the above books of the *Bible* was a lying impostor and a fraud! Using Reason's Tribunal in the search for scriptural truth will prove, too, that Moses is a plagiarized, fictional character stolen from the ancient mythology and creation-lore of Arabia, Assyria, and Phoenicia. This fact is of great importance because believers of Islam, as well as Judaism and Christianity, regard Moses as an actual historical person and an infallible prophet; therefore, any theology that places emphasis on Moses and his intimacy with God should be exposed as being founded on the reworked Pagan mythology of anonymous authors. The first five books of the *Old Testament* which constitute the foundational literature of Judaism and Christianity should be regarded as complete fabrications because the mythical Moses is credited with writing them. In Thomas

163

Paine's proving that Moses is not their author, the *Bible* **"ceases to have authority."**

> **Take away from Genesis the belief that Moses was the author, on which only the strange belief that it is the word of God has stood, and there remains nothing of Genesis but an anonymous book of stories, fables, and traditionary or invented absurdities, or of downright lies.**

---Thomas Paine

> *Clever fellows, these Hebrew mythologists!   Not everyone can deceive his enemies and still be praised and defended by them.*

---Lloyd M. Graham

Clever fellows, indeed, who justify their selfish, script-writing pursuits and their vile aggressions by attempting to make the non-Jewish world believe that it was their beloved, Semitic God, Jehovah, who expressly authorized and demanded such activities be conducted for the personal benefit of Jews and Jews only---that their beloved God had made a promise to them that they would be possessors of a homeland and God surely keeps His promises! Clever fellows, indeed, who acquire what they want by attempting to make everyone believe that it is God who demands it---by attempting to make everyone believe that it is God who wants His "chosen" beneficiaries to be given, by any means necessary, this thing or that thing regardless of who must suffer or die in their acquiring of them. Isn't it quite interesting that Jehovah, who created the world in record time just by saying a few words, didn't think to make the earth a tiny tiny tiny bit bigger with just a word or two in order to give His "chosen" the land they so eagerly sought after without having to impose upon others or murder them to achieve His ends? ---very very very interesting! Clever fellows, indeed, who seek to deceive everyone with the inquiry-deflecting phrase: *"thus saith the Lord,"* in order to fulfill and secure their own self-interests without most folks becoming the wiser—and as we all know, or should know, that throughout much of the religion-dominated centuries, it was generally not a good idea to question what the Lord *"saith,"* ---that is until Reason's Tribunal made its appearance!

To prove beyond doubt that Moses is a manufactured man of myth, because of his older Pagan parallels, is just one of the keys that will help

164

unlock the mental shackles that keeps us in bondage to Semitic theologies—one of the keys that will help pull the plug on their fraudulent scriptures that have been imposed upon mankind for millennia. I leave this noble task of unshackling and plug-pulling to those more qualified to do so such as Thomas Paine, Thomas Jefferson, and other more recent inquisitors. The knowledge gained by their bold efforts to examine and retro-engineer the *Bible* and the *Koran* is vitally important for it reveals the ***"facts and evidence"*** of the older, Pagan sources of "revealed" Semitic scripture. It also reveals the ***"facts and evidence"*** that proves their prophets: Adam, Noah, and Abraham (Ibrahim), to be resurrected, mythological characters conscripted from more ancient Pagan sources as well. Since the Islamic faith considers it a denial of "divine truth" to reject any of its infallible prophets—revealing their previous non-Semitic existence in antiquity is of crucial importance in our noble attempt to debunk Semitic religions. In doing so, we will end the scripture-authorized madness that inspires their devout believers to indulge in terror and atrocity in the name of God—we will end the primacy, veracity, and literary authority of all Semitic scripture thus laying bare the fraudulent, self-serving claims of Judaism, Christianity, and Islam.

The destruction of all evidence of Christianity's gnostic and pagan source was 'the first work.' It was the evangelists themselves who started it, in Antioch, as stated in Acts. ...And of their followers, Edward Carpenter wrote thus: '...they took special pains to destroy the pagan record and so obliterate the evidence of their own dishonesty.'

---Lloyd M. Graham

The following religious elements and ideas, nearly all of which Christians believe to have been divinely revealed, and to belong exclusively to their religion, are of Pagan origin:

---John E. Remsburg, *The Christ*

(Son of God
Messiah
Mediator
The Word
The Ideal Man

Annunciation
Immaculate conception
Divine incarnation
Genealogies showing royal descent
Virgin mother
Angelic visitants
Celestial music
Visit of shepherd
Visit of Magi
Star of Magi
Slaughter of innocents
Temptation
Transfiguration
Crucified Redeemer
Supernatural darkness
Resurrection
Ascension
Descent into Hell
Second Advent
Unity of God
Trinity in Unity
Holy Ghost [Spirit]
Devil
Angels
Immortality of the soul
Last judgment
Future rewards and punishments
Heaven, Hell, and Purgatory
Fatherhood of God
Brotherhood of man
Freedom of the will
Fall of man
Vicarious atonement
Kingdom of God
Binding of Satan
Miracles
Prophecies
Obsession
Exorcism
The priesthood

Pope and bishops
Monks and nuns
Worship of Virgin
Adoration of Virgin and Child
Worship of saints
Worship of relics
Image worship
Inspired Scriptures
The cross as a religious symbol
Crucifix
Rosary
Holy water
Lord's Day [Sunday]
Christmas
Easter
Baptism
Eucharist
Washing of feet
Anointing
Confirmation
Masses for the dead
Fasting
Prayer
Auricular confession
Penance
Absolution
Celibacy
Poverty
Asceticism
Tithes
Community of goods
Golden rule and other precepts)

The Old Testament consists largely of borrowed myths. Nearly everything in Genesis, and much of the so-called history that follows, are but a recital of Assyrian, Babylonian, Chaldean, and other legends.

---John E. Remsburg

From such Assyrian sources, the legends of the creation of the earth and heaven, the garden of Eden, the making of man from clay, and of woman from one of his ribs, the temptation by the serpent, the naming of animals, the cherubim and flaming sword, the Deluge and the ark, the drying up of the waters by the wind, the building of the Tower of Babel, and the confusion of tongues, were obtained by Ezra.

---Dr. Draper, *Conflict*

For a thousand years the Hebrews were "polytheists" who "borrowed" their worshiped gods, (including Jehovah), from Assyria and Babylonia.

In addition to their national god, Jehovah, many of the Jews worshiped Baal, Moloch, and Tammouz, male deities, and Astarte, Aschera, and Istar, female deities. (the worship of the Semitic deity, Moloch, was marked by the sacrifice of children by their parents a tradition of a people who, later, found favor with the Lord of the *Bible*—imagine that! ---kvk)

---John E. Remsburg, *The Christ*

Monotheism existed in Pagan culture long before the Jews of a later period in their history came to practice it—Zoroaster and his earliest followers were monotheists! The monotheism of the Jews did not result from a divine revelation or intellectual superiority; it was chiefly the result of their religious intolerance—Jewish priests and kings tolerated no rivals to their dreadful God and made death the penalty for disloyalty to him. Intolerance, fear, and the threat of death—what would Semitic religions be without them!

The Jewish nation became monotheistic for the same reason that Spain, in the clutches of the Inquisition, became entirely Christian. (Intolerance, fear, and the threat of death---Oh those treasured Judeo-Christian traditions and principles that Americans are so proud to honor for laying the foundation stones of our nation! ---kvk)

---ibid.

Thanks to Jewish mono-mania—the belief in a personal and partisan, bloodthirsty and vengeful, national God—the Semitic roots of the religious mindset of terror began to grow and flourish becoming firmly established as evidenced and enumerated, time and again, in their Chutzpah Chronicles. In Reason's Tribunal, the unpleasant realities of the imposed monotheism of Judaism, Christianity, and Islam will be truthfully "revealed" as a pernicious blight, not as a perceived blessing upon society.

Thomas Paine contends, as do I, that the *Koran* was not written in Heaven and "revealed" to Muhammad by an angel as we are indoctrinated to believe; it was fabricated, as was the *Bible*, to be a Chutzpah Chronicle—designed for priestly purpose by the script-writing hands of ungodly, control-seeking parasites:

All national institutions of churches, whether Jewish, Christian or Turkish, appear to me no other than human inventions, set up to terrify and enslave mankind, and monopolize power and profit.

It bears repeating that a founding father has warned us that religions are but *"human inventions, set up to terrify and enslave mankind, and monopolize power and profit."* How right Mr. Paine was in describing mankind's religious past and in anticipating mankind's religious future. The following is an example of Mr. Paine's inspired "revelations" concerning "revealed" religion:

Admitting ...that something has been revealed to a certain person, and not revealed to any other person, it is a revelation to that person only. When he tells it to a second person, a second to a third, a third to a fourth, and so on, it ceases to be a revelation to all those persons. It is revelation to the first person only, and hearsay to every other, and consequently they are not obliged to believe it. It is a contradiction in terms and ideas, to call anything a revelation that comes to us at second-hand, either verbally or in writing. Revelation is necessarily limited to the first communication—after this it is only an account of something which that person says was a revelation made to him; and though he may find himself obliged to believe it, it cannot be incumbent on me to believe it in the same manner. For it was not a revelation made to me, and I have only his word for it that it was made to him. When Moses told the children of Israel that he received the two tables of stone from the hands of God, they were not obliged to believe him, because they had no other authority for it than his telling them so; and I have no other authority for it than some historian telling me so. ...When I am told that the Koran was written in heaven and brought to Mahomet by an angel, the account comes too near the same kind of hearsay evidence and second-hand authority as the former. I did not see the angel myself and, therefore, I have a right not to believe it.

We all have the right to disbelieve the delirium of those who are certain they have had intimate conversations with God in their dreams and those who claim of having had chats and visitations with an angel. We all have the right to disbelieve the information that results from anyone's so-called communication with imaginary friends. We all have the right to disbelieve miracles—we did not see Jesus walk on water or raise the dead to life, therefore, we all have the right to disbelieve such events ever occurred---we all have the right to disbelieve the only "written" evidence in existence that supports them. For if such evidence of miracles is not a complete fabrication, as I contend it is---it is, at best, based on nothing more than the second-hand, hearsay evidence "revealed" in Semitic scripture. We have only the words of impostors and anonymous authors who were never eye-witnesses or ear-witnesses to the events they write about; we have only their bogus words telling us Jesus did such and such a thing long long after the time it supposedly happened; we have only the words of unknown authors who tell us of events that supposedly occurred in the non-existent, make-believe, mythological Garden of Eden, events that no *Bible* script-writer could possibly have been witness to—duh!

In Matthew every message respecting the child Jesus is communicated by means of a dream; in Luke every announcement is made through the agency of an angel. Yet, after all, these Evangelists differ only in terms; for Luke's angels are created out of the same stuff that Matthew's dreams are made of, and the world is fast coming to a realization of the fact that this whole theological structure, founded on sleeper's dreams and angel's tales, is but 'The baseless fabric of a vision. (so, too, are the angel's tales that the whole theological structure of Islam is built upon! ---kvk)

---John E. Remsburg

*It's time also we examined that repeated statement, 'And God said.'
Why is it so persistently used throughout the Bible? This same book
tells us no man has seen God, yet every scriptural writer declares
he heard Him. Is this but primitive man mistaking his own inner
promptings for the voice of God, or is it a trick of the priestly trade?
It is the latter and used only to give what they wanted divine
authority. Spinoza, himself a Jew, said, whatever the Jews thought,
they asserted God said it. God speaks not until he speaks as man.
Once this simple fact is known, the trick no longer works.*

---Lloyd M. Graham

In the past, it was the *Bible*—today, the *Koran* is Public Enemy #1. It is the unwavering adversary of freedom-loving people everywhere for it instigates an Allah-ordained Holy War against all who cherish the **"Blessings of Liberty."** It is a radical book from which the radical religion of Islam arises and spreads its radicalism with its attempts to eradicate the entire non-Muslim world! It is a radical book that got its start and inspiration from Jewish radicals and their radical book that justified the radical annihilation of entire non-Jewish nations! It would be redundant to use the term: "radical Islam" or "radical Islamist" as if the religion of Islam itself played no part in creating terrorists and their radical behaviors—as if terrorists were somehow "misinterpreting" the *Koran* as I've heard some Islamic apologists declare! Would Islamic apologists prefer instead to have everyone believe that Allah "revealed" His "perfect" Word in such an imperfect, unclear, and obscure way in the *Koran* that it could possibly be subject to misunderstanding or misinterpretation? Really?

Even the mere act of one's merely touching the *Koran* without gloves or without one's prior purification, or holding it below one's waist or talking about this book without proper respect being shown can have "fatal" results—how radical is that? Upon its radical, jihad-encouraging pages, *Koranimals* find their radical authority and inspiration for oppressing, persecuting, killing, and committing atrocity against all who appear to stand in their way—Jews and Christians TAKE NOTE! —you are perceived by Muslims to be the Canaanites of this age—you are now on the receiving end of God's wrath this time around. Sometimes, it does appear that what goes around, comes around, too! Under the guise of sacred duty, the radical *Koran*, like its kindred, uber-radical *Bible*, incites intolerance, terror, death, and martyrdom against all unbelievers, against all non-Muslims in general and even certain Muslims in particular, with Allah's blessing:

...slay the idolaters wherever you find them.

---Allah (refusing His meds! ---kvk) ---*Koran* 9:5

To advance the radical agenda of Islam, the *Koran,* in essence, even instructs its believers to lie and to use deception such as feigned friendship (called taqiyya) as a radical yet necessary means to hide their jihad intentions—gullible, trusting Americans, (infidels) BEWARE! The wickedness of mind that is required for one to be willfully false in order to deceive unbelievers has been approved by Allah for doing His "sacred" work—imagine that (see quote below)! Imagine the above quote, a mere seven-word statement that, certainly, is not subject to any misinterpretation as written upon one of the *Koran's* undoubted pages---a mere seven-word statement is all that is necessary for the mindset of terror to manifest itself and justify its murderous activities—seven words! —seven words written on an "imperishable," always-in-existence tablet no less—seven words that were written an eternity before an idolator ever existed! Pass the lemonade, please!

> *Let not the believers take for friends or helpers unbelievers rather than believers. If any do that, in nothing will there be help from Allah; except by way of precaution, that ye may guard yourselves from them.*

---*Koran* 3:28

An early koranic scholar, Ibn Kathir, sheds light on the above verse, *"Allah prohibited His believing servants from becoming supporters of the disbelievers, or to take them as comrades with whom they develop friendships, rather than the believers."* Another early Koranic scholar, Al-Tabari, explained this verse: *"If you* (Muslims) *are under their* (infidels) *authority, fearing for yourselves, behave loyally to them, with your tongue, while harboring inner animosity for them. . . .Allah has forbidden believers from being friendly or on intimate terms with the infidels in place of believers---except when infidels are above them* (in authority). *In such a scenario, let them act friendly towards them."* Somebody, please break the news to the POTUS, his Cabinet members and to the members of Congress that Muslims, because of their belief in the *Koran,* cannot be trusted, but don't have them take my word for it!

172

The terror-filled tribulations of our times result from the scripture-generated, Muslim devotion to Allah and His seven sacred Words written in *Koran* 9:5 being put into practice at the highest level of veneration. To better understand the similar, terror-filled tribulations of Christianity's past, compare the above *Koran*-words of Most Merciful Allah with the following *"highly esteemed" Bible*-words of Most Merciful Jesus that, likewise, are not subject to any misinterpretation while keeping in mind the world-loving words given in *John* 3:16 that are so often repeated:

But as for these enemies of mine who did not want me to be their king: bring them here and slay them before me.

Jesus---*Luke* 19:27

I came to set the earth on fire; how I wish it were already kindled.

Jesus---*Luke* 12:49

Do not think that I have come to bring peace to the world; no, I did not come to bring peace, but a sword.

Jesus---*Matt.* 10:34

"Yes, Virginia, Jesus was a terrorist jihadist with many less-than-sacred interests similar to those of the Taliban, Al Queda, and Isis fanatics but, again, don't take my word for it! Yes, dear Virginia, Jesus has 'revealed' to us by His very own above Bible-words that He was neither a 'loving' nor a 'merciful' Guy but rather someone like the megalomaniac, Osama bin Laden, someone who much preferred, for the love of God, to add to the miseries of this world and deal in death and destruction. Jesus has 'revealed' to us by His very own Bible-actions that He was not someone who was willing to man-up and behave like the sacrificial lamb He was 'divinely-destined' to be—behave like someone who would willingly offer-up His own life in order to make an 'atonement' (at least in the minds of primitive-minded, uncivilized folks!) for Adam's sin and wipe the slate clean of all of the sins of the world. He has 'revealed' to us by His very own Bible-babble that He was not someone who, in strict obedience to Jewish-justice and Jewish-tradition would willingly become a scapegoat for "all" the trespasses of "all" others. He, however, has boastfully 'revealed' to us by His infallible Bible-words that He was someone who would shortly be returning

to earth 'in the clouds of Heaven' with great fanfare after His death on the cross in order to receive the power and the glory He so yearned for---Matt. 24:30---a promise, dear Virginia, His script-writers, obviously, couldn't make Mr. Pants on Fire deliver on---a promise He certainly didn't keep."

One would think that Jesus would have been over-the-moon to be mocked, beaten, and nailed to the cross knowing, as He did, the importance of His death and, consequently, what His martyrdumb held in store for Him and for all the world---knowing as He did, that He'd only remain dead for a very short time! Who wouldn't want to give up their physical existence knowing, with absolute certainty, that it would result in their becoming an Almighty, imperishable God as in the case of Jesus or as in the case of religious martyrs who also know, with absolute certainty, their deaths will result in their being in God's eternal presence? Hasn't Osama bin Laden become such a one in the minds of his Islamic fan club who picture him enjoying his eternity in Allah's warm and loving embrace and in the company of sex-crazed virgins whose only function is to dispense carnal pleasures to Islamic martyrs? (News Flash: The latest word on ObL is that he is enjoying His blissful eternity, not reveling in a Martyr's Paradise cavorting with scores of slutty virgins, but rather in preaching the "imperishable" *Koran* to the ocean's bottom-feeders about the greatness of Allah and the uber-concern that He has for His noble warriors who die in His service---"Allahu Akbar"!)

Does any of the above *Bible*-BS about Jesus truly impress you as being the unimpeachable designs, the unimpeachable efforts, and the unimpeachable words of an unimpeachable Divinity who *"so loved the world"* or do they impress you as being the fraudulent contrivances of primitive folks who created their personal God in their own ignorant, personal image to suit their own ignorant, personal, paleo-minded reckonings about what God should be and act like, and about what God should do for their exclusive benefit? Isn't it time for the bold questioning of Reason's Tribunal to separate the worthy wheat (if there be any!) from the worthless chaff of the Chutzpah Chronicles?

In *Matthew* 24:29-34, *Mark* 13:24-30, and again in *Luke* 21:25-32, Jesus declared that His "Second Coming" would occur before the folks who were *"alive in His time"* had all passed away, I repeat, "His 'Second Coming" would occur before the folks who were *"alive in His time"* had all passed away. Unfortunately, for members of His Christian fan club, due to the timely deaths of everyone who was *"alive"* in His generation, the "Second Coming" of Jesus and its accompanying "Rapture" will not be taking place as stated in the *Bible*. Reason's Tribunal has pulled the plug on this very telling Gospel-tale about Jesus' encore performance! This may come as a great shock and disappointment to all of Christendumb who look forward, with such longing in their hearts, to the destruction of the world---the torments of *Revelation* being imposed upon the unfaithful---the eternal punishment of all the sinful inhabitants of planet earth, and Jesus' highly anticipated coming in the clouds with great power and glory to gather up and reward His *Bible*-clutching ***"fools and hypocrites."*** Reason's Tribunal has "revealed" that the "Second Coming" of Christ is one of the greatest lies ever told in the *Bible* and we have the glaring, inerrant, literal words of Jesus Christ that prove it. The ***"fools and hypocrites"*** who cannot accept the fact that Jesus lied, want us now to believe that Jesus' foretelling about His "Second Coming" must undergo yet another "spin" cycle---they want us now to believe Jesus' encore performance was just put on hold momentarily—postponed for a more suitable time known only to God and, it seems, to certain Jehovah Witnesses who don't let their previous failures at determining Jesus' return date impede their efforts at determining another return date, which is certainly ANY MOMENT NOW!

Has anyone ever heard of a JW who, in anticipation of that glorious day taking place, gave away all that they had? Hmm! Is more proof required to show that the comings and goings of the *Bible* are but a human invention and not the inerrant Word of God? Doesn't a single error, a single falsehood, a single statement of Jesus that can be misconstrued found written upon on one of the *Bible's* perfect pages, destroy its credibility and its infallible status? Is more proof required to show that "all" Christians are compelled to be selective-believers when it comes to choosing which literal words of Jesus are the Gospel-truth worthy of belief and which literal words are embarrassments to His apologizing followers? Is more proof required to show that "all" Christians who proclaim their unwavering belief in "all" of the words supposedly authored by Jesus are, in the words of Thomas Jefferson, either ***"fools"*** or ***"hypocrites"*** or, more likely, both?

Based upon the above lie uttered by Jesus and the "spin" that necessarily followed it, the Pope and his miscreant minions along with all of the Mega-Church Moguls, in fact, "all" Christian leaders, clergy, and advocates who, incidentally, never deny themselves the physical pleasures of this world (nor spurn them like their "exemplary" mentor, Jesus, supposedly did), are beyond any doubt, the real deceivers of men whether they know it or not---for common-sense reveals that the Gospels are a fraud but yet they, all of the above, persist in keeping the Christ-story going for they are the only ones with a vested interest in spinning and spouting its reason-perverting, lie-infested, bogus tales in order to keep the longest-running, ever-lucrative scam afloat—for they are the only ones who benefit from the ignorance of **"fools"** who treat Christian clergy and Christian leaders as pedestaled aristocrats while supplying them with the financial support necessary for them to meet all of their pleasure-filled desires, their worldly needs, and more!

Incidentally, if the Pope (someone whom we are to believe is directly "guided" by God!) finds it necessary to leave his plush digs in Rome and journey to Canada to "apologize" for the actions of his beloved, Christian followers who acted under papal instruction, then it is self-evident that God's spokesman on earth is surely an impostor---an impostor who reveals not only his spiritual incompetence but that of the inerrant and infallible God who "guides" him! ---yet this is the befrocked buffoon that Christians the world over seek "spiritual" direction from---incredible! ---Man help us!

Incidentally, too, no amount of papal apologizing can undo or make right the brutality and the abuses committed by the Pope-directed Catholic Church against the indigenous peoples of Canada---has any Pope ever apologized for the hellish, unspeakable tortures and horrors of the Inquisition that their beloved Catholic Church carried out with papal approval? If the present Pope is truly intent on doing the right thing now, he should step-up and admit that the Catholic Church has "always" been about **"power and revenue"** and not about the spiritual improvement of mankind---he should have the decency and the humanity to put an end to the parasitic fraud---the deceiving scam known as Christianity---and end his days living amongst Canada's indigenous peoples to learn, first-hand, about each and every sin that Catholicism inflicted upon them and other innocent people in the name of his beloved and blessed Jesus! It is beyond comprehension why anyone would allow such an impostor with such a papal track record to tell us what spiritual and moral behavior is all about.

"Yes, Virginia, the Pope, his miscreant minions and Mega-Church Moguls will always have a scripted-sermon ready to assure you of Jesus' certain return and of His earnest desire to take you back home with Him to His many-roomed mansion in the sky—just be sure to drop off your earthly possessions and money to them before you go—the sooner, the better, for Jesus could arrive and take you away at any moment! After all, it does require a lot of money, goods, and services to keep these 'hypocrites' living in luxury and their institutions going strong, especially the Catholic Church!"

It does take a lot of money, too, to keep the non-Catholic, Christian Mega-Churches and their profit-seeking, pampered ministers living in their tithed-splendor. As for the ever-in-need, Catholic Church, there's the expense of running the grandiose, palatial estate known as the Vatican, an estate that a pious, self-denying, unmaterialistic Jesus would never have stepped foot in---would never have considered as His residence. There's the expense for the upkeep of extravagant Catholic cathedrals and churches around the world, and, of course, the very costly legal settlements between thousands of pedophile clergymen and the many thousands of their child victims.

Why the Pope doesn't sell the Vatican along with all of its many, many, many valuable treasures to pay-off the many many many victims of pedophile, Catholic priests is beyond me. Why the Pope doesn't do it just to give the many many many millions of dollars the sale would generate, to the poor as Jesus commanded, is also beyond me. *"Yes, Virginia, it is impossible for Christians---to believe that Jesus lied about His returning 'in the clouds of Heaven'—to believe that the Pope, his miscreant minions, and Mega-Church Dandies are deceivers and hustlers, not followers of Christ, since they all possess much more, I repeat, "much more" than just one shirt! ---Luke 3:11. It is impossible for Christians to believe that Christian clergy rape children---that Christian Churches cover-up their many transgressions---that Christian Churches are corrupt institutions always in need of the financial support of **'fools'** to fill the collection plates so that the above scammers can carry on their 'sacred' mission to prosper and live their 'exemplary' lives as pious **'hypocrites'**! Certainly, all Christians believe the words of the God-inspired, infallible script-writer who penned Acts 26:23, telling us in their "inspired" way that Jesus would be the very first to rise from death, I repeat, the very 'first' to rise from death—even though, according to the inerrant and infallible, God-inspired accounts of the other Gospel script-writers, regarding the supposed life-restoring miracles of Jesus alone, that He, Jesus, was not the first to rise from death—or the second—or even the third! Yes, Virginia, the Bible's words are not worthy of anyone's belief and neither are the words of its preaching advocates who cleverly enrich their pious-pretending-selves touting the Bible's disdain for the pleasures of this world! ---yeah, right!"*

> *Christ's birth in a manger and death on a cross are the lodestones that have attracted the sympathies of the world, and kept Him on the throne of Christendom; for sentiment rather than reason dominates mankind.*

> ---John E. Remsburg, *The Christ*

To evoke *"the sympathies of the world,"* the *Bible's* clever script-writers pulled out all of the stops when they obliged poor ol' Jehovah, a heartless murderer and an ethnic-cleansing tyrant who favored a chosen few, to be removed (in a third-part!) from a virgin's "immaculate" womb in the humblest of surroundings and so they presented us with the heart-warming, yet heart-saddening image of an adorable, little baby boy lying in a rustic hay trough within an animal enclosure reeking, no doubt, of feces and urine. Aaaahhh, poor baby, Jesus! Remember, that no matter how innocent or humble the Gospel-tale writers tried to make Jesus appear, it was all smoke and mirrors for He is still the criminal, Jehovah, after all—never forget that—oh, those cunning script-writers! Isn't it interesting that God, who, it is supposed, is genderless, could just as easily have chosen to be born a female? Hmm! Isn't it interesting, too, that the God of the *Bible,* a spiritual being with no sexual identity, is always represented as a male figure? Hmm, again! When you think about it, why would God have sexual identity in the first place? ---because the God of the *Bible* was made in man's image—He is man's creation—that's why!

And thus, Almighty God chose to be born (in a male human-form!), not in a palatial estate like the Vatican, but in the meekest of settings (of course!) in order to atone for an apple having been eaten by an innocent-minded child thousands of years earlier. Remember folks, this is the Guy---who after having gone ballistic over a food-tasting event in Eden—condemned and cursed "all" life on the planet---punishing some forever because of it. This is the Guy who later attempted to destroy the entire planet—who was pleased to command the murder of nations of innocent people just so a nomadic horde of idol-worshipers, who often pissed Him off en masse because of their unfaithful behavior, would have a homeland—never forget that! How else could a powerless people get what they wanted but by making others believe that their "scripted" *Bible*-God assigned it to them?

Who would dare to doubt God's mercy and tenderness when He, being of sound mind of course, condescended to be born (as His own son) in a manger (in the guise of being one of the lowliest and poorest among us) in His never-ending attempt to save only His "chosen" people. Aaaahhh, again—are your eyes beginning to well-up, too? And thus, mighty Jehovah, who couldn't prevent the Jews from becoming "lost" ---not even after giving them His undivided attention and direction in the *OT*---opted to "disguise" Himself as a meek and mild man whose entire life's mission in the *NT* was, again, none other than His wanting to save only *"the lost sheep of the house of Israel"* —a mission that, sadly, heartbreakingly, came to naught because of the Jews' total rejection of poor ol' Jesus, even to this day!

One would think that an all-knowing God would have had a better handle on figuring things out in His dealings with ignorant, paleo-minded people—would have enjoyed experiencing, at least, a few successes with his favorite folks instead of having to face failure after failure with them! How sad, too, that the very folks Jesus came to save, cried-out for and demanded His execution by "crucifixion" —(imagine Jews wanting to kill Jehovah!---OMG!) ---are you in full weep-mode yet? And thus, after having misspent all of His time conducting an unsuccessful ministry attempting to save *"lost sheep,"* Jesus' versatile script-writers decided it was time (after having Him morph into His spiritual body days after His horrific, human death coming at the hands of Jews) to become a Savior to "all" whom He had previously avoided like the plague, and for that, Gentiles should give their whole-hearted thanks to Jesus' ever-clever, business-minded script-writers. If not for their last-minute *Bible*-efforts, Gentiles would still be regarded as *"dogs"* unworthy of receiving a loving God's attention at all—so please, in the name of the sacred heart of Jesus, empty your pockets into the passing collection basket---you owe them everything! Oh, those script-writers! Oh, the **"fools"** who believe their fraudulent and manufactured words!

Could it be possible that such an innocent and adorable manger-occupant, the proverbial apple (Son-of-God), could fall so far from the malevolent tree that produced it? No, it isn't possible! This rotten apple (Jesus) of the *New Testament* fell within an inch of its *Old Testament's* putrid source—the God of whom it is said: *"so loved the world"* that He lovingly drowned all but a boat-load of the earth's teeming inhabitants! What a world-lover! Anyone who believes the words stated in *John* 3:16, please let me know if you have any interest in buying the beautiful bridge I have for sale in a much-traveled area of NYC? As you know, in regards to real estate, it's all about location location location. And, as you are beginning to know, in regards to religion, it's all about deception deception deception!

The Nativity scene of an adorable, innocent little baby lying serenely in a hay-strewn manger is in need of a reality make-over. Jesus, who, in reality, wants His enemies to be murdered before His eyes and wants them to suffer eternal torment should, in reality, be depicted, in His rustic li'l baby crib, grinning while holding His baby-sized, flaming, bloodied sword, for He is but a third-part of a Semitic Trio of Terror—Jehovah the Gentile Murderer, Jesus the Homicidal Arsonist, and Allah the Infidel Annihilator! While they may differ in some respects, they all share the same DNA and genetic disorder---a disorder that allows their script-writers **"to terrify and enslave mankind and monopolize power and profit"** as a means of control.

To master the mentality of the masses---to control and dominate their entire lives---these clever fellas knew how to utilize the powers of God's "Word" for their own benefit as well as for their tribes'. They knew that if belief in God could actually cause people to murder their own children (as in the example of Abraham) without giving it a second thought, what else could be done in the name of God? Could nations of people be exterminated and their lands taken away if God ordered it to be done? Could God's "chosen" acquire a homeland by making others believe that God commanded that one should be given to them even if it had to be stolen-away from its rightful owners whom they had to murder in order to acquire it? Could the *"lost sheep"* gain the assistance of powerful nations to assist them in their sacred efforts? The answer to these questions is, sadly, quite obvious.

The clever script-writing priests of the Chutzpah Chronicles knew well how to use the power of God's "Word" to make people truly believe they are sinners-all just for being born---they knew well how to use their expertise at conniving and deception in order for their power-tripping, parasitic priesthood to enrich themselves and their tribes by feeding on peoples' supposed transgressions against God and against man---they knew well how to use a sinner's guilt and his/her fear of a never-ending torment in a Hell made just for sinners---they knew well the power that existed in having folks believe that priests can absolve sins (according to the beloved song, "Amazing Grace," aren't we all "wretches" in need of God's "grace"?) ---they knew well the power in promising all devout believers that after their death they will all experience an eternal life of joyful bliss in a heavenly paradise made just for them---they knew well how to use their cunning modus operandi to gain command and control over not just a few folks, but nearly everyone on the planet. And, for over two thousand years they have succeeded in imposing their scam. Reason's Tribunal, however, can and will administer the mental enema needed to flush and cleanse our cranial cavities in order to remove the morbid excrement of their malevolent machinations that endeavors to *"enslave"* us all!

To master the mentality of the Muslim masses, the *Koran* instructs its mindless followers that when Allah "wills" to lead someone astray to be an "idolater" (sinner), no one, I repeat, "no one" can guide him or even change him---*Koran* 7:186. Imagine---no idolator on the planet ever having the ability to change their beliefs or their lives! ---I'll call Allah out on this point---"liar, liar, pants on fire"!

Devout Muslims believe, however, that in order for them to be obedient to God and His "Word," they have a sacred duty to *"slay"* all idolaters, (all sinners), as a script-written God has "commanded" them to do because Allah, seemingly, is unable or unwilling to do the killing all by Himself. Hence His never-ending need for the assistance of devout Muslims to help Him out---what a steaming pile of Islamic chutzpah! It is quite interesting to note here that Allah, with seemingly little effort on His part, supposedly instantly created the gazillions of galaxies that exist in the Universe without needing anyone's help, but slaying infidels is not something He can handle all by Himself! ---really?

Because of His obvious inabilities and shortcomings at certain tasks, He has delegated this most "just" and most "sacred" of Islamic duties---to *"slay the idolaters"* ---to His ever-faithful Semitic subjects who, of course, are themselves incapable of sinning, incapable of screwing things up, and who are, most assuredly, completely immune-from-error and completely immune from making infallible judgments and, besides, they always know with certainty who each and every sinner on the planet is! Hmm! Hmm! Hmm! The Semitic God who obviously had failed in His efforts to destroy all of the "violence-producing" inhabitants of earth with His "violence-cleansing" flood relies now on the assistance of some of the Deluge's surviving descendants to get the job done with impeccability! Hmm! Hmm! Hmm, again! I find it quite interesting, however, that a "violence-detesting" God should now have as His most devoted followers none other than mindless *Koranimals*---the most "violent" of all creatures that a Semitic God ever made!

Shouldn't God, the Knower of Everything, have known "beforehand" that things would not improve after the "cleansing" floodwaters had subsided as He, obviously, had known "beforehand" of Adam and Eve's disobedient decision before they had actually made it? Wouldn't the "ever-existing," redeeming words of the "imperishable" *Koran* be proof of such knowing? Apparently, God's foreknowledge of events does not result in any benefit to Himself or to anyone else—it only results in more bad decision-making on His part! In assigning abilities to God, a being whom we are told "knows" everything and who is responsible for "creating" everything, the problem arises for His Semitic, control-seeking script-writers as to where to begin and where to end His foreknowing skills in order to make them somewhat credible and somewhat practical—where to begin and where to end His responsibility for "creating" sin in the first place---where to begin and where to end His having to mete-out "punishment" upon not only all who are guilty of sin, but upon the innocent as well!

Strangely, it is not a matter of concern for Muslims, and their mental health, that Allah deliberately "wills" the disobedience of sinners then deliberately "wills" their deaths because of it---what "injustice" is tolerated in the name of God! What injustice is tolerated in the Islamic "necessity" of deliberately punishing sinners for the diabolical actions of Allah who, with knowledge aforethought, purposely leads folks astray to be His enemies! HOW MERCIFUL DOTH RELIGION MAKE US! Hmm! Hmm! Hmm! Such is the insane "will" of Allah and the pitiless, reason-perverting, humanity-destroying power of "undoubted" belief in His "Word." This is the glorious Guy whom Muslims want you to believe is a praise-worthy, justice-loving and merciful Semitic Divinity! ---really? In my humble opinion, such would be the equivalent of bestowing Adolf Hitler with the Nobel Peace Prize! "Lemonade, anyone"?

If Muslims truly believe that nothing happens unless Allah "wills" it to happen—if they truly believe that it is Allah who "wills" the creation of "everything," they should, therefore, accept and abide by His "will" that is totally responsible for giving existence to the good, the bad, and all the ugly features of this Allah-willed world---everything that exists in the world (even sinning) is because of Allah's doing and that's the way He wants it, obviously! All Muslims should simply accept that the very existence of evil in the world along with its touted architect, Satan, both came about as the result of a "willful" act on Allah's part—that America and her *Koran*-dishonoring ideals of ***"Life, Liberty and the pursuit of Happiness"*** along with the blasphemy and disobedience of sinners and infidels are, likewise, the result of Allah's "willful" doing and, as Allah knows best, He should be the one, and the only one, to take care of the problems that He alone "willfully" created and, therefore, is completely responsible for—a case of the watchmaker being held responsible for all the flawed watches that he, and no one else, has made!

Shouldn't the "eternal" torment imposed by God upon sinners for their "finite," and often "momentary" transgressions be considered an "intolerable" injustice and a "shameful" example of God's "merciful" and "compassionate" nature---a nature that His mindless fan club loves to promote? Shouldn't the eternal torment imposed unjustly by God upon sinners be considered by decent-minded human beings, especially Americans, to be an abuse of power and a disgraceful example of Divinity at work? Doesn't every Jew, Christian, and Muslim worship such a sadistic abuser? ---doesn't the majority of Americans?

Whose needs are being served in meting out eternal torment? Would anyone with an ounce of humanity in their heart consider such punishment as being fair and just? Of course not! Would the God-trusting U.S. Supreme Court uphold such cruel and unusual treatment to be an honorable and just act? Of course not! Shouldn't everyone's physical death (non-existence for all eternity) be punishment enough to please a vengeful, immortal God and end the matter once and for all? If it is so that every sinner and infidel must suffer and endure eternal torment to please a Semitic God, why does Sinner/Infidel #1: Satan, go unscathed for each and every one of his transgressions made against Him? Hmm! Is it not possible to see the ungodly hand of power-seeking, vengeance-loving men being involved in this purposeful perversion of fairness and justice?

Since Muslims believe that nothing happens unless Merciful Allah, in His perfection, "wills" it to be and that He certainly wouldn't will something into existence that He didn't want to exist in the first place, it is important, therefore, to give credit where credit is due based on such thinking. It was Allah (God) who "willfully" created Satan—it was Merciful Allah who 'willfully" created Satan's infidelity and his evilness—it was Merciful Allah who "willfully" allows his home-boy, Satan, to exist unhindered and unrestricted to torment Merciful Allah's "Creation" from the Eden of long ago until the present time and evermore! Hmm! Since everything that happens in the entire Universe, according to Islamic belief, is the result of Merciful Allah's deliberate and divine doings—so, too, therefore, is this book, *Reason's Tribunal,* the very result of His perfect "will" and we should all give Him credit for "willfully" inspiring me to write it---I certainly could not have written these pages without His help---"Allahu Akbar"!

Shame on you, Muslims, who dare to interfere with Allah's divine "will" that is responsible for creating everything in the Universe exactly the way He chose to make it! Shame on you, Muslims, for thinking that you, not Allah, must correct, by your own ungodly hands, the imperfections He deliberately intended every human being in the Universe to have! Shame on you, Muslims, for "judging" the works of your God or for second-guessing His deliberate designs! Shame on you, Muslims, for disrespecting and detesting the work of your beloved Allah whom you say has "willfully" created me, my infidelity, and this book. I cannot, therefore, be held responsible for being the way I am, for the thoughts I think, and for the blasphemous words I write—it is, after all, all Allah's doing—it is God's "will" that sin and sinners exist—Blessed be Merciful Allah and His "Akbar" Works!

As the God of Israel is the one and the same God of Arabia (for there is not a separate God that Muslims worship), it was He, the God of all Semites, who said in *Deut.* 32:35:

Shouldn't all Muslims who seek to impose suffering and death in Allah's name be deemed blasphemous infidels themselves for the "willed" vengeance they visit upon those they judge to be sinners? Shouldn't all Muslims, instead, offer-up their lust for *"vengeance, and recompense"* to their Merciful Allah who should be the only one to enjoy making life miserable for everyone who rejects Him because He purposely caused their rejection in the First Place—such is His "will" and His purposeful way of doing things, according to Islamic belief, and His followers should "respect" His immune-from-error methods, abide by them, and not seek to do what He alone is totally responsible for doing and, therefore, He is totally responsible for dealing with?

According to Islamic belief, Allah is to be regarded as a responsible Guy, someone who is quite capable of creating and running the Universe all by Himself without requiring the assistance of folks who are not immune-from-error having to stick their noses, their righteous egos, and their religious zeal into His "perfect" business of deliberately making sinners and meting out punishments upon them. Surely, the religious beliefs of Muslims reveal that their Almighty Allah is incompetent, impotent, and desperately in need of their muddled, misguided meddlings to manage His malicious affairs and deliver His divine justice? Shame on you, Muslims, for audaciously assuming that you are gifted with knowing the mind of God and for adding to the miseries of this world based on such knowledge— shame on you for assuming that you are doing God's work when imposing misery and malevolence upon those who, because of Allah's "will," differ in their thinking and in their beliefs—shame on you for the inhumanity you dispense upon others in order to put a smile on Allah's face---shame on you for involving yourselves in malevolent activities because you believe that Allah needs your help in locating and killing those He purposely made to be God-damned infidels! If all Muslims are duty-bound to kill infidels as stated in the *Koran*, shouldn't Allah have set the example for them to follow by killing Satan, the very first infidel He created?

"Yes, Virginia, Allah purposely created Satan to be His enemy, but apparently, for some reason, He is not 'willing' or able to 'slay' His constant opposer or 'impede' his evil efforts. Hmm! As it turns out, the bad-guy character is ofttimes a necessity in fictional literature—removing the bad-guy, (Satan), from fictional, Semitic scripture would, obviously, spell the end of Semitic religions altogether because there would be no need for the services of clergy and their amazing abilities to absolve us of our Allah-

It is apparent also, that Muslims do not consider Allah's divine justice—His eternal Hell of torments, I repeat, His "eternal Hell of torments" —to be punishment enough for sinners because they believe the scales of justice can only be balanced by imposing their own personal *"vengeance, and recompense"* in this life upon those whom their Word of Allah, the *Koran*, tells them are destined to suffer without end, I repeat, "to suffer without end" in order to please God! Shame on all Muslims who are bent on such behavior and for your disgraceful disregard of Allah's ultimate handling of the situation—His ultimate solution for the actions of sinners and His never-ending, "perfect" justice He has "prepared" for them! Shame on all Muslims who deem Allah's solution not to be punishment enough for the damned? Shame on all Muslims who indulge in atrocity against others in God's name! Shame on all Jews, Christians, and Muslims, for allowing religion to take away our truly "blessed gifts" of existence as human beings who possess a sentient nature—who possess the ability to feel, to think, to reason, to doubt, and to question—who possess the ability, above all else, to be compassionate and humane!

Shame on all of you in the Muslim world who think the only way to please God is by adding to the more-than-abundant miseries and sorrows of this world—that inflicting additional wickedness and cruelty upon certain others will, somehow, make things absolutely right with Allah! Shame on all who desire in the name of God to increase the suffering of those whom you are convinced, by belief in Semitic scripture, will never again experience anything but never-ending agony, I repeat, "never-ending agony"! Sadly, pity and mercy, while often preached about in sermons, are seldom, if ever, employed beyond the pulpit as favored and cherished practices of Semitic religions---seldom are they employed by the followers of the religion that dominates the Muslim world—certainly never to the extremes with which devout Muslims desire to carry out, in the name of God, the fundamental wickedness, terrorism, and vengeance prescribed and promoted in the *Koran*. HOW MERCIFUL DOTH RELIGION MAKE US! Man help us!

What audacity of mind there is in the Islamic belief that Allah is unable to operate the Universe without the help of His Muslim followers! What audacity of mind there is in the Islamic belief that only Muslims have the amazing ability to get things done perfectly right every time they act— unlike their beloved Satan-Maker and Evil-Enabler, "Allah"!

> ***What can be of greater blasphemy than to ascribe the wickedness of man to the orders of the Almighty?***
>
> ---Thomas Paine

If Semitic religions were truly conducted as the loving and merciful enterprises they claim to be, shouldn't the loving and merciful followers of Jesus and Allah---who truly know for certain (because of words written in certain books) that they are destined to experience the never-ending pleasures of Heaven---shouldn't they, therefore, be attending to the earthly needs and yearnings of the less fortunate (sinners and infidels) whom they also know for certain (because of words written in certain books) that they are destined to experience nothing but "eternal" torment? Shouldn't loving, merciful, and spiritual-minded folks, therefore, be moved by the gravity of the situation that has themselves spending eternity in a glorious, pleasure-filled Heaven, while so many others will be spending their eternity roasting and agonizing in Hell. Shouldn't they be doting on sinners and infidels in order to increase, in any way possible, their short-lived joys of life on earth knowing they will soon be suffering never-ending torments in their life after death?

If death-row inmates are allowed by their decent and compassionate jailers to partake of the simple pleasure of selecting their last meal or allowed to have a final, simple request honored, why aren't Hell-bound folks afforded the same courtesies and much more by the Heaven-bound? Shouldn't every devout Christian and Muslim I encounter be over-the-moon ecstatic to send me, a blasphemous infidel, on a vacation cruise or pay off my debts or buy me dinner or a box of chocolates or, at least, send me a consoling "Sympathy" card because of their knowing with certainty what lies in store for me after this life? Hmm! Isn't it strange that God-minded folks who profess their love for enemies wouldn't buy me so much as a cup of coffee but, instead, would prefer to slit my throat or otherwise add to the miseries that I and so many others must endure before we leave this world to begin receiving our greater, eternal torments—isn't it strange, indeed! HOW MERCIFUL DOTH RELIGION MAKE US! Man help us!

Because Semitic scriptures always seek our subjection, never our emancipation, the *Koran*, like its kindred *Bible*, does not teach *"that all men are created equal"* and endowed with certain *"unalienable rights"* — it teaches and demands everyone's total obedience and mindless submission to Allah's Word, OR ELSE! ---comply or die! The only thing missing from the *Koran's* blood-spattered pages is a HOW-TO section instructing faithful *Koranimals* on the correct, spiritual way, of course, to create suicide-vests and IED's while detailing, of course, the heavenly rewards that result in using them in Allah's name. Missing, also, is a chapter or two devoted to teaching Allah's finest murder-missionaries about the finer, sacred details of beheading, torturing, and mutilating the bodies of sinners—the blessed and bloody sacraments of Islam's fundamentalist practitioners—the blessed and bloody sacraments that, when carried out, must surely warm the "merciful" heart of Allah and put a smile on His grim face! Isn't it interesting (and disgusting!) that "spiritual living" in the Islamic faith involves and tolerates so much blood being shed in order to please Allah, the most spiritual of spiritual beings? ---with Semitic religion, it's always about the blood isn't it---the goddammed blood!

The *Koran*, no doubt, is the handbook of an organized religion that sanctions organized crime against all non-Muslims whose very existence is considered a blasphemy---a handbook whose murderous hate speech against blasphemers preaches "Death to America" while its radical pages receive her Constitutional protection to do so—incredible! Because "belief" in the "undoubted" directives written in the *Koran* is the most powerful armament in the mindset of Islamic terrorists, we must confront the *Koran's* religious authority which results in mindless acceptance and mindless actions by its mindless devotees: *Koranimals*! We, Americans, must convince ourselves beyond a doubt that any scripture-based, "spiritual" enterprise that authorizes, endorses, demands, and/or inspires doing harm unto others is not a religious institution, I repeat, "is not a religious institution" and should never be granted favorable, protected status anywhere freedom exists and is honored. Would any decent American ever consider the extermination of nations of people as being a spiritual and religious endeavor? ---of course not, and yet we call Judaism a "religion" and give it Constitutional protection! Would any decent American ever consider burning people to death, impaling, torturing, and beheading them as being spiritual and religious endeavors? ---hell no, yet we call Christianity and Islam "religious" institutions and grant them *"the free exercise thereof"* in our freedom-loving nation!

All Semitic religions should be exposed as being the intolerant, hateful, malevolent, vengeance-based, liberty-destroying, criminal enterprises that they are—criminal enterprises that use the pretense of being sacred institutions because, they tell us, they are acting only under the guidance and direction of God as "revealed" in "inspired" Semitic scripture—a God who just happens to be an intolerant, malevolent, vengeance-based, liberty-destroying, criminal-minded-bastard who commands us to hate our families---*Luke* 14:26! No doubt, the Taliban, Isis, and Al Queda act under the guidance and direction of such a tyrannical madman!

Is there a difference between the dreadful deeds done by Jews who fervently followed the death-dealing dogmas of Jehovah and the dreadful deeds done by Muslims who fervently follow the death-dealing dogmas of Allah and the dreadful deeds done by Nazis who fervently followed the death-dealing dogmas of their leader! Is there really a difference between abominations done in the name of God and abominations done in the name of Hitler? There is no difference—religion is as religion does, and religion only does what its Word of God requires it to do—ditto for the followers of the Word of Hitler! We need to face that reality and use the clarity of mind that will result from Reason's Tribunal to be able to see clearly what all religions have always been, what they have always done, and what they all will always continue to do when allowed to operate without any checks and balances.

We, Americans, a freedom-loving people, should never aid or abet our death-dealing enemies and their freedom-destroying endeavors by giving their maniacal, Islamic religion free-rein, and by granting their sacrilegious scriptures the honor and privilege of Constitutional protection without any limiting conditions. We can no longer turn our heads away when any evil is done in the name of any God—the dark side of all Semitic religions, especially Islam, must be addressed and dealt with sanely, once and for all, by an enlightened, common-sense people concerned with the future welfare of our planet. Killing terrorists will not end the madness—neutralizing their "undoubted" written Word of Terror: the *Koran*, will!

Under the pall of carried-out executions and the constant threat of death, some have tried to confront Islam's inviolable religious authority and global mission via published cartoons and ridicule. While it is acknowledged that such deserved satire and derision tends to exacerbate religious fervor, we must never abandon their use because of the intimidating threat of retaliation by those who feel the need to kill us for opposing their righteous, malevolent madness. Protected speech and free expression are rights that don't exist in Islamic culture or countries---protected speech and free expression should not be extended as gifts to those who call, literally or figuratively, for our physical deaths and the destruction of our nation, her honored ideals, and her Constitution. Without imposing limits, religion should not be given carte blanche in our freedom-loving nation to preach and to encourage "Death to America.

We who speak out against the enemies of civilization, even if only to ridicule them, should never succumb to their intimidations or feel compelled, because of political correctness, to hide literally or figuratively under our desks while those who would destroy us are empowered and encouraged to rail against us without restriction. We must never forget that the War on Terror is being fought for the very survival of America, her freedoms and her honored ideals. We must never forget, too, that there was a time in Judeo-Christianity's inviolable past when any expression of derision or contempt for its spiritual authority was dealt with in like manner by Jewish and Christian fanatics carrying out their global mission to "improve" and "purify" the world!

Today, because of the fear of lethal reprisal by *Koranimals*, Americans and many other peoples around the world have become subdued into silence rather than openly denounce any repugnant aspect of Islam which, incidentally, warms the mindless hearts and heartless minds of jihadists by emboldening them in their imposing endeavors to "improve" and "purify" the world—to deliver "Death to America," and to destroy civilization for Allah's sake. Our reluctance to exercise our Constitutional rights in confronting the virulence of the so-called "religious rights" of Islam as it marches onward without organized, secular resistance to establish a worldwide Caliphate, under Sharia law—amounts to cultural suicide. Americans must decide whether our attempts to appease the imposers of Islam and turn a blind eye to the freedom-destroying effects of Muslim devotion to Allah's Word is in the best interest of those who are blessed to live in *"the land of the free and the home of the brave."*

We must decide whether, acting out of weakness, we are willing to countenance the establishment of Islam's brutal laws and dogmas upon our shores and go shopping for our mandatory prayer-rugs to prostrate ourselves upon while acquiring the "sacred" shrouds that hide the entire female-form from the lusting eyes of less-than-sacred, intemperate men who might, otherwise, have a "lawful" *Koran*-excuse to "sin" against women---rape and brutalize them—or we must decide whether, acting out of strength, we are willing to defend our "sacred" First Amendment right to exercise free speech without threatening or endangering anyone and make a stand against tyranny like the embattled, politically-incorrect Patriots at Lexington and Concord did on April 19, 1775.

If a mere defaming cartoon depiction of Muhammad can inspire Muslims to murder, what should non-Muslim Americans—who are considered "infidels" by their very existence—expect from Allah's assassins for the brazen blasphemy of their unbelief in Islam? Our "politically correct" unwillingness to recognize and oppose the opposers of freedom and their noxious, Semitic religion only empowers "them" and emasculates "us"! As a result of such inaction on our part, we have now arrived at a crossroad moment in our country's history because of our fearful tolerance of Islam and our failure to confront our constant enemy— Semitic scripture---we either survive as a freedom-loving nation or succumb to a freedom-destroying religion—we must carefully choose with absolute certainty which path to follow, especially now after America's disgraceful defeat in Afghanistan---especially now when our enemies are uber-energized to wipe us from the face of the earth---especially now when *Koranimals* are achieving success in their endeavors!

"To arms, to arms" was the sage advice of the Infidel and Son of Liberty, Paul Revere, on that long-ago day, but today, it is evident that military force, even when justified and necessary, cannot prevail against the intensity of the Islamic yearning for the return of the Dark and Middle Ages—a time when religion flourished---a time when mankind and civilization withered. Military actions, while necessary at times, only provoke future hostilities and, as a result, help to produce future jihadists. Military actions can only endeavor to contain the latest outbreak of this epidemic disease—they can never remove the source of the contagion. Instead of loosening the imposed mental shackles of the *Koran's* coerced and uncontested dogmas that provide authority for killing and committing atrocity in the name of God— military endeavors against Islamic terrorists only result in tightening the fetters of their incorrigible, homicidal, religious mindset.

There is a widespread mindset in the Muslim world that perceives Muslim terrorists as being "noble" Islamic warriors involved in fighting a Holy War---Islamic warriors who are merely following the "written" orders of Allah! There is no doubt that today's religion-generated chaos around the world is rooted entirely in Islamic theology which, in turn, is rooted entirely in Islamic scripture which, in turn, is rooted entirely in the scriptures of Judeo-Christianity.

Why then do we constantly deal militarily with the effects of Islamic terrorism by bombing here and there with questionable results rather than deal meaningfully and summarily with its constant cause—the written words of the *Koran?* —that's where we need to deliver a really "smart" bomb—that's where we need to focus our earnest, rational energies against scripture-inspired madness instead of continually imperiling our military forces and innocent civilians with less intelligent, less successful warfare. Lethal retaliation on our part only begets further lethal retaliation on their part which only begets further lethal retaliation on all parts! The only lasting way to remove mosques, temples, and churches from the face of the earth is not through violent, destructive endeavors, but by having the very folks who built them be the very ones to dismantle them because of their greater enlightenment! One sane way to prevent the wounding and killing of America's warriors---one sane way to prevent their PTSD episodes and their less-than-honorable, shameful surrenders (departures) from occurring is to recognize who the real enemies of civilization are and end our futile warrings against their uncontested Islamic beliefs and fanaticisms. In the least, we should not be sending our Caretakers of Liberty off to contend with enemies without supplying them with the "weapons" they will need to prevail---"weapons" that have the potential to prevent future wars! Man help us!

Islam—as it is interpreted and practiced by these people (Muslims)—is, quite simply, incompatible with freedom the way we understand it. It is incompatible with open elections, rights for minorities, trial by jury, and all the other institutions familiar to the Western way of life. It is incompatible with basic morals and decency. It is incompatible with man-made laws and the rights of mankind to adapt and progress and modernize. ...those motivated by extreme fundamentalist Islamic faith have demonstrated their willingness to kill millions and terrify the world with their brutality. None of this will change until we all stop lying to ourselves and accept that these acts and beliefs are rooted in the religion of Islam itself. ...Totalitarian (Islamic) ideologies provide ready answers to everything. They obliterate freethinking and debate, and in their place they prescribe an entire way of life, right down to the minutest of details. They define enemies and friends ("us" and "them" ---kvk) in black-and-white terms that leave nothing to the imagination. ...Anything done to help achieve the goal of bringing about their vision becomes justified, including the murder of children and women. ...Islam is on a crash course with the free world.

---Glenn Beck, *It Is About Islam*

It should be obvious at this point in time, that in order to cease the growth of religious terrorism, we must attack and kill its roots—its jihadist, Judeo-Christian foundation. To fight the fires of today's religion-generated madness, we must extinguish the sparks and flames enkindled by all related Semitic scripture. If we truly wish to end the nightmare known as the War on Terror, we must initiate Reason's Tribunal to neutralize its scriptural support system beginning with the pages of the beloved *Bible* and ending with the pages of the beloved *Bible*-begotten *Koran* simply because, as believers and followers of a greater religion: the Golden Rule, we cannot expect to do unto another related Semitic religion what we refuse to do unto our own! We must initiate Reason's Tribunal against the Judeo-Christian dogmas responsible for the birth of Islam's religious mindset of terror in order to debunk and defeat them both.

Before we begin this noble task, it is important to understand that Muslims are as devout, if not more so, in honoring their long-standing, unquestioned religious beliefs as Jews and Christians are in honoring their own. Any attempt on our part to change the inertia of the entrenched religious thinking of Muslims and their mindless devotion to the *Koran* for the better will require us to overcome in a similar way the inertia of our mindless devotion to its parental scripture—the *Bible*. Changing the malicious-minded, supremacist-thinking habits of our enemy will require changing our own closely related Judeo-Christian mindset—such changes are long long long overdue!

Most would agree about the importance of updating and advancing our thinking when it comes to gaining new knowledge in matters of science, medicine, and technology but, when it comes to our religious thinking, we allow the non-progressive, non-sacred, superstition-filled thoughts of primitive, paleo-minded peoples—their fearful-minded religious ideas, rituals, and customs—to continue to exist unchallenged—to continue to exist without receiving virtually any improving modifications throughout the millennia. Can you imagine if doctors and hospitals practiced medicine today with knowledge that was a thousand years old or even a hundred years old? Certainly, all of the advancements in our lives and living conditions---from food production to the manufacture of clothing, etc., --- from science and medicine, etc., ---everything that I can possibly think of has been improved by increased knowledge being gained throughout the centuries---everything but Semitic religions---which have failed to progress beyond the cave entrance even with their greater knowledge about the finer points on how to fleece a flock to the max.

The best that the *New Testament* could produce was a God who, even after two thousand years, tells us in His "inerrant" and "infallible" *Bible* that "devils" are continually settin' up shop inside us and raisin' hell when we experience sickness because as every Christian knows, all disease is caused entirely by the activities of "gremlins" taking up residence in our bodies! --- God, how stupid can you get? ---yet, we still allow those who would manipulate us with their outdated and uneducated religious beliefs---their outdated and uneducated God---the unhindered ability to impose their will on us without any checks and balances---without any challenge being made to the legitimacy of their Word of God scriptures. We still allow the backward and uneducated paleo-reckonings of life's mysteries founded upon ignorance, fear, and false assumptions, as well as its racist and sexist attitudes, to be passed along to our children in hopes of preparing them adequately for an enlightened future, a future where they will take the helm, man the controls, and guide our ships of state—incredible! Man help us!

> *...religion was the race's first* (and worst) *attempt to make sense of reality. It was the best the species could do at a time when we had no concept of physics, chemistry, biology or medicine. We did not know that we lived on a round planet, let alone that the said planet was in orbit in a minor and obscure solar system, which was also on the edge of an unimaginably vast cosmos that was exploding away from its original source of energy. We did not know that micro-organisms were so powerful and lived in our digestive systems in order to enable us to live, as well as mounting lethal attacks on us as parasites. We did not know of our close kinship with other animals. We believed that sprites, imps, demons, and djinns were hovering in the air about us. We imagined that thunder and lightning were portentous. It has taken a long time to shrug off this heavy coat of ignorance and fear, and every time we do there are self-interested forces who want to compel us to put it back on again.*

—Christopher Hitchens, in his Introduction to *The Quotable Atheist*

If you, the reader, don't think that America is still being affected by the unenlightened paleo-reckonings of supremacist-minded folks who don't live by the Golden Rule, just watch or listen to a national news program! If you don't think America is a victim of Semitic theology, just remember how pleased Jesus was to declare that His mission was to bring division to the earth and discord among its peoples---*Luke* 12:49,51; *Matt.* 10:35 and then watch or listen to a news program to see how successful Jesus has been in making His dreams for America and the rest of the world come true--- *"Praise the Lord"*!

Reason is the noblest weapon a civilized society can use against the indoctrination and deluded thinking of those who find just-cause for their actions on the pages of glorified murder manuals or in the status quo mentality derived from them. These exalted books of human invention constantly manage—through the mental conditioning instilled by one's religious education and upbringing—a mental conditioning supported by one's haughty national beliefs, family and social traditions, spirited church gatherings, songs and sermons, peer pressures and political correctness, etc., —to remain above suspicion and, therefore, beyond scrutiny and beyond reproach. To this day, these exalted books remain out of bounds to those who would seriously attempt to question their authority, no holds barred, in a public forum.

The survival of *"Life, Liberty and the pursuit of happiness"* demands that we put an end to this imposed ignorance, lack of critical scrutiny, and the absence of bold questioning of Semitic scriptures. The evidence "does" exist that will expose the deceptions and delusions dealing with our own bogus Judeo-Christian Divinity and His fraudulent Word, but only if we have the courage of Thomas Jefferson to seek it out in Reason's Tribunal and reveal its sane and sober findings to a religion-dominated world. In doing so, we will have earned the right to seek and reveal the evidence that will expose Islam's Divinity as a fraudulent, man-made object and His Word as a fraudulent, man-made object, too. We will have earned the right to *"Question with boldness"* even the existence of Allah!

Because of the elation-producing, habit-forming nature of religious beliefs, the mindset of every Semitic God-worshiper: Jew, Christian, and Muslim, as a rule, is averse to intervention and resistant to any investigation into its perceived authority—a stifling intoxication which thwarts the very means that could result in ending the constant threat of scripture-based terrorism. The stupefying, pleasurable effects of the so-called "opiate of the masses" is a formidable, life-threatening disease for which we need to find lifesaving, curative treatment. Because of its addiction to belief in a personal God and His perfect Word, the religious mind is programmed to totally accept and defend its pious delusions, never to question them, never to reject them. There is, however, a one-step program available for folks to overcome their habitual use of mind-dulling, mind-perverting Semitic religions and it only requires their accepting Reason and Truth as their Redeemer!

In our noble pursuit to change, via Reason's Tribunal, the status quo thinking of the religion-based mindset that is so disruptive to society and to the peaceful advancement of civilization, we should not be intimidated or frightened away from this formidable task because of the difficulties and dangers involved in being critical of religion and its scripture-inspired pathologies. We should not stop or shy away from discovering and disclosing the necessary *"facts and evidence"* that will someday cause a trace of doubt to enter where it seldom has entered before: the closed religious mind of God addicts. Every little effort made in this regard will eventually have its intended effect—for even a tightly closed door can often be made to open with a slight but determined push!

> Dripping water hollows out stone, not through force but through persistence.

> ---Ovid

> ***Of all the animosities which have existed among mankind, those which are caused by a difference of sentiments in religion appear to be the most inveterate and distressing, and ought to be deprecated.***

> ---George Washington

Of course, it is naive to think that Islamic fundamentalists intent on waging jihad can be reasoned with any more than their Jewish or Christian counterparts could ever be reasoned with, but, they can be influenced by family, friends, and others who can be reasoned with---the justification for the ***"inveterate"*** ***"animosities"*** inherent in their ***"distressing"*** fundamentalist beliefs can, therefore, be ***"deprecated,"*** debunked, and made inconsequential over time by their associations with more enlightened folks. If you, the reader, had to choose between facing the wrath of enraged Islamic fundamentalists waving the *Koran,* or facing the wrath of enraged secularists waving the Bill of Rights, which group would you prefer to contend with? The obvious answer speaks volumes for the immediate need to ***"Question with boldness"*** all the fundamentals, dogmas, and extrapolations of religious fanaticism. Only by revealing the unbiased, undoubted, ***"facts and evidence"*** that will result from such bold questioning will future terrorist candidates have an opportunity to begin to acquire skepticism about the *Koran's* infallibility—to begin to develop doubts and second thoughts about embracing jihad. Only by such boldness of investigation will future terrorist candidates become enlightened enough to begin to question what today's terrorist candidates will not simply because of the inertia of Islam's uncontested religious beliefs. Newton's first law of motion tells us that nothing can change the fixed direction of an object in motion unless outside force is applied—Reason's Tribunal is the outside force needed to change the inertia of the fixed direction of Islam—may the Force be with us!

The mindset of those who are inspired by religion's mass delusions and deceptions—the mindset of those who believe they are living and acting under God and carrying out His Word—the mindset of those who are certain they have Allah directing them and that those who oppose them oppose Allah—this mindset and its potential for terrorism must be recognized as the most formidable weapon of mass destruction in the world, a weapon that can only be neutralized by *"reason and free enquiry"* not by military force which should be quite evident to Americans post-Afghanistan! Because the tyranny of religion affects billions of people, it remains the most widespread, entrenched, and unchallenged despotism existing in the world today—it is time to end its constant impositions and control over our lives, its potential for madness and malevolence, its virulent history, and its evil reign over humanity and civilization.

The thing that makes churchmen (mosque-men, temple-men---kvk) *such dangerous citizens is their belief that they have a God directing them and that those who oppose them are opposing God. A man alone is subject to evil impulses enough, but a man and a god are a thousand times as dangerous.*

---Rupert Hughes

Foremost among our *"unalienable rights"* as human beings is the unrestrained freedom to think about anything of our choosing and the unrestrained freedom to doubt anything of our choosing—these mental abilities which go by the name of "free-thought" result from the natural functionings of our brains—functionings which are deemed abominations in Semitic scripture for they, obviously, pose a dire threat to Semitic religious dogmas. Without "free-thought," our Constitutional guarantee of "free-speech" becomes meaningless! When we are made to believe that the *Koran* and the *Bible* are infallible and inerrant and, therefore, not to be doubted, we are no longer human beings with natural functioning brains, we are mind-controlled robots!

The malevolence-filled scriptural dogmas preached by Semitic religions are most egregious because we, unknowingly, aid and abet the abominations they inspire and instigate with our willingness to blindly accept their doctrines without question and without any opposition or limiting-control—we allow their proselytizing advocates and robust institutions to grow and prosper without their even having to pay taxes while those who would be critical of their abuses must pay them which, in effect, gives financial support (State-aid) for the support of religion but not for the support of its opposers---a clear violation of the separation of Church and State. We allow all Semitic religions to promote their insanities without contention or suspicion—we allow them to intimidate our thinking processes with real or imagined punishments, their potent penalties for daring to question their imposed beliefs—we allow their sexual predators, disguised as sheep in priest's clothing, access to the minds and bodies of the most vulnerable among us—we allow the diabolical dogmas of sociopathic theologies replete with atrocious histories to exist in our midst without any concerns about the mindsets inspired and energized by their pious pathologies.

We allow the mental shackles of blind beliefs to be imposed upon blinded believers without the slightest protest—believers who, unbelievably, accept their spiritual fetters willingly because of the encouragement and pressures of societal and social influences along with the Hallelujah, pie-in-the-sky promise of eternal, heavenly rewards. Sugar-coated imposition sanctioned by tradition is still imposition after all, and spiritual bondage sanctioned by tradition is still bondage after all, and such may help to explain Semitic theology's unfettered ability to enslave gullible hearts and minds throughout the ages because their chains, though ofttimes imperceptible, are still binding chains after all. What else can account, aside from insanity, for a race of people (Americans of African descent) who continue to sing the praises of a God who condoned, justified, and sanctioned the enslavement of their ancestors? Freedom from such mental and physical oppression will only be possible for "everyone" when we begin to wage Reason's Tribunal against the freedom-opposing, scriptural dogmas of Judaism, Christianity, and Islam.

It would be most fitting, therefore, for an American of African descent---who is a descendant of slaves and who finally realizes that he or she has been living in spiritual "bondage" to belief in a bogus, tyrannical, Semitic deity, Jehovah/Jesus, who sanctioned the slavery imposed upon his or her hapless forebears and who is solely responsible for the all of the many iniquities, sufferings, and injustices that are still being heaped upon their race—to begin America's ***"revolution in the system of religion."*** Surely, a God who commanded the annihilation of nations of unoffending people and innocent children just to make room for His racially preferred folks to prosper without their having to endure "coexistence" amongst un-preferred neighbors who merely held different religious beliefs doesn't give a damn about the sufferings of black people past or present! ---to Him, "Black Lives Don't Matter"!

Doesn't such a deity deserve to be brought in for questioning and held without bail until His innocence or guilt in the above matters can be determined in Reason's Tribunal? In their ongoing, daily efforts today to seek justice for the injustices that are still being carried out against people of color in America---injustices that were carried out upon each and every one of their enslaved ancestors, they have yet to recognize and take remedial action against the cause of it all—their beloved Christian religion and its beloved God---their beloved Christian *Bible* and its rabid Baptist preachers who are rewarded to promote its God. And last but not least, African-Americans who continue to *"Praise the Lord,"* every chance they get, have yet to realize that their slavery-condoning Lord and Master, Jesus Christ, was a racist, Gentile-hater who never spoke a word against slavery or sought to end it---He, in His Jehovah disguise, established slavery to be imposed forever!

Instead of being outraged over God's sanctioning of slavery, Americans of African descent prefer, to this very day, to sing songs of praise and Hallelujahs to His not-so-loving heart that sanctioned their history of bondage---His not-so-loving heart that gave slave-masters, not only the right to abuse servants, but gave them instructions for dealing with their disobedience: the least offending servants are to be beaten a few times with a whip while the more offending servants are to be severely whipped as stated in *Luke* 12:47,48! Kneel down---all descendants of slaves---before your Sweet Lord, Jesus, and Praise Him! Kneel down and open your heavily-worn *Bibles* and read *Lev.* 25:44-46---then turn its sacred pages to *Titus* 2:9 and learn that Christianity teaches slaves *"to be obedient unto their own masters, and to please them well in all things."* One can only wonder how many white, Christian slave-masters, in their own loving, spiritual way of course, made certain that verse was laid down! Americans of African descent should have no doubt, after reading all of the *Bible*-texts dealing with slavery, which side of the Civil War—the pro-slavery side or the anti-slavery side—their beloved Jesus, would have supported.

It is hoped that one day soon, every Baptist minister who promotes the *Bible's* chapter and verse to black America, but neglects to include the above verses or a word about God's role in justifying the *"abomination"* of human "bondage," will begin to be held responsible for their part in all the harm they have caused by keeping their sheep in ignorance about the source of their past and present oppressions. It is hoped that one day soon, all clergy who encourage the worship of a slavery-promoting God will come to be regarded by the descendants of slaves with the same disdain and disgust they have now for the symbols of their family's servitude and segregation in the South. If the removal of Confederate symbols is deemed as doing the "right" thing, at the present time, for the ancestors of those forced into servitude, why are the symbols of the religion that sanctioned racism, the enslavement and the abuse of blacks—the symbols of the religion that still give comfort and care to their *Bible*-inspired abusers—allowed to remain in place and unscathed? It is hoped that one day soon, the words of *"We Shall Overcome"* will be sung by Americans of African descent in the past tense: *"We Have Overcome"* but it will only happen when *"all"* slavery-promoting institutions are identified and reckoned with!

It is further hoped that one day soon, a great-grandchild of an African who was ripped-away from their family and their African homeland to be sent-away to America in chains to toil as a slave because of God's "Word" and God's "Will," as expressed in the *Bible*—will be able to overcome his or her programming by their revered reverends, ministers, preachers, and others who sing animated praises to the "author" of their ancestor's abominable treatment through the ages. It is hoped, too, that such a person will find the strength to rise up against the everlasting cause of the dreadful woes and the continuing inhumane discriminations imposed on their race to initiate the long-overdue marches and protests—the long-overdue ***"revolution in the system of religion"*** that will commence their race's journey to total human emancipation from the source of their enduring oppressions.

It will take a courageous, truth-seeking person with the determination of a Rosa Parks, a person with the fortitude to take the first step on another long-needed, human rights march and journey in this country and beyond, by standing up for what is right, decent, and just! It will take a person of color who refuses to kneel down before the God of the *Bible* who was responsible for their ancestor's bondage both physically and spiritually—a person who refuses to continue living in mental servitude to a make-believe Semitic God and His less-than-sacred, slavery-promoting religion—a person who refuses to honor and support the subjugators of her race especially those with a *Bible*-in-hand---for they have aided and abetted in the taking-away of their ancestors' natural rights and their ancestors' natural freedoms to enjoy ***"Life, Liberty and the pursuit of Happiness"*** in the way white America enjoys them. And thus, in freeing themselves from their subjugation to the Christian religion, today's Americans of African descent, whose relatives were made to live, toil, and suffer in captivity in a freedom-loving land, will be free, at last, from the final vestiges of their *Bible*-condoned enslavement as they remove their last set of chains that were placed upon their race, in the sweet name of Jesus!

It surely won't commence, however, from figuratively climbing to the top a make-believe mountain to get a glimpse of the bogus "Promised Land" of mythology—a "land of segregation" that God's chosen stole from the Canaanites---a land they continue to lay exclusive claim to. The journey to justice for the descendants of slaves will begin and end only by their utilization of the gifts available to all citizens living in this liberty-loving land, a real "Land of Promise" where the truth about the Christian religion can finally be "revealed" to all. For it is only such truth that can remove, at last, the mental shackles imposed upon Americans of African descent who have succumbed to the lies and deceptions of their religious indoctrination. For, incredible as it sounds, they, out of ignorance of the *Bible's* ***"facts and evidence,"*** continue with willing hearts and willing minds to submit themselves to living under the thumb of their spiritual masters. For it is only truth that can break the chains of their bondage to the *Bible*, its despicable God, and its intimidating fire and brimstone Baptist preachers—truth that results from utilizing the freedom to doubt and the freedom to question the authority of all who have compelled their race to accept the yoke of a bogus, Semitic God and His theology for the purposes of ***"power and revenue"***!

When Americans of African descent begin to experience their Great Awakening, their Great Enlightenment—when they begin to realize that they are still living in servitude—when they begin to realize the extent of their enslavement to the spiritual deceptions imposed upon their race—when they begin to understand the "reasons" for their joyful acceptance of bondage to the fraudulent scripture of Christianity and its racist, supremacist deity—when they begin to realize why they have embraced being dominated by Christianity's many thundering advocates who aid and abet their race's subjection by keeping them in ignorance and down on their knees, there would, inevitably, soon be marches, protests, and demonstrations carried out from coast to coast across America to protest the mental-manacles imposed upon them---manacles that their brainwashed ancestors, for generations, have allowed to be placed upon their hearts and their minds without question—incredible! Perhaps, it may have something to do with the irrational condition known as Stockholm Syndrome, a condition where, for some strange reason, the abused find a sense of comfort and security at the hands of their abusers! If the **"revolution in the system of religion"** does not begin with such imposed-upon folks, it should begin with other oppressed victims of Semitic religion—homosexuals! —folks who are finally beginning to stand up for their human rights to partake of **"Life, Liberty and the pursuit of Happiness"** —to stand up against religious teachings that regard them and their natural behavior as an *"abomination"* in the sight of a Semitic God who prefers their remaining, not in closets, but in caskets and graves for He has commanded:

> *If a man lies with a male as with a woman, both of them shall be put to death for their abominable deed; they have forfeited their lives.*

---*Lev.* 20:13

All of Judeo-Christianity's leaders (especially the well-to-do Televangelists who are so eager to appear time and again on TV to inform us what is currently on God's mind and what He expects from each and every one of us) should have the theological testosterone to proclaim from the rooftops that everyone must "believe" every word in the *Bible* and "follow" all of God's explicit commandments including the above quoted example. Let them loudly and proudly proclaim which *Bible*-God is to be believed: (A.) ---the one who commands His followers: *"Thou shalt not kill"* or (B.) ---the *Bible*-God who commands His followers in *Lev.* 20:13: "Thou shalt kill homosexuals"? Let them loudly and proudly proclaim, too, which, if any of the following, is an *"abomination"* to their *Bible*-God: (A.) ---stoning people to death or (B.) ---being a homosexual? If their Televangelist testicles have not retreated north after preaching their shameless support for the "abominable" Word of God given above then, perhaps, they might recommend what size stone works best for carrying out God's brutal decrees---my guess is that small stones are favored because they will prolong the agony of those being set upon which would result, of course, in increasing and prolonging the joy of the stone-throwers who are so happy and eager to please God by partaking in this sacred activity! Be assured, folks, that each and every Jew, Christian, and Muslim condones the use of stones being hurled at homosexuals in order to torture and kill them because it is their God's "will" that it be done, yet, they all lack the stones to condemn this God-given commandment whether or not it is still being carried-out today which it is in certain parts of the world dominated by a God-loving, Semitic religion! ---sick, sick, sick!

Let me see if I have this right: If America is truly a nation founded on the Judeo-Christian principles and traditions recorded in the *Bible*---if the *Bible* (and the *Koran*) is truly infallible---if God's Word is truly immutable---if Jehovah, Jesus, and Allah are truly the same God—then homosexuality is truly a God-damned *"abomination"* and stoning homosexuals to death truly pleases God even today—is exactly right! Because Televangelists are always "exactly right," too, when it comes to preaching God's Word to the letter, I wonder why these Testament-touters never have the kahunas to command their righteous, Christian audiences that they should be keeping "all" of God's commandments including the one given in the quote above? Their inability to neither condone nor condemn *Lev.* 20:13, is evidence of a castrated clergy who lack the balls even to hurl figurative stones at literal abominations!

Thankfully, due to the enlightened efforts of mere mortal men, America was not founded on any of the barbaric principles and paleo-traditions glorified in the *Old Testament*: Death, (not ***"Life"***) ---Submission, (not ***Liberty***) ---Wretchedness, (not the ***pursuit of Happiness***"). Thankfully, America was founded on the ***"unalienable rights"*** of "all" human beings and not on the "untenable wrongs" of religion. The founders of America, thankfully, placed a wall of separation between the mindless, heartless, scripture-inspired stone-throwers who seek to "purify" the world with bloodshed—and their many many victims. Thank you, America's founders! Thank you! Thank you!

A man or woman that is a wizard, shall surely be put to death: they shall stone them with stones: their blood shall be upon them.

---*Lev.* 20:27

Religion had its share in the changes of civilization and national character, of course. What share? The lion's. In the history of the human race this has always been the case, will always be the case, to the end of time, no doubt; or at least until man by the slow processes of evolution shall develop into something really fine and high—some billions of years hence, say. ...if man continues in the direction of enlightenment, his religious practice may, in the end, attain some semblance of human decency. ...The Church, after doing its duty in but a lazy and indolent way for eight hundred years, gathered up its halters, thumbscrews, and firebrands, and set about its holy work in earnest. She worked hard at it night and day during nine centuries and imprisoned, tortured, hanged, and burned whole hordes and armies of witches, and washed the Christian world clean with their foul blood. Then it was discovered that there was no such thing as witches, and never had been. One does not know whether to laugh or to cry. (one should not laugh, Mr. Twain, one should cry! ---kvk)

---Mark Twain

The time has come for God's "personally selected" representative on earth, the Pope, to tell his fleeced flock, in no uncertain terms, whether he, the Prince of the Church, faithfully follows "all" of the commandments of Jehovah/Jesus, his loving Lord and Prince of Peace, or not, and whether he, too, considers homosexual behavior and so-called witchcraft as "abominations" that must be lethally punished and thus wiped from the face of the earth as God has commanded, or not. The Pope, who pretends to be the guiding light for Christians, who pretends to know the fickle mind of his vacillating *Bible*-deity, chooses not to "reveal" the answers to the above questions preferring instead to tiptoe around in his velvet slippers in the Vatican on this vital subject rather than take a valiant stand in them. Why is it that the Pope, in his role as God's spokesperson on earth, rises to his feet to tell us that the Christian Church cannot bless anything having to do with homosexuals for homosexuals are considered "sinners" by Jehovah/Jesus merely because a verse in the *Bible* has his God saying it is so in *Lev.* 20:13? Yet, the pious fraud known as the Pope, in his hypocritical, Christian fervor to promote God's "Word," lacks the spinoculars to tell us what his God commands His believers to do to every homosexual in the very same verse: they *"shall surely be put to death."* Consider, if you will, that if someone, after reading *Lev.* 20:13, was inspired to murder a homosexual person because of what they had read in the *Bible*, wouldn't that person think he or she was doing God's work? I certainly think so!

Could it be possible that the Pope, the "Vicar of Christ," in purposely omitting God's command to kill homosexuals in his sacred sermons demanding our belief in, of all things, God's every Word is, in reality, telling folks not to believe everything God says---just some of what He says? Surely, the infallible Pope has some vigorous "splaining" to do when it comes to his "reasons" for imparting to us, "only in part," what his God has commanded in *Lev.* 20:13! For those with eyes to see and a brain to comprehend the words written in the twentieth chapter of Leviticus, there is a very telling reason why silence is golden at certain critical times when it comes to preaching "all" of God's "Word." For the Church and its less-than-honest Pope would certainly not be able to continue fleecing their imposed-upon flocks today, in this more enlightened age, if they were ever foolish enough to take a stand to "uphold" God's "Word" that demands the death of homosexuals. For obvious reasons, the Pope cannot publicly admit which of the following his God truly considers to be an *"abomination"*: (A.) --- same gendered folks having loving, intimate relationships or (B.) ---killing all who do? If you don't believe me, just ask His Holiness to give his answer to the above!

Ask the Pope, too, if His peace-loving, merciful, and compassionate God wants all homosexuals to be stoned to death---if he answers "Yes," ask him why he worships and wants us to worship a mass-murderer? ---if he answers "No," then the Pope, according to the inerrant and infallible *Bible*, is a goddammed liar! Thankfully, in America, it certainly would never be considered okay to stone homosexuals to death just for their being the way they are or for any other reason---why then are Jews and Christians proud of their shared religion that authorizes such an abomination? ---no "decent" American should be okay with this "un-American," Judeo principle and tradition that seeks to punish someone just for being who and what they are---no "decent" American should involve themselves with glorifying any "sacred" scripture that promotes the shocking and shameful sins of Semitic theology!

The Pope, unfortunately, is still unable, at this late date, to step away from the darkness of the Church's doom and gloom, ignorant past and take a big big big step into the bright light of the 21st century without continuing to stumble about in his comfortable footwear---a stumble that still sanctions the discrimination and the racial, sexual hatred of certain folks and adds to the malevolence and miseries of this world---nice goin' holy man! But, on second thought, what would you expect from someone whose mindset and religious thinking was formulated during the earth's "flat" period---what would you expect from his fawning ring-kissers!

(NOTE TO POPE: please make the attempt to get over your pathological, Judeo-Christian obsession with sex and seek psychiatric care for your homophobia. I know it will help things along if you would get out of your pleasure palace and your Pope-clothes more often and see what life is really like beyond the walls of the Vatican---read more books that are not *Bible*-related and broaden your *Bible*-stifled horizons. Begin to see people for what they are and not for what the *Bible* tells you they are. Sell all of your Vatican possessions and spend the millions upon millions upon millions of dollars thus derived on improving living conditions around the world. Begin your exemplary, spiritual career by living not in the lifestyle of the rich and famous, but in the lifestyle of your Lord and Mentor, Jesus, who, it is supposed, never wore rings or hats or slippers---who never had bank accounts or lived in luxury digs, etc., etc., etc. Spend your days healing the sick and ending the suffering of others, like Jesus said you'd be able to do, unless you know in your heart of hearts that what Jesus said in *John* 14:12 is not to be believed either just like the words He spoke in *Lev.* 20:13. And lastly, ditch the ring, the silly hats, the silk wardrobe, the Pope-mobile, and your foppish footwear. Otherwise, put down your *Bible* and back away slowly---hands in the air---and nobody gets hurt . . . and, really, nobody gets hurt!)

Sadly, as we all should know, there was a time, several times in fact, in ages past, when the Church and its stone-throwers could and did get away with such paleo-minded brutalities but thanks to the efforts of those who struggled against their oppressions served up in the name of God, the world has slowly changed for the better. Has anyone noticed that when Man prevails in his secular efforts, the world improves and when God prevails in His sacred efforts, the world declines?

One shouldn't expect direct answers to the above direct questions coming any time soon as the Pope, along with the entirety of the world's Christian clergy who rely on his authority and direction in all matters, all have a vested interest in defending their religion and its written "Word" (as best they can!) no matter how indefensible it may be, hence the silence of the lambs on the "entire" text of *Lev.* 20:13!

Thankfully, in America today, if "anyone" were to call for the "killing" of people because of their sexuality, that person would be considered a psychopath, a threat to society, and dealt with as a criminal, however, when God calls for the very same "killing" to be done in His name, we purposely overlook or dismiss His malevolence, preferring instead to defend and worship Him—incredible! Such is a prime example of the mindless nature of religious belief!

Why does the Pope, who Christians believe is the Almighty's #1 go-to-guy, prefer to dance around in his slippers rather than answer the direct question whether or not a loving, merciful God authored *Lev.* 20:13 and *Lev.* 20:27. His reluctance to provide an honest answer is indicative that he, the Pope, "doesn't believe" everything he reads in the *Bible* is the absolute truth and the unchangeable Word of God that must be obeyed without question.

Is it possible that America, in reality, doesn't "trust" in this God or live "under" Him and His Word as all Christians "pretend" to do while boasting about it? One should be asking members of the Christian clergy why God's commanded stonings which He wanted His believers to carry out "forever" without any exceptions or interruptions, are never carried out today in America, a supposed Christian nation? The answer is because Man, not God, is slowly being recognized and credited for shining the guiding light that leads us to a more enlightened understanding about our lives and our world!

The tyranny, terror, intolerance, injustice, inhumanity, and mass destruction embedded and embraced in the scriptures of all Semitic theologies continue to be the greatest threat and impediment to civilization, the advance of freedom, and the ***"Blessings of Liberty"*** around the world. Owing to the sanctified status of Semitic scriptures, we dare not expose these so-called "sacred" texts ever, root and branch, to the light of reason, sanity, and truth. Everyone must unconditionally accept and believe their words without inquiry as we are reared and nurtured, educated and instructed, indoctrinated, obliged, and/or coerced to do—or else we'll end up suffering the excruciating agonies of a tormented eternity that a loving, Semitic God has prepared for us!

> *Christians, like slaves and soldiers, ask no questions.* (add robots and morons to your list, Mr. Falwell! ---kvk)
>
> ---Jerry Falwell

Owing to such mental conditioning and its potential for malevolent manifestations, we must begin to disarm and disable the Armageddon mindset of all Semitic religions. If Christians are able to believe their beloved, meek and mild Jesus is none other than the animal-mutilating, burnt-flesh savoring, homosexual-killing, unruly children-stoning, mass-murdering monster known as Jehovah, they will likely believe any other Christian absurdity simply because it is "written" in the *Bible* and, therefore, "must" be true! What is true for Christendumb, however, is the following:

> ***The authenticity of the books of the New Testament was denied, and the books treated as tales, forgeries, and lies, at the time they were voted to be the Word of God.*** (that bears repeating! ---kvk)
>
> ---Thomas Paine

Seeing how the folks who run the Catholic Church resorted so readily to involve themselves, in recent years, in ongoing immoral and sinful activity by covering-up and destroying evidence that "revealed" their prior knowledge about the actions of their pedophile priests and the Church's lack of concern for their molesting and raping of children—except for reassigning some of these bottom-feeders in an attempt to avoid any civil consequences or criminal responsibility for their egregious crimes. Such immoral behavior on the part of Church leadership is nothing new—it is evidence of their conducting business as usual. Let us not forget, in our scrutiny of these matters, that these pedophile priests, hypocrites all, while making themselves appear that they were diligently treading upon their righteous, carnal-desire-denying path to priesthood during their seminary years, knelt before graven images of their Almighty God and swore a vow of lifelong chastity along with the devout promise to act always as morally perfect "Soldiers of Christ" —every one of them!

(Note to Catholic parents: it was your revered, black-robed "Soldiers of Christ" who have not only sexually molested so many of your children, they have mentally molested all of the most vulnerable among you as well---for who but malevolent-minded *Bible*-terrorists would instruct naive and impressionable children (I being one of them) about the Devil, his cruelty, and his eternal Hell of torments that lays in wait for everyone who doesn't believe and follow their intimidating, imposing *Bible*-words? Is the Taliban's method of coercing others, using the words of the *Koran*, any different? Haven't all children of Catholic parents (and Taliban parents) been psychologically wounded---suffering nightmares and lifelong trauma to their psyches---believing they will be tortured forever for their "sins"? What an egregious thing these black-robed bastards have done to the innocent-mindedness of children---destroying their mental serenity and their childhoods of wonder, joy, and excitement!

In your role as parents of these children, do you think you bear any responsibility for their sexual and psychological defilement and for enabling their abusers? ---if not, you should! Do you continue to support the Church and its child-molesting clergy? ---if you do, you shouldn't! Raping the bodies of children is quite damaging enough to those who have experienced it--raping their minds using frightening, brutal tactics in the name of all that is holy is an act of terror and a violation against humanity, human decency, and the ***"unalienable rights"*** of all! For all the horrors the Catholic Church and its terrorizing clergy has caused to be done in the name of God, they should be considered, like Al Queda and the Taliban, a terror-dispensing organization and dealt with accordingly---for the Pope and the likes of Osama bin Laden are but like-minded, kindred beings who act only out of devotion to their God and His terror-filled words---"believe, or else"!)

It is inconceivable that any decent Catholic of sane mind would still find a spiritual need for the "sacred" services of such miscreants who, when dressed in their austere and ominous priestly garb are indistinguishable from those priests who are not morally corrupted (there may be a few!). It is inconceivable that any person claiming to be a Catholic would still find a need for continuing their allegiance to a Church that knowingly abetted the criminal, sexual predatory behaviors of its parasitic, pious-pretending priests. It is inconceivable that the blessed sacraments of the Catholic Church: hearing confessions and forgiving us of our sins, performing baptisms, confirmations, marriages, and the giving of last rites, etc., ---all of these sacred activities have been and will continue to be carried out by sinful-minded wolves in priests' clothing and their hypocritical holy performances will still be considered valid, God-pleasing practices by the Church and all of Christendumb! One wonders how Catholic folks are able to know with certainty whether they are confessing their sins to a child-molester/child-rapist or worse? Who, one wonders, do sick, child-molesting/child-raping priests go to hear their sick confessions? ---probably another of their sick kind! How are Catholic folks to know if the absolution-giving, black-befrocked sickos who hear their confessions, can be counted upon to truly wash-away their sins? Don't worry folks, if Father Jack-the-Ripper were to hear your confessions, rest assured, his absolutions would still be counted as valid by the Vatican! ---which makes one wonder about the "need" for priests in the first place!

While on the subject in part, many people, myself included, can't remember ever being baptized as a tiny infant so, not wanting to take the chance of spending the rest of my life-after-death life in Hell, I was fortunate to find a DIY Baptism Kit online that one can use in the comfort and safety of one's own home. The DIY Kit contained a small bottle of water and a Post-It Note with some strange writing on it and it had a money-back guarantee assuring me that an invisible flying fowl would descend from heaven and land somewhere on my body---and it only cost me $150.00 plus a small shipping and handling fee---such a deal! The Note instructed me to dump the water out upon my head while reciting the words that Jesus spoke during His baptism---that's why some of the Note was written in Hebrew because Jesus didn't speak a word of English---now I can finally rest assured that I'll be hanging-out in Heaven forever and ever!

Wait a sec---that's where child-molesting priests and prostitute-procuring ministers who perform baptisms will be hanging around, too---Christ, I hope I can get my money back! ---LOL! Referring back to the topic of hearing confessions:

"Once upon a time," I heard about this fella who would go to a couple of different Catholic Churches in his town, and confess to being a murderer (or was it a puppy and kitten torturer?) just to find out what the penalty would be: Church "A" imposed 3 "Hail Marys" and 4 "Our Fathers" while Church "B" only imposed 2 "Hail Marys" and 3 "Our Fathers" for the same crime---obviously, this fella stopped going to Church "A" to seek absolution of his sins! After this fella's confessing, at Church "B," to really having sexually molested a child, the priest, hearing his "confession" and, of course, demanding to know every sordid detail of the molestation, told this fella to *"Forget about it"*! ---God is truly merciful, wouldn't you say? ---but, I digress . . .

Who knew that evil priests, in their disguise as good priests, are considered by the Catholic Church to be just as worthy in the administration of their pious duties as the less wicked ones (there may be a few)? Who knew that such evil priests are perfectly capable, even without the use of magic wands, of accomplishing "transubstantiation"—the turning of bread and wine, by their focus on hocus-pocus, into the perfect body and blood of Christ without having to change the appearance of either—what an incredible skill—I don't think any Las Vegas magician can top that—what an incredible skill for sinful-minded bastards to master in order to forgive the sins of others!

It is inconceivable, too, that any Christian who is truly concerned with their spiritual behavior and who is committed to living a holy and exemplary life would continue to support, in any way, the Catholic Church, a criminal and parasitic enterprise that has resorted to egregious immoral, criminal, and terrorist activities throughout its tainted history—an enterprise that common sense reveals as being totally unnecessary for the improvement of anyone's spiritual yearnings. As stated previously, the "first" duty of freedom-loving people is to see, clearly, that benevolent human conduct and ethical behavior is "not" in any way dependent upon any Semitic religion's beliefs or "mysterious" rituals.

One has only to investigate the matter with an open mind rather than blindly accept the accounts rendered by dishonest Catholic scholarship which has always sought to cover-up and destroy evidence of the sins of the Church—nowhere is this more evident than in its whitewash of its wicked Popes. Reason's Tribunal will expose the disgraceful behavior of the

Princes of the Church who were murderers and debauchers—men whose wickedness had even turned the Vatican into a brothel where carnal excesses were unashamedly indulged in—excesses that were "recorded" by Catholic "scholarship" as the *"love of good cheer"*! Such disclosures will shock the minds of devout Catholics and rightly so—their Christian mindset has been complacent and unchallenged far too long. It is time to reveal the "truth" about the Catholic Church and its less-than-sacred doings to those who blindly accept its imposed religious beliefs—to those who blindly accept every word (every selected word!) in the *Bible* as "truth" --- truth that they state they have belief in but never seem to follow. It is time for Reason's Tribunal to expose and challenge such dogmas and such beliefs---so let's begin *"In the beginning."*

> ***As to the account of the Creation, with which the book of Genesis opens, it has all the appearance of being a tradition which the Israelites had among them before they came into Egypt; and after their departure from that country they put it at the head of their history, without telling (as it is most probable) that they did not know how they came by it. The manner in which the account opens shows it to be traditionary. It begins abruptly; it is nobody that speaks; it is nobody that hears; it is every criterion of being a tradition; it has no voucher. Moses does not take it upon himself by introducing it with the formality that he used on other occasions, such as saying, 'The Lord spake unto Moses, saying.'***

> ---Thomas Paine

If we are to believe that it was Moses who is the one telling us that his *Bible*-God said, *"Let there be light,"* ---*Gen.* 1:3 to whom were these "inspired" words of God spoken, I repeat, "to whom were they spoken"? We surely have a right to know! How the writer(s) of *Genesis* was able to know and certify what God had said, *"Let there be light: and there was light"* ---able to know that *"God saw the light"* and that God thought in His own mind that *"it was good"*? On whose eye-witness, ear-witness, or thought-witness authority should we believe these events actually occurred?

It certainly could not have been Moses or any of the so-called *Bible*-authors, or even the illiterate Adam and Eve, for they had not yet been fabricated at that time and neither had anyone else. Therefore, it is of utmost importance to learn the name of this person, the *Bible's* "First Deceiver" who time and time again gets an exclusive, personal audience with God to hear Him speak and to make a record of His every word, His every thought, His every feeling in His heart, and His every action? Does anyone know the name of God's "First Witness," the person to be credited with telling us in the very first "scripted" sentence of the *Bible*: *"In the beginning God created heaven and the earth"*? Whoever this creative-thinking, masked-man may have been, he (not she!) might just as well have begun his *Bible*-story with the words: *"Once upon a time,"* for that is how most fairytales begin their bogus, beguiling accounts—for it is in fairytales where exaggerated, concocted fish-stories belong and where the invented testimonies and story-lines of fabulous fables and fictional folktales are told!

"Let there be light," indeed, to enable us to see, with absolute clarity, why there is an absolute need for concealing the identity of the *Bible's* script-writers, *"In the beginning"* and throughout the *Bible*-tales! In reality, what fool would really want to sign his name in order to take credit for writing the concocted BS shoveled deep upon the *Bible's* pages? The *Bible* with its many unknown, script-writing authors certainly tops the list of whodunit books! Take a good whiff of the anonymously written words found on its every page and see if you can detect the odor of deception and dishonesty!

Is there any Pope, Cardinal, Bishop, Mega-Church Preacher, Baptist Minister, or Televangelist who can reveal this mystery person's identity to us? —for the above always preach that they have all of the correct and infallible answers for everything because of their absolute belief in the *Bible* and their ability to converse with God any time they choose. Surely then, these spiritual know-it-alls have an obligation to tell us the exalted name of God's "First Witness" and we have a right to demand to know it, for if God's very first words and the very first person to declare he heard them spoken are contrivances, as obvious conclusions and common-sense reveal they are, why should anyone believe, as true, the tales that follow, I repeat, "why should anyone believe, as true, the tales that follow"? If the *Bible* can be found to contain just one lie (which certainly has been proven!) then "every" word of it becomes suspect. Thanks to the bold questioning of Reason's Tribunal, the credibility of the *Bible* is DOA—destroyed by the ***"facts and evidence"*** of the falsehoods it has ***"revealed"*** to us on page one of chapter one!

As to the second chapter of *Genesis*, why should anyone believe the lies and nonsense told by God's unidentified "First Witness" about the Almighty needing 6 days to create the Cosmos and that He had to recuperate from the fatigue of His labors on the day after completing the job---labors that amounted to nothing more than His having to "speak" a few words.

Wouldn't a nano-second snap of a pair of God's gifted twelve fingers have sufficed in both cases? How long was a day before days ever existed? Did God really have to physically exert Himself? If so, perhaps with all the heavy lifting involved in making the Universe, He suffered injuries to His back and was forced to go on disability as a result—such might account for His frequent bouts of absenteeism in today's world—don't laugh! —crafting Semitic-scripture is a very serious business! I am of the opinion that an "Almighty" God could have created the Universe in under 2 days—3 days max—had He really put His mind to it—imagine the Almighty needing 6, twenty-four-hour days to complete anything and getting physically exhausted as a result of His efforts—incredible---sounds like God has a bit of man's weaknesses! *"Once upon a time"* . . . there's that smell again! *"Wait, what's that, Virginia? Yes, my dear, God has twelve huge fingers, three tiny ears, one eye, seven noses, and a mouth as big as an elephant (the Guy is truly hideous!) ---and you thought He looked like one of us? ---really? ---imagine that! And, 'no', you really don't want a graven image of this Frankenstein hanging around your neck!"*

(NOTE TO READER: never underestimate the amazing abilities of words---words that can not only instantly create a Universe when voiced, but can instantly reveal a fraud upon hearing them spoken! Oh, the mighty power of words!)

Why should anyone believe the nonsense about Adam and Eve's bogus existence and their world-changing "sin" and the nonsense about Jesus having to be the innocent scapegoat who "had to die" in order to make an "atonement" for it, when the teller of these tales has shown himself to be a deceiver, a conniving contriver, and a liar? *"Let there be light,"* indeed, to dispel the darkness and deceptions of Semitic religions! *"Let there be light"* to reveal to us the name of God's very own confidant, His personal recording secretary, and His confessor—the only person who had intimate knowledge about what God saw with His own eyes, what He felt in His heart, what He regretted doing, and exactly what every word was that God had spoken to no one—the only person who was an eyewitness and earwitness to events in Eden and yet, we don't even know his name! Shouldn't we investigate the matter in Reason's Tribunal in order to find out? If willful lying is not a characteristic of spiritual behavior, but rather a characteristic of evil-mindedness, be assured the *Bible* was not authored by any Divinity revealing Himself, it was authored by ungodly men revealing themselves!

When the Lord saw that the wickedness of man on the earth was great, and that man's every thought and all the inclinations of his heart were only evil, he regretted that he had made man on the earth and was grieved to the heart---(imagine God having regrets about something He'd done and grieving as a result of it---really? ---sounds like He's a bit fallible to me! ---kvk) *Then the Lord said, 'I will wipe from the earth man whom I have created—man and beast, crawling creature and bird of the air as well—for I regret that I made them.' But Noah found favor with the Lord.* (Judging by the way world #2 has turned out, I bet God must surely have regretted making that decision too--probably wept like a baby over it! ---kvk)

---Genesis 6:5-8

And God said unto Noah, The end of all flesh is come before me; for the earth is filled with violence because of them; and, behold, I will destroy them with the earth. (We are to believe that these words were spoken by a "peace-loving," "world loving" Guy who, after having removed all *"violence"* from the planet, commanded that nations of innocent people should be brutally annihilated---commanded that homosexuals and unruly children should be stoned to death---commanded the abuse of women and animals---all being carried-out, one would assume, in a non-violent manner of course---really? This Psychopath scares the hell out of me! ---how about you? ---kvk)

---Gen. 6:13

And of every living thing of all flesh, two of every sort shalt thou bring into the ark to keep alive with thee; they shall be male and female.

---Gen. 6:19

...and I will cause it to rain upon the earth forty days and forty nights; and every living substance that I have made will I destroy from off the face of the earth.

---Gen. 7:4

213

...and Noah only remained alive, and they that were with him in the ark.

---Gen. 7:23

What a "revelation" it is to learn that the "perfect" and "infallible" God of Judeo-Christianity has confessed, I repeat, "has confessed" to being incompetent when He admitted above to having made a very big mistake when He created the *"flesh"* of *"every living substance"*! His very own words prove, beyond any doubt, that the Semitic God of the *Bible* was not suited for the job at hand—that He lacked the skills necessary to create a non-violent world, not once, but twice! His second attempt to create a better, peaceful world was, quite obviously, not worth the tremendous, miracle-laden effort He undertook in order to destroy the first one. If God had regrets over His bungled first attempt at making a world free of *"violence,"* He must surely have kicked Himself in the ass for finding "favor" with Noah and for realizing the extent of all the blunders He had made in His second attempt to create a non-violent world! No one, I repeat, "no one" should expect a better, blissful future is in the works for us with this Guy in charge!

If we are to believe the above words of the regretful Maker of all *"flesh"* telling us that man and beasts, crawling creatures, and the birds of the air were filling the earth *"with violence,"* and, as a result, needed to be destroyed because of it, who should be held responsible for making all *"flesh"* with this evil propensity in the First Place? All fingers point to the Creator of *"all flesh"* ---it is He who should be held responsible for making *"flesh"* the way it was, the way it is, and the way it still continues, post-flood, to behave? Who else is to blame? Are we to believe, in man's case, that it was his *"knowledge of good and evil"* and his free-will that gave cause to his violence? In the case of the animals who, obviously, lack the *"knowledge of good and evil"* and who have no free-will to act contrary to the urgings of their instincts---why did God blame and punish them for something they, obviously, had no part in doing? What had birds, bees, and butterflies done to deserve the damning wrath of God? Shouldn't those of sound and sane mind be seriously concerned about the mental health of someone who observes *"violence,"* I repeat, *"violence"* in the wondrous, innocuous industries of birds, bees, and butterflies? God definitely has some more "splaining" to do!

Imagine the "Creator" of these non-threatening, sinless creatures, regretting having unleashed their marvelous *"living substance"* upon the

214

face of the earth, but not regretting having created Satan and allowing his wickedness and evil to be unleashed against everyone—incredible! More "splaining"! Who would've ever suspected that birds, bees, and butterflies, aside from being fruitful and multiplying as part of God's plan for planet Earth, were up to no damn good flitting from tree to tree, from flower to flower in order to fill the earth *"with violence"* —those evil, scheming bastards, those rampaging agents of the Devil in their beguiling disguises! Isn't it a bit surprising though, that one never ever hears a sermon about what the animals had done that caused the earth to be *"filled with violence"* especially since that violence was responsible for God's destruction of the planet? Believe it or not, I'd make the pilgrimage to Joel Osteen's extravagant palace of worship just to hear him "reveal," in one of his spectacular, "Come to Jesus" sermons, how it came to be that the activities of butterflies caused the destruction of the world---I'm all ears, *Bible*-boy!

How laughable it is, when the obvious conclusions gleaned from this imposing *Bible*-tale and others are told in this extrapolated manner—how laughable it is to believe such incredible nonsense contained in Semitic scripture concerning the *"violence"*-producing nature of *"all flesh"*! Here we have a, supposedly, "compassionate" and "loving" God who is divinely-distraught about the savage nature of *"all flesh,"* ---a nature that He alone created by making animals the way they are---instinctual creatures unable to act on free-will. And yet, He decides to kill, non-violently, of course, nearly every one of them in order to erase the big mistake He had made in giving them life in the First Place. And yet, in His own "loving" way, He prepared a tormenting, eternal Hell where burning coals and pitchforks are to be constantly shoved, non-violently, of course, into the asses of innumerable humans who have forgotten to invoke or utter the sweet name of Jesus with their dying breath! Let's not forget that these destined-for-Hell humans are all descendants of Noah---a guy that God thought to spare from His drowning flood because he seemed like such a nice fella---another big mistake on His part---more "splaining! And yet, with His track-record of utter failure in being able to successfully complete any of His well-thought-out projects, we're told to believe that He was able, beyond any doubt, to create a "perfect" Heaven to reward every person who has belief in Him whether He is thought of as Jehovah, or as Jesus, or as Allah---really? ---but, as so many Americans know with certainty, ---having belief in Jesus is really the "only" way to go!

How sad it is that millions upon millions of Jews, millions upon millions of Christians, and millions upon millions of Muslims believe such crapola as stated above because it is part of their imposing Word of God. They continue to worship, without any concern whatsoever, a genocidal Monster whose evil deeds would surely shame Satan and his like-minded minions if ever they truly existed! How sad it is that billions believe in unbelievable Semitic scripture---in every word they contain that tells of the perfections of a "loving" Creator and the imperfections of His detested creations---really? Man help us!

Have you, dear believers in the "Word of God," noticed how the malevolent imperfections of World #1 have continued, post cleansing-flood, to fill World #2 evermore so with the *"violence"* that the Maker of all flesh is totally responsible for in both cases---an "all-knowing" Creator, who only figures things out too late and who reacts rather unmercifully when He does! Remember, dear believers, the reasons for Noah's flood were #1: to destroy *"all"* of the flesh responsible for filling the earth with *"violence"* and #2: to *"destroy"* the earth. Since, obviously, neither event happened as a result of the flood, for the earth and its *"violence"*-producing inhabitants continue to exist, God has been caught once again wearing blazing pants! Please rest assured, dear believers in the "Word of God," in the absolute certainty of the blissful, future Paradise He has promised to share with all of you---for God, after all, is a man of His Word and, after all, it is written in the *Bible* and what could be more truthful and reliable than that?

It is interesting to note here that Mr. Pants Afire, who was so intent on destroying the world and all of its violent inhabitants, would be content (or have need) to wait day after day, week after week, month after month, year after year after year after year, to allow 4 boneheads (Noah and his three sons) with no building experience and no shipbuilding tools to build a humongous, seaworthy boat, fill it with "every" animal species that existed in the area and in the far-off reaches of the world and load it with enough provisions to feed an army in order to embark on an ocean cruise of unknown duration aboard a vessel teeming with (and reeking of) raw sewage.

Why didn't an impatient, vengeful, Almighty God create the ark and fill it with animals and food all by Himself in a blink of an eye with just a snap of His fingers? Or, why didn't He just destroy the earth and all of its violent inhabitants in a "VOILA" moment and be done with all of the dramatic doings and the countless miracles that were obviously needed to accomplish His world-destroying goals as they have been "revealed" to us in *Genesis*? Why didn't the overburdened and exhausted ark crew beseech their favoring God to put an end to their stinking, miserable sufferings---their seemingly endless 24/7 labors caring for the welfare of *"every living thing"* on board? ---I don't think the reeking animals enjoyed their ordeal at sea either, being unable to move about in their cramped quarters for months and months on end!---if, as God supposedly stated in *Ex.* 6:5, *"the wickedness of man was great in the earth, and that every imagination of the thoughts of his heart was only evil continually,"* ---what the hell was in God's malicious *"imagination,"* in His wicked *"thoughts,"* and in His malevolent *"heart"* when He resorted to *"evil"* to correct the problems inherent in His Creation? Why is it that the *Bible*-God can do no wrong no matter the number of malicious and brutal, abominable acts He commits? Surely, it was the *"wickedness"* of God that *"was great in the earth"* ---it was His thoughts and His doings that was *"only evil continually"*!

Why, too, does an all-powerful God, the one and only Creator of the Universe, have to rely (and wait!) on the assistance of others to get the job done? Why, too, does the God of Semites always endeavor to involve Himself with murder and destruction, with boatloads of misery, with punishing the innocent, etc.? Is it because the God of Semites is as incompetent and as reprehensible as His anonymous script-writers---His power-seeking, sicko creators? ---or, is it because the God of Semites, the God of the *Bible* and the *Koran* is just a mythic leading character---a purposely designed "bully" made to intimidate others into accepting the self-interests of His designers---a tyrannical madman who makes the revealing of *"Once upon a time"*-tales much more interesting, intriguing and dramatic? Ask yourself why a God who created the world in less than a week would allow decades to pass in order to achieve His (drama-filled!) goal of destroying it! ---something He, in His incompetent role as Almighty God, according to *Bible-evidence,* had obviously failed to accomplish!

Returning to the boatload-tale, according to the revered justice system proudly promoted by Semitic religions, birds, bees, and butterflies are now to be counted among God's chosen scapegoats who were made to pay unjustly, of course, for the sins of others with their innocent, innocuous lives—scapegoats who, we're told by God, were "all" deserving of annihilation except for a boatload of animal and human refugees who, excepting Noah, were all possessors of the evil minds and the evil hearts that God so detested and yet, it was because He had found favor with one human being that He greatly admired, He decided to save Admiral Noah and all of the other degenerate human/animal passengers who sailed the seas with him onboard the ark! What the hell was God thinking?

According to God's very words, it was solely because of the actions of *"all"* men and *"all"* beasts that the earth had become filled with *"violence,"* in the First Place and that that was the reason behind His wanting to destroy the entire earth and "all" of its evil occupants. Yet, lo and behold, this uber-

Genius replenished the earth with what else but more of the very same evil-minded, evil-hearted, "violent" creatures that He was responsible for creating in the First Place—creatures who were filling the earth with you know what! ---need I say, "Duh!'"? What was the point of God's well-thought-out destruction of all the violence-producing inhabitants of the earth, and even the earth itself, if not to make the planet a better, new and improved, non-violent place after His cleansing flood? Let us all, therefore, give a great big shout-out to God for cleaning up His act and for a (long-delayed) job well done in His perfect efforts to purify the world perfectly! ---what an incredible "inspired" boatload of BS God's infallible and inerrant script-writers would have us believe!

Is there any member of the Christian clergy who can tell us, without grin-suppression, why it is absolutely necessary that we believe, with the mindset of a kindergartener, every word given in the *Old* and the *New Testaments*? Why we must believe, without question and without having second thoughts about it, that Noah, a 600-year-old man well past his prime and his three sons (1 man and 3 boys!) were capable of building, without setbacks, a large, seaworthy vessel using only green, unseasoned "gopher wood," pine-pitch and stone tools? Without the use of metal tools, how were they able to fell trees, saw, chisel, and plane raw timber into finished lumber? ---without knowledge of the use of a square (a device used to make right angles) ---without knowledge of a plumb bob (a device used to determine verticality)---without knowledge of a "cubit" being a unit of length (approx. 20" long) ---surely, such things were in only in existence at a later time when the script-writer(s) of this tale wrote it!

How were they able to assemble such a sturdy, sea-worthy cargo ship without any knowledge of shipbuilding or of wood-joinery techniques which, like metal tools, didn't exist at the time? The lack of technical advancements that had to occur in tool-making, woodworking, and boat-building, from the time of Adam down to Noah (nine generations!), to make building the ark possible would certainly be enough to sink, not float, such a boat—a 500 ft. long x 84 ft. wide x 50 ft. high un-ballasted, 3-decked boat with its thousands upon thousands of precision wood joints supporting thousands upon thousands of pounds of cargo that incredibly never sprung a leak except when common-sense went aboard to check on conditions!

In doing the math, each deck contained 42,000 sq. ft. (with partitions this number would be even less) ---if one allows 50 sq. ft. of deck space (10' x 5') for each pair of animals, then 840 pairs of animals could have occupied each deck (840 pairs of animals x 2 decks would allow for a total of 1680 pairs of animals being on board the ark if one allows for the third deck being used entirely for food/water storage. When one considers that there are more than a million animal species on the planet, it doesn't require a genius to figure out that the *Bible*-claim of *"every living thing"* being onboard the ark (which would have to include the entire plant kingdom!) is an outright BS fabrication for the *Bible* also tells us with *Bible*-certainty that every living thing outside the ark had perished as *"Noah only remained alive, and they that were with him in the ark."*! Is more proof needed to expose God's Word as an absolute fraud and a purposeful rewrite of mythology by its self-serving script-writers?

Certainly, the amount of food and water that would be needed to sustain the lives of the ark's teeming passengers for the amount of time that the ark supposedly remained afloat would have required Noah to have built another ark, or two, or three, for food storage alone and towed this flotilla alongside the ark for an unknown period of time for God never told Adm. Noah how long he, his crew, and his passengers would have to tread water! (To those of you who have not lost brain function because of your *Bible*-beliefs---if you believe the Noah-tale to be a true, infallible and inerrant *Bible*-event and not a mythic story from pre-*Bible* antiquity, who was the *Genesis* script-writer who told us with absolute certainty that every living thing outside the ark had perished? ---who was the *Genesis* script-writer who told us with absolute certainty that the mountains were covered with 15 cubits of water? ---I have no doubt that it was the same guy who heard God say, *"Let there be light"*! I think it is possible that it was the same guy who later-on ran a concession stand for years in Coney Island---this guy knew everything about everything---I think his name was Joel, but I could be mistaken!)

From the day of Adam's creation to the day that Noah's flood began covered a span of 1656 years if one believes the *Genesis* timeline—a timeline "revealed" by an amazing and unknown (of course!) record-keeping-ancestral-historian and script-writer who, long after the fact, tells us with absolute accuracy exactly how many years passed in each generation and exactly when each generation began to "begat" other generations—an impossible undertaking for present-day ancestral historians to accomplish without error over that length of time even with the use of computers! Extrapolating on the amazing rate of technological advancement and accomplishment that we are imposed upon to believe occurred in those nine biblical generations in order for Noah and his sons to have experienced no difficulty in building the ark, it should have only taken a few more generations of Adam's great-grandchildren to be able to develop the skills, the technology, and the science necessary to build a spaceship capable of sending men to the surface to the moon! Perhaps, it may turn out after all, that some future astronaut exploring the lunar surface will stumble upon the remnants of a strange craft built from gopher wood and pitch, and, most likely, an extraordinary amount of what Thomas Paine called ***"salamander wool"*** !

Why must we believe, as naive kindergarteners do, without having second thoughts about it, that Noah's ark contained Antarctic penguins, Arctic polar bears, Asian panda bears, Australian kangaroos, South American anacondas, North American grizzly bears and bison, along with countless numbers of vertebrate and invertebrate, warm and cold-blooded creatures most of whom only existed in unknown and remote locations from the ark's supposed locality? Why must we believe, too, that Noah was somehow able to catch whales, get them on board, and keep them alive as every living thing outside the ark had expired as stated in the undoubted, God-inspired words given in *Gen.* 7:23? *"Yes, Virginia, we are told to believe everything in the Bible, even the obvious lies, for it is the purpose of all Semitic scripture to make us believe the unbelievable and believe it with certainty!"*

Is there a *Bible*-pounder who can tell us with absolute certainty how Noah was able to know about the existence of these exotic animals in the first place and how he was able to know about their special needs in regard to diet, and how he was able (without the use of miracles!) to trap and transport a male and female member of each species across continents and oceans, mountains and deserts along with tons and tons of their sustaining foods back from the far reaches of the world to Arkville in the Middle East. On arriving there, these amazing animals, who had been filling the earth *"with violence,"* would then be placed aboard a seaworthy, ocean-going vessel that Noah knew, with certainty, would be capable of floating for an "unknown" length of time upon the anticipated flood waters that were soon to inundate the earth. This was done, we're told, in order to "save" these God-damned creatures and their God-damned DNA from God's planned destruction of every living thing which had to include all of the God-damned plant life on the planet as well! How many thousands of miracles does it take to create the ark-tale and then make us believe its every word?

Perhaps, there is a *Bible*-Pounder who can tell us what the members of the plant kingdom had done to deserve God's wrath? Perhaps, there is a *Bible*-Pounder who can tell us with absolute certainty, how Noah was able to determine the difference between the males and females of so many close-in-resemblance members of a particular species that he and his sons had never seen before? Perhaps, they can tell us with absolute certainty why the "infallible" chapter 6 of *Genesis* tells us the animals came aboard the ark only in pairs including cattle and fowls while its "inerrant" chapter 7 tells us the *"clean"* cattle and fowls came by sevens even though no one onboard the ark knew what a *"clean"* or an "unclean" animal was? --- surely, such knowledge was in existence only at a later time when the script-writer(s) of this tale wrote it! Perhaps they can explain with absolute certainty why in the former chapter, God told Noah He was going to destroy *"all flesh in which there is the breath of life,"* and *"all that are on the earth shall die"* (by drowning!) —which must have included the drowning of all of the fishes! —certainly, the air-breathing fishes such as whales, seals, manatees, etc. Certainly, they would not be in existence today unless their forebears were listed as passengers on the ark's manifest—and that's according to the ***"facts and evidence"*** of the indubitable *Bible*, folks!

Was it possible that Noah had two (or seven) of every "sea creature" in the world on board as well, for we are told in the latter chapter given above that only Noah and those with him in the ark *"remained alive"* which could only have meant that all of the world's aquatic creatures—*"every living substance"* —outside the ark had ceased to exist including every living plant and every living seed on the planet. This might explain the disappearances of the "tree of life" and the poor little cherubs left to stand guard over it, but how many "inerrant" *Bible*-Pounders are aware that the ark, without doubt, must have been carrying the living seeds of every plant, too, in order to reestablish their kind after their wantonly imposed extinction, otherwise, how would Noah be able to replenish all the planet's plant life that God destroyed? I think it only right, therefore, to give Noah all of the credit and all of the heartfelt thanks that he and each of his crew mates deserve for their astounding deeds---crew mates that must have included an infallible, unknown, God-inspired, Semitic script-writer as well---in order to memorialize the incredible events of such an unbelievable sea-odyssey! Thank you, Noah and crew, and the unknown chronicler of Ark-tale events, thank you so much for saving our scapegoat planet and for all of your unbelievable efforts in assisting God to make the world over into a non-violent, uncorrupted, and improved place for *"every living substance"* to live in, unlike the world that existed before the flood! Interestingly, the following is a post-flood account of this New World described in the *Wisdom of Solomon*:

All is a raging riot of blood and murder, theft and deceit, corruption, faithlessness, tumult, perjury, confusion over what is

What incredible nonsense it is to believe such a contrived story as the Noah-tale—a story plagiarized from ancient, Pagan mythologies— mythologies that floated their own versions of Noah and the ark long before the *Bible's* corrupted version of them came to be! What incredible nonsense it is to believe that Noah could possibly have loaded enough provisions and drinkable water aboard the ark to sustain the lives of millions of land, air, and sea animals (and to keep the onboard plants alive) for an odyssey of unknown duration and that 8 people (9 people if one includes the script-writer of this tale!) would be able to care for them all. As it turned out, their time spent aboard the ark I have calculated to be more than a year (375 days) for the *Bible's* **"facts and evidence"** provides us with the exact day of the ark's boarding by Noah and crew and the exact day of the ark's disembarking by Noah and crew:

On the seventeenth day of the second month of the 600th year of Noah's life, the floodgates of heaven were opened according to *Genesis* 7:11. Two verses later it is stated that in that selfsame day [the seventeenth day of the second month of the 600th year of Noah's life] *'entered Noah and Shem, and Ham, and Japheth, the sons of Noah, and Noah's wife, and the three wives of his sons with them, into the ark.'* They remained aboard the ark until the twenty-seventh day of the second month of the 601st year of Noah's life, as told in *Genesis* 8:13-19. That was the day God ordered Noah, his crew and his animal (and plant!) cargo to abandon ship. Their time spent aboard the ark, therefore, is reckoned as one year plus ten days for a total of 375 days. It is interesting to remember that it took God only 6 days to create everything in the Universe with no one helping Him and His having absolutely nothing to work with. Yet, He needed the assistance of Noah and his three sons---to spend what must have taken years (decades?) to accomplish---to build a seaworthy ark, fill it with animals from all over the world and then had them spend more than a year's time living aboard it caring for its live cargo while the remainder of *"every living thing"* existing in the world perished in a flood that only God could create. All of these mighty unbelievable works were done in order for God to destroy one gazillionth of one gazillionth part of the Universe: the earth---an effort that He, obviously, could not achieve even with the help of others! Hmm! Hmm! Hmm! As remarkable as this epic cruise turned out to be, there was also the remarkable but little-known event that took place on one of those unbelievable days spent onboard this ocean-going vessel. Because of the turbulence caused by stormy, tossing seas, the lions were able to escape their confines aboard the ark and devour the only remaining, mating pair of pink unicorns in existence. A sad day indeed, that such amazing animals should become extinct in order to satisfy the hunger urge of two large cats. Thankfully, however, the rarely-seen pair of flying pigs brought aboard the ark by Noah himself and who shared the same stateroom as the unicorns, were spared the unfortunate fate of their bunkmates, for they were able to escape the marauding felines by utilizing their ability to fly out of harm's way just in the nick of time. Today, however, they can still be seen, at times, when ***"fools and hypocrites"*** speak about the veracity of their *Bible*-tales. There is no doubt, however, that my words that tell of the amazing animals I've included as being onboard the ark are as reliable as any words revealed in *Genesis* and elsewhere throughout the *Bible*—at least, in this particular case, the author is known! ---kvk

What incredible nonsense it is to believe that any man or animal could have survived the miserable, stifling conditions imagined to have existed aboard the manure-laden and urine-reeking ark which had but one small ventilation window for the entire stinking vessel—an odor that still seems to linger on the pages of the *Bible* after all these many years. Wouldn't Noah be compelled to butcher some of the animals that were aboard in order to feed the ark's many ravenous carnivores to keep them from starving to death month after month after month? ---I think PETA should be informed about Noah and his boatload of abused animals!

On release-day, if one believes the many impositions of the ark tale, the carnivores left the ark alongside the herbivores and waited patiently for them to be fruitful and to multiply before attempting to devour them—what incredible nonsense! What incredible nonsense it is to believe that the herbivores, after being released from the ark, could find anything to subsist on when God, whose heart is always filled with compassion and whose head is always filled with wisdom, had just destroyed *"every living substance"* on the face of the earth with His killing flood---*Gen.* 7:4! What incredible nonsense it is to believe that the world's only existing penguins, polar bears, pandas, kangaroos, anacondas, grizzly bears and bison, etc., were released, under God's all-knowing direction—not back into their native lands, but somewhere into the mountains of Turkey where *Bible*-thumpers would have us believe they were to begin replenishing the earth with their kind! How many miracles does God have to perform in order to destroy the earth and rebuild it when all He had to do to create the entire Universe was to speak a few words? Upon reflection, Turkey would be the perfect place, after all, to release the many turkeys contained in this tale!

(NOTE TO READER: the reason so many *Bible*-tales are lacking in details, logic, and believability is because they were purloined from mythological tales, a form of storytelling that long pre-dates the *Bible*. Mythology is not historical narrative but a fanciful means (without having printed books) to account for something in a memorable way in its attempt to explain the origins of the world, the creation of life forms, and other perplexing mysteries in story-form without going into great detail to explain them. Mythological tales with their wild exaggerations and perplexing gaps were never meant to be literally believed---they, for obvious reasons, always suffer from a lack of essential information and clarifying details, hence the *Bible*-tales lack of essential information and clarifying details in its borrowed and re-purposed myths from more ancient cultures where story-telling was used to educate, not indoctrinate like the Christ-myth was meant to do.)

The script-writers of the mythic Gospels knew well how to tweak the religious ingredients (the bogus prophesies of the *OT*) needed to deceive us into believing that their non-physical God (their creation!) could be made into a physical human being (their creation, too!) ---they knew well how to bring Him into this world and they knew well how to take Him out of it in such a way that would evoke the pious sympathies needed to serve their interests of ***"power and revenue."*** What they didn't know well, however, was how to fill in the missing years (decades) of the mythical life of Jesus by telling us where He was and what He did for all of those years, those many years---where and when He learned the identity of His real father---where and when He suddenly became aware of His superhuman powers---where and when He became aware that He was God and decided to reveal His true identity, etc., etc., ---I can only assume, that for all of those many many many years when God, Himself, walked in sandals upon the earth with no one able to record His every move (as was so common in the *OT)* - --there must have been a shortage of *Bible*-authors hangin' around in the bushes! Thankfully, however, because of God-given "inspiration," I am able to fill in some of the blanks of Jesus' life that no one, including the Pope and every Pampered Preacher, can dispute because of the lack of evidence needed to prove me wrong!

"Once upon a time," Jesus, as we all know, was the leader of a parasitic, street gang known simply as the "Disciples"---twelve guys who hated (*Luke* 14:26) and abandoned their families, their livelihoods, and their pastimes (if they had any besides fishing!) ---guys who survived, not by sowing, reaping, fishing or otherwise working for a living as all exemplary, pious parasites continue to do to this day---but by hanging around the streets, panhandling and living off the generosity of others as did their revered, racist Ruler---a racist Ruler who told His homies not to worry or give a thought or a damn about tomorrow or their bodies---not to worry or give a thought or a damn about where their food, their drink, and their clothing shall come from as such necessities of life are the concerns of Gentiles only, not the superior, spiritual-minded Jews---really! ---thirteen guys who, not having underwear, toilet paper, a bidet, or a change of clothes (*Matthew* 6:25,31, *Luke* 3:11), wore the same reeking rags on their reeking bodies day after day after day (their modern-day-look sporting heavenly haloes is but a religious improvement on their ring-around-the-collar existence) ---thirteen stinking guys who seemingly never bathed themselves at least on a regular basis and yet Jesus is usually depicted as wearing a sparkling white frock and smelling probably like a fresh rose petal instead of a warm manure pile- --really! ---imagine God being in need of a bath! ---imagine Jesus not being in need of one! ---what's that goddammed smell?

Being the product of a dysfunctional family, Jesus was a troubled youth who had His share of problems growing up which were quite evident by the disrespect He showed His mother---*John* 2:4 and a pleading Gentile woman---by His loathing of Jewish Temple-authorities and their less-than-sacred religious practices---by His hatred and disdain for every Gentile He encountered throughout His entire earthly life---by His occasional outbursts of anger, paranoia, and hypocrisy to the point of arming His gang with swords to annihilate, not to "love" His enemies---Jesus even suffered from bouts of megalomania thinking He was none other than Almighty God! As we all know, too---God, with all of the many reports of His *OT* thuggery and His *NT* arrest record---His criminal past is just too well documented in the *Bible* to deny!

Quite often Jesus wondered, while growing up, why Joseph, His father, (the only father He ever knew!) never really regarded Him as His own son! His real father in heaven above, as we all know too well, was a criminal with a rap-sheet so big, it required chapters and verses to reveal it in its entirety---everything from creating Satan and then rewarding him for his malevolent activities to animal abuse and butchery---from His disdain for women and for Gentiles---from His attempt to destroy the world to the brutal murder and annihilation of unoffending folks and the raping of their virgin daughters---from His desire to punish only the innocent for the misdeeds of others and on and on and on! There seemed to be little hope for Jesus, a boy who had a psychopath for a father, and a mother who was a descendant of another sicko known simply as David, a deranged criminal who, today in Judeo-Christian America, would be on Death Row awaiting execution for his "divine" Semitic activities! Like Father, like Son, Jesus, too, was an animal abuser who was responsible for the horrific deaths of two thousand swine---an arsonist who desired to turn planet earth into a pile of ashes---a lying, tree-cursing individual who was obsessed with devils and their removal from our bodies---a man who prepared an eternal Hell to punish the many and an eternal Heaven to reward the few---but what would you expect from someone who was a carrier of such Divine DNA?

Because of His inherent penchant for violence along with His inexplicable hatred of family members, His loathing for Gentiles and for Jewish religious traditions that had something to do with money (of all things!), Jesus desecrated and vandalized a Jewish temple and was sent away to a juvenile detention center for psychological evaluation and rehabilitation. While there, He happened upon His cell-mate playing with his wand and proceeded to pluck his eyes out and cut-off his hands--- imagine that! These brutal acts earned Him several years behind bars at Jerusalem State Penitentiary. Luckily, because of His knowledge of carpentry, Jesus caught a break one day and was able to leave his well-deserved confines to work, while on supervised release (community service!), making repairs to the very temple He had ransacked years before. While there, He removed part of a damaged wall in order to fix it and, lo and behold, a strange looking snake-headed rod tumbled out and landed in Jesus' arms (perhaps, the very first "Come to Jesus" moment?)! Because of the hissing sound it made when He held it, Jesus knew there was something very unusual about this rod and the powers it possessed so He decided to hide it in some nearby bushes until His release-day finally came and He was able to go and retrieve it. After handling and playing with His rod for a time, Jesus had actually created a tremendous swarm of locusts and He realized then, at that moment, that the rod He had found was, in reality, the magic wand used by Moses and Aaron to lay waste to Egypt!

Understandably, the rod with its God-like, magic powers (God-rod!) was always in Jesus' possession and He often used it just to impress His homies attempting to make them believe He was God Almighty---turning water into wine (which turned out to be quite a useful thing based on the drinking habits of His gang!) ---turning a few measly fish and bread morsels into banquet meals where thousands upon thousands received their fill! (a useful skill, no doubt, for sponges who neither toiled nor tilled for their sustenance!) ---turning dead folks into living folks once more only to have them die again! (not-so-blessed events when you think about it!) ---walking on water in order to be able to cross bodies of water without having to raise a sweat rowing a boat or to pay for boat-fare! There you have it folks---the missing years of Jesus and a bit more! If you have evidence to the contrary about any of the above statements I've made, please notify your local religious authorities at once! Now back to where I left off describing where Noah left off his millions of foul-smelling passengers:

Based upon such a boatload, I believe that adventurous, wealthy *Bible*-believers, instead of broadening the search to find remnants of a bogus wooden ark somewhere in the vicinity of Mt. Ararat in order to prove the veracity of the *Bible* and its Noah-nonsense—they should be narrowing their fruitless endeavors to finding, instead, some physical evidence that proves that the abounding occupants of the ark were all deposited there, on Mt. Ararat, and nowhere else according to the infallible *Bible*, to re-establish their kind. Perhaps then, they can explain how the pair of released kangaroos were able to make their way back to Australia? What an incredible journey that must have been! My bet is that *Bible*-believers won't find any evidence to prove their ridiculous *Bible*-claims---that they won't find any evidence of koala bears ever having been in the vicinity of Mt. Ararat nor any evidence of the eucalyptus trees that provide their only source of food growing anywhere in the region. What I am certain of is that a fat rat or two will definitely be located in the telling of this uber tall-tale to prove the veracity of Reason's Tribunal---just more evidence that the *Bible* is a Chutzpah Chronicle: a book of grandiose lies and deceptions written for the benefit of its script-writers and their tribes only!

Unbelievably, and counter-intuitively, the very "first" thing Noah decided to do after disembarking from the ark in order to "non-violently" restore and replenish the formerly *"filled with violence"* earth with the animal survivors that he went to such great lengths to acquire and keep alive and well during their long odyssey at sea—was to build an altar in order to "kill" and to roast a member of the various *"clean"* beasts and the various *"clean"* fowls in order to produce a *"sweet savor unto the Lord."* What a wonderful, Semitic way for the few, God-selected, privileged survivors of a life-destroying flood of mythic proportions, to celebrate the beginning of a new world and a new age—with what else but more violence and more bloodshed! What a wonderful, Semitic way to initiate the reestablishment of animal life upon the planet by indulging in the slaughter of some of the ark-survivors, especially since God had just finished eradicating the entire animal (and plant) kingdom from the face of the earth except for those fortunate enough to have survived their ordeal at sea onboard the lifesaving ark!

At that extraordinary moment in time, Noah deemed that what the new "violence-free" world needed was some more death-dealing activities—the bloodshed and butchery of *"clean"* animals! This is especially noteworthy, I repeat, "especially noteworthy" since Noah had no idea what a *"clean"* animal was, and he had no idea why such animals should be ritually butchered and burnt upon an altar as a means to please God because the "inspired," paleo-minded script-writers of "inerrant" Jewish scripture had neglected to inform and instruct Noah about these basics of Semitic theology from a later period in the Jews' fabricated history! It was not possible for Noah to know that God so loved smelling the *"sweet savor"* of burnt flesh when such ungodly behavior was unknown in the *Bible* before the ark-tale! ---duhhh! The idea of Noah's wanting to build an altar to give thanks to God, for ensuring the ark's safe voyage to the new world, is an anachronism. Noah's attempt to please and appease, in a ritual ceremony, God's sensuous, carnal nature with the slaughter of *"clean"* animals and the cremation of their mutilated remains was never a part of the *Bible's* Eden-tale which immediately preceded that of Noah's water-logged tale. The ritual sacrifice of animals, therefore, was never a part of Noah's life experience! Hmm! Hmm! Hmm! Doesn't lemonade really taste great?

When you, dear *Bible*-readers and *Bible*-believers, disembark from reading the boatload of BS contained in this tale about the leaking flagship of Semitic chutzpah, the very first thing you should do is to reflect upon its many subliminal subtleties. When you learn of the many extraordinary efforts undertaken by your Semitic ancestors aboard the ark—with whom everyone on the planet now completely owes their new and improved existence to---with whom everyone on the planet now shares their DNA---with whom everyone on the planet is indebted to because of the many hardships they must have endured to make the world a much better place for everyone and everything on the planet---bet you didn't know that everyone on the planet is of Jewish descent! Oy vey! How is it possible, therefore, for anti-Semitism to even exist when everyone on the planet is, in effect, a Semite? Oy vey!

It was only because of our Semitic ancestors' aiding and abetting in the most heinous ecological atrocity the earth has ever been subjected to that we are here at all today! These "chosen of God" assisted Mr. Clean in implementing His "final solution" to the problems "He created" with His attempt to "cleanse" the post-flood world of all *"violence"* by KILLING, I repeat, "by KILLING" *"every living substance"* which He declared had been causing it.

Fortunately, Mr. Clean had allowed only world-saving Semites to book passage aboard the lifesaving ark. Therefore, I would like to give a big "Shout Out" to Mr. Clean and His cleansing ark-crew and thank them for their help in ridding the world of every evil-hearted, evil-minded substance that had been filling the old world *"with violence."* I would like to thank them all for our very existence today in this, His new and improved, non-violent world---we surely have been blessed! Wait a GD minute---has anyone noticed that the world is still filled with violence---what the hell? ---get Mr. Clean, or one of His enablers, on the phone right now! As I think about God's competency in this world-changing matter, Moe, Larry, and Curly come to mind for some strange reason!

As a result of God's cleansing flood, the transformations that must have taken place on a global scale to abolish the *"violence"* in man's nature, should be quite apparent to everyone, or else God's tremendous efforts to improve the world were certainly done in vain. Out of decency, respect, and gratefulness, shouldn't the rightful duty of everyone---like you and I---who has benefitted from the extermination of every *"violence"*-producing lifeform on the planet---be to honor our Semitic superheroes, our Jewish ancestors aboard the SS Steaming Pile? Nine people (8 crew + 1 script-writer) who, I'm sure, were quite pleased to participate in purifying the planet with their peace-loving God—a God who sought to "eliminate" *"violence"* by dispensing more of it in order to make the earth a totally "peaceful" place for all—incredible! Since it has been established that annihilating everyone who displeased them or got in their way is an honored Jewish tradition that a loving God "demanded" His "chosen" to indulge in, it follows then that the destruction of the entire earth was just a precursor of things to come in God's futile attempts to keep improving the world for the benefit of His favorite folks only. Are you getting this? There's absolutely no limit as to what God will do for His homies and what they, in return, will do in His name!

Because of their obsession with the Judaic roots of their religion,

Christians have completely obligated themselves to believe the fabricated, Judaic Word of God, the Semitic Chutzpah Chronicles known as the *Old Testament*. Being among the blessed beneficiaries of today's new and improved, nonviolent world, Christians have thus obligated themselves to pay honor and homage to their sea-faring Semitic saviors aboard the ark for their part in helping God purify the earth and make it a better place, post-flood, in which we all now live. All Christians, it seems, appear to be over-the-moon to serve the Jews for all of the spiritual blessings that their God-pleasing endeavors have bestowed upon the Gentile world as stated in *Romans* 15:27:

> *For if the Gentiles have been made partakers of their spiritual things, their duty is also to minister unto them in carnal things.* (why the Jews, a spiritually motivated people, should have any interest in carnal things is beyond me! ---kvk)

Seemingly then, all Christians should be over-the-moon to minister unto the Jews *"in carnal things"* for their incredible favor with God, for their assistance in helping God rid the earth of *"violence,"* for their setting the example for everyone on how to live a spiritual life, and for their knowledge on how to please God through the shedding of blood, which seems a most curious way to worship a Deity whom they want us to believe, abhors *"violence"* and who sought to end its existence on earth---just another example of God's ineptitude---another example of His hypocrisy---another example of religion having it both ways. The only consistency with Semitic religion appears to be its many inconsistencies!

Since the violent, barbaric custom of sacrificing children to please God and its replacement—the violent, barbaric custom of sacrificing animals in order to please Him—are no longer considered kosher for modern, new and improved God-heads to indulge in, a small number of proud, "ultra-orthodox" Jews, however, still persist in carrying-out their paleo-reckonings and pious pathologies upon *"clean"* chickens in order to wash-away their Semitic sins and, therefore, improve the blissful state of their ultra-Semitic existence. This incredible bit of Semitic hocus-pocus transfers, with God's approval of course, their ultra-orthodox sins into the scapegoat bodies of innocent chickens who are then religiously improved with a knife to their necks, swung three times around overhead, and "VOILA"! —the sins magically disappear! —it's as simple as that and quite an amazing sacred and blessed Jewish spectacle to behold! Incidentally, the small number of God-heads who piously carried-out the 9/11 attacks with a knife to the necks of the innocent airplane pilots who were murdered that infamous day, to no one's surprise, were proud, "ultra-orthodox" Muslims who were merely washing-away America's sins in order to improve the state of their world—"VOILA"!

(NOTE TO THE ABOVE ULTRA-ORTHODOX JEWS: be ultra-careful fellas not to exceed the limit of swinging your bleeding chickens around three times above your heads---any more than that, you run the risk of stopping the earth's rotation or, possibly, making the moon disappear which would eliminate one of your God's hiding places! Because you are messin' with mighty powerful and unpredictable forces, I advise you to be ultra ultra-careful that you don't overdo this religious ritual of such great importance and consequence to sinful, ultra-orthodox Jews! ---do not take your God-gifts lightly---you could actually endanger the earth with your sacred activities!)

By drinking a bit of God's blood (wine) and eating a bit of God's flesh (bread), paleo-minded Christians, the proud beneficiaries of the religious endeavors and religious rituals of Jews, are able to indulge in what is little more than a cannibalistic ritual I call "Swallow the Leader." What better way for them to show how much love and respect they have for someone who killed gazillions of sentient creatures (man included) when He drowned the world and later commanded the annihilation of untold numbers of Canaanites---than by drinking and eating some of God's body parts! ---for paleo-minded reasoning believes that doing such things bestows some of the power of the eaten to be transferred to the cannibalistic consumer of them!

Never forget, dear Christians, the biblical fact and logical conclusion that it was "Jesus" who drowned the world and destroyed the Canaanites for, we are told that God and Jesus are one! How strange is it then that Jesus, who appears to have been afflicted with divine amnesia, never mentioned a word or acknowledged in any way His prior evil doings---His indulgence in atrocities. How strange, indeed, that "logical conclusions" can have such a devastating impact on infallible and inerrant *Bible*-babble!

Isn't it logical that God, who *"so loved the world,"* would "not" have cursed all of its human and animal inhabitants---would "not" have drowned almost every one of them in an attempt to destroy the world He *"so loved"*? Isn't it logical that God, who instructed "us" to *"forgive men their trespasses,"* ---*Matt.* 6:14, would "not" have *"prepared"* an *"everlasting fire"* ---25:41, for most of the world's post-flood survivors whose *"trespasses"* He will not forgive? *"Do as I say, not as I do"* ---right? Logical conclusions---right? One wonders what God would have done different if

He had "so hated the world" instead of *"so loved"* it? I almost shudder when I hear a freedom-loving person say the words: *"God Bless America"* as if a murderous God's "blessing" is any better than His "love" for us!

"Yes, Virginia, Jesus is a murderer and an unrelenting tormenter for we're told in the Bible that Jesus is God and we're also told in the Bible that God is a murderer, therefore, Jesus is a murderer---right? If A=B, and B=C, it follows then that A=C---right? Do the algebra or, at least, do the simple math involved with having belief in the Trinity: that 3=1 and that 1=3. The Father, the Son, and the Holy Ghost are the 3 that add up to 1--- right? ---you shouldn't be drinking that much lemonade, my dear!"

If vicariously consuming God's body is symbolically insufficient in providing enough evidence of the adoration and admiration Christians have for Him and His loving concern for the *"world,"* as told above, then we, as proud Americans living in a Judeo-Christian nation, should honor our Judeo-Christian God on every piece of American currency and in America's Pledge of Allegiance, etc. If that still isn't enough adoration being shown to the worst, violent character in the history of the world, at least according to the *Bible*, than we should all drop to our knees and plead for His mercy and grovel for His attention in hopes that He may throw us a bone like He begrudgingly did to the pleading female "dog" of Canaan as is proudly told in the fifteenth chapter of *Matthew*—but, I, in my uber-infidel way, digress again . . . back to the hidden realities of the ark-tale . . .

Isn't it strange that the *Bible* never reveals the name of Mrs. Noah, the obvious grandmother of us all, I repeat, "the grandmother of us all"? Isn't it strange that the *Bible* never reveals the names of the wives of Noah's sons who, obviously, are the mothers of us all, I repeat, "the mothers of us all"? *"Yes, Virginia, the Bible teaches us, in so many ways, some subtle, some not, that women are not the equal of men! They, the gals aboard the ark, certainly must have been extraordinary women to have endured the extraordinary perils of their extraordinary voyage. However, the misogynist, male script-writers of the Bible deemed them undeserving of the courtesy and decency of having their names mentioned for posterity to honor them and their extraordinary efforts—how extraordinary! Because of all of the extraordinary indignities and long-sufferings that women have had to endure throughout the history* 'revealed' *on the pages of the Bible and the Koran, you, dear Virginia, should pride yourself knowing that none of the script-writers of either book were female—'God's Word' is entirely the 'word' of men—men who were inspired, not by anything of a spiritual nature, but only by* **'power and profit'**!*"*

Isn't it strange, too, that Noah, the world-saving sailor, after taking such incredible efforts to preserve the lives of his precious cargo of animals, at all costs, at the beseeching request of God, would have decided on his own that it was suddenly proper for him to purposely begin killing-off some of those assigned to his life-sustaining care in a Semitic religious ritual that was unknown to him and to his family? Shouldn't he have feared incurring the wrath of God for performing such egregious acts of savagery and butchery, acts that should have angered a life-preserving, *"violence"*-detesting deity? How strange, too, that God should be so immensely pleased with Noah's animal-holocausts so shortly after His drowning by the gazillions all the remaining animals and every other lifeform on the planet! I suppose the stench of the rotting carcasses of these animals would not be deemed as pleasurable as the *"sweet savor"* of the burnt flesh of *"clean"* animals arising from Noah's altar and reaching God's sacred nostrils which, evidently, are never too far away as He is always sticking His nose in everything! And for that *"sweet savor,"* we should give thanks to God's barbecue-craving, male script-writers—script-writers who, earlier, had their God preferring Abel's flesh-offering over that of Cain's vegetable garden offering! Hmm! ---I wonder if Abel knew beforehand that he had killed and butchered a "clean" animal and, if he did know, ---how did he know it---how did he, an Eden-dweller, know that his brutal actions would please God? ---and, I'd like to know as well, how God is able to know the difference between the *"sweet savor"* of a "clean" animal and the *"sweet savor"* of an "unclean" animal? ---and, I'd like to know, why the killing of an animal was so pleasing to a loving God? Lemonade, anyone?

How strange, too, that God, who commanded the inhabitants of Eden to eat only the seed-bearing herbs and fruits for their sustenance—for their *"meat"* ---*Gen.* 1:29, was not shocked by the news of Abel's act of animal butchery and the sight of the gory flesh he offered to Him as a result of it. One wonders how Abel was able to know how to kill anything and where he got the implement(s) needed to dismember his victim and which body parts should be removed and offered as "gifts" to God---since butchery, the tools needed to butcher, and which cuts of meat he should remove to please God were skills and knowledge that existed only at a later time in Jewish history when the script-writer(s) of this tale wrote it. How was Abel able to come up with the idea to "kill" when death and flesh-eating were unknown to him and to his family. Where the hell did he get the idea that such acts would be pleasing to God? Instead of horrifying the "loving" Creator of *"every living thing,"* we learn, incredibly, that it was God, not Satan, who was rather pleased to learn that the earth was now home to a "killer" whom God had even voiced His *"respect"* for! ---*Gen.* 4:4. Imagine God respecting Abel for slaughtering and dismembering an animal as a bloody food offering to Himself but not having respect for Cain's bloodless food offering---one wonders whether it is man or God who has been made in the likeness of the other? ---wonder no more!

The earth was now home to a butcher whose brutal-minded, free-willed action to commit animal slaughter and dismemberment were entirely the result of Abel's own volition and not the urgings of a deceiving, talking reptile—actions that, strangely, were not deemed sacrilegious or offensive to the author of *"THOU SHALT NOT KILL"*! This, the same God who was appalled by an apple having been eaten by a cunningly deceived and naive innocent named Adam—incredible! If anyone should be suspected of enjoying Abel's offering, who would you presume? —a loving, merciful God who is above being tempted or His bogus script-writing story-tellers who, I'm quite certain, because of their "carnal" nature, were uber-pleased to have their God enjoy the odor of burnt flesh as much as they did.

Surely, if one allows that God found joy in the acts of animal-slaughter and animal butchery, why wouldn't one also assume that God would find joy in devouring the flesh that results from such brutal activities---why wouldn't one also assume that God has the needed body parts for eating and digesting it? Is it not a *Bible*-mystery, therefore, that we never hear of God desiring to consume the flesh whose roasting odors arising to His nose put Him over-the-moon? Could it be possible that meat makes Him gassy? ---or could it be that He is on a restricted, meatless diet? ---or that, with His huge appetite, He has run out of "clean" animals to eat? ---His script-writers surely have some more "splaining" to do! My guess is that God having been made in man's image, He, like some of mankind, has a somewhat weak digestive system and a very sensitive nose which savors the smell of burning flesh but, one assumes, utterly detests the *"abomination"* of having to endure the "unsavory" aroma of His own gassy, flatulent bowels---however, I'm not a doctor so I really can't say for sure! FARTERS BEWARE! ---of the harm you may be causing to others, especially to the Creator of the Universe and His uber-sensitive nose---if you dare to pass gas in His presence, you'll probably be deemed deserving of spending your eternity in a stinkin' Hell! ---but I digress again . . .

Returning, once again, to the deluge of lies and the flood of deceptions in the *Bible*-tale dealing with a water-logged boatload of stinking excrement, and after learning about all of the unbelievable hardships that its captain and crew had to endure on their epic odd-yssey to re-start the world, I was, nonetheless, saddened to learn of Noah's sinking into the desperate straits of alcoholism. It saddened me to learn that such a talented boat-builder and sea-farer, ocean-crossing navigator and world traveler, discoverer of continents and other unknown lands and their fauna, animal trapper and animal transporter extraordinaire, zoo-keeper and distant grandfather of us all—a man who should have been credited with the discovery of America long before 1492—a man who almost singlehandedly saved the entire animal and plant populations of the planet from becoming extinct due to the wrath of an invisible, audible God who hasn't mastered His anger-management or found a way to control His rage—would become, in the end, are you ready? —a passed-out, naked drunkard and an embarrassment to his sons and to me, his great-grandson.

Perhaps, the realization of his agreeing to assist the person behind the demanding voice in his head carry out His global genocide, finally got to him! Noah, as a close confidant and personal friend of this phantom God, had to resort to the numbing effects of alcohol to deal with his grief in aiding and abetting a maniacal Madman to "purify" the planet. Being the lush that he was, Noah, nevertheless, managed to stay afloat to reach the vine-ripened age of 950 years! One would think that such a loyal servant of God would have been rewarded, by God, with a more blissful existence than that found in the bottom of a wine bottle! Sorry, Noah, because you have *"found grace in the eyes of the Lord."* this is the Guy with whom you'll be sitting alongside, at the head table in Heaven, for all of eternity—"care to see the wine-list?"

This is the Guy that so many ***"fools and hypocrites"*** can't wait to "permanently" reside with in the flawless Forever-Land He created just for the purpose of His being able to wait hand and foot on everyone there (His dreaded, abominable Gentiles no less!) and provide them with every delight imaginable for ever and ever and ever! Unlike God's other failed endeavors to improve the world, somehow, He and His script-writers were finally able to achieve "perfection," in the Paradise #2 that He created to reward only His faithful—the rest of the world, as you well know, can all go to Hell! *"Yes, Virginia, God's Word, the Bible, cannot be 'perfect' if it is unbelievable in any of its parts. If, my dear, you consider the Bible to be perfect in all of its parts, you have only to visit the replica of Noah's ark in Kentucky that is open to the public and request to see where all the various pairs of whales were kept aboard it and where the orcas, who feed on whales, were kept, for the 'perfect' Bible tells us in 6th and 7th chapter of Genesis:*

And God said unto Noah, the end of all flesh ("all flesh," folks!) *is come before me; for the earth is filled with violence through them; and, behold, I will destroy them with the earth . . . And of every living thing of all flesh* ("all flesh"!), *two of every sort shalt thou bring into the ark, to keep them alive with thee . . . And they that went in unto Noah into the ark, two and two of all flesh* ("all flesh"!), *wherein is the breath of life* (the breath of life, folks! ---that certainly must have included the air-breathing whales---a fact about whales that the *Bible's* ignorant script-writers (and the God who inspired their words) were obviously unaware of at the time they wrote this tale because they failed to invite or include the air-breathing sea animals aboard the ark!) . . . *And all flesh* ("all flesh," folks!) *died that moved upon the earth . . . Noah only remained alive* ("remained alive," folks!), *and they that were with Him in the ark* (which could only mean that there must have been whales on board the ark because every whale outside the ark would not have remained alive! ---*Bible*-evidence, folks---*Bible*-evidence! ---kvk"

If any "literal" Word of God cannot be believed as written in His inspired *Bible*, which of its words are we to believe is the absolute "truth"? If God deliberately meant to spare the fishes and the air-breathing whales in His destroying flood, He, in His perfection, should have made note of it, yet, in His very own perfect words to Noah He stated: "*. . . the end of all flesh is come before me.*" No exceptions, folks! Surely, the flesh of sea-creatures was as guilty of filling the earth with *"violence"* as were the birds, the bees, and the butterflies! ---have you ever witnessed a pod of orcas attacking a whale or its calf, or witnessed a great white shark attacking a seal? Are we to believe that God, in His quest to end the lives of all the creatures who were filling the earth with *"violence,"* would have spared the *"violence"*-producing denizens of the deep oceans whose *"flesh"* certainly outnumbered the "flesh" of all the land-dwelling animals? Of course not! ---mythology was never meant to provide answers to its logical extrapolations. Who then has the temerity to make excuses, apologies, or adjustments to God's "Word" in order to make them more credible? The answer is: everyone! ---everyone who chooses to believe in God's pathological *Bible*-persona---who chooses to believe in the absolute veracity of His words even when they cannot be believed as written, that's who---Man help us!

As many *Bible*-apologists, excuse-makers, spin-doctors, and adjustors would "now" have us believe, in their attempts to promote *Bible*-perfection (in the Noah-tale) regardless of scientific proof to the contrary---that *"Once upon a time"* (a mere 6000 years ago or thereabouts) all the earth was one big continent when it was instantly created by God---a place where polar bears, kangaroos, three-toed sloths, etc., etc., were all instantly created, too, and could have easily walked its level, mountain-less terrain, without hunger, thirst, or distress of any kind, to Arkville (surely, it must have taken the uber-slow-moving sloths several years to make the trek unless they had the good fortune to hitch a ride with the kangaroos!). Fortunately, however, none of the Ark-critters had stepped off the earth's edge and fallen to their deaths in their journey there because believers in the perfect, God-inspired *Bible* also held the belief that the earth that God had instantly created was four-cornered and perfectly flat and anyone who thought otherwise---well, you know what became of them! *Bible*-believers, of course, are obligated to tell us "anything" in order to prevent God's perfect "Word" from being taken "literally" as written when it shows a lack of crystal-clear and "perfect" clarity in the "perfect," inspired words of a "perfect" God written by the *Bible's* "perfect" script-writers! Like the ending of so many other cartoon tales, this *Bible*-tale should end as well with these words: "*That's 'all,' folks*!"

One should keep in mind that God could have instantly destroyed every living thing that He had instantly created in Eden and, later, regretted ever making---destroyed every living thing that in Noah's time was filling the earth with *"violence,"* ---with just a snap of His fingers! ---no need for a boatload of lies, no need for the innumerable miracles required to gather-up mating pairs of every living thing, no need for a killing flood, no need for a miracle to increase the water level on the planet in order to inundate the mountaintops and another miracle to decrease it, no need to destroy any innocent life in the process, no need to make us believe the ark's animal survivors released on Mt. Ar-a-rat, were able to return back to their native lands even if it involved crossing oceans or even one tremendously large, plant-less continent, no need to go to the extremes that were undertaken in this unbelievable, mythological, ark-tale drama---for nothing is impossible for God and His amazing speech or fingertips to accomplish---"VOILA"!

One mustn't forget that the *Bible* tells us that God created "heaven" and "earth" in a single day---that He removed Adam and Eve from Eden the very instant He cursed them, for God, one assumes liked to get things done, but yet He, in His fervor to destroy the earth and all that lived upon it, was content to wait year after year after year for Noah and crew to build the ark, fill it with animals, gather enough food to sustain them on a voyage of unknown duration, and successfully complete (as it turned out) their year-long sea-trial in order to get the job done in a less-than-perfect way---for the earth continues to be filled with *"violence,"* in case you haven't noticed---much of it, nowadays, because of what else: belief in a Semitic God---imagine that! Man help us! If only God had been able to get His hands on

Moses' magic wand, He could have ended the old, violent world in an instant and begun the new one in a heartbeat! ---(more on magic wands ahead).

Apparently, if you can be made to swallow this Semitic whale of a fish-tale about Noah and his ark, you'll surely be able to swallow with ease the unbelievable antics performed by Jesus that are "revealed" in the Gospels which, incidentally, include their own whale of a fish-tale about Jonah's swallowing of one, or was it the other way around---either occurrence would certainly be worthy of belief as long as it is stated in the *Bible*! You'll even be able to play "Swallow the Leader" by eating bits of God's flesh and by sipping some of God's blood which has been miraculously transubstantiated, (in a hocus-pocus, "VOILA" ritual of course), from bread and wine only through the sacred abilities of Catholic priests when their attention is not focused on the molestation and the raping of children! Surely, a civilized world will no longer have interest in or need for the malevolent, vengeful Gods of religion as they have thus been "revealed" to us by their paleo-minded script-writers---no need for their bloodshedding, bloodspreading paleo-rituals and endeavors---no need for their less-than-spiritual, bogus tales and their less-than-spiritual, devoted followers---no need of clergy. A civilized world will have no need for temples, churches, or mosques--no need for the Semitic Chutzpah Chronicles known as the *Bible* and the *Koran*!

As in Noah's day, the ever darkening, threatening skies of our religion-troubled times indicates to me that it is time to begin constructing another extraordinary, ordeal-worthy craft: the *USS Reason's Tribunal*. It is time for this mighty destroyer of myths, lies, and deceptions, to finally be launched, to weigh anchor and set sail on its noble, reason and truth-mission to sink the leaking, stinking ark, and the other unbelievable tales put afloat by chutzpah-laden scripture. It is time to rescue the entire population of the world from the stifling impositions of Semitic religions—and do it all without having to annihilate any living thing and without having to erect a flesh-burning altar afterwards in order to please God! ---for it is evident that the lies, deceptions, religious absurdities, and Semitic chutzpah found on the very first page of the "inspired" *Bible* were not confined there on page 1 of *Genesis*.

Man puts words into the mouth of his creations then later believes these creations spoke.

---Lloyd M. Graham

238

In religion what damned error but some sober brow will bless it and approve it with a text.

---Shakespeare

What damned error would have us believe that Moses was the author, the authority who we are supposed to believe wrote the first five books of the *OT*: *Genesis, Exodus Leviticus, Numbers, Deuteronomy* for they are called the books of Moses? Where is the *Bible*-evidence that proves such a claim? The unknown script-writer(s) of the *Bible*-tales contained in these *OT* books tell us, with utter perfection, what God had supposedly said to Moses: *"And the Lord spake unto Moses"* ---they tell us, with utter perfection, what Moses supposedly had said: *"And Moses had said unto the people"* which is a strange way for any author (especially a God-inspired one!) to have Moses speak of himself---which amounts to further doubt that he, Moses, was the author of these books! How would it have been possible for Moses, by his own hand, to flawlessly record, without error and without angelic assistance, every single "Word" of God as quickly as, we are supposed to believe, they were being *"spake"* unto him, chapter after detailed chapter after detailed chapter after detailed chapter in the *Old Testament*? If Moses was the author of these books, how was he able to tell us in *Deut.* 34:5,6 where he had died and where he had been buried—that's seems to me to be a bit too "inspired" and much too much to swallow wouldn't you say? Pass the lemonade, please!

Surely, if Moses was the author of these five books, he certainly possessed a most imposing hand that was able to record, without error, all of the many, many events "revealed" in them. I wonder how he was able to find the time to write them down, in some form or other, each and every word given in these books. Especially during the times he was engaged in killing, injuring, or imposing upon every non-Jew he could find during his 24/7 terror campaign to annihilate, with God's blessing, every Gentile who was perceived as standing in the way of His "chosen" and their spiritual endeavors!

To Moses' list of astounding accomplishments—besides being able to inflict the plagues and pestilence imposed upon Egypt with the assistance of Aaron, his partner in crime, and his incredible parting of the Red Sea just by stretching out his rod-holding hand (and by stretching the truth!)—we must add speedwriting skills that defy logic to his unbelievable résumé! Another accomplishment of Moses was his amazing serendipity at being "chosen" by God to be His personal assistant, spokesperson, and go-to-guy. Moses even hand-delivered God's Commandments (written in duplicate!) on "perishable" stone tablets to the Jews---something which God was seemingly incapable of doing all by Himself.

The Decalogue was fabricated---not for the edification and moral improvement of Gentiles, but in order to make the Jews treat other Jews in a less-ruthless manner than before and to make the Jews fear the power of the Almighty lest He, in anger, seek revenge against them for their "sins." This was done so that the Levites, their control-seeking priests, would be able to benefit by the sin-offerings (money, food, etc., etc.) that came their way from "sinful" folks who believed these pious parasites could keep God from following-through with His terrible wrath against them as only priests can do! Sadly, however, for those with a vested interest in promoting God's Word, no original copy of Moses' written accounts of his many contacts and conversations with God can be found anywhere—it seems that mythological beings and their mythological Gods are never quite competent enough, even with their amazing ability to perform astounding miracles, to write down their own personal experiences with the Almighty and preserve them for posterity!

For some unknown reason, it was not possible for a Semitic God to leave a permanent record behind of the all-important contracts He made with the Jews inscribed (ala the Ten Commandments) on stone tablets and guarded in perpetuity (ala the tree of life) with another flaming sword manned by cherubs—it just wasn't possible to do even though *Matt.* 17:20 tells us that nothing is impossible for *Bible*-believers to accomplish, for sure, nothing would be impossible for God to accomplish either—just another example of religion having it both ways! It is quite hard to believe, too, that the Jews, upon learning that they were "favored" by God above all others, would not have wanted, as part of the deal to worship Him only, to get such a declaration in writing carved upon an "imperishable" tablet by God's own hand---what a game-changer that would have made for Jews and their supremacist endeavors—what were they thinking! Imagine having the opportunity to reveal to the world a valid contract written on an imperishable tablet and signed by God entitling Jews to acquire anything and everything they desired and their not taking full advantage of it! Oy vey!

The Old Testament is by no means a unified book in terms of authorship, date of composition, or literary type, it is instead a veritable library. . . . By no means did all the books of the Old

Testament originate at the same time and in the same place, rather, they are the product of Israelite faith and culture over a thousand years or more. . . . For most Old Testament books it was a long journey from the time the first words were spoken or written to the work in its final form. That journey usually involved many people, such as storytellers.... (Storytellers! --- imagine that! ---kvk)

---*Funk & Wagnalls New Encyclopedia, Vol. 4*

Take away from Genesis the belief that Moses was the author, on which only the strange belief that it is the word of God has stood, and there remains nothing of Genesis but an anonymous book of stories, fables, and traditionary or invented absurdities, or of downright lies. ...As to the ancient historians, from Herodotus to Tacitus, we credit them as far as they relate things probable and credible, and no further; for if we do, we must believe the two miracles which Tacitus relates were performed by Vespasian, that of curing a blind man in just the same manner as the things are told of Jesus Christ by his historians. We must also believe the miracle cited by Josephus, that of the sea of Pamphilia opening to let Alexander and his army pass, as is related of the Red Sea in Exodus.

---Thomas Paine, *The Age of Reason*

The religious doctrines and dogmas of the Jews, as related in the *OT* that announced their superiority over the Gentiles---that established their claim to a "God-Promised Land" and their deserving of special treatment from high above (and the rest of the world!) ---that required them to perform animal sacrifice and engage in rituals involving genital mutilation and changes in their physical appearance to look a certain way, etc., —which were all based upon their supposed exclusivity with a favoring God and their binding deals (covenants) made with Him as relayed to them by Mr. Moe-Says—were not written by the sacred hand of authority on an imperishable tablet---they were deceivingly written by pious impostors (script-writers!) pretending to be something they were not for their own exclusive benefit and that of their tribes which, obviously, were lacking the ability to acquire what they wanted in any other way.

Moe-Says, the mythological storyteller, who is credited with writing the Chutzpah Chronicles of the Jews, their supposed "inerrant" and "infallible," self-aggrandizing, self-serving religious history—the man who because of his intimacy with the Almighty was able to convey God's will to God's favorite folks—the man upon whose script-written words in the *Old Testament* the Jews base so many of their traditions, principles, rites, and rituals—never existed, except mythologically---his persona being "borrowed" from older Pagan sources---namely Arabia, Assyria, and Phoenicia where he went by the name of—are you ready? —"Mises!" Oy vey, again! Quite a coincidence wouldn't you say?

We should keep these facts in mind when we learn that God, along with the helpful assistance of Moses and Aaron, engaged in a juvenile-minded, show-off contest with the magicians of Egypt to see who could outperform the other with mighty wonders as told beginning in the seventh chapter of *Exodus*. At that time, the Jews, lacking a "working" magic wand, did not have the power to escape their enslavement for they claim, according to the *Bible*, that they were all being held in bondage in Egypt by its heart-hardened Pharoah. However, after gaining freedom from their oppressors, (with the use of a "working" magic wand!), we learn that they, too, indulged in doing unto others as the Egyptians had supposedly done unto them. Why is it that the inhumanity of enslaving others was an approved, kosher activity for the Jews to engage in, but not so for the Egyptians whom the Jews considered bastards and worse for doing the same thing to them? Hmm!

When the above trinity-of-terror (God, Moses, Aaron) commenced their magic wand assault on Egypt with their "Presto!" performances of mighty wonders, the amazing Egyptian magicians, without any divine assistance whatsoever, were easily able, for the most part, to match each and every impressive and destructive effect the Israelites conjured up with their mighty wand (Moses' rod) and the divine assistance of their diabolical Deity—turning their magic wand into a serpent (as Mises had previously done elsewhere)! You can almost hear Moses, playing the role of a schoolyard-bully saying to the Egyptian magicians, "I bet my magic wand can beat all of your magic wands!" ---and, waddayaknow---it did just that by morphing into a snake and eating "all" of their competitor's magic wands after they, too, had miraculously morphed into snakes! *"Yes, Virginia, the Egyptians possessed a magic wand, too, in fact, they had several of them! It should be obvious, therefore, to those of sane and sound mind, that all Semitic religions are based on myth and make-believe for what could be more mythic and fanciful than a bunch of magic-wand-wielding, comic book characters performing their juvenile-minded, cruel antics, never for anything good and decent, of course, but only to show-off their impressive, abracadabra skills like some Las Vegas prestidigitator?"*

Moses and Aaron then used their magic wand's powers of "mass destruction" when held on high to turn all the water sources in Egypt into blood which caused all this fish-tale's fish therein to die, rot, and create quite a stench. I can still smell it every time I open the *Bible* and read the *Exodus*-tale---can you? Amazingly, instead of every Egyptian being outraged over this act of terror---instead of their wanting to kill the bastards who had just destroyed every fish in Egypt and every drop of their drinking water---the Egyptian magicians made no attempt to restore these vital resources with their own *"enchantments,"* ---they, incredibly, only thought to try their hands at re-performing the very same catastrophe, which, the *Bible* claims, they had succeeded in doing---even without the use of their magic-wands for, a short time earlier, their wands had all been turned into tasty snakes and eaten by a Jewish magic wand that had instantly morphed into a sacred serpent on a strict, kosher, snake-diet---this is *Bible*-truth, folks!

Somehow, with their wand-less *"enchantments,"* they, the Egyptians, were able to turn all of Egypt's water, that the Israelites had already turned into blood a moment before, into blood again and re-kill all of the fish that had just been entirely killed off—I'm not making this stuff up, folks! Not even in the make-believe world of fairy-tales would one find such illogical nonsense and foolishness as portrayed in the *Bible*. However, such foolishness is "revealed" to us, beginning with Chapter 7 of *Exodus*, not as fanciful fiction, but as flawless fact! Imagine any Egyptian of sane and sound mind wanting to play a part in poisoning all of their country's drinking water---wanting to annihilate every fish in their waters! —the Chutzpah Chronicles of the Chosen are, certainly, quite hard to swallow at times. Hopefully, there's enough lemonade for everyone!

Because Egypt was perhaps the most advanced culture the supremacist-minded Jews had ever been exposed to, it became necessary to disparage the uber-tolerant Egyptians in any way possible in their exalting Chutzpah Chronicles even if doing so exposed their own stupidity. They obviously needed to "reveal" to the world the inferiority of the Egyptians when pitted against the exceptional, superior abilities of a God-chosen people, a desert-dwelling tribe of nomads in whom God had taken an interest to provide for their welfare alone at the expense of everyone and everything else! Exceptional, superior abilities that when deployed with the use of a magic wand, nearly destroyed the entirety of Egypt even though historical accounts of the time have, somehow, failed to take note of Egypt's near demise---failed to take note of any of its tremendous, ecological disasters and its tumultuous, turbulent times! How stupid of the Chutzpah Chroniclers to think that recorded history would not have exposed the fraudulent, religious claims of the Jewish race.

Acting under the guise of being selected by God to be His master race, the Jews would have us believe, too, that they were given permission and a license by God to murder others and thus acquire their lands, and to take whatever they wanted when they wanted it---they would have us believe that God commanded them to annihilate anyone whom they deemed to be standing in their way in their efforts to purify the world and promote their Semitic self-interests---sound familiar, folks? ---9/11! Who but God-denying infidels would dare to question, or otherwise impede, the efforts of a people who tell us they are merely following God's express orders and doing, in His name, what God expects of them? Hmm! Pretty slick!, but I digress . . .

Moses and Aaron, we are told, then used their magic wand to cause such a plague of frogs to emerge from the very same blood-filled, toxic rivers and ponds that their incalculable numbers *"covered the land of Egypt,"* an incredible historic event that historians of the time had failed to take note of! Amazingly again, instead of killing the wicked wand-wavers for the pestilence and destruction they were causing to their Egyptian homeland, the much-less-than-intelligent magicians of Frog-land responded by repeating, somehow, this very same act of terror upon their croaking land. Rather than make any logical attempt to undo the harm caused by the Israelites, the Egyptian magicians, we are supposed to believe, intentionally used their wandless, hocus-pocus *"enchantments"* to recreate another plague of frogs which, one assumes, must have re-inundated their homeland well beyond what M&A had just achieved—great job fellas! — you really showed those Israelites who they were messin' with!

Shortly thereafter, however, the good fortune of the Egyptian magicians to match each and every one of the malevolent, magic wand performances of M&A began to wane even though their very own magic performances had also imposed exceedingly bad fortune upon themselves and their country. They, regrettably, were unable to match the Israelites' ability to transform mere dust particles into tormenting lice which, seemingly at the time, was a trade secret known only to the above Israelites and their aiding and abetting God! ---nana—nana—boo—boo! ---I'm so very impressed, aren't you? God really showed those Egyptian showmen not to mess with His wand-wielding wizards---wand-wielding wizards whose torments, obviously, had to afflict, not only the Egyptians, but the Jews as well unless God was able to distinguish them from the Egyptians and thus spare them from receiving His wrath---something He was unable to do at the Passover without "blood" being sprinkled on each of their doorposts! ---incredible!

The poor, lice-tormented, Egyptian magicians surely must have been very, very disappointed at not being able to increase their own suffering as well as that of their countrymen and countrywomen by not being able to produce more intolerable lice! Hmm! Hmm! Hmm! As freedom-loving Americans who find themselves being tormented by this tale, we should be very thankful that the religion-inspired Middle-Easterners who performed their acts of terror on 9/11 were not able to get their hands on a magic wand!

If only God had been able to get His hands on Moses' *"rod"* in Noah's time, He could have "instantly" destroyed the earth and all of its violent inhabitants, on the land and in the water, in one dramatic "VOILA" thrust of Moses' rod---for that boy, Moses, using his "hot" rod to the max, knew how to get things done and make good use of his time! But, in enchanted storytelling and unbelievable fish-tales, it makes for far more interesting reading to be told a beguiling tale about God's destruction, by flood, of a planet *"filled with violence"* and all of its evil inhabitants---a beguiling tale that relates how Noah was chosen by God to become a super-hero---a man who, along with three sons, spent years building a life-saving ark in order to replenish the earth, after the killing flood, with the release of the onboard animals, etc., etc., rather than having all of these really impressive events occur in a "Presto," magic wand moment!

The above magic-wand abuses and the following, factual *Bible*-events "reveal," in some detail, the tormenting plagues the "chosen of God" Israelites were able to inflict upon the Egyptians (and themselves!) with their malevolent, hand-held, God-rod---events that history could not have failed to note when the Jews smote the Egyptians with a *"grievous"* swarm of flies---smote them with a disease to kill all of their cattle---smote them with painful, blistering boils---smote them with a barrage of hail that killed not only man and animal but destroyed every herb and broke every tree in their country---smote them with locusts in such great numbers that they covered the face of the earth, I repeat, "covered the face of the earth" --- really? ---and ate up all of the plant life that, somehow, had escaped the previous plant-annihilating plague---smote them (and themselves!) with 3 days of total, black-out darkness which, I believe, the Israelites had secretly prepared for by bringing along a few magic lanterns: flashlights! ---(that shouldn't be so hard to believe since we know with certainty that flashlights exist and magic wands don't!---except in the minds of those who believe with certainty that magic wands are real because of what is written in the *Bible*!) Following these wicked, inhumane, despicable activities directed against Egyptians, the God of the Israelites began killing all of Egypt's firstborn of man and cattle---cattle which, shortly before the baby-massacre, had all been plagued to death!

It was then that the Israelites---the most spiritually "endowed," spiritually "inspired, spiritually motivated" people on the planet---then *"borrowed"* from these devastated people, their jewels of silver, their jewels of gold, and their clothing as if the hapless victims of Moses and Aaron's wanton "wandings" hadn't suffered enough miseries and losses. And all of this occurred because the *Bible* tells us that the Pharaoh of Egypt would not let the Israelites leave his country—why? —are you ready? —because Mr. Smotely had *"hardened"* the Pharaoh's heart against releasing them, I repeat, "because Jehovah bin Laden had *'hardened'* the Pharaoh's heart against releasing them!" How ridiculous it is to believe then that God blamed the captivity of His "chosen" people in Egypt upon its Pharoah who was unable to release the Israelites because of a heart-condition that God had imposed upon him! Who, rightfully, should be blamed, therefore, for keeping the Israelites in bondage? Who was it that was severely afflicted with a hardened heart? Really, folks, it's a no-brainer, again!

While on the subject of enslavement, haven't vast numbers of people, through the long, religion-darkened ages, been living in bondage long enough to this heart-hardened, Semitic Ruler of the Universe? Haven't we suffered long enough? Haven't the hearts and minds of Jews, Christians, and Muslims been either *Bible*-hardened or *Koran*-hardened to feel a certain way towards certain others (us and them), to think a certain way about certain others (us and them), to act a certain way towards certain others (us and them)? I only wish there was a magic wand we could get our hands on that would allow us to break our bonds to religious thought and religious dogma---to free ourselves, at last, from the plague of religious "enchantment," religious "inspiration," and religious "imposition." Wait a sec---there is such a divine, hand-held device---it's a book called *Reason's Tribunal* ---Hallelujah!

Any human being who can stomach to read about the above sinister activities carried out against the Egyptians, as proudly told in *Exodus*--- about the demonic God of the Israelites' deliberate abuse of these tolerant people and their imposed-upon, "heart-hardened" Pharaoh who, obviously, was not personally responsible for keeping the Israelites in captivity--- should harden their hearts, too, but only to avoid having belief in Him and His malevolent Word as "revealed" in the *Bible,* a book that continues to cause destruction whenever it is lifted into the air by religious fanatics!

Incidentally, the "chosen" *Bible*-word that the clever script-writer of *Exodus* 12:35 used to describe the Israelites plundering of the Egyptians of their treasure was: *"borrowed"* as if the goods taken were intended to be given back---really! ---"stolen" would be a much more honest description of these events!

(NOTE TO THE PEOPLE OF ISRAEL: I'm certain the Egyptians would like the immediate return of all the jewels, silver, gold and whatever else you *"borrowed"* from them---exactly what was in that big *"ark of the Lord"* box that your ancestors carried around everywhere they went---the big box that no one dared to peek inside? Hmm! Also, shouldn't you, the people of Israel, who deem yourselves a decent people with un-hardened hearts, of course, be seeking to right the wrongs of the past---if you believe they really occurred! ---by making efforts to compensate the Egyptians for all of the undeserved havoc your God and your ancestors imposed upon them and inflicted upon their animals and their environment with your sinister plague and pestilence-dispensing wand? In the least, the Egyptians deserve a televised, public apology from the Head of State of Israel—an apology conducted before the General Assembly of the United Nations for all the physical harm and libelous slander done to an innocent, tolerant people regardless of when it happened. And, while you are at it, how about conducting a televised apology in memory of the hapless Canaanites and the other Victimites whom your ancestors exterminated!

It is time to begin doing the right thing, for once, in the name of God—it is time to pay off your spiritual debts---or else abandon the contrived fictions in your Chutzpah Chronicles that establish and proclaim your "chosen" status and your less-than-honorable, spiritual history—a shameful, sinister, malevolent legacy that no one, who calls themself an American, should be proud of! Try for once to make the effort to do as your God has commanded you to do---LOVE THY NEIGHBOR, the native Palestinians, AS THYSELF---instead of attempting to *"smite every male thereof with the edge of the sword"* ---which has been your historic response to neighbors who are non-Jewish---or else, admit that this "commandment" was only meant to apply to your Jewish neighbors!

Try easing up a bit on the "us" and "them" attitude that forever prevents WORLD PEACE from becoming a reality---seriously folks, "WORLD PEACE" ---just think about the role Israelites could play in achieving it! For all of their long history of close encounters and fellowship with Almighty God, the people of Israel should be the most tolerant, the most forgiving, and the meekest people on earth. Try setting the example, therefore, for the entire world about what a godly people and spiritual living are all about---just give it a try! Give peace a chance! In the very least, the people of Israel should be asked, in a "YES" or "NO" poll, if the extermination of the Canaanites was an honorable part of Jewish history? ---every Christian, every American, every believer, every politician, every POTUS needs to know the answer! If "YES," is their answer, Jews should be ashamed of their religious heritage---if "NO," is their answer, Jews should be ashamed to be counted among the less-than-spiritual-minded folks who have increased the sorrows, sufferings, and atrocities of this world done in the name of their God!

Since, for some mysterious reason, God is no longer hanging around in the clouds above Israel or in its bushes---since He no longer personally involves Himself in driving-out the folks who you now perceive to be standing in Israel's way---since He no longer "speaketh" constantly to His "chosen" day after day after day as in and around the time of Moses, in fact, to say the least, He, surprisingly, no longer "speaketh" to anyone anywhere in Israel today---how strange---right? ---or anywhere else for that matter, except to the deranged, to the delusional, and to the deceivers of men who tell us they regularly converse with Him.

Perhaps, you might assume that He, the God of the Jews, no longer gives a flying fig about your future as He unrelentingly cared about your most remarkable past where "all" of His attention and concerns, day and night, night and day was only for the welfare of Israelites---or, maybe, He just decided to give up on His "chosen" with all that golden calf business going on! ---or maybe, God's script-writers went into forced retirement because of the difficulty they faced in remaining anonymous in today's world? Whatever God's reasons may be for hiding out and avoiding even a camouflaged, cameo appearance now and then to the Israelites---Reason's Tribunal should be able to shed some light on the cause of it all!)

No decent person who calls himself/herself a Christian should be proud of such a contrived legacy either, for the God you worship is the same God that the Israelites and Arabs worship—the same God that many Americans and their beloved institutions, such as the American Legion, are proud to proclaim their love for and their trust in:

...the American Legion recognizes the influence of Almighty God in all worthwhile endeavors and declares the allegiance of Legionnaires to both God and Nation.

---American Legion Preamble

Thank goodness, the Constitution of the United States doesn't recognize God in any such way---in fact, it doesn't recognize God in any way at all! Is it possible, therefore, that the American Legion is, in reality, a religious institution---an institution that, based on the above quote, discriminates against honorably discharged, wartime Veterans who happen to be agnostics or atheists and who might aspire to become Legionnaires? ---a missive sent to the AL's National Cmdr. seeking an answer to the American Legion's un-American position on the above matter has gone unanswered!

Incidentally, why aren't the folks who are searching far and wide for any trace of "Noah's Ark' and the location of the "Holy Grail" also looking for Moses' Magic Wand, God's terror-rod, which, like the flaming sword, is still out there somewhere. Why isn't the United Nations making a concerted effort to find and retrieve this wicked weapon of mass destruction in order to keep it out of the prayerful hands of those who believe it should be used for godly purpose? As for myself, I don't think I'll be able to enjoy another peaceful night's sleep ever again until it is found and safely secured! Therefore, in an effort to make the world a much safer place, I am kicking-off the start of the "FIND THE WAND" campaign—volunteers will be needed, of course, to search every attic, every basement, and every shed around the globe until it is found. To the person or persons who may happen upon it, please remember not to handle it or to point it at anyone— treat it as you would any loaded weapon—keep a safe distance away from it and notify the authorities immediately. In the name of God, never never never raise thine hand heavenward while holding it!

Interestingly, it has never been reported and for good reason! —that shortly before the above-mentioned plagues and pestilences took place in Egypt, a postal strike there curtailed deliveries of *Magician's Monthly* which, ironically and sadly for the magicians of Egypt, contained a clear and concise article with step-by-step instructions for producing lice from dust! —who knew? Who knew that one lousy magazine article could possibly have made such a huge difference concerning Egypt's fate if only her magicians had been able to match the Hebrew's lice-from-dust performance? Who knew that rather than M&A having to try to outdo the magicians of Egypt with their destructive wandings, their juvenile-minded playground torments—all that these show-off Israelite bullies had to do to really shock and awe the Egyptians, to out-perform and thus overpower them—all that the Israelites had to do in order to gain their freedom was to have Egypt's Pharaoh and his magicians observe Moses, at the outset of the Wand Wars, divide the Red Sea into two separate pieces just by hoisting his mighty God-rod skyward—divide and conquer—that is: divide (the sea) and conquer (the land), and nobody gets hurt---wet, maybe! As a footnote to the above miracle, Mises, the Pagan myth-man whom Moses was modeled after, was able to part a body of water also! —who knew? Who knew that Mises, a Gentile, could beat a member of the "chosen few" to the punch in the performance of unbelievable miracles?

Wouldn't the Pharaoh's witnessing such a stupendous, visual spectacle at the outset of Moses and Aaron's wicked and wanton wandings have done the trick and secured the release of the Israelites without their God having to take delight in inflicting punitive, malevolent measures or resort to killing the firstborn of man and animal in Egypt? The answer, of course, would be "Yes!" if we were talking about a decent deity, but the God of Jews, Christians, and Muslims being demented and lacking any self-control over His anger, had to impose His wrathful temper-tantrum, as He would so often do, by punishing the innocent yet again! What a sick bastard! Only Jews, Christians, and Muslims can happily persist in their worship of this mass-molesting, mass-murdering, malevolent Miscreant whose "miracles" were meant only to impress and to intimidate others into submission—an infant-killing Bastard who is deemed worthy of receiving solemn tribute in America's Pledge of Allegiance and upon America's currency---an infant-killing Bastard who is honored in the American Legion's Preamble. *"In God We Trust"* is still a favored slogan of bullies, thugs, show-offs, and even institutions who use this hypocritical motto to impress and to intimidate others with their supremacist-minded smugness---a smugness that endeavors to make the world believe in the Christian-godliness of "all" Americans which, obviously, would include criminals, underhanded politicians, and child-raping clergymen who, I'm certain, would all agree on the truthfulness of this phrase's four words.

The mythic tales of mythical Moses, known as the *Old Testament,* comprise the steaming pile of Semitic crap that Judaism has used to construct and impose its contrived dogmas and its bogus timeline from the moment of Creation to the present day in order to convince everyone of the legitimacy and the exclusivity that all Jews have always had with their degenerate God. How is it possible for such excrement to be taken seriously at a time when man has already stepped foot on the surface of the moon and is planning to step foot on the surface of Mars in the not-too-distant future. How is it possible that such ignorance is still in control of our lives when advanced technology, personal computers, and the internet are commonplace in the modern world? —such is the phenomenon of the tenacity of the religious mindset, its paleo-reckonings and its propensity to resist change. Reason's Tribunal thankfully reminds us that the earth was considered flat for centuries only because of religion's imposed ignorance—it quickly became a globe when folks began to boldly question the orthodox, widely accepted thinking of the flat-earthers who were certain it was so because of their belief in the *Bible*—obviously then Phase 1 of the critical thinking needed to undo such imposed, ignorant religious beliefs via Reason's Tribunal has, apparently, been successfully completed! Phase 2 is now underway!

"*What damned error*," to borrow the words of Shakespeare, would have us believe, with certainty, any so-called "revealed," Word of God scripture of Judaism, Christianity, and Islam when no original copies or valid evidence of their existence or authorship can be found? Where are the original writings of the *Old Testament* done in Moses' hand---where is there any evidence proving that Moses authored the first five books of the *Bible*? There is none!

> *In the first place, there is no affirmative evidence that Moses is the author of those books; and that he is the author, is altogether an unfounded opinion, got abroad nobody knows how. The style and manner in which those books are written give no room to believe, or even to suppose, they were written by Moses, for it is altogether the style and manner of another person speaking of Moses.*

---Thomas Paine

Where are the original writings of *Matthew, Mark, Luke,* and *John*? Where are the two stone tablets inscribed, not once but twice, by God's very own hand that, seemingly, would make them "imperishable tablets, too? Where is the original copy of the *Koran*, especially the one that should have been written during Muhammad's lifetime after his receiving revelations from Gabriel for no other possible purpose than to memorialize these revelations in book form? Where are the golden tablets embellished with the enigmatic symbols from which Joe Smith, another hocus-pocus charlatan, with the aid of a hat and a magic "seeing stone" was able to reveal to us, the mighty Book of Moron—er, excuse me, Mormon? "*What damned error*" would have us believe, with certainty, that the Almighty achieved "inerrant" success in getting His vitally important, "infallible" and "unchangeable" Word out to everyone in differing editions? *"What damned error"* would have us believe unbelievable Semitic scriptures?

Those who are not much acquainted with ecclesiastical history may suppose that the book called the New Testament has existed ever since the time of Jesus Christ, as they suppose that the books ascribed to Moses have existed ever since the time of Moses. But the fact is historically otherwise. There was no such book as the New Testament till more than three hundred years after the time that Christ is said to have lived. At what time the books ascribed to Matthew, Mark, Luke and John began to appear is altogether a matter of uncertainty. There is not the least shadow of evidence of who the persons were that wrote them, nor at what time they were written; and they might as well have been called by the names of any of the other supposed apostles, as by the names they are now called. The originals are not in the possession of any Christian Church existing, any more than the two tables of stone written on, they pretend, by the finger of God, upon Mount Sinai, and given to Moses, are in the possession of the Jews. And even if they were, there is no possibility of proving the handwriting in either case. At the time those books were written there was no printing, and consequently there could be no publication, otherwise than by written copies, which any man might make or alter at pleasure, and call them originals. Can we suppose it is consistent with the wisdom of the Almighty, to commit Himself and His will to man upon such precarious means as these, or that it is consistent we should pin our faith upon such uncertainties? We cannot make, nor alter, nor even imitate so much as one blade of grass that He has made, and yet we can make or alter words of God as easily as words of man. About three hundred and fifty years after the time that Christ is said to have lived, several writings of the kind I am speaking of were in the hands of diverse individuals; and as the Church had begun to form itself into a hierarchy, or church government, with temporal powers, it set itself about collecting them in a code, as we now see them, called The New Testament. They decided by vote, as I have before said in the former part of "The Age of Reason," which of those writings, out of the collection they had made, should be the Word of God, and which should not. The rabbins of the Jews had decided, by vote, upon the books of the Bible before. As the object of the Church, as is the case in all national establishments of churches, was power and revenue, and terror the means it used, it is consistent to suppose that the most miraculous and wonderful of the writings they had collected stood the best chance of being voted. And as to the authenticity of the books, the vote stands in the place of it, for it can be traced no higher.

---Thomas Paine, *The Age of Reason*

Mr. Fenning in his dictionary definition of the word Bible, subjoins the following history of its translations: 'The translation of this sacred volume (the *Bible*) *was begun very early in this kingdom (England) and some part of it was done by King Alfred. Adelmus translated the Psalms into Saxon in 709, and other parts were done by Edfrid or Ecbert in 730, the whole by Bede in 731, Trevisa published the whole in English in 1357. Tindal's was brought higher in 1534, revised and altered in 1538, published with a preface of Cranmers in 1549. In 1551, another translation was published, which was revised by several bishops, was printed with their alterations in 1560. In 1607, a new translation was published by authority, which is that in present use.' From this account it appears, that from the first translation of the Bible by Trevisa, into English, in 1357, it has been revised altered, and passed through six different publications, the last of which is said to have been done by authority, which I conclude means that of the king, whose prerogative in giving us a divine revelation, can no more be esteemed valid than that of other men, though he may be possessed of an arbitrary power within the limits of his realm to prevent any further correction and publication of it. As to the changes it underwent previous to Trevisa's translation, in which time it was most exposed to corruptions of every kind, we, will not at present particularly consider, but only observe that those translations could not, every one of them, be perfect, since they were diverse from each other, in consequence of their respective revisions and corrections; nor is it possible that the Bible, in any of its various editions could be perfect, any more than all and every one of those persons who have acted in part in transmitting them down to our time may be supposed to be so: for perfection does not pertain to man, but is the essential prerogative of God.*

---Ethan Allen, *Reason, The Only Oracle of Man*

Lest the fraud be readily detected, manufactured Semitic Deities will

253

always have need for the services of "anonymous" and "untraceable" script-writers to write their Chutzpah Chronicles---"storytelling" authors such as the *New Testament's* authority-lacking, unknown authors who penned their fish-tales using the headings: *"According to" Matthew, "According to" Mark, "According to" Luke,* and *"According to" John* in order to fabricate and impose their deceiving Gospels on everyone while keeping their personal identities hidden. Is mankind/womankind so desperate to have belief in God that we will abandon all reason to acquire it? Shame on us for accepting the above impostors' bogus words as being the perfect Word of God—shame on us for accepting their contrived tales without their having any authority, without any questions being asked, without any doubts about their veracity---shame on us for believing the outright lies, the hearsay evidence, and the invented and contradictory testimonies of pious impostors as being above suspicion in matters of religion!

Shame on us for our part in promoting and spreading the man-made, malevolent fictions of Judeo-Christianity! "According to myself," if *Matthew, Mark, Luke,* and *John* truly had anything of immense importance to tell us about their first-hand, personal experiences with Jesus Christ, they should have each written about it themselves during their lifetimes—their silence during their lifetimes on such matters, however, is quite telling! Can you imagine yourself as being any one of the twelve disciples and not wanting to put pen to papyrus in order to tell the world of your personal experiences living day and night in the physical presence of God---imagine yourself as being any one of the twelve disciples whose eyes had witnessed Jesus walk on water and raise the dead to life---not wanting to memorialize, in writing, such miraculous events after Jesus' death? How strange that not one of these guys who were personally hand-picked by God to become another "chosen few" and spread His "Word" was inspired enough while they possessed the breath of life, to pen their God-Diaries! Not one out of these twelve men made a record of their experiences with the Creator of the Universe! But, oh!, what wondrous Gospel tales suddenly appeared in writing centuries after the passing of all of the Gospel's fervid characters known as the disciples! Hmm! Hmm! Hmm!

> ***The study of theology, as it stands in Christian churches*** (Jewish temples and Islamic mosques---kvk), ***is the study of nothing; it is founded on nothing; it rests on no principles; it proceeds by no authorities; it has no data; it can demonstrate nothing; and it admits of no conclusion. Not anything can be studied as a science, without our being in possession of the principles upon which it is***

founded; and as this is not the case with Christian (Jewish and Islamic---kvk) *theology, it is therefore, the study of nothing.*

---Thomas Paine

"*What damned error*" would have us believe any word of testimony given "*according to*" *Matthew, Mark, Luke,* or *John*—whom the *Bible* tells us were despicable, deceitful disciples who were able to look into the eyes of Jesus while swearing to Him that they would never, I repeat, "never," I repeat, "never" deny Him even if it meant losing their own lives—despicable disciples who, to a man, ran away and abandoned Jesus during His arrest in order to save their own pitiful, cowardly asses? Such shameful, disgraceful behavior on the part of Jesus' hand-picked confidants who were the only human beings ever granted the exclusive privilege of living day in and day out in the glorious, intimate presence of God---human beings whose treasonable actions should not only be an embarrassment to every Jew, to every *Bible*-believer, to every decent-minded person on the planet, but to the very Devil himself and all of his loyal and steadfast, non-forsaking disciples as well! Imagine the actions of God's "chosen" disciples shaming and being an embarrassment even to the most evil of all souls that God had supposedly created! ---*Matt.* 26:35,56! The disgraceful disciples of Jesus, rather than stand their ground and defend their Savior to the bitter end, preferred instead to run for cover that memorable, arresting day! Shame on all who believe, or would have us believe, the Gospel testimonies of such ingrates—perjurers and traitors all—shame, shame, shame on you!

Think about it, dear Christians, what possible fear could any of the disciples have had about being apprehended when God, Himself, was standing right alongside of them? Peter, the lying fisherman (imagine that!) who told Jesus he would rather face death than forsake Him---*John* 13:37 became the "ROCK" upon which the Christian Church is supposedly built, a man whose life had previously been saved by Jesus from drowning to death---*Matt.* 14:22-32. Peter not only deserted his Savior during His arrest, he denied ever knowing Him—not once—not twice—but three times! ---*Matt.* 26:69-75—what a guy---what a steaming pile to build the Christian faith upon! To understand the forsaking disciples' inexplicable, baffling behavior at the arrest of Jesus---a man that they knew with certainty, because they, supposedly, were witness to it, was able to walk upon water and return the dead to life---requires the realization that truly devoted followers would never have run away and abandoned Jesus, someone whom they "knew" beyond any doubt was God, yet, their treason had a reason.

Suddenly stepping out of His portrayed passive *Bible*-persona, just prior to His arrest, the disciples had all witnessed Jesus become a very troubled, mentally unstable, and paranoid man wavering in his beliefs, someone who began to act in ways that ran contrary to all that He had previously preached to them and to others. Instead of Jesus following His own inane teachings and commands: to love one's enemies---*Luke* 6:27, to agree quickly with one's adversaries---*Matt.* 5:25, and not to resist the evil of others---5:39, He ordered His bewildered disciples to arm themselves by stripping off their clothes, the only clothes they supposedly had, and selling them in the streets to purchase swords with the proceeds. This call-to-arms by the Prince of Peace was done for no other reason but to confront and defy His "enemies" to prevent the so-called "prophecies" of His final days from taking place. Jesus, the sacrificial lamb, was preparing to lock horns with His apprehenders. Apparently, meekness, humility, and turning the other cheek really doesn't apply when your own life is at stake!

Knowing the dire consequences inherent in brandishing swords---*Matt.* 26:52, Jesus, the "meek and mild," holy hypocrite who we're made to believe would never resort to violence, desired, nevertheless, that He and His divine disciples should perish with them! Where, by the way, could the disciples have possibly found a sword-seller on such short notice, especially one willing to accept used, soiled clothing as payment? Had this event taken place in today's world, no doubt, Jesus would have ordered His disciples to procure hand guns or assault rifles, not swords, to deal with the threat to His life. It certainly must have been quite the spectacle, however, to see Jesus' naked disciples running around the streets like comic-book characters brandishing swords! Perhaps, in an effort to put a spiritual-spin on this unbelievable tale, it was possible that the swords were deemed necessary by a kind and generous Jesus, to be given away merely as gifts to His captors—such a thoughtful Guy!

Observing His manic behavior—the trepidation, indecision, resistance, and inconsistency in His conduct—the disciples, seemingly, must have begun to doubt the divinity and omnipotent spiritual nature of Jesus, a distraught God-pretender having a meltdown—the disciples ran away and abandoned their leader because they now "knew" with certainty that He was not God after all, only a megalomaniac who believed He was! It should also be noted here that just before His arrest, Jesus spoke the following words concerning His disciples: *"Of them which thou gavest me have I lost none."* An unbelievable statement for Jesus to make when one considers that the moment before it was uttered, Judas betrayed Him and the moment after it was uttered, all of His remaining disciples ran off! Perhaps, a delusional Jesus really didn't lose any of His devoted disciples on the day of His arrest---it is possible, after all, that they had merely left His side momentarily during His apprehension in order to find a more serene place that would allow them to have a peaceful opportunity to pray for their Savior and to count their blessings! Had the chosen disciples of God been in possession of all of their hanging parts or had they been Irishmen, I can assure you that the Gospel-tale accounts of the disciples' shameful betrayal of Jesus, at the time of His arrest, would have "revealed" a much different turn of events!

The elephant in the room regarding *Matthew, Mark, Luke,* and *John's* betrayal of Jesus, is a very large elephant indeed! Why is it that the Gospel accounts that carry their names and that we are led to believe, tell of their own personal experiences with Jesus never, I repeat, "never" contain a "Mea Culpa," a heartfelt apology to their Lord for lying to Him and running their asses off to avoid capture on the day of His arrest. Before that day they had all supposedly witnessed Jesus restore the dead to life, walk on water and feed the multitudes with just a few loaves and a few fishes. A few days later, after Jesus' death on the cross, these guys had all supposedly witnessed Jesus' having been physically restored to life---all of them witnessed Jesus walking bodily through walls, all of them witnessed Jesus being physically transported skyward on a cloud! Would there have been any doubt in their minds at that point that Jesus, was in fact, God Almighty? Certainly not! Had I walked in a pair of their wet shoes that day, I would have been sorrowful and distraught beyond words and so afflicted with anguish that I probably would have wept for days. I certainly would never have written, or caused to be written, my memoirs, about being a disciple of Jesus, that didn't begin with mention of my contrition for my disgraceful actions---with mention of my sadness, my regret, and my utter heartbreak for the dastardly deed I and all the other disciples had done to God, Himself, on the day of His apprehension. I would not have written an account of my life experiences with Jesus that didn't contain, more than once, the words: "God forgive me for what I have done"! It is quite difficult, if not altogether impossible, to believe the Gospels were written "according to" these unremorseful bastards!

Since it is supposed that every word in the *Bible* was put there by God, in one way or another, then it must be assumed that every single word, every single *Bible*-fact is of utmost importance to everyone, therefore, no *Bible*-word, no *Bible*-fact, no *Bible*-claim, no *Bible*-tale should be minimized or dismissed as being of little or no consequence. And, if I could have your undivided attention for an amusing moment or two, I would like to employ the scrutiny and skepticism of Reason's Tribunal to some of the whoppers found in the fish-tales alluded to above about Jesus' feeding of the hungry multitudes---events significant enough to be mentioned by all four Gospel writers:

"Twice upon a time," Jesus fed His "even-numbered," sushi-eating, fan club in the desert! The men alone in the first feeding totaled 5,000 in number; in the second, their exact number was 4,000! ---both of these figures, of course, did not include the vast number of women and children who were also in attendance but who didn't deserve to be mentioned in the undoubted headcount of those who really mattered to God and His disciples. Hmm! Both meals consisted, obviously, of tons of bread and raw fish that miraculously materialized from just a few loaves and even fewer uncooked fishes---talk about fast food! Yet, both meals ended up with more food being left over after each feeding than what each meal had begun with---for a combined total of 19 basketfuls of leftovers! Is this an example of God's bounty and generosity or is this just another example of God's incompetence?

Had God miscalculated the amount of food needed to satisfy the hunger of the multitudes? ---you decide! What was the importance of Jesus' ordering His disciples to, *"Gather up the fragments that remain, that nothing be lost" ----John* 6:12? What became of these leftovers that were gathered with such care? Where the hell did the baskets come from? ---did they, like the multitude's main course, suddenly materialize, too? Instead of having need of toting around heavy, fish-reeking, doggie-bag-baskets, why didn't Almighty God think to reduce the size of the leftovers back down to the manageable, miniscule morsels from which they had begun---perhaps, to the size of after-dinner mints to be handed out to each of His departing, desert-diners?

Imagine the tiring members of the bread and fish-fed hordes milling around after receiving their fill of food on a warm, if not hot, desert evening with baskets of leftover, raw fish! Can you smell it, too? Who, one wonders, was tasked with carrying these heavy, stinking baskets around? Were these leftovers meant to be a late-night snack for all, or perhaps, breakfast for everyone? Would 12 baskets of food be enough to feed 5,000 people? Surely, the gathering of leftovers in both feedings without redistribution plans would be pointless endeavors! And why, one wonders, did the disciples ask Jesus, "Where will we find enough food in the desert to feed this (second) crowd 4,000 + people?" ---when, previously, they had miraculously fed 5,000 + folks in the barren desert with just a blessing from Jesus? Why didn't the disciples know, with certainty, where the food was going to come from for the second feeding? With night coming on, as was the case in the first feeding, why didn't Jesus or His disciples, who were so concerned about the hunger of the crowd (and the gathering of leftovers), show any concern for the plight of the multitudes (women and children included!) who were now having to face spending a long, uncomfortable night in the desert? Why was bread and fish a necessity but not beds and blankets? ---Reason's Tribunal raises so many logical questions about detail-lacking, mythological fish-tales, don't you think?

Apparently, the miracle-promoting script-writers of these miraculous "VOILA" meals had missed a really great opportunity to make an even bigger, more impressive spectacle of the day's events that could easily have included a better-tasting fish-dish being on the menu they served-up at this amazing dinner in the desert! As every reader of the *Bible* knows, these unbelievable meals were catered by none other than God, Himself, who didn't think to include any butter or any oil for the bread that had to be as dry as was their desert location---no beverages of any kind to quench their growing thirst (no turning sand into water!) and no tartar sauce to accompany the fish-dinner---no tartar sauce---OMG! Surely, it would only have required just another miracle or two to make these dessert-free, desert meals truly be out of this world? Turning water into wine---no problem! ---turning meager morsels into a meal for the multitudes---no problem! ---turning desert sand into water, or tartar sauce, or beds---no way! Hmm! Whatever these *Bible*-tales are trying to feed us, they're giving me indigestion! Where's my lemonade? ---I think I've had my fill of fabricated *Bible*-fare, haven't you? ---but I digress . . .

Returning to the above-mentioned departing disciples, it is quite interesting and amusing to note here that the *Bible*-tales begin with one snake running off at the mouth in the *OT's* Garden of Eden and end up with twelve snakes running their asses off in the Gospels! Twelve contemptible, slithering, belly-crawling turncoats who are all now, strangely, revered and worshiped as "saints," —amazing! Surely, these men certainly deserved to receive some *Bible*-justice, as have so many others, for denying God by, perhaps, having some of their "chosen" parts roasted in order to fill God's nostrils with their "sweet savor"! ---*Exodus* 29:18.

Can my blasphemous criticisms of Jesus be a worse thing than what the disciples had done to Him? ---I think not! Certainly, their disgusting actions that arresting day were much worse, I repeat, "much worse" than anything that Adam and Eve supposedly did in Eden---that bears repeating. Shame on anyone (Pope included) who promotes the Gospel testimonies of impostors: *Matthew, Mark, Luke,* and *John*—men (if they can be called men!) who deserved to be spit upon for their dastardly deeds rather than glorified and honored! Shame on every Christian who teaches us to have absolute trust, faith, and belief in the words of these despicable, lying cowards! Shame on every Christian who teaches us to believe that the Almighty chose to inform the world of His Great Truth via the anonymously written Gospels given in a book of revised, altered, and amended texts—a book that came to us by way of someone's vote. Shame on those who teach us to accept, without question, the Gospel Word of perjurers and betrayers—men who disgraced themselves by lying to Jesus and turning their backs on Him—men whose scripted, scriptural accounts also abound in contradictions and disagreements regarding time, place, and circumstance! I think I should open a lemonade stand! *"What damned error"* would have us believe the following Gospel accounts concerning the death and resurrection of Jesus as given "according to" one of the above pieces of human excrement:

Now, (says Matthew), behold some of the watch (meaning the watch that he had said had been placed over the sepulcher) came into the city, showed unto the chief priests all the things that were done; and when they were assembled with the elders and had taken counsel they gave large money unto the soldiers, saying, Say ye, His disciples came by night, and stole him away while we slept; and if this come to the governor's ears, we will persuade him, and secure you. So they took the money, and did as they were taught.... ...He [Matthew] tells a story that contradicts itself in point of possibility; for though the guard, if there were any, might be made to say that the body was taken away while they were asleep, and to give that as a reason for their not having prevented it, that same sleep must also have prevented their knowing how and by whom it was done, and yet they were made to say that it was the disciples who did it. Were a man to tender his evidence of something that he should say was done, and the manner of doing it, and of the persons who did it, while he was asleep, and could know nothing of the matter, such evidence could not be received; it will do well enough for Testament evidence, but not for anything where truth is concerned. ...According to Matthew the eleven were marching to Galilee to meet Jesus in in a mountain, by his own appointment, at the very time when, according to John, they were assembled in another place, and that not by appointment, but in secret, for fear of the Jews. The writer of the book of Luke contradicts that of Matthew more pointedly than John does; for he says expressly that the meeting was in Jerusalem the evening of the same day that he [Christ] rose, and that the eleven were there— (see *Luke:* 24:13,33---kvk). *Now, it is not possible, unless we admit these supposed disciples the right of willful lying, that the writer of those books could be any of the eleven persons called disciples; for if, according to Matthew, the eleven went into Galilee to meet Jesus in a mountain by his own appointment, on the same day that he is said to have risen, Luke and John must have been two of that eleven; yet the writer of Luke says expressly, and John implies as much, that the meeting was that same day in a house in Jerusalem; and, on the other hand, if according to Luke and John, the eleven were assembled in a house in Jerusalem, Matthew must have been one of that eleven; yet Matthew says the meeting was in a mountain in Galilee, and consequently the evidence given in those books destroys each other.*

---Thomas Paine, *The Age of Reason*

"What damned error" would have us believe as true anything else the above disciples have to tell us about Jesus when they couldn't even agree on the location of the most important meeting they had ever attended in their lives? How long would it have taken the forsaking disciples to walk from Jerusalem to the mountains of Galilee? —an estimated distance of between 30 to 60 miles? Could they have completed such a march in a single day? Wouldn't they all have remembered making such an arduous journey that ended in such an unbelievable, memorable way? *"Yes, Virginia, if the truth be told, the Gospel-writers are liars and their Bible-testimonies prove it along with the doubt-free certainty that the Bible is neither an 'infallible' nor an 'inerrant' scripture---it, surely, too, is neither a 'decent' nor a 'holy' book? If, dear Virginia, these guys, 'according to' the Bible, could lie to Jesus, I repeat, "could lie to Jesus," why should anyone believe their Gospel-words to us?"*

"What damned error" would have us refuse to question the boastful and self-flattering belief that America is a "Christian" nation, a nation that proudly declares—IN GOD WE TRUST—but relies on a nuclear arsenal—just in case? We dare not question the boastful and self-flattering

261

belief that we are—ONE NATION UNDER GOD—when our Constitution's Preamble clearly establishes that America is one nation under ***"WE THE PEOPLE"***! We dare not question the hypocrisy of the Christian mindset that espouses—LOVE THY NEIGHBORS—then places locks on doors! *"Yes, Virginia, even the pretentious Pope, his parasitic priests, and the pompous "Good News" profiteers known as 'Televangelists' have locks on their doors and it's not because of their professed love for neighbors, but for fear of them—trust me! We dare not question the hypocrisy of the Christian mindset that espouses—LOVE THY ENEMIES—then makes attempts to kill them—for I have yet to hear of any Christian declaring his or her "love" for the perpetrators of 9/11---have you? What **"fools and hypocrites"** Christians be!"*

We dare not question the "spiritual" nature of a "loving" and "merciful," "meek" and "mild" Jesus regarding His despicable treatment of a desperate Gentile woman who was pleading with Him to heal her ailing daughter. Jesus attempted to dismiss her concerns outright because He told her, in a most despicable, insulting way, that she was, in effect, a piece of Gentile garbage unworthy of receiving His compassionate attention. He told this distraught woman: *"It isn't right to take the children's bread* (the spiritual food meant only for Jews) *and throw it to the dogs"* (the Gentiles) ---*Matt.* 15:22-26! When the beseeching woman beggingly replied, *"but even the dogs eat the crumbs that fall from their masters' table,"* the master-minded Jesus, impressed now by her groveling, self-degrading behavior, reluctantly relented and healed the woman's daughter. What a Guy! What a glorious Guy who *"so loved the world"*! ---what an example of His "good will" towards others!---what an example of the "God-like" behavior of Jesus! *"Praise the Lord"*!

Jesus could hardly have been more insulting to this woman had He actually spit in her face that day! And this is the beloved, sacred-hearted, holy-hypocrite whom the Christian world wants everyone to bow down to—amazing and incredible! Had that God-despised woman been my mother and I heard her being spoken to in such a humiliating way, Jesus would have required immediate medical attention! Imagine if someone had said such a thing to Jesus' mother . . . "Hey bitch, it ain't right to take food meant only for Gentiles and throw it to a stinkin' Jew"! Nasty stuff, right? ---but weren't the words Jesus spoke to this distraught, beseeching, Gentile mother just as offending? Yes they absolutely were! ---that's what Semitic Divinity teaches us by His exemplary example!

Apparently, in regards to the above example of Semitic Divinity at work, silence is golden when it comes to Papal proclamations and Sunday sermons given by wealthy Mega-Church Entrepreneurs, TV Evangelists, and other pious frauds who publicly promote and *"Praise the Lord"* but who, for some doggone reason, are careful never to promote and "Praise" these Gentile-renouncing, Gentile-loathing "Words of God" to their adoring, crumb-eating "Gentile" audiences today! Imagine a loving God inspiring someone to write a *Bible*-account of such a mean-spirited, disparaging account about His less-than-sacred doings!

To Gentile *"dogs"* who hath eyes to see and ears to hear, it should be quite evident that Jesus was an "us" and "them" kinda guy---a racist whose life's mission and whose life's labors, actions, and preachings, were devoted to saving only His *"sheep,"* the Jews, and not the *"dogs,"* the Gentile garbage. He came into this world in order to atone for a Jew's sin (Adam's!) certainly not to atone for any Gentile's sin! ---He came into this world for the welfare of the Jews only, as Jesus was born, we are told in *Matt.* 1:21;2:2, to be *"King of the Jews,"* not to be King of the Gentiles! He was, as confirmed by His shameful conduct with the woman of Canaan, "anti-Gentile," a bigoted, denigrating, supremacist, ("us" and "them"-minded), racial separatist who despised non-Jews and promoted "anti-Gentile-ism" throughout His entire biblical ministry.

He commanded His Jews-only disciples to avoid Gentiles and their territories, and to deal only with the *"lost sheep of the house of Israel."*---10:5,6, *"For the Son of Man is come to save that which was lost."* ---18:11, *"...all my teaching was done in the synagogues and in the temple, where all the Jews come together"* ---*John* 18:20, *"He helps the descendants of Abraham."* ---*Hebrews* 2:16, *"...He will send out His angels to the four corners of the earth, and they will gather His chosen people* (guess who they are?) *from one end of the world to the other."* ---24:31. To His *"lost sheep,"* He offers "life eternal" while the rest of mankind's groveling *"dogs"* who eat whatever might fall from their masters' tables, can all go to Hell! ---25:31-46. Jesus even went so far as to use the slick and crafty manner of speaking in parables in order to deceive and to exclude Gentiles from sharing in the blessings He wanted bestowed only upon Jews: *"...lest at any time they* (the Gentiles) *should be converted, and their sins should be forgiven them."* ---*Mark* 4:11,12---yeah, God forbid that should happen! The above *Bible*-verses make it quite obvious that Jesus, during His lifetime on earth, didn't intend or desire to be a Savior to everyone, as we are led to believe by *Bible*-promoters. (NOTE TO GENTILES: read *Mark* 4:11,12 over and over again until you can clearly perceive and clearly understand the clear purpose for Jesus' use of parables.)

It was only after the death and supposed resurrection of Jesus, I repeat, "only after the death and supposed resurrection of Jesus," did the script-writer of *Matt.* 28:19 suddenly decide to have Jesus, the Jew-savior/Gentile-shunner, finally throw a bone to the *"dogs"* that He previously snubbed and rejected—suddenly decided to have Jesus undergo a posthumous change of heart (Hmm!) allowing Gentiles (the losers) to partake of the special privileges He previously had intended only to be given to His *"lost sheep"* who, by the way, "rejected" Him and continue to do so even to this day! This late script-change became a requirement if Semitic priests were going to continue their parasitic, prosperous lifestyles bestowed upon them by the sweat, the labors, and the financial support of others---if they were going to keep the scam of Semitic religion alive, it became necessary for the script-writer of *Matthew* to make this drastic, last-minute script-change. If the Jews weren't going to buy into the "Jesus is the Messiah" tale, it became a priestly priority to allow, by addendum to *Matthew's* closing words, the more numerous Gentiles to enter the fold. Besides, it would certainly be good for business to have a bigger flock to fleece which, obviously, would cause an increase in ***"power and revenue"***! Lose the flock of disbelieving sheep and gain a gullible bunch of crumb-eating dogs---such a deal! The combining of the bogus *OT* tales with the added contrivance of the bogus *NT* Gospels now---"VOILA!" ---becomes the inspired "Loser's Manual"!

For Jesus, even as an afterthought, to have radically changed, with His final utterance, the message He delivered only to Jews throughout His entire ministry—to reverse Himself in regards to His utter disdain for Gentiles and their total exclusion from God's Kingdom, is the equivalent of Jesus' telling us to "believe not" all of His previous preachings in which He regarded Gentiles as being unworthy and unwanted folks in the eyes of God. Before His death, Jesus, who stated in *Luke* 19:27 that He preferred "to kill" His adversaries not "love" them! He didn't want Gentile *"dogs"* to be granted eternal membership in His exclusive, pie-in-the-sky-savoring, elitist, Jews only, Country Club Estate located just beyond the clouds. After His supposed "resurrection" it appears that Jesus had His own "Come To Jesus" moment when He decided to state without any reservations at all that He now, after taking His final breath as a mortal human, wanted to be a "Savior" to Gentiles, too! ---now wanted to be "everybody's" Redeemer! Okay, Jesus, based on your parting words in *Matthew,* I will "believe not" a word you preached before your death as told in the contrived Gospels! As for believing the words you spoke after your death, that were told to us centuries later "according to" the voted-upon testimonies of traitors and perjurers, I think not!

We dare not question, too, the sanity of the mental state of Jesus, the lifelong Gentile-hater and excluder ("anti-Gentite" for short!), when He declared (to Jews only as He didn't preach to Gentiles!), the conditions everyone must meet in order to become His follower (everyone except for the Gentiles of that time of course!) and what actions should be expected from each and every one of His *"lost sheep"*-believers in order to be considered a member of His flock "According to" Jesus, one must—"hate" their family members---*Luke* 14:26, "love" their enemies and "do good" to those who hate you---*Luke* 6:27 (commonplace activities that every Christian is so proud to undertake in the sweet name of Jesus---LOL!) "According to" Jesus, all who believe in Him will have the ability to: perform greater works than His own! ---*John* 14:12—drink any poison without harming oneself! ---*Mark* 16:18. "According to" Jesus, Christians must: sell all of their possessions and give the money to the poor (or buy swords with them!) ---*Luke* 18:22—never own more than one shirt! ---*Luke* 3:11—never save money or anything of value! ---*Matthew* 6:19—never be concerned for your life (except when being arrested!), or for your food, (except for the hungry multitudes who followed Jesus into the desert!) or for your clothing! ---*Matthew* 6:25—never think about or make plans for tomorrow or, therefore, have thoughts or concerns about making the world a better place for all---what a world-lovin' Guy! ---*Matthew* 6:34. These "lowly esteemed," Jew-rejected commands and directives of Jesus which are now *"highly esteemed"* by Gentiles and especially every "Do as I say, not as I do" Pope, Mega-Church Mogul, TV Evangelist, and Sunday-School Teacher who would have their deluded "Gentile" flocks believe and obey are, curiously, never followed or lived up to when it comes to their own "exemplary," Christ-obeying, Christ-following behaviors---Hmm! Hmm! Hmm!

The same "Do as I say, not as I do" behavior holds true for non-clergy Christians, as well. Jesus, apparently, has many faithful believers, but lacks even one faithful follower---incredible! (Not even Mother Teresa was a Christ-follower for she had in her possession tens of millions of dollars that folks had given to her charity for the care of the infirm, the needy, and the dying and yet, she refused to spend a penny of it to alleviate the pain and suffering of the poor people that she was, undeservedly, "renowned" for helping! Mother Teresa considered their suffering to be "Christ-like" and, therefore, was not highly motivated to alleviate it in the most humane way possible to those under her care such as administering pain relievers to the terminally ill, or seeking an available doctor's attention, or a local hospital visit for others who should have and could have received such care and treatment. However, Mother Teresa was not above seeking such care and treatment for her own infirmities!) *"Yes, Virginia, Mr. Jefferson was right---there are only two classes of Christians: **'fools and hypocrites'***!" To confirm the truth of Mr. Jefferson's assertion, just ask anyone, from the Pope to Joel Osteen---folks who proudly proclaim to have belief in the words of Jesus, in this case, the words He spoke about doing *"greater works"* in *John* 14:12---just ask them to restore a dead person back to life---a task that any non-foolish, non-hypocritical "CHRISTIAN" should have no problem performing! ---right? . . . *"C'mon Lazarus, get up off your dead ass! ---there's a Revival Meeting goin' on in town and I don't want to be late." "LA-ZA-RUS!"*

Helpless infants, abandoned derelicts, lepers and the terminally ill are the raw material for demonstrations of compassion. They are in no position to complain, and their passivity and abjection is considered a sterling trait. It is time to recognize that the world's leading exponent of this false consolation (Mother Teresa) *is herself a demagogue, an obscurantist and a servant of earthly powers.*

---Christopher Hitchens, *The Missionary Position*

Returning to the topic of Jesus having no followers---a stellar example of Mr. Jefferson's ***"fools and hypocrites"*** statement occurred not too long ago when Jerry Falwell Jr., the pious-pretending President of Taking Liberty University—er—Liberty University, and, one assumes, a devout Christian leader who certainly must have been a "paragon" of Christian virtue and Christian living, was booted from his college post for taking a few "liberties" with his wife and a pool boy! ---I wonder if Jesus had a pool boy? Jerry Falwell Jr.---the son of his school's founder, another pious pretender, Jerry Falwell Sr.---apparently "fell well" in his ouster as head of this Gospel-indoctrinating college with his pockets filled with millions for his less than evangelical behavior as head of Liberty U., a stellar Christian University—shocking isn't it? —that those who make their living promoting the Gospels—those who tell us they are certain of the dire consequences that everyone will face for their disobedience to their Lord and Savior, Jesus Christ—should be counted so often among the violators of God's "Word."

Would JF Jr. have "sinned" if he truly truly believed he'd caused an ache in God's heart or that he'd possibly be spending an eternity in Hell for his actions? Wake up, folks (and students of "higher" learning at TLU), there's a lesson to be learned here! The Gospels of Jesus Christ are a contrivance used by scammers who study human weaknesses in order to manipulate them in the guise of a pious-pretending religion whose main concern and interest is in *"power and revenue"* and, quite often, in having sex—it definitely is not in having folks own only one shirt or having them sell "all" of their possessions in order to give the money to the needy. Mr. Falwell, like all of his evangelical kin such as Franklin Graham and Joel Osteen, is a stellar example of a dishonest Gospel advocate and promoter, Christian hypocrite, owner of many shirts, and possessor of many unsold possessions! In *Matt.* 5:42, Jesus stated, *"When someone asks you for something, give it to him."* ---I'm certain, therefore, that if I were to ask Jerry, Franklin, or Joel for some of their millions, my pockets would soon be filled with God's bounty in no time at all! ---don't you think so, too? I find it ironic, however, that a school founded on promoting the Gospels in order to impose its dogmas on others and to shackle the hearts and minds of its students should contain the word "Liberty" in its title? Certainly, one of the Ten Commandments of Secularists should read thus: "Thou shalt not use the word: 'Liberty' and 'religion' in the same sentence!"

Today, it is said, the world contains between one and two billion Christians: folks (like the Falwells, the Grahams, and the Osteens) who are so eager and so proud to proclaim their unwavering faith and belief in the *Bible*-words of Jesus Christ, yet, strangely, not one, I repeat, "not one" (including the above hypocrites) can be found in all of Gospel-Land's multitude willing or able to follow the mandates Jesus gave to His believers—not one can be found in the entirety of Gospel-Land's multitude who can demonstrate the things that Jesus said was possible for them to do! With faith the size of a tiny mustard seed, according to Jesus, nothing, I repeat, "nothing" shall be impossible for His faithful followers, (including the Falwells, the Grahams, and the Osteens) to accomplish---*Matthew* 17:20.

They, (all of the above-named and their blessed, brainwashed brethren), will be able, by faith alone, to surpass Jesus' own miracles---*John* 14:12— they will all have the ability to turn water into wine—walk on water—calm the wind and waves—feed the world's starving populations with a few meager morsels—heal every known affliction—return the dead to life— uproot and hurl trees at whim without moving a finger---*Luke* 17:6---re- locate entire mountains without any physical effort---*Matthew* 17:20——and they will not experience any harmful effects from ingesting poison---*Mark* 16:18. Yet, not a single person (including the Falwells, the Grahams, and the Osteens) in two billion *"fools and hypocrites"* can be found in possession of enough faith, I repeat, "enough faith" to move even the "tiniest" of tiny mustard seeds a fraction of a nano-fraction of an inch—incredible! Incredibly, Jesus stated in *Matt.* 13:32 that mustard seeds are the "smallest" of seeds and that they grow into the "largest" of plants---I guess He must have forgotten creating poppy seeds and redwood trees!

The existence of the power of faith is easy enough to prove or disprove in a world awash with fruitful believers who are "moved" by their belief in the Word of God! However, to give dear Jesus another chance to prove His case, I am going to leave instructions not to be cremated for as long as possible after my death because a faithful Christian might just happen to walk by and take note of my Lazarus-condition and---"Voila" ---who knows? On second thought, when my mortal remains begin to stink to high Heaven like the words of Jesus, just go ahead and light the fire that will turn my flesh and bones into a splendid *"sweet savor"* unto the Lord! ---now what could be more God-pleasing than the roasting of an infidel? Mmm, Mmm, Mmm!

To be fair, Reason's Tribunal would certainly allow for any Christian (including the Falwells, the Grahams, and the Osteens) who wishes to demonstrate his or her mustard seed-sized, faith-based abilities, to be given a chance to show the world how such an insignificant amount of faith in Jesus enables one to walk on water, e.g.---two billion genuflecting Gentiles should be able to generate at least one, I repeat, "one" Christ-believer willing to take a faithful plunge on national TV! Any Christian who wishes to show the world that "faith" is all one needs to accomplish any of the above miracles, should contact "America's Got Real Talent" TV show for the chance to prove that Jesus is surely not a liar and, therefore, is totally worthy of belief in all that He has said.

(NOTE TO READER: —PLEASE PLEASE PLEASE PLEASE PLEASE---DO NOT DRINK POISON—I repeat, "DO NOT DRINK POISON"—in an attempt to prove your faith in the truthfulness of Jesus' exact words as given in *Mark* 16:18 about those who believe in Him being able to drink *"any deadly thing"* without doing harm to themselves. Believing in the insanity of this *Bible*-tale delivered from the lying lips of Jesus will harm you or kill you—believe me! From *Bible*-evidence only, we know that Jesus, the holy-hypocrite, despised His enemies and wanted them killed before His very eyes---*Luke* 19:27---perhaps, it was just His way of "loving" them to death! What a glorious Guy! ---can't you just feel the love? One would think that God, who only had to speak a few words (to no one!) in order to create the entire Universe, would be able to communicate clearly in a most perfect, literal manner when He, in His

Jesus disguise, stated that His believers would not be harmed by ingesting poison---I suppose the death of all of Jim Jones' Kool-Aid drinkers was the exception to that blessed announcement! If Jesus really didn't mean to convey to His believers the thought that they could drink poison and handle deadly snakes with impunity, He, the Perfect Communicator, should have told them so, in no uncertain terms, I repeat, "in no uncertain terms." Apart from our being poisoned to death or fatally bitten by Jesus' "Word" ---His reason for having everyone love their enemy has nothing to do with "love" at all—it is done, in keeping with Judeo-Christian tradition---it is done in order to *"heap coals of fire"* on their heads---*Romans* 12:20, and you thought that was the Devil's job! —really! ---asbestos hats and lemonade anyone?

...the author of Christianity (Jesus) *warns us against the impositions of false teachers, and ascribes the signs of the true believers, saying, 'And, these signs shall follow them that believe, in my name shall they cast out devils, they shall speak with new tongues, they shall take up serpents, and if they drink any deadly thing it shall not hurt them, they shall lay hands on the sick and they shall recover. These are the express words of the founder of Christianity, and are contained in the very commission, which he gave to his eleven Apostles, who were to promulgate his gospel in the world; so that from their very institution it appears that when the miraculous signs, therein spoken of, failed, they were considered as unbelievers, and consequently no faith or trust to be any longer reposed in them or their successors. For these signs were those which were to perpetuate their mission, and were to be continued as the only evidences of the validity and authenticity of it, and as long as these signs followed, mankind could not be deceived in adhering to the doctrines which the Apostles and their successors taught; but when these signs failed, their divine authority ended. Now if any of them will drink a dose of deadly poison, which I could prepare, and it does not 'hurt them,' I will subscribe to their divine authority, and end the dispute; not that I have a disposition to poison anyone, nor do I suppose that they would dare to take such a dose as I could prepare for them, which, if so, would evince that they were unbelievers themselves, though they are extremely apt to censure others for unbelief, which according to their scheme is a damnable sin. ("Yes, Virginia,*

beware of the impositions of false teachers, but don't take my word for it!" ---kvk)

---Ethan Allen

Believe my words when I tell you it is not to Jesus' credit that He supposedly lived as a merciful, humble man who had the ability to end the miseries of this world with just a snap of His fingers, and yet He *willfully* chose, I repeat, "He *willfully* chose" to let them continue—something, I assure you, that no decent human being, who possessed power over everything in the Universe, would allow to happen. Think about it folks, how could the heart of God who *"so loved the world" ---John* 3:16, be content to allow tribulation and oppression to exist—sickness, suffering, and sorrow—hunger and famine—disease and death—bloodshed and war—pestilence and crime—tyranny and injustice—eternal damnation and torment? SHAME ON THEE and SHAME ON YOU who believe that mankind is deserving of such a fate! If Osama bin Laden was deserving of his fate for adding to the miseries and sufferings of this world, why then do we choose to worship a mega-terrorist God instead of condemn Him and remove Him from our midst? I would have terminated the above-mentioned human miseries out of my love and concern for the world were it possible for me to do—does not the compassion of an imperfect human being, therefore, exceed that of a perfect, merciful Semitic Divinity? *"Yes, Virginia, it does!"*

If I had the power that the New Testament narrative says that Jesus had, I would not cure one person of blindness, I would make blindness impossible; I would not cure one person of leprosy, I would abolish leprosy. (way to go, Joe! ---kvk)

---Joseph Lewis

It is plain that there is one moral law for heaven and another for the earth. The pulpit assures us that wherever we see suffering and sorrow, which we can relieve and do not do it, we sin, heavily. There was never yet a cause of suffering or sorrow which God could not relieve. Does He sin, then? If He is the Source of Morals He does—certainly nothing can be plainer than that, you will admit. Surely the source of law cannot violate law and stand unsmirched;

270

---Mark Twain

And yet, Christians are shamelessly content to glorify Jesus and revel in the depth of His "compassionate" heart for allowing war, hunger, disease, etc., etc., to continue even though His scapegoat death was, we're told, an atonement for Adam's high-crime of apple-eating! If this were the case, where, oh where then is our restored Garden of Eden now that the God-damned lien on the place has been satisfied? Incidentally, what had Eden's innocent animals done to deserve their banishment from their Paradise home? Did they begin filling the world with *"violence"* on the very day of their instant creation in Eden---a day when they began living their bloodless, idyllic existence for, surely, predatory behavior was unknown in such a place? Surely, every creature there existed, like Adam and Eve, on the produce of lovely fruit trees---surely, every creature in the world, at the time, must have lacked fangs, canine teeth, claws, and the violent, unremorseful nature needed to use them the way God intended they be used!

Surely, vultures and Venus flytraps must have been fruit-eaters at the time, too! Or, was every animal on the planet, like the cursed Adam, being "disobedient" to God, too? Why did they deserve to suffer and die because of Adam's apple? Everything, it seems, is upside-down and backwards when it comes to Semitic religions and their child-minded reckonings and ridiculous beliefs, especially the savage-minded, vengeful actions on the part of their *loving* God—it is the reverse of what merciful and ethical behavior, benevolence and compassion, reason and sanity, justice and holiness should reveal and condone.

The karmic price tag Jehovah/Jesus placed upon all of mankind because of one man's disobedience, according to Judeo-Christian justice, has surely been duly PAID-IN-FULL by the sacrificial death of Jesus. On the day of His supposed resurrection, Jesus, one would rightly assume, should have announced, from that moment on, that the idyllic Garden of Eden would be re-established on earth, a place where suffering, sorrow, violence, and death would no longer be permitted, but, alas, He didn't because His *Bible*-storytellers couldn't deliver on such a fair and square deal! The scamming script-writers of the *Bible*, obviously, couldn't deliver on their concocted tale about sin and redemption---they, obviously, couldn't restore Eden even though they had us believe that Jesus' sacrifice was a "perfect" atonement for Adam's "sin" and so, this time, with a little more word-tweaking here

271

and there in the Gospels, our Paradise home was no longer to be found here on earth but kept hidden now beyond the clouds high above our heads. And all that one was required to do now, in order to eat a piece of the promised pie-in-the-sky and become a permanent resident of the Heavenly Kingdom of the Chosen, was to die without sin or simply call out to Jesus to remember your sad ass when you take your final breath, an example of which is given in *Luke* 23:42,43 where Jesus tells His double-crossed neighbors: *"Today shalt thou be with me in paradise"* which, incidentally, doesn't agree at all with Jesus' dying words as given in *Matthew* and *Mark.* The rest of the world's residents who die without doing either of the above, can all go to Hell—for God *"so loved the world,"* He willfully torments the greater part of it forever! ---can't you just feel the LOVE?

Interestingly, within our present Earthly Kingdom of Sorrows, a world teeming with suffering and need, there exists legions, I repeat, "legions" of Christians who Jesus, Himself, has told us will "outperform" His own miracles. Yet, in spite of all the troubles facing the world, God is content to squander His miracles making folly---for why are Jesus' "prophesied" miracles of this day and age seemingly limited to novelty such as weeping or bleeding statues, weeping or bleeding pictures, and curious images of "Himself" appearing on a water-stained rug, on tree bark, on toast, etc.,— even though no one knows what Jesus looks like—even though graven images of Jesus exist in virtually every Christian home—even though possessing such images is considered as sinful as engaging in the act of murder according to *James* 2:10—even though having such images is a Commandment-breaking, first-class ticket to Hell?

I, nonetheless, was blessed to witness firsthand the miracle of God's facial image showing up in the darndest of places---while wiping-up after a BM---Holy Shit!---there He was! ---His face suddenly appeared on the TP---God surely does work in mysterious ways! I'm thinking about sending it to the Pope so that it can be proudly displayed in the Vatican and, perhaps, become another one of its many valued treasures and sacred relics---it surely would be a shame just to flush it down since God, Himself, had performed a miracle in order to produce it! The Shroud of Turin will now have to share the spotlight with The Shred of Charmin! Think about it, folks, is what I said in irreverent jest about God's face appearing on used TP worse than what Jesus said in earnest to the beseeching woman of Canaan? ---I don't think so!

Why, oh why is it we never hear of any Christian paragon who possesses the Gospel-guaranteed ability to surpass the works of Jesus---I'm talking about the Pope and those charismatic, Televangelist, Mega-Church, *"Praise the Lord,"* Mustard-Seed-Preaching, Hallelujah Hustlers (like the Falwells, the Grahams, the Osteens) going "Hands-On," like Jesus stated in *Mark* 16:18, and emptying all the beds at a Children's Hospital? What could possibly prevent these pious frauds from accomplishing, in the name of God, what they all profess to be is His "Word" ---a 'Word" that they are so fond of preaching, promoting, and profiting from?

> *...they shall lay hands on the sick and they shall recover.* (except for the above hustlers and hucksters who aspire to *'lay hands'* on your wallet instead! ---kvk)

---*Mark* 16:18

Perhaps, it is because Christian belief in the powerful abilities of faith as small as a tiny mustard seed requires having an intellect of similar size! Perhaps, too, it is because Jesus lied and the *Bible* confirms it! *"Yes, Virginia, Christians, obviously, do not exist, but don't take my word for it, take Jesus' 'Word' for it as He has stated in John 14:12! Because of our reluctance, as Americans, to reveal our own religious credulity, we cannot expect to expose the religious credulity of our enemies who desire, in the name of God, to destroy all of our freedoms while adding to the miseries and sorrows of our world instead of trying to ease or end them, hence the dire need for Reason's Tribunal to begin to reveal 'the rest of the story' to the imposed-upon multitudes in an effort to improve the living conditions of everyone!"*

It is interesting to note here (in this digression!) that in *Matt.* 10:3-8, Jesus, the Jewish-race-favoring God, gave "each" of His disciples miraculous powers along with orders to avoid Gentile lands and to heal the sick, to raise the dead back to life, to end the sufferings of only the members of *"the lost sheep of the House of Israel."* Twelve guys with superhero abilities on a mission to cure disease and overcome death, yet, the *Bible* neglects to give us even one example of their mighty "great works" ---remarkable events that should have filled many of the *New Testament's* pages especially the pages written *"according to"* Matthew, Mark, Luke, and *John* who, we're told, were possessors of these amazing God-talents! Had I been a disciple of Jesus who had been blessed with such awesome powers, there would not have been a sick, dying, or dead person anywhere I ventured and, I'm quite certain, history would have recorded my extraordinary exploits as well as those of the twelve "Miracle-Men"! Yet, Jesus, who possessed the power to end these things: disease, death, and all of the sorrows of this world, chose not to---"do as I say, not as I do," once again---what a spiritual Guy! Returning to where I left off . . .

Shame on you, Jew and Christian! Shame on you for your total acceptance of the totally unacceptable! Shame on all of you who consider Jehovah/Jesus bin Laden worthy of worship and adoration after reading chapters 7-12 of *Exodus* that describe in detail the "divinity" He and His hooligan henchmen, Moses and Aaron, dispensed upon Egypt! Shame on you for not knowing what you are worshiping—for upon such God-damning infamy: the terror-filled plagues and pestilences imposed upon Egypt's blameless citizens and the murder of their innocent firstborn children and animals, commanded by your personal God—your shameful religions are founded!

Can we imagine a conduct more abominable, than that ascribed by Moses to his God, towards the Egyptians, where that assassin proceeds boldly to declare, in the name, and by the order of his God, that Egypt shall be afflicted with the greatest calamities, that can happen to man. Of all the different ideas, which they (the first founders of all sects) wish to give us of a supreme being, of a God, creator and preserver of men, there are none more horrible, than those of these impostors, who believed themselves inspired by a divine spirit.

---Baron d'Holbach

Thus stands the record (of Egypt's tribulations), *and upon that record religion must stand or fall, for if it be literally true and historical, this monster* (God) *should be damned instead of worshiped; and if it be but mythology, the Bible's authority is gone forever. The latter, we claim, is its true nature. That the race can read it, believe it and still worship its monstrous God is an index of our intelligence, our knowledge of Causation, Reality, Truth. It is that of the child and the savage, yet this is the intelligence that is running our world; this is the intelligence that sustains our religion, nationalism, commercialism—and the giving away of countries on the words of a myth. These are not the fruits of wisdom and understanding but of incredible ignorance. Do you wonder then that we have war and oppression, crime and corruption? What would you expect of beings still in the God-worshiping stage? ...What we offer here is admittedly and intentionally a one-*

---Lloyd M. Graham

What would you expect of *"beings"* who condone religious tyranny---who deem Moses, the murderer, and Muhammad, the pedophile, worthy emissaries for carrying out or relaying anything of a spiritual nature---for bringing and revealing God's loving "Word" to the world? What would you expect of religions advanced by a killer and a child-molester? *"Yes, Virginia, God does work in mysterious ways!"* What would you expect of *"beings"* who surrender their intelligence and their sanity to the oppressive, malevolent rantings of these and other demented terrorist-criminals of Semitic scripture? What would you expect of *"beings"* who, because of their religious beliefs or religious customs, are compelled to dress, and to style their hair in a certain way—beings who enslave their entire lives to peering out of the eye-slits of death shrouds called "burkas"—beings who enslave their entire lives to performing monotonous, robotic rituals to the point of strapping little cases (phylacteries) containing scriptural texts to their foreheads and their left arms, to performing pointless genital mutilation upon their male infants, to performing prayer sessions five or more times every day while facing in the direction of Mecca, the birthplace of Muhammad the child molester? According to God's anonymous script-writer(s), God spoke the following words to Abraham:

off from his people; he has broken my covenant. (God seemingly has an obsession with junior's li'l pee-pee and with cutting-off certain things! ---kvk)

---Gen. 17:10-14

Why should anyone believe that God uttered such a cutting remark to Abraham? We have only an unknown script-writer's word for it—never Abraham's word for it—never a known eyewitness or a known earwitness to tell us what was seen or what was heard in the detailed events being described in the above chapter and verse! If circumcision was such a big deal to God, why is it that Jesus, who, evidently, suffers from *OT* amnesia, never promoted it in "His" role as the Almighty? ---why did His advocate, Paul, state, in *Galatians* 5:6, that neither circumcision nor the lack of it makes any difference at all? ---just another example of religion having it both ways!

The Judaic circumcision ritual imposed upon male babies is based solely upon a supposed verbal pronouncement, a command, from God to Abraham, but who was it that was able to record and relay every syllable of that pronouncement to us? Was it the mythical God of the Israelites, Himself? Was it the mythical Abraham? Was it the mythical Moses? Or, was it an unidentified, mysterious witness hiding out in the bushes with pen and papyrus in hand, ready to write down every God-spoken word verbatim? Who was this person who was fortunate enough to always be in the right place at the right time to hear God speak and was always prepared to memorialize it? Who was it that had the astounding, amazing ability, I repeat, "the astounding, amazing ability" to tell us in *Gen.* 17:17 what Abraham had *"said in his heart"*? Really? ---what an extraordinary gift of extrasensory perception all of the script-writers of Semitic scripture possess---what an extraordinary large, steaming pile! *"Yes, Virginia, when someone tells you what is in another person's 'heart' ---know, with absolute certainty, that you are absolutely being lied to! Know, too, with absolute certainty that it takes an extraordinarily large, steaming pile of fog-forming chutzpah to make such an audacious claim in a supposed book of 'truth'! Think about it, dear Virginia, ---only a lying, conniving, contriving script-writer of the Chutzpah Chronicles could have reported such obvious 'fake news'!"*

Sadly, it is solely because of such concocted pronouncements made throughout the *Bible* by unknown authors, that Jewish male babies (under God's supposed express orders) must undergo genital mutilation (even

276

though we're told, later on in the *Bible,* that this barbaric ritual makes no difference at all---a top priority in the *OT,* but not so much in the *NT!*) --- concocted pronouncements that, aside from God demanding the mutilation of babies' genitals, has Him demanding entire nations of innocent people to be put to the sword—incredible! Yet, no one knows the identity of these script-writing *Bible*-bastards who were God's "only" witnesses---the "only" bastards---to ever make the claim that they knew with impeccable certainty, what God had thought about in His head!---what God had said in His heart (I wonder what was in God's heart and mind on 9/11?)---what God had spoken to others---the "only" bastards with the chutzpah to try to make us believe these BS communications and close encounters with God really occurred and wrote them down as such upon the pages of the *Bible*---a book that the imposed-upon are supposed to swallow whole! The *Bible's* lack of authority is as prevalent as the lack of foreskins in Israel! The mutilation of Jewish males' members is not based on any infallible, *Old Testament* truth but only on the imposing lies and the imposing deceptions found throughout it. I only wish that all believers in the *Bible* had the miraculous *Bible*-ability to read my thoughts and know what it is I'm saying in my heart when it comes to my efforts to reveal the "revealed" Word of God for the fraud that it is!

If something was ever truly needed to be forcibly excised from anyone's person as part of a "spiritual" endeavor, it should be the bogus *Bible* with its insentient, brutal rituals and destructive dogmas that is removed from one's person! No matter how you slice it, lopping off part of an infant's genitalia is a gruesome, grotesque act—a barbaric, religious ritual that the violated victims have no say in since eight-day old, male babies are non-verbal in their vocalizations of pain. If Jewish "men" had the "choice" to willingly submit (or not) to having someone take a razor to their manhood, it is my opinion that they would all behave like Jesus' disciples on the day of His arrest! Jewish fellas should be thankful, however, that Abraham, in his chat with God, wasn't told to increase the length of the shortening by another inch! Phwhew! Since eight-day old, male babies are considered spiritually mature enough to have a Jewish religious ritual imposed upon them, I wonder why are they not made to wear tassels on the sides of their diaper or made to sport a li'l scripture-case on their forehead and left arm, or wear a yarmulke on their skull? Why are eight day old, male babies, in the name of God, forced to undergo ritual, genital mutilation but not old enough to wear tassels, phylacteries, and skullcaps in the name of God? ---my guess is that it wouldn't be proper to impose upon babies in such a loving, sacred way!

Why in any case is it necessary for God to intervene in human history, in human affairs, as almost every religion assumes happens? That God or the gods come down and tell humans, "No, don't do that, do this, don't forget this, don't pray in this way, don't worship anybody else, mutilate your children as follows." Why is there such a long list of things that God tells people to do? Why didn't God do it right in the first place? You start out the universe, you can do anything. You can see all future consequences of your present action. You want a certain desired end. Why don't you arrange it in the beginning? The intervention of God in human affairs speaks of incompetence.

---Carl Sagan

We are told that God is omnipotent, omniscient, and benevolent; yet He behaves like a petulant tyrant, unable to control his recalcitrant subjects. He is angry, He is proud. He is jealous: all moral deficiencies surprising in a perfect Being. ...What can we say of the rather curious psychology of a Being who creates humans—or rather automata—some of whom are preprogrammed to grovel in the dirt five times a day in homage to Himself? This obsessive desire for praise is hardly a moral virtue and is certainly not worthy of a morally supreme Being.

---Ibn Warraq, *Why I Am Not a Muslim*

Shouldn't every Jewish male, after arriving at a mature age in life, have the opportunity, at that "point," to decide for himself whether he wants to enter into this penis-shortening covenant with God or not? After all, a covenant is a solemn agreement made between "consenting" adults who supposedly have been given (by God) the "free will" to act as they "choose" to act. An eight-day old baby is not a willing, consenting party to the "covenant" of circumcision—he is an imposed-upon, innocent child who has no choice or voice in the matter. I'm sort of surprised, however, that God didn't "choose," for "all" of His chosen people both male and female, a more visible body part to be removed such as an ear lobe or the tip of the nose or the tip of a finger in order for all of the non-chosen world to easily bear witness to, and be impressed, by God's power to impose His will upon His devoted followers and for His devoted followers to openly reveal to others, their strict adherence to their loving God's "Word." I'm sort of surprised, too, that proud members of this exclusive, first-ever covenant-with-God-club of Jewish males don't parade around exposing themselves to everyone to show-off the lengths (or lack of) that they have undergone as a sign of their exclusive contract with God—a sign of their love and devotion to Him! Without seeing a guy's genitalia, how is anyone able to get the point that certain males are spiritually-special? —why do male Jews keep their exclusive covenant with God hidden from view? Shouldn't Jewish fellas be proud to show the world their spiritually improved member as proof of their identity as being a "member" of God's chosen elite—be proud to show the world that they are a cut above everyone else on the planet!

Small children are too young to decide their views on the origin of the cosmos, of life and of morals. The very sound of the phrase 'Christian child' or 'Muslim child' (or 'Jewish child' ---kvk) should grate like fingernails on a blackboard. ...Let children learn about different faiths, let them notice their incompatibility, and let them draw their own conclusions about the consequences of that incompatibility. As for whether any are 'valid,' let them make up their own minds when they are old enough to do so.

---Richard Dawkins

Besides, how would it be possible for anyone attempting to abide by *Gen.* 17:14 to be able to determine if a male has been circumcised or not in order to ascertain if he should be *"cut off"* from his people? I'd be willing to bet that many Catholic priests and other clergy members would be over-the-moon to have the opportunity to make that kind of determination! Isn't it just a tad weird that the Creator of the Infinite Universe, I repeat, "the Creator of the Infinite Universe," would concern Himself with such perverse rituals as messin' with junior's li'l pee-pee or the minutia of forbidding the wearing of clothes made with two different kind of threads? ---*Lev.* 19:19—or by indulging His mighty nature obsessing about the need to place tassels on clothing with violet-colored cords no less? ---*Num.* 15:38—or by obsessing about the number of times that Aaron, in performing a sacred sacrifice, sprinkled the victim's blood from the tip of his finger? ---*Lev.* 16:14---or by obsessing about when to eat unleavened bread and when not to? ---*Ex.* 12:18-20---or by obsessing about whether Jews are wearing shoes and holding onto a rod while eating? ---*Ex.* 12:11--- or by His obsessing about smearing the blood of a fresh-killed lamb on certain parts of the front door so that an All-Knowing Almighty will be able to "know," when He or His accomplice comes to town during the indiscernible darkness of night if the people who lived behind those bloodied doors are Jewish or not (it's always about the "blood" isn't it? --- the freakin' ritually-begotten and ritually-spread blood!) ---why not just hang a foreskin on the door instead so there'd be no doubt as to who lived inside? ---better yet, shouldn't an Almighty God have used His loving God-powers to determine, with inerrant perfection and infallible precision, whom to pass over and whom to smite! Hmm! Why would an All-Knowing God need help to locate Jews when He was obviously quite capable of finding the firstborn of Egyptian families and animals without any assistance whatsoever? Hmm! Hmm! Obviously, the Jewish script-writer of this *Bible*-tale made his created God to have only one overriding concern in His entire operation of the entire Universe: the welfare of Jews! Hmm! Hmm! Hmm!

Because Passover is deemed a religious event---an event that begins with bloodshed (the killing of the Passover lamb) and ends with even more of it (the killing of all Egyptian first-borns) ---any people calling themselves "God's chosen" should be ashamed to make such inglorious, malevolent activity a part of their celebrated religious history for there is nothing in the sick Exodus/Passover-tale that has any spiritual dimension---nothing! Isn't it quite interesting, too, that the Creator and Operator of the entire, infinite Cosmos is singularly concerned with the performance of paleo-minded rituals and completely obsessed with all things Jewish? ---quite sick and quite slick at the same time! Isn't it just a tad weird, too, that a loving and merciful, *"Thou shalt not kill"* Creator would order His "chosen" to slaughter the Canaanites and not have any concerns about indulging in such an *"abomination,"* but God forbid they should boil a baby goat in its mother's milk---*Deut.* 14:21! I suppose God had to draw the line somewhere when it comes to what He considers to be acceptable behavior and what isn't---what thou *"Shalt"* do and what thou *"Shalt not"* do— incredible, just incredible! What an honor it must be to be considered a member of God's favorite folks---folks who are intent to do His cruel and unusual bidding---folks who would have us believe that their God's malevolent behavior directed against man and animal is sacrosanct--- malevolent behavior that they are damned proud to honor, celebrate, and promote!

Taking one of the male lambs, the priest shall present it as a guilt offering, along with the log of oil, waving them as a wave offering before the Lord. (I'm performing a wave offering right now as I write this! ---kvk) *This lamb he shall slaughter in the sacred place where the sin offering and the holocaust are slaughtered; because, like the sin offering, the guilt offering belongs to the priest and is most sacred.* (Mmm! I bet! ---kvk) *Then the priest shall take some of the blood of the guilt offering and put it on the tip of the man's right ear, the thumb of his right hand, and the big toe of his right foot.* (Once upon a time, the priest accidently put some of the lamb's sacred blood on the man's li'l piggy instead of on his big toe and, lo and behold, the poor guy's right ear fell off! I suppose it's just one of the risks involved in having your sins removed by sacred Semitic ritual! ---kvk)

God speaking to Moses---really, folks! ---*Lev.* 14:12-14

"Yes, Virginia, the exact location where the above 'offering' must take place and the precise locations on a sinner's body where the blood of the sacrificed animal must be smeared are among the foremost concerns of a so-called Almighty Maker of Worlds who, one would think, would have much greater concerns than expecting a certain peoples' conformity to inane customs and rituals and making Himself the obligated record-keeper of them. One such custom in the Muslim world has Muslim women wearing shrouds and head scarfs as a sign of respect, but to whom are they being respectful if not to their male rulers?—men who treat women as chattel and sexual servants whose rights are not the equal of themselves—men who (Allah forbid) might be caused to have a sexual thought upon seeing a woman's curving contours under snug-fitting clothes or seeing an inch of a female's uncovered flesh—men who do not share the same clothing restrictions as women are forced to do---that's because it was men who penned the pathological, puritanical rules that regard most, if not all, sexual behavior as an evil! Watch out, world! —when Muslim women begin to burn their burkas and head-coverings in protest and begin to acquire and enjoy their long-deserved liberation from male domination as a sign of respect to themselves! Watch out, world! —when Christian women begin to read what suffragette Elizabeth Cady Stanton wrote in an article titled 'The Degraded Status of Women in the Bible':

The Bible and the church, they have been the greatest block in the way of her development. The vantage ground woman holds today is due to all the forces of civilization, to science, discovery, invention, rationalism, the religion of humanity chanted in the golden rule

281

round the globe centuries before the Christian religion was known. It is not to Bibles, prayer books, catechisms, liturgies, the canon law and church creeds and organizations, that woman owes one step in her progress, for all these alike have been hostile, and still are, to her freedom and development. . . . Here (in the *New Testament*), *in plain English, woman's position is as degraded as in the Old Testament* (and as degraded as in the *Koran*! ---kvk)"

Surely, the Almighty Maker of Worlds would have a much greater reason for creating the Universe than to establish and record the mindless repetitions of mindless trivialities that He imposed upon His mindless-chosen—trivialities that are to be considered as being of profound importance such as foreskin removal and having a certain hairstyle, the profound importance of the color and the number of different threads used in clothing, and in dressing a certain way in order to stand apart ("us" and "them") from all other people---these are, without doubt, the concerns only of the control-and-conquer crowd—the power-seeking, ritual-promoting, script-writing priests of Semitic theology and not the concerns of a World Maker (with obvious OCD issues!). Likewise, are the mindless mumblings of Christians who are compelled by the control-and-conquer crowd to recite time and again: "Our Fathers" and "Hail Marys" in robot-fashion until their eyes bleed---until God, who must spend every second of every minute of every hour of every day and every night counting and recording each and every prayer and every genuflection---each time someone's hand makes the sign of the cross or fingers a Rosary-bead—until He decides to forgive His "robots" for each and every one of their trespasses the instant they achieve the magic number of repetitions, a number known only to God and to Catholic priests, even the ones who rape children when they're not involved in hearing confessions and meting-out sacred penance to others in order to wash away their sins—incredible!

It is also incredible that God, whose uber-concern is only for our compliance to His asinine rituals, would have created the Universe with a gazillion other worlds that man will never see, visit, or make use of---a gazillion other worlds that serve no purpose whatsoever and are absolutely of no importance or benefit to His foremost of interests: Jews and their ritualistic religions! Hmm! Sadly, it appears that God has wasted His amazing talents on creating such an uber-abundance of stars, black holes, galaxies, etc., ---the mere trivialities of His ever-expanding Universe when compared to the highly consequential mumblings of His fan club members! (News Flash: I have just learned from very reliable dream-sources---like those often mentioned in the *Bible*---that Heaven has finally entered the Computer Age and has gone "DIGITAL"! The counting of everyone's "Sins" and "Prayers," a never-ending, 24/7, thankless task that used to commandeer every nano-second of every minute of God's attention, now takes less time than a wink of the eye for God to get a print-out of someone's "good" and "evil" accountings---the very same "naughty or nice" list that God likes to share with Santa!

Thankfully, God spared no expense in acquiring the latest technology in the upgraded version of the "S&P-2000" system which, thankfully, responds to voice-commands just like in His early days. Because He no longer has to tabulate every sin, every prayer, every fingered bead, God is now able to get more couch-time in in order to play His favorite video-games---much to His latest wife's annoyance. She is constantly nagging Him to drag His ever-growing hind parts---OMG! ---to "Fitness Planet" to prevent them from getting any bigger. *"Yes, Virginia, God, like the Universe, is constantly expanding and now you know why! He also has a wife and tons of kids who are made in His exact image---no problem establishing paternity here! He even has a few exes, but He has lovingly prepared a special place for those bitches to spend their eternity!"* ---but I---LOL---digress . . .

For the Lord had said unto Moses, 'Tell the Israelites (after they had rejected Jehovah and worshiped a golden calf instead): *You are a stiff-necked people. Were I to go up in your company even for a moment, I would exterminate you.' ---Ex.* 33:5. (It is nothing less than astounding to be told in the *Bible* that God who favored the Jews also had it in mind to exterminate them! ---kvk) ... *'Speak to the Israelites and tell them that they and their descendants must put tassels on the corners of their garments, fastening each corner tassel with a violet cord.' ---Num.* 15:37-39 ...tell them they must not *'put on a garment woven with two different kinds of thread'* ---*Lev.* 19:19 ...tell them they must *'observe my precepts and be careful to keep my regulations, for then you will dwell securely in the land.'* ---25:18. ...tell them they must *'stand in fear of your God.'* ---25:17. (Stand, also, in fear of God's followers who do His bidding, that's my greatest fear! ---kvk) ... *'Thus you will remember to keep all my commandments and be holy to your God'. ...'To me, therefore, you shall be sacred; for I, the Lord,* (as if Moses was uncertain who was speaking to him! ---kvk) *am sacred, I, who have set you apart from the other nations* ("us" and "them"!) *to be my own.'* ---*Lev.* 20:26. (And there you have it folks, and it only took a few scripted sentences from God's lips to establish it: the power-lacking, tribal Jews now have Almighty God completely on their side which makes them, at least according to their Chutzpah Chronicles, the most powerful and the most important people on the planet whom God has personally selected to be His favored folks just as long as they carry-out what God has written they must do as stated in their Chutzpah Chronicles---such as destroy their neighbors, steal and plunder their lands, and rape their women children, etc., etc., and they are to do it all under the guise of obeying and complying with God's express orders in order to please Him and gain His blessings. How slick! How absolutely necessary it is then that God-loving Christians should back the God-following-Jews in their every endeavor and support them in all of their sacred biddings---all in the name of God, of course! Slick, super slick! ---kvk

It appears, judging by the apparel being worn by many of the chosen people I see today, that they no longer tussle with tassels and, therefore, no longer stand in fear of their God. They, as a religious sect, no longer keep "all" of God's commandments, precepts, and regulations which set them apart from all others. Because of the way the majority of them now dress, they have apparently become a stiff-necked people once again like the idol-worshiping heathens they once were and nearly exterminated by God because of it. I wonder what Jehovah's response will be this time to His stiff-necked, non-God-fearing, favored followers now that Moses is no longer around to plead their case and make the Almighty change His mind---*Ex.* 32:9-14? Perhaps it might have something to do with their dwelling securely! Hmm! ---kvk

Circumcise therefore the foreskin of your heart and be no more stiff-necked.

---Deut. 10:16

Now there's a ritual that the chosen people choose not to take to heart! Who knew that the heart had a foreskin and that it could be circumcised? Who knew that the call for the removal of foreskins should not always be taken literally? —a tip-off to Jewish males!

Who knew that circumcision prevented Jewish males from having stiff necks? ---kvk

Aside from the above nonsense about the obsessive, compulsive behavior of God in establishing His silly, inane rituals for certain folks to observe, there are other inane customs that deserve the scrutiny of Reason's Tribunal such as the swearing of oaths upon the *Bible*.

Why is it considered a matter of great importance in America, where Church and State are kept separated from each other on purpose, to have folks swear an oath to tell nothing but the truth in whatever matter that is before them by raising one hand skyward while placing the other hand on a *Bible*, a Chutzpah Chronicle that glorifies (deep deep breath, folks!) — atrocity, intolerance, inhumanity, oppression, deception, slavery, lying, cheating, criminal activity, animal and human cruelty, jealousy, trickery, thievery, conniving, lechery, debauchery, rape, revenge, wickedness, terror, tyranny, murder, infanticide, genocide, supremacism, manipulative cunning, and everything else involved with non-spiritual activity. The ceremonial hand-placement on the *Bible* during oath-taking in court proceedings is done, amazingly, in order to swear to the sanctity, the purity, and the truthfulness of one's statements or intentions while attempting to impress others with one's supposed reliance on this "pretended" Word of God for one's righteous, spiritually guided testimony---it's really quite amazing and beyond comprehension!

Using the Judeo-Christian *Bible* for swearing an oath to tell only the truth in matters of the State violates the First Amendment of the Constitution—for the State, in doing so, prefers the *Bible* over all other religious books for this singular purpose and, in consequence thereof, establishes and confers legitimacy to the *Bible* for being accepted, in our nation, as a book of truth, I repeat, "as a book of truth" —incredible! --- what an incredible accomplishment for the *Bible*'s script-writers! Obviously, the hidden message here is: if it is good enough for someone to place his or her hand on the *Bible* in order to become POTUS then it surely must be good enough for everyone else to believe in! When taking the oath of office, the President of the United States should, instead, place a hand on a copy of *The Age of Reason* or a copy of the Golden Rule if truth, justice, fairness, and decency are matters really worth acknowledging, upholding, and swearing to! The customary, traditional, and habitual use of a *Bible* in swearing an oath to something certainly cannot be used as an excuse to justify its continuance—the killing of people perceived as outsiders, while being a long-established, Semitic religious custom and tradition, is certainly not reason enough to continue the bloody practice! As to the long standing, Judeo-custom and tradition of killing animals in order to please God:

Why, one wonders, did the cherished rituals of animal sacrifice come to an end when they were such an important and glorious feature of the religious ceremonies of Jehovah's chosen worshipers especially since God had commanded such brutal activities to be carried out without end, I repeat, "without end"? Why had God spent so much of His precious time giving Moses and his tribe precise instructions for killing, butchering, and dismembering animals? ---in His divine, sacred manner of course

God took great pains to give His fan club a biblical, How-To-Course covering the basics of blessed animal butchery beginning with the slitting of their throats (a Semitic tradition that, no doubt, has survived the ages), the mandatory sprinkling of their blood here and there in the most sacred of areas, and last but not least, the removing with surgical precision of their various body parts and the barbecuing the choicest of cuts for their amazing aromas and their astounding, sin-absolving, atonement abilities. These God-given, divine, blood-shedding instructions have, remarkably, not been "revealed" to us in just a few *Bible*-paragraphs either---they have been expounded not only in verse after verse, but in chapter after detailed chapter after detailed chapter in *Leviticus,* perhaps making up the greater part of God's "Word" on any subject demanded of His followers!

Why, therefore, has animal sacrifice been abandoned by Jews since their God has ordered that it *"be a statute for ever unto them throughout their generations"* ---*Lev.* 17:1-7? Surely, even today after such a long hiatus from this sanctimonious activity, Jehovah, no doubt, would still relish smelling the cremation odors resulting from the ritual, brutal acts of animal slaughter that He took such great efforts to instruct, ad nauseam, to His priests of long ago—which included, (the always popular among the pious!) the wringing-off the heads of turtledoves---*Lev.* 1:15---an act that today is considered criminal animal abuse and dealt with as such in America, a supposed Judeo-Christian nation that "trusts" in God! Why then are such spiritual activities never ever the topic of sermons preached today to His faithful who believe His every "Word"? Why do sermons only tell us about God's great love and mercy? ---never about His great brutalities---why is that? Reason's Tribunal holds the answer!

Surely, a carnally stimulated God would still find sensual pleasure with the *"sweet savor"* of roasted flesh, barbecued in His honor, arising to His nostrils! ---who even knew that God has nostrils? ---was He, perhaps, made in man's image? Why do the majority of Jews of this day and age refuse to reconnect, reinstate, and re-indulge in a "sacred" endeavor meant to honor and appease their bloodthirsty God, a God who placed such tremendous importance on animal sacrifice? Why do today's Jews choose to avoid---choose to abstain from such a God-commanded, God-pleasing, religious ritual begun in their most sacred of times: their exemplary and honorable past when God personally dealt with Jewry on a daily basis? Why are the majority of Jews of this day and age inclined to distance themselves from an activity that, thanks to the civilizing effects of human progress (Man's help!), is viewed in a more enlightened age as a rite and a ritual of a less-than-civilized, paleo-minded people who, because of their ignorance of the world around them, lived in fear of their thunder-making, lightning-making God---using sacrifice to appease Him in hopes of avoiding His wrath? Why do the Jews of this day and age view as unworthy (except for a small number of ultra-orthodox types who like to fowl-around) only one of the religious rituals from their barbaric past while the remainder of their religious customs established during that time are carried forward and strictly adhered to by Jehovah's most devoted Jewish fans? Why? Why? Why?

Strangely, the Israelites of today, free from any outside constraints on their religious practices, choose not to conduct animal sacrifices any longer in order to please Jehovah with the bloodshed/butchery of animals and the *"sweet savor"* aroma of their burnt flesh that He enjoys sniffing so immensely! Hmm! Why aren't sacrificial altars found anywhere in Jerusalem or elsewhere in Israel in this day and age? Perhaps, in this day and age—because of the absence of ritual animal slaughter being conducted by His fan club to pay homage to their Almighty God on a regular, daily basis—we might assume that the God of the Jews has finally tired of the custom. Perhaps, He has seen the error of His deplorable, wicked ways and has become a meek and mild Veg-Head living on the simple, bloodless fare He initially commanded everyone to eat in *Gen.* 1:29.

Perhaps this God, along with His followers who were made exactly in His image and vice-versa, at least to some degree, have become the product of progressive secularism---the enlightened improvement and civil evolution of mankind due to the increase of knowledge, scientific achievements, and cultural advancements occurring throughout the ages in spite of religion's best efforts to keep us in ignorance and living in the darkness of its primitive past where fear, threats, and bloodshed reigned. Even the *"highly esteemed"* Christian custom of eating the symbolic flesh and drinking the symbolic blood of Christ, that was supposedly shed to atone for Adam's disobedience, had its origin in the everyday, commonplace rituals of human and animal sacrifice occurring during the honored and exalted God-filled days of early Jewish history. Surely, animal sacrifice was the product of the primitive mindsets and the primitive habits of a primitive people living in that primitive, barbaric age, the heyday of Judaism. Thankfully, however, as Man evolves, so too, ever so slightly, does his stiff-necked God! Unfortunately, however, progressive secularism tends to be a very slow process, judging by the fact that here in the Space Age, billions still believe in Him and worship Him: the despicable God of Semitic scripture.

The Chutzpah Chronicles known as the *Bible* and the *Koran*, written by unknown authors whom we are made to believe were incapable of lying, have created their Creators of the Cosmos (Jehovah, Jesus, and Allah) to have a singular, preeminent concern—the welfare of a few chosen specks of parasitic dust particles existing upon a minuscule grain of sand (planet Earth) found on Universe Beach. What would you expect of beings who are only capable of making the Gods of Judeo-Christianity and Islam in their own self-serving, self-centered, self-indulgent, vengeance-seeking, carnally-driven, compulsive, capricious, misogynist, xenophobic image— Gods who always act, understandably, for the exclusive benefit of their homies, especially for the exclusive benefit of the gender of all of the script-writers of Semitic scripture---for Gods, not surprisingly, are made in the exact image of the men who created them, the men who invented and wrote their Gods' "inviolable" words!

The creation of the *OT* God was the handiwork of primitive, savage-minded men---for their Jehovah is surely a primitive, savage-minded deity, yet as Man slowly improves through increased knowledge, education, and evolution, so too, does his bogus God and man's thoughts about Him tend to improve, too. Today's Christian God-addicts now choose to believe in a more enlightened Almighty who is loving of everyone on the planet, merciful to all, and impartial in meting out His blessings and His justice—a God who would never involve Himself in the wanton killing of animals--- never involve Himself in punishing anyone, certainly not eternally, for their breaking of any Commandment which today are regarded more like the Ten Suggestions! Yet, it is only in the minds of today's slightly-more enlightened God-addicts that their slightly-more enlightened Deity exists, for the inerrant and infallible *Bible*, as it is "now" written, describes Jehovah as a malevolent tyrant and Jesus as an unenlightened man who certainly was not loving of everyone, an unenlightened man who was certainly not merciful to all, an unenlightened man who was certainly not impartial in His doings, for only an unenlightened man would seek to send out His angels to gather up legions upon legions of sinners in order for them to be thrown into the fires of Hell where: *"There shall be wailing and gnashing of teeth,"* but don't take my word for it, take His as stated in *Matt.* 13:41,42!

It is unfortunate for believers, however, that the Gospels, as "now" written, still require many more "slight" revisions in chapter and verse in order for more-conniving script-editors to finally fabricate a more tolerable Jesus! *"Yes, Virginia, God's angels are going to locate each and every sinner that ever existed on the planet, even cave-men, and send them off to you know where. And, yes, they are going to find every live sinner and all of the dead ones even though their bodies may have been cremated---even though their bodies have long ago turned to dust over the ages. Yes, it will include their finding the nano-remains of everyone who perished at sea and whose bodies were eaten and excreted by ocean predators, and their finding each and every animal (sinners all!) especially the long, long-dead ones who were responsible for filling the earth 'with violence.' These bastards will all be found, their bodies will, of course, be completely restored in order that they be roasted forever if only for their God-pleasing aroma and their joyful-noise-making!*

It is my opinion, dear Virginia, that God, in uber-underestimating the number of sinners the world would produce, was totally unaware of the scope of the exhausting, daunting details and efforts listed above that He would need to undertake in order to accomplish His forever-goals and He may have gone into cardiac arrest as a result of His learning of them. That could explain God's puzzling absence during the Vietnam War when our nation surely needed to experience the warm fuzzies of knowing that He was on our side. Instead, America's Mighty Protector led us into a disgraceful defeat by a nation of non-Christians which surely inspired and emboldened Islamic fanatics, which led to the horrors of 9/11! ---and where the hell was our God on that day? ---where was America's beloved God during the 20 long years our nation, once again, sacrificed her young Caretakers of Liberty in Iraq/Afghanistan and invested a trillion-plus dollars in order to rid the world of religious fanatics? ---how'd that work out?

How many more times will we have to listen to a POTUS say, in sincerity: 'God bless America!' and 'God bless our nation's troops'? If Americans truly believe that God is on our side and watching out for us and answering our prayers, why is there a need for our nation to have a military force? ---God is taking care of us---right? ---Americans are such infidels at times! Is it not hypocritical to be relying, instead, on our armed forces to protect us? ---is it not blasphemy to suggest that God is incompetent in carrying out

His sacred duties to guide and guard America? How much longer will it take to realize the utter futility of such entreaties made by our nation's brain-washed leaders?

On the other hand, Virginia, when God is truly on one's side like the time when He was caring for the Bible-Jews, nothing could impede their land-grabbing conquests---hell, the Bible-Jews were unstoppable and with God acting as their Protector, they could not have failed!---they could have easily defeated the military might of the Greeks and the Romans during their glory days and taken over their heathen countries if they had chosen to---and why wouldn't they have chosen to do such things for the glory of God? ---hell, if the Bible-Jews had brutally murdered each and every Greek and Roman, their loving God would have been over-the-moon as long as they, His chosen people, benefitted from their raping and plundering genocides---(had Christians existed at the time, they would have genuflected and brought them water!) ---wait a minute---that's exactly what happened to the Canaanites, the unoffending neighbors of God's chosen people---OMG!

Today, it is apparent and quite strange, too, that the Jews of Israel no longer rely on their favoring, script-written, absentee God for their protection---they no longer rely on their mythic, papyrus-tiger deity for their security, instead, they rely on a strong military force! ---imagine that! ---imagine the Jews choosing jets over Jehovah oy vey! ---what does that tell you? And, by the way, where was the Jews' beloved Jehovah when they were being rounded-up---placed in concentration camps, and slaughtered by the millions? Where was the above loving God, His protection, and His blessings when our Judeo-Christian nation and her Caretakers of Liberty were most in need of them? The belief that America, too, has this God on her side and that all Americans 'trust' in Him, is literally destroying our country---a country where the Bible is purposely placed on a protecting pedestal out of the reach of investigators to be preached and promoted from coast to coast without question! Ask yourself why---ask, like a former POTUS did, what you can do for your country!

Does anyone know of God's whereabouts and why He doesn't answer His voicemail? Could it be that God has lost His secret hiding places? ---could it be that God has lost His health and His power due to His many regrets of having made the world the way it was and the way it continues to be? Perhaps, America's Commanders-in-Chief and anointed clergy who rely so heavily on the God of the Bible for His aid should, instead, be beseeching Santa Claus for his generosity and his blessings as he, seemingly, delivers on so many of the prayers and requests made to him and don't forget, Santa keeps a list of who is naughty and who is nice---a real asset these days when child-molesters disguised as priests are so abundant!

Yes, Virginia, there is a Santa Claus---he does exist and his whereabouts 'is' known to all. Maybe, it is time to begin questioning, with boldness, if America should continue calling herself 'One Nation Under God' ---to begin questioning, with boldness, if America should continue having 'Trust' in God!---surely, it is time for America to finally WAKE UP from her Judeo-Christian coma!---surely, it is time for America to finally realize what it is that inspires America's enemies to want to destroy us---surely, it is time for America to establish a Department of Common Sense founded upon Reason and Truth to guide her "God-blessed" Department of Defense---surely it is time we develop the weaponry that will enable us to deal effectively with religious fanaticism! Please, Virginia, send a request to Mr. Claus to locate our AWOL God and beseech him to assist in God's speedy recovery as America needs His services now more than ever to keep us safe from, of all things, another set of His 'chosen' Semites! ---its always about the God-blessed Semites isn't it?" ---oops!, I've digressed again . . .

What we can expect from the Chutzpah-Chroniclers mentioned above (before my long reply to Virginia!), along with those who believe their scripted words, is their "knowing" with certainty what their mirror-image, man-made God is always thinking, what actions He wants them to engage in, and what He plans to do on their behalf because they all believe that God "speaks" directly to them inside their heads! Hmm! How anyone would know with certainty that the voice they say they hear is that of God is anyone's guess for they never reveal the reason for their having such confident belief, especially since the Devil's words can supposedly be heard in like manner. However, because their God was purposely made to be incapable of communicating directly with everyone, He is always, I repeat, "always" in dire need of angelic or human assistance, pulpiteers and dreams to deliver His hearsay messages to a few chosen recipients, including any day-to-day changes in His divine plans! Hmm!

Because their God was purposely made incapable of directly communicating His directives with impeccable clarity in His ambiguous chronicles penned by anonymous authors, everyone, especially the clergy, is free to pick and choose, interpret, and embellish their infallible and inerrant "Word" of God to suit their own personal needs! Hmm! It is nothing short of amazing that these folks, being but humble dust particles, have the power, always to anger or to please their incompetent Semitic deity at will or at whim, to vengeful or loving actions, undertaken on their behalf! Hmm! Hmm! They know, always, that they can impose upon their steadfast God to make Him alter His plans to suit their purposes, when needed, with their mumbled prayers, their quid pro quo tithes, and their oft-repeated, mindless rituals for He is so moved by their trifles! Hmm! Hmm! Hmm!

> ***...for what is the amount of all his prayers but an attempt to make the Almighty change His mind, and act otherwise than He does?***
>
> ---Thomas Paine

They know, always, that their God must constantly rely on them, sinners all, to carry out His imposing will and His "sacred" life-destroying endeavors! Hmm! They know, always, that Jehovah/Jesus, the God who favors only the Jews, the God who, like His meat-eatin' male manufacturers, savors the smell of burning flesh—Mmmmmm! ---*Lev.* 1:9---(it being the only sensory stimulation that seems to get His total attention and put Him in "Forgive-Mode"!) *"Yes, Virginia, if Jesus was anything like His Father, He, too, must have savored the delights of smelling burnt flesh and, just like dear ol' Dad, His attention was solely focused on the Jews, not the Gentiles."* In His Allah disguise, the God who favors only the Muslims, He makes exclusive edicts for His incompetent Prophet Muhammad to be provided with all the sexual partners he desires to indulge his stiff-necked nature---*Koran* 33:50! Hmm! Hmm! Hmm!

> *If he* (a sinner) *presents a goat, he shall bring it before the Lord, and after laying his hand on its head, he* (the priest) *shall slaughter it before the Meeting Tent; but Aaron's sons shall splash its blood on the sides of the altar. From it he shall offer as an oblation to the Lord the fatty membrane over the inner organs, and all the fat that adheres to them, as well as the two kidneys, with the fat on them near the loins, and the lobe of the liver, which he must sever above the kidneys. All this the priest shall burn on the altar as the food of the sweet-smelling oblation.*
>
> Jehovah, Meathead and Butcher,---*Lev.* 3:12-16

Mmmmmmm—nothing but the best cuts will satisfy a God who is above temptation! Hey, "Meathead"—lay off the fat, —you're gaining weight and getting quite lazy as a result—pretty soon you won't be able to get your humongous hind parts off the couch to perform your amazing magic acts and continue visiting with your fans and having those intimate, intra-cranial chats with them. You're slowly becoming a has-been, Big Guy! ---sorry, folks, I was just "savoring" the moment! ---kvk

Could a being create the fifty billion galaxies, each with two hundred billion stars, then rejoice in the smell of burning goat flesh?

---Ron Patterson

Yes, Ron, he could because He is made exactly in man's image! ---kvk

The carnally-stimulated, carnally-rewarding, Muslim-favoring Creator, Allah, is, apparently, not above pimping and pandering to bestow the chauvinist perks of Prophet-hood on His hand-picked, cave-dwelling, pedophile messenger, Muhammad. Even those males who are "fortunate" enough to be martyred while committing atrocity in His holy name are rewarded with 72 virgins (as many Muslims believe!) —Allah is surely an "Akbar" Guy! *"Yes, Virginia, the God of Islam has been made entirely with a male-gendered, male-favoring, sensory image—I think He bears a striking resemblance to Osama bin Laden—maybe it's the eyes—the glazed eyes!"* Since the God of Islam is made, like all other Semitic Gods, to "resemble" their male creators, Muslims are entitled, like the Jews and Christians before them, to make their own "borrowed" deity in their own image in order to suit their own religious requirements. I find it somewhat astounding, however, that Arabs would accept, without question, without batting an eye, the God of the Jews. They have, for the most part, accepted the religious beliefs of a people they historically mistrust even though the script-writers of the *Koran* made their own blistering alterations to the "Word" of this Hebrew deity and His death-dealing dogmas! Palestine, apparently, was not Jewry's first Muslim-takeover—never underestimate the beguiling and imposing powers of religion and their "Word" of God and "words" in general!

If it weren't for the ignorance and backward-reaching effects of Semitic religions being shoved down our necks and up our lower parts throughout the centuries, such as believing the earth was flat and that no one should ever question such a *Bible*-reckoning, today's world would have advanced by a millennium, at least—the result of inquiring minds and scientific genius being put to use, instead of their being put to torture and to death! Shame on everyone who resorts to the *Bible* or to the *Koran* to seek the "ultimate" answers to explain the reasons for our existence, the purpose of our lives, and the moral guidance for our conduct as ethical human beings! ---really? Shame on us all for accepting, believing, and supporting their words without question. Fabricated, fictional, fraudulent scriptures, after all, are but ***"human inventions, set up to terrify and enslave mankind and monopolize power and profit,"*** —they were not intended to teach us and enlighten us about *"Causation, Reality, Truth"* except by imposing upon us with their unquestioned kindergarten child-minded reasoning and paleo-reckonings of the world around us!

The primitive-mindedness of Semitic, religious scriptures was intended only to indoctrinate us through fear and intimidation to believe that we are sinners all and, therefore, ever in need of God's merciful Word and His sin-absolving priests to avoid the painful, everlasting fires of Hell that God had so painstakingly prepared for so many of us to be tormented forever---*Matt.* 25:41---*"for God so loved the world"* ---yeah, right! What incredible BS! ---what incredible chutzpah it takes to create infallible Semitic Gods and their inerrant Words! —what incredible chutzpah it takes to foist these fabricated, man-made-monsters and their fabricated man-made-manuals of deception upon the entire world to be honored, worshiped, and adored! The losses that humanity, society, and civilization have incurred as a result of religion---its brutalities and its enforced stiflings to the increase of knowledge with its potential to enlighten us and to promote the humane progress of mankind---is incalculable. Please, dear God, stop loving the world so much!

It could have been in the year 492 that ships of discovery set sail in the name of science and understanding instead of a thousand years later in the name of ***"power and profit."*** It could have been around that same year when slavery was discovered to be an "abomination" and homosexuality "accepted," for by this time, the Golden Rule had been in existence (but rarely practiced!) for nearly a thousand years! Had slavery not been given God's approval in the *Bible*, Africans by the tens and tens of thousands would not have been stolen away from their families, their loved ones, and their homeland. They and their descendants would not have had to endure the brutalities of their forced imprisonment and the hardships of living in menial servitude to others and being treated as something less than human in the "civilized" Christianized parts of the world even to the present time. The Civil War would never have occurred in order to keep this reprehensible Christian practice continuing-on in America—Christianity certainly has a lot of African misery and bloodshed to atone for, as well as the harm its white supremacist followers are still causing to retard the moral progress of our nation! How long must Homo sapiens endure the outdated relics of our ignorant, religion-dominated, paleo-minded past and continue to give the *Bible* and the *Koran* credence and allow them to hinder man's evolution as a progressive species?

Religion is certainly a relic from humanity's distant past, a device used by unenlightened minds to help explain the cause of the physical phenomena that could not otherwise be determined or understood at the time. Fortunately, our need for stone tools and Semitic religions, both of which have served practical purpose in mankind's infancy, have outlived their usefulness because of the religion-retarded, religion-stifled increase in mankind's knowledge. While tool-making has certainly improved beyond a rock and a stick throughout the centuries, Semitic religions, unfortunately have only slightly, very slightly progressed during the same ages. They have been able, unfortunately, to maintain their death-grip over mankind to the present day only because fear, ignorance, and guilt can still be cunningly utilized by those who know how to continually benefit from using them. Semitic religions, unfortunately, to this very day, continue to retard and stifle the moral and scientific progress of mankind; they have not been able to keep pace with the religion-retarded, religion-stifled scientific knowledge that is responsible, in great measure, for all of the progress made by enlightened men and women. For ages, Semitic religions have promoted and enforced their paleo-reckonings, with rocks, sticks, fire, and brutality in order to have us believe the earth was as flat as a pancake, and they continue to this day to promote and enforce their belief that homosexuality is not to be accepted! Let us never forget that thanks to the efforts of Man, not God, we have learned that the earth is a globe; thanks to the efforts of Man, not God, we no longer stone homosexuals to death except in a few countries that continue to promote, enforce, and impose God's "Word" as the law of the land!

Let the fossil-record of an evolving humanity bear witness to man's need early-on for stone tools, stone weapons, and stone-cold religions---let it bear witness to their use and to their passing. Let such a record bear witness, too, that, at the present time, we no longer kill and roast animals in order to titillate a man-made God's senses, or annihilate, in His name, those who are considered to be standing in the way of His preferred people. Let it show that we, a more enlightened people, no longer indulge in or otherwise condone slavery or the murder of homosexuals, unruly children, witches, and infidels, etc., etc., in order to please a vengeful and sadistic, Semitic deity. Let it show that we no longer have need to create an angry God to explain the phenomena of lightning and thunder or have need to use His scripted, threatening words to manipulate the masses into submission for the enrichment of a few---surely, religion made its debut in the Stone Age when some proto-Levite, power-tripping caveman figured out how to manipulate others to do his bidding through the use of man's natural fear of the unknown! As the Universe and our knowledge of it expands, we have learned to utilize better, more useful tools and ideas—there is no further need or purpose for our paleo-reckonings and primitive practices to accompany us as we now begin our attempts to head off-planet to experience a future of cosmic exploration! There is no cogent need in the Space Age to bring Moses to the Moon, Jesus to Jupiter, or Muhammad to Mars unless their Semitic fables and fomenting legacies are deemed useful and necessary to our extraterrestrial endeavors to gain understanding of the Cosmos where, on touching down on distant, planetary shores—"We Come In Peace"!

Shame on us all—Jehovah-worshiping Jews, Jesus-worshiping Christians, and Allah-worshiping Muslims—we are all guilty of imperiling the world with our ignorant devotion to bogus, ungodly Deities and their cruel and unusual dogmas! Those who do not wish to know the *"Causation, Reality, Truth"* regarding their personal, Semitic religion are sustained, unfortunately, by those who, through ignorance, are unwilling and/or unable to divulge them. I am sustained, however, by the hope that I have made my case and convinced you, the reader, about the dire need for Reason's Tribunal, the dire need to institute your own personal investigation into your own personal religious beliefs. I am sustained by the hope that such an enlightening investigation, as proposed by Thomas Jefferson and undertaken by Thomas Paine, will result in a public one that will ***"Question with boldness even the existence of a god"*** for the entire world to behold and benefit from. In Reason's Tribunal, we will determine the root cause of the past and present mindset of terror that constantly emanates from Semitic religions—we will mitigate their virulent outbreaks by exposing their fraudulent authority and end, at last, the pathological effects of their pandemic disease upon civilization and the ***"Blessings of Liberty."*** The following is not an example of the decency and the justice inherent in practicing the "Golden Rule" of heathens—it is an example of the "Iron Rule" of God-favored folks. Their practice of the "Iron Rule" I express as—"Do unto others ruthlessly until you get what the hell it is that you want":

A typical example of how religion causes bloodshed, war, hatred and unhappiness is the Bible-inspired invasion of Palestine by the Jews. As a result of having been taught from earliest childhood that the Jews are God's chosen people, and with the example of God having ordered the Jews to exterminate the Canaanites, the original inhabitants of Palestine, modern Jews have propagandized their racial and religious adherents so that many actually believe they have the right to take Palestine away from the Arabs who have lived there for many centuries. They have driven the Arabs out, killed those who have resisted and taken their lands, goods and lives—all as a result of the teaching by their fanatical rabbis. It means nothing to the Jews that for generations they have lived in Europe, Asia or America, that they do not speak Hebrew, and that the Arabs have lived in their land for more than a thousand years. Cruelly, with great cunning and finally as they grew stronger, by force of arms they are taking the homes away from the weaker Arabs. By using political manipulation in Britain, the United States and the United Nations, and with the great financial support from the United States Jews they are able to obtain the support of the great powers in thus invading the land of the Arabs and setting up their own country. The foolish Christians in America think that this is foreordained by the Bible and few think it wrong. Apparently in order to obtain the votes of the American Jews, the politicians gave support to the Palestine invaders. A great hatred is being engendered among the Arabs, apparently helpless to protect themselves from the might of the great powers who are backing the Jews. The Arabs not only hate the Jews but Americans, British and other foreigners who support the Jews in their invasion. The hatreds, injustices and wrongs, thus engendered will probably last for several generations and thus another center of bloodshed, trouble, possible future war and world distress can the traced directly to religion.

---James Hervey Johnson

(this "prophetic" piece was written in 1949 well before the age of political correctness! ---kvk)

Open the newspaper or turn on the television and see what the parties of god are doing in Iraq, in their attempt to reduce a once-

*advanced society to the level of Afghanistan or Somalia (the last
two countries where the parties of god had things all their own
way). Observe the menacing developments in the neighboring Iran,
where the believers in the imminent return of a tooth fairy known as
the Twelfth Imam are reinforcing their apocalyptic talk by the
acquisition of doomsday weaponry. Or shift your gaze to the
western bank of the Jordan, where Messianic settlers hope, by
stealing the land of others in accordance with biblical directives, to
bring on Armageddon in their own way. The chief international
backers of these religious colonists, the American evangelical
fundamentalists, are simultaneously trying to teach stultifying
pseudo-science in schools, criminalize homosexuality, forbid stem-
cell research, and display Mosaic law in courtrooms.*

---Christopher Hitchens, in his Introduction to *the Portable Atheist*

*The Jews have no more right to Palestine than any other people;
they never conquered it, they never owned it. ...They* (the Jews) *are
in bondage in Egypt 430 years, in Babylon, 70. These alone make
500 years. Add to this 40 years to the Philistines, to Hazor 20, to
Eglon 18, to the Midians 7, and in Mesopotamia, 8. Add to this
several others scattered throughout the Bible and it makes nearly
700 years, practically their entire authentic B.C. history. If this is
racial history, the Jews should be ashamed of it instead of proud.
And again, if it is racial history what becomes of their B.C. claim to
Palestine? They never owned it, save mythologically.*

---Lloyd M. Graham

*Actually, there is no historical proof that the present state of Israel
ever was the ancestral homeland of the Jews.*

---Rabbi Elmer Berger

Returning back to the subject of America being labeled a "Christian
nation,":

America's founding fathers: Jefferson, Paine, John Adams,
Washington, Franklin, and Madison were not Christians, I repeat,
"were not Christians"—they were Unitarians and Deists—they

were Semitic theism-rejecting Infidels and Secularists! ---kvk

Strip the theists of their mythological authority and you see the atheists have been right, not in denying a Creator, which they do not, but in denying the God of religion, which they do and rightly so. It is from these that all enlightened government comes, including that of our founding fathers, most of them atheists and we could fill pages with their atheism.

---Lloyd M. Graham

Yes, Virginia, the author of the Declaration of Independence along with the above-named Founders were atheists because they did not believe in the existence of the God of Semitic religion! ---kvk

Out of England Deism was borne to France by Voltaire, where it became the creed of nearly all the skeptics who labored at the Encyclopedia and at the new philosophy of naturalism and humanity. From various directions the doctrine came into America, spreading widely among the intellectual leaders of the American Revolution and making them doubly dangerous characters in the eyes of Anglican Tories. When the crisis came, Jefferson, Paine, John Adams, Washington, Franklin, Madison, and many lesser lights were to be reckoned among either the Unitarians or the Deists. It was not Cotton Mather's God to whom the authors of the Declaration of Independence appealed; It was to "Nature's God." From whatever source derived, the effect of both Unitarianism and Deism was to hasten the retirement of historic theology from its empire over the intellect of American leaders and to clear the atmosphere for secular interests.

---Charles and Mary Beard, *The Rise of American Civilization*

God has infinite wisdom, goodness and power; he created the universe. . . . He created this speck of dirt and the human species for his glory; and with deliberate design of making nine-tenths of our species miserable for ever for his glory. This is the doctrine of Christian theologians, in general, ten to one. . . . Wretch! What is his glory? Is he ambitious? Does he want promotion? Is he vain, tickled with adulation, exulting and triumphing in his power and

the sweetness of his vengeance? Pardon me, my Maker, for these awful questions.

---John Adams

The Christian god is a three headed monster; cruel, vengeful and capricious. . . . One only needs to look at the caliber of people who say they serve him. They are always of two classes: fools and hypocrites. . . . Christianity is the most perverted system that ever shown on man. . . . perverted into an engine for enslaving mankind . . . a mere contrivance (for the clergy) to filch wealth and power to themselves.

---Thomas Jefferson

The way to see by faith is to shut the eye of reason.

---Benjamin Franklin

Religious bondage shackles and debilitates the mind and unfits it for every noble enterprise.

---James Madison

The Bible is a book that has been read more and examined less than any book that ever existed.

---Thomas Paine

The United States of America should have a foundation free from the influence of clergy.

---George Washington

While we are led to believe that our nation was founded upon "uplifting" Judeo-Christian traditions and principles—it was not—because there were none! Our nation was founded upon religion-suppressed, secular traditions and principles and we have the above words of Americas founders to prove it.

300

Theologians of every sect, school, and persuasion, in struggling to maintain their empire over the intellect of the modern world, were fighting a losing battle against fate. In the colonial age, between the founding of Jamestown and the Declaration of Independence, that is, between 1607 and 1776, there was taking place throughout western civilization a radical upheaval in the affairs and thought of mankind. The discovery and exploitation of the New World, with its luxuriant natural resources, multiplied the number and piled higher the riches of the bourgeoisie, a class which was in conduct and interest, whatever its professions of faith, primarily secular.

---Charles and Mary Beard

Our secular-minded founding fathers bestowed the credit for America's origin on this ***"radical upheaval in the affairs and thought of mankind"*** believing, in opposition to Judeo-Christian beliefs, ***"that all men are created equal"*** with ***"unalienable rights"*** to ***"Life, Liberty and the pursuit of Happiness."*** These ***"self-evident"*** truths and ***"unalienable rights"*** much to the disgrace of so-called "civilizing" religion, were never granted or even expressed in any Judeo-Christian traditions, principles, or scriptures—never! —just ask the Canaanites! Sorry, folks, that would be impossible to do—the Canaanites were exterminated and their lands stolen by a "superior" race of people who were not created equal to everyone else on the planet—people who were "chosen" by God to have superior rights to take what they wanted from others, to kill anyone who got in their way just as long as it was done in God's holy name!

Thank heavens it was not Jehovah/Jesus to whom the authors of the Declaration of Independence appealed; it was to ***"Nature's God"***! Americans should never forget that it was the *"highly esteemed"* Judeo-Christian tradition of slavery---*Lev.* 25:44-46 that almost destroyed our nation! The following quotations denouncing the cruelty and wickedness of Judeo-Christianity are from four of our founding Infidels:

> ***As I understand the Christian religion, it was, and is, a revelation. But how has it happened that millions of fables, tales, legends, have been blended with both Jewish and Christian revelation that have made them the most bloody religion that ever existed?***

---John Adams

Millions of innocent men, women and children, since the introduction of Christianity, have been burnt, tortured, fined, imprisoned; yet we have not advanced an inch towards uniformity. What has been the effect of coercion? To make one half the world fools, and the other half hypocrites; to support roguery and error all over the earth.

---Thomas Jefferson

If we look back into history for the character of the present sects in Christianity, we shall find few that have not in their turns been persecutors, and complainers of persecution.

---Benjamin Franklin

What influence, in fact, have ecclesiastical establishments had on society? In some instances they have been seen to erect a spiritual tyranny on the ruins of the civil authority; on many instances they have been seen upholding the thrones of political tyranny; in no instance have they been the guardians of the liberties of the people.

---James Madison

The above words that the above fathers of America spoke against the outrages of Judeo-Christian traditions and principles would be just as relevant today in denouncing the outrages of Islam's traditions and principles. We should honor, therefore, the true ***"guardians of the liberties of the people,"*** —our nation's secular-minded founders for their courage to speak and act against the ravages and realities of Judeo-Christianity, especially for their efforts to keep Church and State separated. Think about it folks, if having religion was ever a good thing why did our founding fathers' want to remove it from the affairs of State? ---if religion is not good for politics, why is it seen as good for every other purpose? The separating of religion from our affairs must continue until it is removed not only from government, but from our thinking and from our conduct as freedom-loving Americans! It is my opinion, that if the secular-minded Framers of the Constitution could have anticipated the horror and terror that Islamic ***"fools and hypocrites,"*** and their religious ***"roguery"*** would visit upon America, I believe they would have written the First Amendment so that it contained caveats and constraints against certain religious activities rather than unconditionally allowing for *"the free exercise thereof"*!

The framers, who could not have anticipated the nightmare of 9/11, wanted no "infringement" on religious practices just as they wanted no infringement on the right to bear arms yet every State in the Union violates (regulates) the Second Amendment as each sees fit to do! Is it not an "infringement" on one's Second Amendment rights to prohibit any American from bearing (possessing) surface-to-air missiles or other advanced "arms"? Of course it is! As an example of one founder's mindset at the time, it made no difference to Thomas Jefferson whether his neighbor believed in one God or twenty, since *"it neither picks my pocket nor breaks my leg."* In hindsight, however, It should have made a difference to an infidel like Mr. Jefferson knowing that his neighbor might have believed in just one God whose "Word" in the *Koran* demanded his death and the deaths of other freedom-loving Americans! Such complacent thinking— that the government should neither enforce, encourage, nor otherwise intrude on religion—found its way into the Constitution in the form of the First Amendment. Sadly, today, because of belief in just "one god": Allah, —American pockets are being picked to finance the War on Terror and to keep our homeland secure from His intruding, fanatical followers who prefer to slit our throats rather than break our legs!

If our founding fathers had the ability to foresee the horrific, tragic events and the freedom-destroying effects that Islamic religious beliefs would impose upon the *"unalienable rights"* of today's Americans, Thomas Jefferson, most likely, would have penned another Declaration of Independence to address the grievances of a free people against the tyranny and oppression carried out in the name of God. Because our nation's founding fathers could not foresee the shocking, *Koran*-generated atrocities and impositions that are taking place in the world today, it is necessary, in order to secure the *"Blessings of Liberty to ourselves and our Posterity"* and *"insure domestic Tranquility,"* that *"We the People,"* use the remainder of our **"unalienable"** Constitutional rights—freedom of conscience, free speech, and a free press to address the unanticipated blight of Islam upon not only our nation and her founding ideals, but upon the entire world.

"We the People," the beginning words of our Constitution's Preamble, is a concept that originated in the enlightened minds of secularists, a concept that is repugnant to religious minds which prefer to discriminate and divide people into "us" and "them." *"We the People"* proclaims the secularist effort to unite Americans over and above the exclusionary, selfish interests

of Judaism, Christianity, and Islam, an effort to advance human progress rather than allow the divisive, intolerant, and narrow-minded pursuits of Semitic theologies to continually impose upon and hamper it. It is an obvious certainty that the Preamble to the Constitution and the Bill of Rights which follows it were not composed in any temple, church, or mosque—they were composed in the sacred, secular sanctuary known as Independence Hall!

If I could conceive that the general government might ever be so administered as to render the liberty of conscience insecure, I beg you will be persuaded, that no one would be more zealous than myself to establish effectual barriers against the horrors of spiritual tyranny, and every species of religious persecution.

---George Washington

Inexorably, therefore, the national government was secular from top to bottom. Religious qualifications for voting and office-holding, which appeared in the contemporary state constitutions with such profusion, found no place whatever in the federal Constitution. Its preamble did not invoke the blessings of Almighty God or announce any interest in promoting the propaganda of religion.

---Charles and Mary Beard

Since it is the business of Semitic theists to please their God even if it involves imposing upon everyone's basic rights to ***"Life, Liberty and the pursuit of Happiness"*** it is, of necessity, the business of secularists to secure and defend our ***"unalienable"*** freedoms, hence the secular scriptures: the Declaration of Independence and the Constitution of the United States of America! Because the God-pleasing aspirations of Judaism annihilated, not tolerated, all who were perceived to be standing in its way: Canaanites, Hittites, Girgashites, Amorites, Perizzites, Hivites, Jebusites, Midianites, et al., so too, the God-pleasing aspirations of Islam are to annihilate, not to tolerate, all Infidelites who are perceived as standing in its way, and to establish a global Islamic State conducted under Sharia law by "any" means necessary. The naïveté of our assumptions about Islam being a peaceful, loving, and tolerant religion must be abandoned, especially our attempts at Islamic appeasement—we cannot appease the unappeasable— for how would it be possible for any Muslim to *"slay the idolaters* (infidels)" in a peaceful, loving, and tolerant way?

We should never seek to minimize or excuse the inexcusable behavior of Muslim terrorists, as it is sometimes politically correct to do nowadays, by believing the reasons behind the animosities they wage against us results from something America has done. We must never forget that the Muslim mindset of terror that was unleashed on 9/11 and continues in operation around the world is the exclusive result of religious indoctrination. It originates in the radical scripture of Islam that assures its believers they alone please God, and that all *"idolaters,"* non-believers in the *Koran* and freedom-loving people who, by their very existence, are a blasphemous offense to Allah---an offense that America, the "Great Satan" of the world---teeming with freedom-lovers---must summarily be lethally punished---in the name of God, of course! The terror and atrocities directed against us by the scripture-inspired madness of Muslims is but a form of Islamic worship: a sacred, *Koran*-justified, Allah-honoring affair for which ***"We the People"*** of America, should never offer apology or our naive assistance to those who would destroy us and our way of life. We, the Caretakers of Liberty, owe a tremendous debt of gratitude to those responsible for acquiring and safeguarding our freedoms and for bestowing upon us the fruits of a liberty-loving nation worth defending:

A new nation conceived in Liberty, and dedicated to the proposition that all men are created equal.

Abraham Lincoln, *Gettysburg Address*

We should have a higher regard and respect for the humanity-honoring, progressive nature of the freedoms we enjoy as Americans, a nature that the religious indoctrination of Muslims perceives as an abomination to Allah and, therefore, deserving of His followers' wrath.

To them, America, as stated above, is seen as the "Great Satan" of the world simply because we are a nation that endeavors to "honor" the sanctity of mankind's ***"unalienable rights,"*** not to "destroy" them. We should never be ashamed of our noble efforts in this regard—we should never be ashamed of efforts that offend a God who sanctions wife-beating, child-rape, Sharia law brutalities which include stonings, floggings, and forced amputations, the atrocities of Islamic terrorism, and the annihilation of the free world—such a God deserves to be offended! We should have a higher regard and respect for those who have struggled, suffered, and sacrificed so much throughout the ages to allow for our nation's sacred ideals to finally gain a foothold in the stifling, oppressive world that existed under the rule or influence of Semitic theologies and their liberty-rejecting, freedom-destroying dogmas.

We should honor and reflect often on the noble sacrifices, the abject miseries, and the insufferable deprivations experienced by the Patriots, the Caretakers of Liberty, who wintered with General Washington at Valley Forge, Pennsylvania (1777-1778) without having adequate shelter, food, or clothing---many going without socks and gloves, and even hay or straw on which to sleep---the bodies of some men, as a result, actually freezing to the raw, frozen ground they attempted to sleep on. Imagine the strength of will it took for twelve thousand starving and freezing men to endure the hardships of their ordeal knowing that some of their neighboring countrymen-farmers were taking wagonloads of farm produce to Philadelphia to sell to their well-fed enemies because they paid in sterling rather than their having to accept the questionable value of Continental script offered by the America's "rabble in arms"! The personal tribulations these men were willing to endure under such extreme and deplorable conditions should instill in us a higher regard and respect for our nation, its ideals, and its Patriot defenders whose noble sufferings, sacrifices, and sorrows should instill in us a new appreciation for the Legacy of Liberty that has been acquired and bestowed upon us by the tremendous, inspirational efforts and indomitable spirit of others!

Can you imagine how long the cowardly-minded, self-serving, ass-saving disciples of Jesus would have lasted living under similar conditions in order to defend and fight for the glorious cause of their Almighty God? *"Yes, Virginia, these valiant men of Valley Forge fame were truly the saviors of 'all' of mankind---it certainly wasn't Jesus Christ whose life's aim, 'according to' His NT script-writers, was to be a Savior only to the Jews and to spread a slightly revised edition of the OT's doom and gloom, paleo-minded, dogmatic endeavors of His tribe's religion. Surely, the very lives of these men who wintered at Valley Forge were as precious to themselves as Jesus' life was precious to Himself. To a man, they were willing to lose the only life they had (unlike Jesus!) for the cause of Liberty. To a man, these thousands of men willingly offered-up every comforting aspect of their lives, risking injury and death in doing so, for the betterment of "all," not the "few," as in the case of Jesus and His despicable disciples. In the entire world, there doesn't exist a greater 'Holy Land' than Valley Forge, Pennsylvania where these lovers of Liberty (many dying of starvation and exposure, and more than half of them being unfit for active service because of such dire conditions) lay in bodily need and poorly clad on frozen ground for an entire winter so that 'We the People' could finally experience something that never before existed, I repeat, 'never before existed' in a religion-dominated world: 'Life, Liberty and the pursuit of Happiness.' Is there a more sacred, hallowed place on earth than here where so many sacrificed so much and struggled so hard to acquire our nation's greatest treasure: Liberty?*

Tyranny, like hell, is not easily conquered, yet we have this consolation with us, that the harder the conflict, the more glorious the triumph. What we obtain too cheap, we esteem too lightly---'Tis dearness only that gives everything its value.

---Thomas Paine

"Fortunately, Virginia, thanks to the noble efforts of these noble men to secure such hard-won freedoms---America is now home to these cherished ideals. Thankfully, these hard-won, secular ideals still maintain their 'dearness' and are still being honored, protected, and defended today by our nation's Caretakers of Liberty and, in part, by our secular-minded Constitution which has provided us with a peaceful means to deal with America's enemies---to deal somewhat with the religious hate speech contained in the Koran with its incitements to violence, warfare, annihilation, and Islamic supremacism---to deal with the destroyers of civilization. One of those non-violent means, which does not involve picking our pockets to fund the costly and ever-expanding use of arms abroad and the ever-tightening security measures at home, is Reason's Tribunal, our greatest ally in the War on Terror."

We must use every reasonable means at our disposal to "disarm" those who, because of religious indoctrination, despise our way of life and seek our total demise before resorting to a shocking "final solution." ***We the People,*** as a matter of self-preservation, need to fear a religion that seeks to utterly destroy us. We need to acquire an educated Islamophobia that results from knowing what is written in the *Koran* and what it holds in store for unbelievers. We need to begin to use the gifts of America's freedoms to great advantage in order to undo Semitic Theisms' constant potential for malevolence and terrorism and their constant stranglehold on the advance of freedom around the world. We need to challenge and disable the arrogant claims of Semitic religions that credit their dogmas for instituting all that is good, decent, and sacred in the world. We need to finish the anti-tyranny work begun in 1776 by a freedom-loving people and, once again, ***begin*** *the world over"* with ***"a revolution in the system of religion"*** to create, at long last, a sane and safe future for "all" of mankind. We need to rekindle our inherent, rebellious spirit and make a stand against the tyranny we face today from undoubted belief in the sacred scripture of Islam—another imposing Semitic religion rooted in abomination and atrocity.

Are intolerant, Judeo-Christian dogmas, doctrines, principles, and traditions that burned scholars at the stake, instituted slavery, denounced the Magna Carta's challenge to divine rights as "Devil-inspired," opposed science, medicine, enlightenment, human-equality, equal justice for all, and virtually any advancement or improvement in the human-condition, century after misery-filled century, to be credited with laying the foundation of a freedom-loving Republic in order to bestow its deity-detested abominations of ***"Life, Liberty and the pursuit of Happiness"*** upon all of its inhabitants---really? ---did I mention that I have a lovely bridge for sale in NYC?

What had Jesus' disciples to fear if not the Judeo-traditions and religious authorities of their time? What had the Pilgrims of Plymouth escaped from in the Old World if not the Judeo-Christian traditions of persecution in their homeland? What had they established in the New World if not their own Christian tyrannies?

We know the clerical party; it is an old party. This it is which has found for the truth those two marvelous supporters, ignorance and error. This it is which forbids to science and genius the going beyond the Missal and which wishes to cloister thought in dogmas. Every step which the intelligence of Europe has taken has been in spite of it. Its history is written in the history of human progress, but it is written on the back of the leaf. It is opposed to it all. This it is which caused Prinelli to be scourged for having said that the stars would not fall. This it is which put Campanella seven times to torture for saying that the number of worlds was infinite and for having caught a glimpse of the secret of creation. This it is which persecuted Harvey for having proved the circulation of the blood. In the name of Jesus it shut up Galileo. In the name of St. Paul it imprisoned Christopher Columbus. To discover a law of the heavens was an impiety, to find a world was a heresy. This it is which anathematized Pascal in the name of religion, Montaigne in the name of morality, Moliere in the name of both morality and religion. There is not a poet, not an author, not a thinker, not a philosopher, that you accept. All that has been written, found, dreamed, deduced, inspired, imagined, invented by genius, the

*treasures of civilization, the venerable inheritance of generations,
you reject.*

---Victor Hugo

*Progress depends on a continuous readjustment of opinion to new
ideas and a widening circle of information. No man and no society
is truly progressive unless beliefs are held as subject to whatever
modifications increased knowledge may demand.*

---James Hervey Johnson

Judeo-Christianity, in essence, had turned off the lights to a European world
full of promise and potential thus ushering in the Dark and Middle Ages of
its imposed ignorance.

*There once was a time when all people believed in God and the
church ruled. This time was called the Dark Ages.*

---Richard Lederer

As century after religion-dominated century passed, the stifling darkness
imposed by Semitic Theism finally began to diminish as the light of Liberty
was, at last, being lit causing a new brightness to appear across the wide
Atlantic.

America, a New World full of promise, was beginning to shine with
freedom's sacred light, a beacon bright with hope for the religion-oppressed,
"huddled masses" of the Old World. Thankfully, her foundation, as noted
above, was not rooted in Judeo-Christianity and its traditions, as is so often
proclaimed---it was rooted in struggles against their embedded, embraced,
and employed malevolence, and its freedom-destroying pursuits:

*God had put kings and superior persons in the world to govern it.
In short, the Revolution, as the Tories saw it, flew in the face of
experience, history, and divine sanction....*

---Charles and Mary Beard, *The Rise of American Civilization*

Unfortunately, a couple of notable Judeo-Christian traditions did manage to
cross the ocean and wash ashore at Massachusetts and Maryland. The

cherished sacraments of Semitic religion: intolerance and corporal punishment were dispensed by the Pilgrims of Plymouth where. . .

...swift and stern punishment was visited upon all who were guilty of blasphemy.... It is exercising restraint to say that a general freedom of conscience had not been up to that time [1649] a cardinal principle proclaimed by Catholics, Anglicans, or Puritans wherever they were in a position to coerce.

---ibid.

The Puritans executed Mary Dyer, William Robinson, Marmaduke Stephenson, and William Leddra on Boston Common for the terrible crime of being Quakers. The Puritans also waged a holy war on the Pequots, setting fire to a village on the Mystic River, killing 700 Native men, women, and children. The survivors were sold into slavery. The genocide was like something out of the Book of Joshua. And indeed, the Puritans saw it that way. They saw themselves as instruments of their god's holy will: 'Such a dreadful Terror did the ALMIGHTY let fall upon (the Natives') Spirits, that they would fly from us and run into the very Flames, where many of them perished.' According to John Mason, the Puritan militia commander, his god laughed while he murdered: 'But GOD was above them, who laughed his Enemies and the Enemies of his People to Scorn, making them as a fiery Oven. . . . Thus did the Lord judge among the Heathen, filling the Place with dead Bodies!'

---Andrew Seidel, *The Founding Myth*

Maryland's Toleration Act of 1649 offers a clear example of these treasured "Semitic traditions" that were transmitted from the Old World via the Judeo-Christian mindset—a mindset of Holy Terror that, ironically, sailed away from the religious repressions of Europe with the hope of imposing its own intolerant version of them here in America—fines, confiscation of goods, public whippings for infidels, and the sentence of death, I repeat, "the sentence of death" to all non-believers of Christ's *"Akbar"* divinity. Certainly, any Old-World mindset that justified and sought to establish these "Jihad" traditions in the New-World was certainly not capable of composing the words telling us ***that all men are created equal, that they are endowed by their Creator with certain unalienable Rights, that*** *among these are "Life, Liberty and the pursuit of Happiness."* By anticipation, it was a mindset that would have sought to destroy, in the name of Jehovah/Jesus, the very lives of America's heretical, founding fathers and America's, infidel Sons of Liberty!

The principles and traditions of Judeo-Christianity and its offspring, Islam, have a long history of opposing human equality, human welfare, and human progress wherever and whenever they have become entrenched—the narrowness of such a mindset allows only for one to be considered a like-minded member (us) or only as one who is to be considered an outsider or infidel (them) and, therefore, subject to much less than equal and civil treatment. Thankfully, America was able to overcome many of the Semitic religious endeavors of her early settlers and avoid the carnage, calamities, and cultural stagnation that had laid waste to so much of Europe during the Dark and Middle Ages.

Whence arose all the horrid assassinations of whole nations of men, women and infants, with which the Bible is filled, and the bloody persecutions and tortures unto death, and religious wars, that since that time have laid Europe in blood and ashes— whence rose they but from this impious thing called revealed religion, and this monstrous belief that God has spoken to man? The lies of the Bible (Old Testament) *have been the cause of the one, and the lies of the* (New) *Testament of the other.*

---Thomas Paine

If ever a "Holy Land" exists, it is Valley Forge, Pennsylvania and America, the *"Land of the Free,"* ---a place where the secular interests of *"Life, Liberty and the pursuit of Happiness"* are promised to be granted equally to all—a place where each and every day is made sacred by the struggles and sacrifices of freedom-loving people throughout the ages. It is the place where the Sons and Daughters of Liberty refused to submit to the impositions of governmental tyranny—it is the place where their heirs are refusing to submit to the impositions of the religious tyranny of Islam. Unfortunately, today, America has yet to fulfill her promise of "equal justice for all" under the law—has yet to overcome the vileness caused by the racist, sexist, and supremacist thoughts of the religion-dominated mindset of vast numbers of her Christianized citizens. The remnants of mankind's religious, Judeo-Christian, paleo-barbarisms are still affecting our lives— still being imposed upon people because of their ethnicity, the color of their skin, their gender, and their sexual preference, but the years of their continuance are surely numbered. Reason's Tribunal will hasten that long-awaited day when the embedded malevolence of all Semitic Word of God scriptures will no longer be accepted and revered—will no longer threaten anyone's life—will no longer be tolerated or indulged in by an enlightened, civilized, and progressive people who will no longer be inspired to slit throats in the name of God or to kneel on them in the name of civic duty. The separation of Church and State was a blessing---the separation of Church from our state of mind---ever more so!

Today, the countries in the Middle East under Islamic rule present to us examples of a people who have further succumbed to religion and its oppressions which is quite apparent in their treatment of women, children, homosexuals, and their disdain for non-Muslims. Without secular influence along with the advance of freedom and human-rights in their cultures, there is little hope for their future and, consequently, for ours. The totalitarian Islamic religion and its rabid rulers have denied the Muslim world its own version of the Magna Carta, the Bill of Rights, and *The Age of Reason* just as Judeo-Christianity attempted here, in Western civilization, to deny us our own attempts at human-progress and free-expression. Americans, therefore, should give thanks and credit where thanks and credit are due for our "Land of the Free" by acknowledging, honoring, and cherishing the noble, secular-minded deeds and the noble, secular-minded doers, the Caretakers of Liberty, whose valiant struggles and sacrifices have surely given us this day to enjoy our daily bread!

The past and present worlds bear stark witness to the bloodshed and barbarisms carried out in the beloved names of Jehovah, Jesus, and Allah. Until we recognize the very source of these religious threats and direct our earnest energies against the chinks in the scriptural armor that protects mankind's ever devout adversaries and determined terrorists, we fight a losing battle in the Middle East and beyond. In our efforts to civilize the world with bomb and bullet, we have neglected to enlist the aid of our greatest ally in the War on Terror: Reason's Tribunal.

> *The most formidable weapon against errors of every kind is reason.*
>
> ---Thomas Paine

With the use of this *"formidable weapon,"* we can correct the *"errors"* of fraudulent and deceptive religions, we can begin to confront and vanquish

America's Judeo-Christian indoctrination which will enable us to begin confronting and vanquishing the kindred Islamic indoctrination of our deluded enemies. Without its use in the War on Terror and the truthful, convincing conclusions that will result from its employment, we will surely continue to suffer the remainder of all our tomorrows fearing Muslims and their undying devotion to Allah and His "Word." Because Muslim supremacy is the fundamental goal of Islam, we must begin to challenge the authority of its persistent instigator—the undoubted words of the *Koran*. We must begin to challenge the orthodoxy of Islam in order to find a way to bestow the blessings of D-O-U-B-T upon the entrenched religious beliefs of Muslims. Neutralizing a formidable enemy's mindset that believes the *Koran* is immune-from-error requires finding and using a formidable means to neutralize their scripture-inspired madness that is not immune from reason and truth.

The freeing of people from their Islamic oppression is a noble but vain endeavor unless and until we attempt to begin the liberation of the Islamic mindset that has been conditioned for centuries to accept and defend the monstrous religious impositions and imperatives inherent in their Muslim faith, e.g., divinely sanctioned death imposed upon homosexuals and infidels, forced mutilations and amputations, wife-beating, abuse of children, etc. Is there any Muslim to be found who is outraged enough to speak out against the *Koran*-authorized, abusive behavior directed against women and children when their beloved, child-molesting Paragon of Muslim manhood, Muhammad, acting under the divine counsel of an angel of God, engaged in and condoned spousal abuse---*Koran* 4:34, a man who, acting under the divine counsel of Allah, married, I repeat, "married" a 6 year old child and consummated, I repeat, "consummated" the marriage 3 years later when he was in his mid-50s and his blushing, baby bride was only 9 years old! ---Allah, the sleazeball-enabler, really knows how to pick 'em!

Procreation was certainly not on the Holy Pedophile's mind when he was attempting to have sexual relations with a pre-pubescent, 9-year-old innocent—such is the reprehensible, lecherous behavior of a cave-dwelling child-rapist whose "heart," his early followers asserted, was cleansed of all "unworthy" thoughts when he was a boy of 12—all but one obviously! From such a bold assertion by his early thought-police followers, it is obvious too, that Muslims (Muhammad's followers), or at least some of them, possess the astounding ability and chutzpah to claim that they "knew" then and continue to "know" now, with certainty, what was in Muhammad's heart---really? Hmm! To the amazing mind-reading, heart-reading followers of Muhammad who today claim to know, with certainty, the worthiness and purity of another's thoughts---had I been the father of that innocent, little girl being pursued, pawed, and preyed upon by this prayer-rug-kneeling pervert, it is hoped that you also have the ability to read what is in my heart and in my "worthy" thoughts on the matter!

Out of concern for a child's safety, would you allow a Muhammad-type to be left alone in a room with your young daughter? If not, why would you, or anyone else, consider such a degenerate worthy of being honored as God's personal messenger to spread God's message about spiritual living? It is quite interesting to note here that God, who knew Muhammad to be a sexual deviant, would order an angel to co-mingle with him in, of all places, the close confines of a cave! ---knowing that men, according to God's Word, are sexually attracted to angels and are not above raping them---*Gen.* 19:1-5. One can only wonder what really happened to Gabriel at the hands of a sexual predator and Most Holy Prophet after decades of up-close and personal, unwitnessed contact? One can only \wonder, too, about the result of the lasting effects of the abuses imposed upon innocent human angels who are obliged to attend Sunday schools and madrasas' where they are ordered to believe everything contained in the Most Holy *Bible* and the Most Holy *Koran*?

It should come as no surprise to learn, and the evidence too well established to deny, that the religion-obsessed and religion-oppressed mentalities of Muslim men (and Catholic priests) and their sexually-repressed lives oftentimes result in extreme and/or brutal, stress-relieving behaviors. Jihad, in this regard, takes on a whole new meaning for hardened, Islamic warriors. If Muslim men can be made to believe that donning and detonating a suicide-vest guarantees sexual relations with 72 virgins (little girls, no doubt!) what Islamite, wanting to please himself and Allah at the same time, could resist the temptation? What Muslim man could resist becoming a sacred Islamic warrior in order to indulge his stifled carnal pleasures---the so-called sins of the flesh---while ravaging and ruining the lives of 72 de-flowered, virgin females who have been purposely created by Allah only to serve and to satisfy the physical desires of His male martyrs? *"Yes, Virginia, "Allahu Akbar!" (God is great!) when meting out injustice to the innocent---when it comes to rewarding males and imposing upon females whom He has made to serve only one purpose and one purpose only!"*

It is difficult to understand why any female would condone a religion that regards their gender so unfairly—that regards them as sex slaves and as the chattel of men! Since the Mighty Muhammad has set the exemplary standard of conduct for Muslim men to follow—parents of female children—BEWARE!

To me it seems certain that the fatalistic teachings of Muhammad and the utter degradation of women is the outstanding cause for the arrested development of the Arab. He is exactly as he was around the year 700, while we have kept on developing.

---General George Patton

Based on the shameful, child-predatory behavior of Muhammad, it is understandable why Islam requires total, "unquestioned" belief in its Most Holy and Merciful Prophet, and the Holy *Koran*. It is understandable why doubters of any Islam-isms receive special, "divine" dispensations to deal with the "unholiness" of their unbelief, a tradition not unlike Judeo-Christian traditions of the past. Because of such inflicted or threatened dispensations there is, in essence, total, undoubted acceptance of the *Koran's* "perfect" Word of Allah in the Muslim world---again, not unlike the results of Judeo-Christian dispensations of the past. Also, not unlike Judeo-Christian traditions of the past, rejection of Islamic beliefs is not a free-will, penalty-free choice for a Muslim to make unless he or she is prepared to suffer scripture-inspired torture, mutilation, and/or death---believe or die! The word "Islam" literally means "to surrender" —surrender your innate knowledge of good and evil---surrender your innate compassionate and sentient nature to the law and the will of Allah—surrender your every thought to Allah, or else! Muslims, understandably, are compelled to surrender to the imposed oppression of their "undoubted" Islamic beliefs—they, seemingly, have no other choice but to comply—while the Sons and Daughters of Liberty, understandably, will always be compelled to defy their imposing oppressors. Rather than submit to the tyranny of his time, another Infidel and Son of Liberty, Patrick Henry, said it best: ***"give me liberty or give me death!"*** Liberty, after all, is the cherished ideal we live and die for as freedom-loving Americans.

The *Koran* "forbids" free-thought and religious doubt by its mind-controlled devotees who demonize secular societies for allowing their use. Atheism is not allowed to exist in Islamic controlled countries—countries where everyone must comply with established religious beliefs or suffer very dire consequences. It is time, therefore, for a freedom-loving people to squarely face that reality and begin to shine the light of truth from Reason's Tribunal into the religion-darkened recesses of our planet. It is time to begin spreading America's very own form of secular "extremism" that will strike fear and loathing into the hearts of Islamic fundamentalists and terrorists everywhere throughout the world. It is time to unleash civilization's unique form of intimidation against the radical ideology of Islam: the dreaded deception-detecting, deception-destroying device known as Reason's Tribunal. When the words of all scripture-based, malevolent dogmas and fanaticisms are exposed via critical scrutiny to the light of reason and truth, the fetters of religion will finally, I repeat, "finally" begin to loosen. Suicide-minded terrorists who now twitch and tremble at the mere mention of free thought, free expression, a free press, and the freedom to entertain religious doubts will be shaken to their core when faced with undeniable evidence that nullifies their religious indoctrination. Thankfully, because of these, the above hard-won, American freedoms, I am able to express my free-thoughts and my free-opinions on the lack of authority, the lack of decency, and the lack of common sense in the revelations upon which all Semitic religions are fabricated. We need to share these secular gifts of our Legacy of Liberty with the religious fanatics who would destroy us because they have never been exposed to the blessings of freedom and the enlightenment that accompanies it!

It is only because of these secular gifts that I am able to express my curiosity about a God who did not care to "spake" directly to His Prophet Muhammad in order to relay the *Koran* to him as He did so often "spake" directly to His Prophet Moses whom, we are made to believe, was able to record His every Word in the *Old Testament* because of his close and personal intimacy with God. I suppose it is possible that the *OT Almighty* may have strained His vocal cords or have been plagued with a hellish case of laryngitis after repeatedly having to bellow His lengthy commands for the commission of battlefield atrocities and exterminations to Moses and Joshua for their murderous tribes to carry out. What else could possibly account for God having "need" to enlist the services of His go-to guy, His able communicant, Gabriel, to relay every word of the *Koran* to Muhammad for more than two decades? Is it possible that God would ever be in need of someone else's assistance? Really? What chutzpah it takes for any man to surmise that "God needs my help"! I suppose it is possible, after all, that God didn't communicate directly with Muhammad because He may have feared saying the wrong thing to an Islamic fundamentalist!

Whatever the cause of His indirectness with His Prophet Muhammad, thankfully, Allah had a heavenly confidant He could faithfully rely on to get His Word out since, apparently, He is seemingly incapable of communicating directly with whom His firsthand message is so vitally important! Where would Muslims be without the assistance of an angel and his secondhand information; where would mankind be without another Semitic scripture that incites violence, vengeance, and terror! Incidentally, when Gabriel initially appeared to Muhammad in a non-verifiable vision and proclaimed him to be a prophet of God, Muhammad, we are told, was greatly perplexed by the experience and had some misgivings about his prophetic mission. Well, guess what? ---so do I! I, too, am greatly perplexed and have a multitude of misgivings about the reality of Muhammad's visions and the certainty of the religious beliefs based upon them.

Why is it that Muslims, today, believe everything they have been told about the "reality" of Muhammad's visions---visions that supposedly took place in the dark confines of a cave---visions that went unwitnessed by others? Yet, today, if any Muslim man were to say, and even swear to it, that he was told by an angel in a vision that he, too, is a prophet of God, would any Muslim believe it to be so based on this man's word alone? ---certainly not! Would he be believed if the event had actually happened? ---certainly not! Would any Christian today believe, with certainty, any girl who claimed she was "overshadowed" by a ghost and "became with child" as a result? ---certainly not! ---would they believe any girl who claimed she became pregnant without having sexual intercourse? ---certainly not! —not even the Pope is foolish enough to admit of the possibility of such a thing happening today! He is foolish enough to admit, however, of such a thing having occurred in the long-ago, unverifiable past and that no one should ever have any doubts about it having taken place! Hmm!

Were any girl that is now with child to say, and even to swear it, that she was gotten with child by a ghost, and that an angel told her so, would she be believed? Certainly she would not. Why then, are we to believe the same thing of another girl, whom we never saw, told by nobody knows who, nor when, nor where?

---Thomas Paine

If Muhammad had received his visions in this day and age instead of fourteen centuries ago, would anyone believe his account of things that went unwitnessed by others? Would anyone, today, accept someone's fanciful tales about their having been personally selected by God to receive His "revelations" via covert encounters with an alien as actual physical events or would they be considered the result of delirium, drug use, or megalomania? *"Yes, Virginia, no one today would believe a modern*

Muham-mad type and his fabulous claims, yet, this was the means we are imposed upon to believe the Almighty Allah chose to 'convince' the Arab world that Muham-mad was His Holy Prophet of Islam, ---the very means that Mr. Paine has proven would not serve the purpose for which it was intended even if his supposed encounters with Gabriel had actually occurred."

> ***...is it more probable that nature should go out of her course or that a man should tell a lie? We have never seen, in our time, nature go out of her course; but we have good reason to believe that millions of lies have been told in the same time; it is, therefore, at least millions to one that the reporter of a miracle tells a lie? ...Instead, therefore, of admitting the recitals of miracles as evidence of any system of religion being true, they ought to be considered as symptoms of its being fabulous. It is necessary to the full and upright character of truth that it rejects the crutch, and it is consistent with the character of fable to seek the aid that truth rejects. ...How strange and inconsistent it is, that the same circumstance that would weaken the belief even of a probable story should be given as a motive for believing this one, that has upon the face of it every token of impossibility and imposture.***

---Thomas Paine

How strange and inconsistent it is that Muslims—and I'm certain of this! — would not consider the visionary claims of a modern Muhammad-type and his unwitnessed, audible encounters with an angel to be real events. I believe that Muslims, instead, would consider them to be the result of a vivid imagination, drug use, or a psychological disorder, and not the result of any divine intervention—that is my contention. To test my theory and the usefulness of this kind of rationale and inquiry being used against the mindset of terror, a poll should be taken in Allah-land to verify the existence of this phenomenon in religious thinking regarding an event of similar circumstance—an event that curiously results in "belief" in the one instance and "unbelief" in the other. If my claim proves to be true, that such visions today would be perceived in the Muslim world to be the result of delusion rather than divine intervention, we should capitalize on such a discovery. We should not underestimate the disquieting effect that such a confirming poll would have on the mindset of the immune-from-error crowd regarding Muhammad's angelic revelations. A seed of doubt will ofttimes sprout when it is sown by truth and cultivated by reason—even Mary's inconceivable pregnancy can give birth to an unexpected offspring—skepticism!

How strange and inconsistent it is that in *Luke* 1:35, Gabriel, the immune-from-error angel, tells Mary that she shall bring forth *"the Son of God"* but in the *Koran*, he, Gabriel, reveals, over and over again, that Allah (God) has no son! To believe otherwise is called *"shirk,"* the cardinal sin of Islam, a crime which is considered worse than murder, rape, genocide, and all the rest of infamy's deeds combined. Christians—BEWARE of the wrath you have incurred in Allah-land by your very existence—BEWARE of the penalty you must pay for the blasphemy of having "polytheistic" Christian beliefs—BEWARE of how you are being perceived in the Muslim world!

How strange and inconsistent it is, too, that Muslims only believe the words of Gabriel as given in the *Koran* but not as given in the *Bible*. After much careful and critical consideration of the above differing accounts that reveal Gabriel to be a liar, at least in one of his revealing statements, I am compelled to disbelieve all of his words—I am compelled to disbelieve, too, the infallible and inerrant nature of the books that contain them along with anything that is founded upon someone's "visions." The following factual observations regarding Muhammad and the *Koran's* immune-from-error status have resulted from employing Reason's Tribunal personally for my own edification and enlightenment, keeping in mind that Muslims believe Allah has power over all things, and that nothing happens unless Allah wills it—now we know why "SHIRK HAPPENS"!:

It required 23 years, I repeat, "23 years" of continuous, Allah-willed, angelic visitation via visions to teach Muhammad, the Holy Prophet of Islam, to memorize (when he wasn't off in pursuit of raping a child) the entirety of the forever-existing *Koran*. This was supremely important because the *Koran*, as relayed word for word by His divine, hearsay messenger, Gabriel, contained the entirety of Allah's profound message and mission for the benefit of Muslims and for the detriment of infidels. Despite Allah's best efforts to communicate to His child-predator-Prophet His vital and vengeful life and death plans to His believers and His non-believers via the visionary Gabriel, Muhammad died suddenly (Allah-willed, of course!) without ever completing his singular, sacred task of producing a copy of Allah's Word given painstakingly and exclusively to him. And the reason for his prophetic nonperformance—the reason Muhammad failed to produce a copy of the *Koran* after 23 years of heavenly effort was—because—are you ready? —he was unable to read or write and remained illiterate even after two decades of divine intercession—Allah can really pick 'em! No chuckles please! ---it's just another example of God's "mysterious" workings and His "not-to-be-doubted" doings!

God, who we're told by His confident promoters, can accomplish mighty and impossible works in the blink of an eye, chose (with all of His infallible and inerrant wisdom!) an illiterate caveman (and a pedophile no less!) to get His sacred written word out to the Muslim world employing the powers of heaven for 23 years with no success---surely, God should have known better don't you think? If God had only sought the counsel of a sane person before making this decision, He could have saved Himself a lot of time and effort! Is it any wonder then why God pulled the plug on Muhammad---need I say more? Personally, I would have pulled the plug on this guy after investing 23 minutes (23 seconds!) with him!

As in the case of Muhammad, even the mighty Moses failed to produce a written copy of his incredible accounts of God's momentous message, meant only for the benefit of the Jews and not for the benefit of mankind, that was spoken only to him in an unwitnessed manner, of course. How Moses, or his script writers, could flawlessly record each and every innumerable word that God supposedly spoke to him in the numerous accounts given in *Genesis*, *Exodus*, *Leviticus*, *Numbers*, and *Deuteronomy* remains a profound mystery. How Moses was able to tell us where he was laid to rest remains an even bigger one---*Deut.* 34:5,6! It is the dubious details of dealings such as those given above, that place the Gods of Semitic religions, their script-writers, and their believers on a par with the Keystone Cops and the Three Stooges. If it weren't for the atrocities and wickedness that resulted from their doings, they would be just as laughable!

What became of Gabriel after his incredible, 23 year-long mission ended in complete failure with nothing to show for his intensive, Allah-willed labors? Was he put on administrative leave indefinitely for his incompetence? Does this explain his notable absence for nearly 14 centuries? Why did Allah willfully pull the plug prematurely on His Prophet, Muhammad after such an intense, heavenly effort to communicate the *Koran* to him? Why didn't Allah think to employ, *Bible*-style, another anonymous script-writer, another "according to" impostor, to write down the "revealed" words of the *Koran* that was supposedly stored in its entirety inside Muhammad's noggin before dispatching him as he was the one and only human being with such important knowledge, especially if keeping the *Koran's* every word immune-from-error was a heavenly priority? What an embarrassing, pathetic, and pitiful tale of ineptitude Muslims have pinned their hopes on!

The inability of the combined efforts of Allah, the Creator of the Universe, Gabriel, a high-ranking official in Heaven and personal messenger of God, and Muhammad, the only human being chosen by God for the task at hand, to accomplish the simple secretarial task of transcription is truly beyond belief and should be a grave concern for all who consider the *Koran* to be of divine origin. The mere recording, by a Prophet of God, of the dictated words of a book with a writing instrument is an endeavor that should have taken days or weeks, yet, decades passed without a single page of the *Koran* ever being produced. What was the purpose, after all, for all the powers of Heaven to become involved in producing Muhammad's miraculous visions if not to "publish" Allah's perfect, divine "Word"? Certainly, if Muhammad, whose memory alone contained the entirety of the *Koran*, was purposely struck down by Allah before he could bring its vital message, in book-form, to the attention of the Muslim world, then that stoppage was the result of Allah's willful doings, too! ---incredible!

Evidently, Allah must have become mightily displeased with the "imperfections" of His Prophet, Muhammad, and had begun to have second thoughts about revealing His "Word" (written on a perfect, "imperishable tablet") to the world by way of a dysfunctional pervert and illiterate caveman. Those who say they accept, honor, and obey the will of Allah should, therefore, accept, honor, and obey His "will" that was totally responsible for the untimely demise of their un-prophet-able Prophet, the only person Allah "chose" to bring the perfect *Koran* to the Arab world— "Praise be to Allah" for His long-delayed mercies dispensed in this case! If it be true that Allah wills everything, then it follows that it was Allah, and Allah alone, who killed Muhammad---"Praise be to Allah"! However, as a result of Muhammad's death, a frantic search for any bits and pieces of the "forever existing book" that, supposedly, "existed" only in Muhammad's memory and that he may have uttered, in part, to someone else over the years, was begun in earnest. This was not done under orders from Allah or Gabriel, it was done in order for the error-free crowd of Muhammad-associates to keep their hopes alive for the Muslim world to obtain their own immune-from-error Chutzpah Chronicles. However, by His own example, Allah has shown the Muslim world that His immune-from-error intentions and actions---His unchangeable "will" in which every Muslim should have no doubt---is the perfect mother-of-all-ironies!

It is apparent that the *Koran*, as it exists today, is not the product of divine "will"—it is the audacious product of the desires of ungodly men who chose to impose their will on everyone. If the Holy Trinity of Islam, Allah, Gabriel, and Muhammad, have "revealed" anything to us by their actions, it is that they are perfect examples of incompetence, perfect examples of pious frauds and pitiful bunglers who are seemingly "immune" only from critical scrutiny of their words, their actions, their thoughts, and their intentions—at least until now. The Almighty (always hindered in His noble efforts to get His Word out!) could just as easily, I repeat, "could just as easily" have made Muhammad literate and handed him pen and paper or, even better, an actual copy of the *Koran* if He had so willed—but, lo and behold—after 23 years of fruitless, heavenly effort—I reckon that Allah had had enough of Muhammad and his pedophilia—or, perhaps, some other reason—and decided to "willfully" end his earthly days instead of allow him to finish his long-memorized, prophetic work! As Allah and fate would have it, in order to finally give written expression to His vital concerns for Muslims---Allah, because of His incompetent doings, was now compelled and completely content to rely on the unreliable, imperfect recollections and dubious writings of others: Muhammad's groupies. Hmm!

These "others" we are to believe, were men who supposedly listened to, or supposedly memorized, or supposedly made attempts to pen Muhammad's every word which Gabriel gave to Muhammad alone, even though Muslims admit that some of the Heaven-sent words that Muhammad spoke to "others"---words that were supposedly relayed from Allah to Gabriel to him, were admittedly forgotten, lost, or changed by others over time. It was upon these fragmentary accounts, recalled from the third-hand, hearsay words of others, no doubt, that the entirety of *"the book in which there is no doubt"* was created, a fourth-hand account of a book that Muslims believe is immune-from-error but is nevertheless open to various interpretations because of its lack of indubitable clarity. (A firsthand account would obviously have been from Allah to Gabriel—a secondhand account: from Gabriel to Muhammad—a thirdhand account: from Muhammad to "others"—a fourth-hand account: from some of these various "others" to us via the pages of the perfectly-penned *Koran*—hence the need for an auxiliary work, the Hadith, to help explain the imperfections found within the "perfect" Word of Allah!)

Are we not being further imposed upon to believe that these amazing non-prophet "others" were perfectly able, unlike the incompetent Prophet Muhammad, to compile Allah's perfect Word—were able to recall and record, word for word, the 114 chapters of the "accepted" version of the *Koran*, and do so flawlessly, from the bits and pieces of their "perfect" memories, without having any divine calling to do so, or any angelic visitation or heavenly assistance whatsoever? No doubt, this amounts to another unrecorded miracle akin to Moses' amazing speedwriting and memorization skills! No doubt, if Muhammad was the wrong guy to complete the job Allah had assigned to him (which he was!) guess who should have known about it beforehand?

No doubt, because of God's inherent inability to get the job done, it became necessary, once again, as usual, for sinful-minded humans to come to the aid of a perfect-minded, Semitic deity in order to accomplish what the Almighty and His mighty messenger-angel could not—bring the inerrant and infallible Word of God to the Arab world without generating the slightest bit of suspicion in its flawless and perfect transfer from high above to far below even if it meant eliminating all who may have thought otherwise. As a result of Muhammad's death, it became necessary for Muslims to locate and burn all of the variant, "dubious" versions of Allah's perfect Word that were then in existence in order to keep Allah and His winged messenger from looking like the inept fools the Islamic Chutzpah Chronicles have made them out to be. (I guess there must have been some "doubt" about these variants being God's "perfect" Word!) Only after destroying all of the other "imperfect" Mother-Of-All-Books that came to light, did the earthly *Koran*, retrieved from the flawless and perfect memories of various "others" who, evidently, must have been immune-from-error themselves---become a "divine" production, an undoubted, "perfect" copy of the heavenly Book in Allah's private library—what incredible BS, I repeat, "what incredible BS"! All of the above events occurring, no doubt, while the Holy Trinity of Islam were smiling from ear to ear, watching with utmost admiration these events unfold from the lofty serenity of their "immune-from-criticism" heavenly abode! What incredible naivete and ignorance exists in the Islamic mindset in order to maintain belief in a personal God—what incredible chutzpah exists in the same mindset that considers it a sacred duty to kill anyone who disagrees with any part of the religious beliefs inserted into the *Koran* by various "others."

Because it is supremely important that every Muslim believe every statement in the *Koran* is the absolute truth and, therefore, absolutely beyond doubt, the book, one would assume, would have been written by God in such a manner as to be very easy to read and very easy to comprehend by every one of its past and present readers but, like the *Bible*, it isn't. Both books are the product of the age in which they were written— each with their God-pretender communicating, of course, in the familiar manner of expression in common use at the time. Because of the changeable nature of language, the *Bible* and the *Koran*, obviously could not have been written to be completely understood for all eternity in the same exact way today as in the time of their writing. Language evolves, God's written Word, while purposely altered at various times, does not!

The continually progressive change to which the meaning of words is subject, the want of a universal language which renders translation necessary, the errors to which translations are again subject, the mistakes of copyists and printers, together with the possibility of willful alteration, are of themselves evidences that the human language, whether in speech or in print, cannot be the vehicle of the Word of God. . . . At the time those books (the Gospels) were written there was no printing, and consequently there could be no publication, otherwise than by written copies, which any man might make or alter at pleasure, and call them originals. (ditto for the *Koran*! ---kvk)

---Thomas Paine

Hence the need for the assistance of the Hadith to help explain and clarify the perfect *Koran's* shortcomings.

How strange, indeed, that God's Word should be "revealed" in ways that require an instruction manual to help explain it. Hmm! To help ease any confusion about the perfect nature of the assembled bits and pieces that various "others" contributed to fabricate the flawless Word of Allah, one would think that Gabriel would have scheduled, at least, a brief appearance (23 seconds would have sufficed!) to the *Koran*-makers to verify the accuracy of the final cut and give his heavenly approval to it. One would think that a profoundly persevering and persistent person—as evidenced by Gabriel's long, tedious years of effort to teach a cave man to memorize every word of the *Koran*—would have, in the least, taken but a mere moment more to reveal his thumbs-up or thumbs down to the final production of the *Koran*-compilers in order to confirm or deny the perfection of their labors. As it turned out, the prodigious patchwork endeavors that were made in assembling, fourth-hand, all of the "proper" third-hand accounts supposedly preached by Muhammad, were disputed for years by the various *Koran*-makers and yet, upon the final contrived assemblage of all the "perfect" bits and pieces into an "undoubted" Islamic Chutzpah Chronicle, the entire world must now submit to Allah's perfect "Word," the *Koran*, and Allah's perfect "will" as expressed in it or perish in this life and suffer eternal torments in the next—the script-writers of Islam's Mother-of-all-Books were finally able to achieve the glorious penned-perfection they were seeking!

Are we, Americans, who are deemed "infidels" upon the pages of the perfect *Koran*, willing to be assaulted or killed for the undoubted, hearsay words contained in the multi-authored *Koran* that Muslims are compelled to believe in? Or are we willing to defend and die for what we, a liberty-loving people believe in? That is the question that needs to be asked and answered by freedom-loving people everywhere. It also needs to be asked and answered why Allah would "will" to have "me" deliberately "write" this very book that places doubt upon His "undoubted" Word—an undertaking which defies explanation like so many of God's erstwhile "willed" endeavors. Perhaps, Allah, growing up without parents, without siblings, and without having the company of friends, playmates, or even a pet, has left Him a very disturbed individual, a victim of a lonely, dysfunctional childhood if ever He had one. Perhaps, His perplexing, ungodly behaviors are but an indication that He's just craving attention—thankfully, Reason's Tribunal will, mercifully, bestow that attention upon Him and all of His incredible, unbelievable doings as well!

In Reason's Tribunal, it will be "revealed" how Muhammad, with his "immunity from error," was able to know, with such certainty, that the person speaking to him in his "visions" was an angel and how he was able to know what an angel even looked like, or if Muslims are being deceived and imposed upon. In Reason's Tribunal, it will be "revealed" how Muhammad was able to know, with such certainty, that his visually indistinct, obscure informant was a good angel rather than a bad one (as all angels are not all angels!) and on what grounds he considered Gabriel to be a trustworthy agent of Allah, or if Muslims are being deceived and imposed upon. A "good" angel, one would think, would have interceded on behalf of Allah and His pious interests of course, to persuade and prevent Most Merciful Muhammad from "marrying" and sexually molesting an innocent child because of his less-than-spiritual urges—God surely does work in mysterious ways!

In Reason's Tribunal, it will be "revealed" beyond any doubt if Gabriel, in order to establish his angel-hood status, handed Muhammad a signed note from Allah to prove his identity, or if he carried an official "Heavenly Choir" photo ID or some other form of identification, or if Muslims are being deceived and imposed upon. In Reason's Tribunal, it will be "revealed" why Muhammad, given his supposed intense desire for knowledge and enlightenment, never once, over the span of 23 years, sought answers from Gabriel about any other subject of human interest or concern---why his lengthy and intimate conversations with such a knowledgeable "INSIDER" did not result in any advancement in science, medicine, technology, etc., or if Muslims are being deceived and imposed upon. In Reason's Tribunal, it will be "revealed" if Gabriel sported sparkling white clothes and golden wings, whether he was capable of flying like a bird and standing on a cloud, or if Muslims are being deceived and imposed upon.

In Reason's Tribunal, it will be "revealed" beyond any doubt why such incredible, constantly reoccurring events—Muhammad's unique, hallucinogenic visions of a non-human-being of extraterrestrial origin, spanning beyond two decades, were never witnessed by anyone else. Could Muhammad's mushrooming visual effects of a horizon-striding entity be attributed to the mind-altering effects of psychotropic plants growing in the Arabian desert or inside his cave retreat? Are we to accept and believe such delusional events, that took place in a light-lacking cave, as certain proof of the mysterious workings of divinity or rather as the result of drug use or mental illness? Hmm! Isn't it strange that Gabriel's prolonged, record-setting encounters with Muhammad—the most important and longest Allah-willed endeavor to ever occur in the entire infinite Universe—a Universe that He happened to create in its entirety in just 6 days—is not deemed worthy of receiving a single sentence in the entire *Koran* or elsewhere to describe Allah's trustworthy emissary in any "doubt-free" detail. Belief in the incredible story about a "perfect" book being "revealed" to an illiterate, mule-man and pedophile in the darkened recesses of a cave in the Middle East by such an incredible character as Gabriel for such an incredible length of time should have produced such an abundance of "credible" evidence to support it. After all, belief in a book in which there is no doubt requires belief in the incredible story of its angelic transmission from Allah to Muhammad in which there is no doubt, too. The miraculous, mystifying, murky meetings between the Holy Prophet and the Mysterious Heaven-sent Messenger and all that their supposed encounters must have entailed, will finally receive the rational-minded, clear-sighted attention-to-detail and critical scrutiny they richly deserve thanks to efforts of Reason's Tribunal!

If only out of curiosity, wouldn't you like to know, with certainty, what Gabriel really looked like? —and who better than Muhammad to tell us. If the darkness of a cave prevented Muhammad (for 23 years!) from getting a good look at Gabriel's features in order to describe him to perfection, how the hell was he able to know with such certainty who he was talking to? We should also know, with certainty, that shining the light of reason and truth into the darkened recesses of religious dogma will often bring the blurry details of obscure objects into much sharper focus. In Reason's Tribunal, every effort will be made to reveal the truth about a "revealed" religion to the reasonable satisfaction of everyone—Praise be to merciful Reason and Truth!

Every freedom-loving American, especially policy-making politicians who consider themselves as being Caretakers of Liberty, should read: *The Complete Infidel's Guide to the Koran* by Robert Spencer who tells us:

> *Those whom the Koran asserts are Infidels need to know what the Koran is saying about them and what must be done about them, because Muslims around the world today are acting upon these teachings. . . . That's why it is imperative for Infidels to know what is in the Koran. It's a simple matter of knowing who those who have vowed to destroy us think they are, and what they think they're doing, and what they hope to accomplish. They themselves tell us the answers to these questions are found in the Koran. . . . And that's why an Infidel's guide to this strange and little-understood book is so urgently needed. It's a question of self-protection. . . . The fact that the Koran counsels warfare against unbelievers should move readers to act in defense of freedom of speech, freedom of conscience, and the legal equality of all people, before it is too late. Jihadist activity will continue as long as there are Muslims who believe that the Koran commands it. And that's why Infidels have a responsibility to themselves and to their children to know what is in the Koran, and act accordingly.*

A religion-ravaged planet has recently entered a new and, perhaps, fateful millennium. Civilization will end here, in this era, if we, the freedom-loving people of the world, are not able to emancipate ourselves from the mental and physical tyrannies of religion---our time is running out, for it is only a matter of time before the destroyers of civilization will acquire and use biological, chemical, and nuclear weapons of mass destruction to rid the earth of ***"Life, Liberty and the pursuit of Happiness"***! Now, more than ever before, as a result of our defeat in Afghanistan, Islamic terrorists---believing our nation's loss there to be a blessing and a message from Allah---have been uber-inspired to carry-on and carry-out the work that they say they must accomplish in His name. Man help us! In America's darkest hour during her initial struggle against imposition and oppression from abroad, it was the words of Thomas Paine that uber-inspired and rallied General Washington's demoralized army to overcome the dire adversity of their situation and achieve, at last, their hard-won victory:

These are the times that try men's souls. The summer soldier and the sunshine patriot will, in this crisis, shrink from the service of their country; but he that stands by it now, deserves the love and thanks of man and woman. Tyranny, like hell, is not easily conquered; yet we have this consolation with us, that the harder the conflict, the more glorious the triumph. What we obtain too cheap, we esteem too lightly; it is dearness that gives everything its value.

---Thomas Paine

These, too, unfortunately, *"are the times that try men's souls."* To deserve the *"love and thanks"* of mankind, we, too, must not shrink from the service to our country and to civilization in their greatest time of need. We must stand by them now to expose every pious fraud in an effort to honor and protect all lovers of Liberty's *"dearness,"* along with their descendants, from the scourge of scripture and its fatal fanaticisms. The religion-generated mindset of terror is *"not easily conquered"* too, therefore, the sooner we gain the courage to investigate and question its constant source---Semitic scriptures---the sooner we can effectively plan a strategic and sane offensive against them.

It has been by wandering from the immutable laws of science, and the light of reason, and setting up an invented thing called revealed religion, that so many wild and blasphemous conceits have been formed of the Almighty. The Jews have made Him the assassin of the human species to make room for the religion of the Jews. The Christians have made Him the murderer of Himself and the founder of a new religion, to supersede and expel the Jewish religion.

---Thomas Paine

And the Muslims will not stop until they have made Allah *"the assassin of the human species"* of unbelievers to make room for His followers—they will not stop until they *"supersede and expel"* all the Jews, Christians, and non-Muslims **"to make room"** for the religion of Islam only. Our continued existence, therefore, lies not in beseeching the mercy and ministrations of any manufactured deity; it lies in our success in revealing the impious, imposing, and murderous hands that wrought them all---the murderous hands that are ever a part of Semitic religions and their destructive dogmas.

We must begin to examine and expose the *Koran's* fundamental fallacies to its followers in our attempts to find a cure for the religious cancer responsible for the atrocities of 9/11---the religious cancer that can rabidly and rapidly break-out and virally spread at any moment—the religious cancer that constantly threatens our very survival on this planet. We must begin to heed the advice of many of our nation's founders and overcome our unwillingness to scrutinize religious beliefs in order to uncover, and proclaim to all, their deceptions and their virulent incitements to violence.

> *...Do not be frightened from this inquiry* (into religion) *by any fear of its consequences.*

> ---Thomas Jefferson

It is time to hold religion accountable for the slings and arrows, bombs and bullets, murders and mutilations, tortures, amputations, decapitations, incinerations, genocides, vengeance, hatred, bigotry, racial divisions, the abuse of women, children, and animals, and other evils that have originated from their inviolable dogmas—the world has suffered long enough from "sacred" Semitic fervor and its "God-worshiping" endeavors. We must not excuse or abide the pious frauds of religion simply because of their possible involvement in "good works" —religion doesn't have a monopoly on ethical behavior, benevolence, philanthropy, or decency. The end of "revealed" religions' reign will not spell the end of spiritual activity or humane, compassionate, and charitable behavior---it will, undoubtedly, increase such activities! We must begin to educate ourselves about God's "Word" in order to enlighten those who, stranded in greater ignorance, believe they are doing God's "Work" in seeking our demise and the end of civilization. We must begin the noble inquisition that will someday convince all of humanity that dying for the contrived written words of Jehovah, Jesus, and Allah is truly MARTYRDUMB! We must begin Reason's Tribunal---the only rational and honorable solution to scripture-based terrorism.

The sectarian divisions are the great dividers in our world; the cause of hatred, bigotry and prejudice. Ethnic divisions can live together until the sectarian enters in; the "melting pot" can fuse all isms except religious fanaticism. This endures and perpetuates the divisions. Today great effort is being made to combat "religious prejudice," but we simply do not know how to go about it; we cannot see that the only way to rid the world of "religious prejudice" is to rid it of religion, its cause and source. The substitute? That truth that would set us free—from religion's errors. This was the goal of all world teachers; it was only the priests who came after them that founded religions on them. These were not based on fact but fiction, the miraculous and the supernatural. So false a basis brought us little save stupefaction, chaos and war. If it ends in total extinction it will not be because we have found a power that would destroy us, but because we have not found the truth that would save us.

---Lloyd M. Graham

Imagine there's no heaven . . . It's easy if you try . . . No hell below us . . . Above us only sky . . .

---John Lennon

If we are unsuccessful in our noble, honorable efforts, there is little hope for the future of our planet! If successful, we will end, at last, the oppression, cruelty, and bloodshed that pious pathologies and toxic theologies perpetually inflict upon the world. Surely, it will be a difficult task to accomplish but we must begin to make the effort. There are no other pursuits that will bring about the final solution to religious fanaticism except, Man forbid, Option II (the "Twin Towers" option).

This method, which "certain Americans" would be very pleased to carry out, but which every person of sane mind should reject, would obliterate (ala the 9/11, "Ground-Zero" attacks carried out in NYC) ---two Sacred, Supreme Shrines in the Middle East that would be perceived, "undoubtedly," in Allah-land as a "Judgment of God," a "divine retribution" directed against the Islamic world that could only have resulted from the anger of their "displeased deity." It would be perceived as such because Muslims believe that "nothing" happens unless Allah "wills" it. The "Twin Towers" option would only require two guided missiles---like the two loaded passenger planes that were used as missiles to destroy the Twin Towers in New York City---to bring Muslim-mania to its supplicating, prayer-rug positions in an attempt to win back the affections of Allah. It must be admitted, however, that two horrific bombs did end the horrors of WWII and that two much smaller bombs do have the capability to halt the ungodly pursuits of Islam and bring to an end the terror and horrors of WWIII. Those "certain Americans" mentioned above would be well pleased with such a course of action, but using terrorism as a means to end terrorism is not an enlightened way for a "good" and "great" nation to prevail over all of the insanity of our times, as vengeful actions taken on our part can only generate more vengeful actions taken against us on their part, which can only generate more vengeful actions being undertaken on all parts. A far better future for the sane pursuits of civilization would result from implementing Option I, (Reason's Tribunal) which prefers that Semitic religions decline and disappear as a result of their being "found out" by those who do believe in them rather than their being "rubbed out" by those who don't.

Americans, as Sons and Daughters of Liberty, must not be afraid to declare our independence and our willingness to free ourselves from the mental shackles imposed by religion, to free ourselves from the tyranny, terror, threats of annihilation, racial discord, supremacist thoughts and hatreds that proceed from belief in unchallenged Semitic scriptures. We must once again, fire *"the shot heard 'round the world"* in this noble war with the potential to finally end all wars: a war whose only casualties will be ignorance, indoctrination, intimidation, injustice, inhumanity, and the threats of scripture-commanded persecutions, racial supremacism, and mass destructions. In this War of Independence from the tyranny of religion and its mindset of terror, the Sons and Daughters of Liberty will ultimately prevail against the Sons and Daughters of Tyranny when we begin, in earnest, to focus the figurative, not literal, cross hairs on the correct target and pull the figurative, not literal, trigger on the singular source of Jihad Johnny and Jihad Jane's perceived literal authority and literal inspiration for killing and committing atrocity in God's name—the literal *Koran*.

We must begin to deal effectively and intelligently with the recurring malevolence embedded, embraced, and employed in the ***"human inventions"*** of sinister, Semitic theologies in our noble efforts to neutralize them. We must begin to ***"Question with boldness"*** the uncontested, sacrosanct beliefs of Judaism, Christianity, and Islam along with the "divine" origin of their "revealed" Word of God scriptures, and even the existence of their Gods if we are ever to permanently cease the cruel and unusual histories of Semitic religions. We must hold Semitic religions accountable for their egregious *"errors"* and their odious offenses conducted against humanity throughout the ages. We must begin to nullify the scriptural justifications for engaging in Jihad if we are truly intent about insuring a peaceful, progressive future for our planet. We Americans should now know with certainty, post-Afghanistan, that the scripture-based pursuits of Muslims and Muslim terrorists are little affected by intense military responses---they, as we've learned the hard way---are emboldened and empowered by them!

> *Soon after I had published the pamphlet "Common Sense," in America, I saw the exceeding probability that a revolution in the system of government would be followed by a revolution in the system of religion The adulterous connection of church and state, wherever it has taken place, whether Jewish, Christian or Turkish, has so effectually prohibited by pains and penalties every discussion upon established creeds, and upon first principles of religion, that until the system of government should be changed, those subjects could not be brought fairly and openly before the world; but that whenever this should be done, a revolution in the system of religion would follow.*

---Thomas Paine

While that *"system of government"* has been changed centuries ago, sadly, Mr. Paine, we have yet to bring *"those subjects"* (the systems of religion) . . . *"fairly and openly before the world."* Reason's Tribunal will commence this needed *"revolution,"* a revolution that will prove to be a slow but sure means to reverse the worldwide, centuries-long, unchallenged bondage to Semitic indoctrination that produces the religious mindset of terror. As part of our efforts to remove the threat posed by Islamic terrorists, we must become aware of their deadly religious disguise (taqiyya)—the sheep's clothing that allows them to dwell unnoticed among us while concealing their homicidal intentions. Depending on the strength and the progress of our edifying, emancipating efforts, it may take years, even decades to accomplish a noticeable effect upon Semitic theologies, their deceptive dogmas, and their deluded advocates. Advancements and setbacks in this regard, inevitably, will occur, but truth, inevitably, will triumph over the lies of false theologies and set us free, at last, from our mindless servitude to their imposed tyrannies and to the violence and carnage they inevitably produce and promote.

As freedom-enjoying, freedom-honoring people, Americans have a duty to decide and to declare if we approve or disapprove of the existence of Semitic religions and their scriptures of death and destruction, whether we consider them necessary for the improvement of civilization, for the betterment of society, and for the advance of freedom around the world, or whether they are quite unnecessary and quite dangerous. And let's not forget what can happen when some religious fanatic gets his hand on a "magic wand"! *"We the people,"* have a duty to decide and to declare, if only to ourselves, whether it is necessary to abide religions that are based on authority-lacking credentials—that inspire and demand deadly atrocity to be carried out in God's name—that are continually and unfailingly linked to terrorism, or whether we should seek to diminish or abolish them and their radical, racial agendas, their never-ending threat to the hopes and dreams of the entire free world. We can no longer delay the start of the American Revolution *"in the system of religion"* for the fate of mankind now hangs in the balance because of our centuries-long reluctance and refusal to deal with the Devil-in-the-Details of "revealed" scriptures. In the darkest hour of the American Revolution, Thomas Paine prophetically wrote:

We have it in our power to begin the world over again.

And, thankfully, the Sons and Daughters of Liberty did make *"the world over again"*! In the ever-darkening hours of our times, *"we,* (too), *have it in our power to begin the world over again"* by vanquishing, in this second War of Independence, the scripture-justified, religion-endorsed mindset of terror. We have it in our power to prevail against those who are educated and programmed to value oppression over freedom, violence over benevolence, and death over life. We have it in our power to prevail against the destroyers of civilization and their God-pleasing, God-inspired madness. We shall overcome!

We all want a peaceful, warless world (all but *Koranimals*! ---kvk) but *we haven't the faintest idea of how to achieve it. ...We are proud of our armies and navies never realizing that if we were civilized there would be no such things. We are proud of the size and efficiency of our police force when this is due only to the number of criminals in our society. We are proud only because we haven't sense enough to be ashamed.*

---Lloyd M. Graham

We are proud of our religious beliefs too, only because we haven't sense enough to be ashamed of them!

According to Christian belief, Jesus is "God" —a third part of Him manifested as a man with all the abilities of a deity, whatever they may be. He, Jesus, in all or in part, was, therefore, the creative genius who evidently possessed, in theory, Ph.D.'s in every known and unknown field of art and science deemed necessary to make the entire Universe out of nothing but His spoken Word (that no one ever heard Him utter!). How strange then that Jesus never "spoke" a single "word" about His Creation's many wonders—never spoke a word about anything but "sin" to his "inquisitive" disciples—men, it appears, whose low mental horizons and understanding of the world barely exceeded the reckonings of present-day kindergarteners.

Imagine yourself being a disciple of Jesus and choosing to remain silent, ignorant, and unknowing about anything in the world when in the frequent presence of God—someone who could provide you with total, accurate knowledge on any subject—someone whose IQ was light-years beyond that of any human being, someone who knew "everything about everything." Hmm! Imagine hanging-out day and night with God for nearly 3 years, as in the case of the disciples, or in the case of Muhammad, hanging-out with God's top agent for nearly 23 years, and their not asking either of their supreme-savants any questions about the multitude of mysteries dealing with our bodies, our planet, and the cosmic curiosities that lie beyond it. Imagine Jesus' disciples and Muhammad "not" asking their intimate, Know-It-All-Teachers about the cause of disease---about what causes the changes in the weather---about what causes rain, rainbows and their unvarying sequence of colors---about what causes snow and ice to fall from the sky---about what causes the eclipses of the moon and the sun---about what causes the lit surface of the moon to increase and decrease in size only to disappear completely on a regular basis and slowly reappear again---about what causes the seasonal changes with their increasing/decreasing amounts of daylight—perplexing occurrences that they were all witness to, I repeat, "that they were all witness to." To be fair, Jesus did disclose to His disciples the cause of all illnesses: dirty boogeymen! ---I repeat, "dirty boogeymen" residing in our bodies---*Luke* 11:14-26.

Do you think an obviously ignorant Jesus or an illiterate caveman could have given educated answers to the above questions? ---I don't think so, hence the curious silence on such matters in God's "Word"! Never forget, folks, that it was Man's enlightening sciences, not God's ignorant, imposing scriptures that have provided us with the answers to the above questions! ---

imagine Jesus giving His disciples a discourse on refracted sunlight being the cause of rainbows! ---I don't think so! ---there is only one overriding reason for the existence of Semitic scripture and it has nothing to do with the education of others! Imagine Moses, whom God "spake" to constantly day in and day out, never having a curious thought about anything beyond sin, beyond ritual slaughter, and beyond the supremacism of the Jews--- when he had the amazing opportunity to converse directly with the Almighty, the Knower of Everything! . . . (Moses to Mr. Know-It-All Smarty Pants! ---"How in Your name do you expect me to write-down, without error, every word You are going to *"spake"* unto me as fast as You spaketh them"? Mr. Know-It-All-Smarty-Pants to Moses---"Donchaworry boy, Daddy will provide you with all the script-writers you need to get the job done and get it done to perfection and you won't have to explain anything!") LOL!

Imagine God, the Great-Informer, not wanting to share any such information with anyone---preferring instead to keep such knowledge all to Himself---preferring to keep His followers in blissful ignorance---preferring to let them continue to believe that the earth was flat and that the sun went around it every day. Not even the *Bible*-prophets with their supposed talent to accurately prophesy about future events knew any better—had they and their script-writers "truly" been "inspired" by God to know the future with certainty, wouldn't they have been able to foretell man's stepping foot on the moon? Shouldn't they have been able to "reveal" to us, somewhere on the pages of the divinely-inspired *Bible,* the name of the very first man to do so with the same familiarity they told us the names of the genealogical cast of characters from Adam to Jesus? If *Bible*-prophecy was unable to predict *"One small step for man, one giant leap for mankind"* why should anyone attach importance to the contrived words of *Bible*-prophets? The following account from *The Age of Reason* tells us about the "prophet," Isaiah, and his "inspired" words of "prophecy" to Ahaz, king of Judah whom he "assures" will not face defeat:

But to show the imposition and falsehood of Isaiah, we have only to attend to the sequel of this story, which, though passed over in silence in the book of Isaiah, is related in the 28th chapter of the second Chronicles, and which is, that instead of these two kings (the king of Syria, the king of Israel) failing in their attempt against Ahaz, king of Judah, as Isaiah had pretended to foretell in the name of the Lord, they succeeded; Ahaz was defeated and destroyed, a hundred and twenty thousand of his people were slaughtered,

Jerusalem was plundered, and two hundred thousand women, and sons and daughters, carried into captivity. Thus much for this lying prophet and impostor, Isaiah, and the book of falsehoods that bear his name.

And, by the way, *Bible*-heads---referring back to the previous chapter, if you think Moses' recording skills were truly legit, try keeping-up with writing-down something you're listening to as fast as it is being voiced—no can do, folks! ---neither could Moses unless he could write in sacred shorthand! ---but I digress . . .

Did the mighty murderer, Moses, and the despicable disciples of Jesus, and the pedophile Prophet of Islam truly have no interest in knowing about those mysterious, twinkling lights in the sky: planets, stars, and galaxies—no interest in knowing how many of them existed (I'm sure the inspired script writers of the *Bible* could have told us the exact even number!) ---no interest in knowing what caused the sun to rise and set---no interest in knowing what caused the rise and fall of ocean waters (tides), earthquakes, volcanoes, lightning, thunder, static electrical charges along with their visible spark and physical jolt—no interest in knowing what caused the light of day and the darkness of night (our planet's rotation)---no interest in knowing what meteors and comets are and where they come from---no interest in knowing the extent of the Universe---no interest in knowing if objects could fall off the edge of the earth---no interest in knowing what caused fog---what caused water (dew) to appear on various surfaces in the morning---what caused women to menstruate? Wouldn't they have wondered and asked about such things and passed such informative answers along in their "revealing" scripture had they possessed it? Had such things been known at the time, the Black Stone, a meteorite encased in a Meccan shrine, would only be a curiosity and not the object of Muslim veneration that ignorance, supposition, and wishful thinking has bestowed upon it.

While on the subject of knowing and not knowing—Jesus, the loving and merciful "Maker" of figs and, of course, the loving and merciful "Maker/Knower" of every season---blasted a fig tree into oblivion for not bearing fruit because, as *Mark* tells us, *"for the time of figs was not yet."* ---11:13,14. To all who hath eyes, to all who hath ears, and more importantly, to all who hath a brain, there's a lot to be learned about Semitic "divinity" in this outrageous Gospel tale of ignorance, intolerance, and injustice—if a tree is known by its fruit, so, too, is it's Maker! Is there any member of Christendumb who can tell us what this unoffending fig tree hath done to deserve receiving a life-destroying curse from God, the Creator of Everything, just for not bearing fruit in a non-fruit bearing season—a season that Jesus alone, being God, had intentionally established for fig trees to grow in and put forth fruit in? Why didn't a loving Jesus, with just a touch from His miracle-bestowing hands, bless the fig tree and turn its barren branches into fruitful bounty? *"Yes, Virginia, you shouldn't give a fig about this kind of Bible-crap that's being imposed upon all of us as a stellar example of sacred activity!"*

I wouldn't be surprised to learn that, for not supplying a hungry God with its tasty, nourishing fruit, this hapless tree will be spending its eternity as a burning bush in you know where! Instead of annihilating this blameless tree, wouldn't it have been more humane of Jesus to have just beaten the living crap out of this heart-hardened, fruitless tree and let that be punishment enough? Imagine what would have happened had a single tree, for one reason or another, pissed off Cmdr. Smotely---Jesus' former self---the Guy who slew 50, 070 men just because a few fellas tried to peek inside a box? I believe He, according to His idea of (vengeful!) Semitic justice, would have wiped out every living thing on the continent of Africa and been damned proud about doing it and so would the many members of His fan clubs! Is there any fruitful, Christian-fan-club-apologist who can invent a reasonable excuse for the vindictive behavior undertaken by God against this fig tree— someone who can "spin" this tale of mean-spiritedness and spitefulness into a merciful and loving act of Divinity? Those of us who possess ears and a brain, should be on the edge of our seats listening for the answer coming from one of Jesus' many apologists . . . did somebody drop a pin? By the way, should anyone ever stumble upon a hangry-looking, tree-cursing individual, especially someone blasting (exterminating) a fruit tree for not bearing fruit out of season, do not approach the subject, leave the area immediately, and notify the authorities---disturbed folks like this tree-totaler should never be allowed to interact with children, animals, or even inanimate life forms---after all, this Guy has a criminal past and a rap-sheet as long as a Torah scroll . . . come to think of it, the Torah "is" His rap sheet!

(NOTE TO ALL WHO HATH A BRAIN AND THE ABILITY TO USE IT SANELY: Please remember always the "Lesson of the Fig Tree" so that this poor, unoffending life form didn't perish in vain. Let its withered branches and its extinction be a constant reminder to you about the wretchedness and the less-than-sacred behavior of Jesus Christ. Is more proof needed to reveal His hateful, malevolent, and vengeful theology. And most importantly, know that the time and the season of Reason's Tribunal has arrived and that everyone should begin now to nourish themselves on its urgently needed, life-sustaining fruits---mmm!)

The silence of Jesus' disciples, the Prophet Muhammad, the *Bible*, and the *Koran* on the elemental and curious matters of human interest speaks volumes about the knowledge-level of their simple-minded chapter and verse writers who were, of course, unable to put words into the mouth of Jehovah, Jesus, and Allah that exceeded their own uninformed and ignorant understanding of the world. Apparently, silence is golden and ignorance is bliss when it comes to being educated and enlightened by the Knower of Everything, or by His "revealing" angel, when it comes to acquiring knowledge and understanding about the mysterious and puzzling environment around us.

It was not so long ago that the advocates of the above Semitic scriptures would have us believe that every attempt by man to gain understanding about such matters or even having a curiosity about them was a heresy, a sin punishable by torture and death. It was a sin to even imagine the earth as a sphere or that it orbited the sun. It wasn't until the overwhelming evidence produced by torture-defying and death-defying, brain-utilizing scientists proved otherwise, helping to rid the planet of the centuries-long, religion-imposed ignorance that prevented any advancement in gaining knowledge of the world and the human condition—it won't be until the overwhelming evidence produced by the bold questioning of Reason's Tribunal that mankind will finally be able to rid itself of its greatest enemy to ***"Life, Liberty and the pursuit of Happiness"*** and the progressive, life-improving pursuits of science—an enemy who, dressed in a Pope's frock, decided in the year 1992 to "absolve" Galileo of heresy!

After three and a half centuries, the infallible, inerrant head and guiding light of the infallible, inerrant Catholic Church thought that it was finally the proper time to "forgive" Galileo of the "sin" of declaring that the earth was not a stationary object but a moving one. It only took three and a half centuries for the Pope, God's chosen confidant and supposed earth-envoy---the paragon of Christian piety, decency, and knowledge---to finally admit of wrongdoing on the part of the Catholic Church. One would think that sometime during these 350 years of having constant communications with God Almighty, at least one Pope would have learned early on from God Himself, that the earth was a globe! Think about it folks, the Pope's claim to fame is that he communicates, on a regular basis, with God about everything worth knowing but is only able to reveal to us God's take on "sin" and nothing else! Hmm! ---and this is the guy much of the world continues to seek guidance from---incredible!

In light of this long-delayed act of contrition on the part of the Church for imposing its ignorant, paleo-reckonings upon a scientific genius, shouldn't it follow then that the Catholic Church, out of respect for "all" of its innumerable victims, admit publicly to "all" of its wrongdoings, all of its "sins" against humanity that it imposed upon innocent victims throughout the centuries? I think not, as Catholic contrition only requires three "Hail Marys" and two "Our Fathers" to wipe the slate clean!

Since faith is "the belief in things unseen," things that do not require certain proof in order for someone to be convinced of their reality, and since having faith in the belief that Jesus is God is all that matters, why then the need for spectacle and supernatural events such as water-walking and raising the dead to life? If the possession of faith alone is the only prerequisite needed for having such a belief about Jesus' divine identity, then miracles are unnecessary. If, however, miracles are necessary for such a belief, then faith is unnecessary—only religion can utilize and maintain both positions and proceed without scrutiny!

> *...either faith is sufficient or else miracles are required to reassure those—including the preachers—whose faith would otherwise not be strong enough. For me, witnessing an act of faith-healing or conjury would simply not be persuasive, even if I could credit it and even if I did not know people who could—and can and do— replicate such wonders on stage.*

> ---Christopher Hitchens, Introduction to the *Portable Atheist*

Would you, on faith alone, believe the words of someone claiming to be God, someone you didn't know? ---certainly not! Would you, on faith alone, believe the same words spoken by someone you did know? ---certainly not! Who then has the "faith" needed to believe such a *Bible*-claim made about Jesus on words alone? ---words by an unknown author claiming that Jesus, a Jewish guy, is the Creator of the Universe—no one in their right mind, that's who---only a Jewish Chutzpah Chronicle would dare to make such a claim! That's why the Gospel script-writers found it necessary to tell us that Jesus performed miracle after miracle—for who else but Almighty God would have the ability to stroll on water and perform instant death cures— Jesus, therefore, must be "God"! ---right? The performance of miracles then, not faith alone, is a necessity for believing the imposing claims made about Jesus in the *New Testament*. Without the mention of supernatural, superhuman performances in its accounts, no one would believe that Jesus is God based simply upon *Bible*-words or upon *Bible*-faith alone! That's why it is so important to check the *"facts and evidence"* of such scamming claims to determine if we have been imposed upon.

> *Inattention to reason, and ignorance of the nature of things makes many of mankind give credit to miracles. ...Nothing is more evident to the understanding part of mankind, than that in those parts of the world where learning and science has prevailed, miracles have ceased.*

---Ethan Allen

If the "Wow-factor" of performing mind-blowing miracles was a scriptural requirement for our having belief that Jesus is God, why didn't He, the Creator-of-Worlds, choose not to reveal "all" of His astounding accomplishments to everyone in order to astonish and amaze them with His uber, mind-blowing résumé? Why didn't He reveal to His disciples the "Wow-factor" about the seemingly flat earth He created—that it is in reality—TADAHHH! —a globe spinning around at tremendous speed on an invisible axis while being orbited by the tide-creating moon while both are circling the Sun, a star traveling at tremendous speed through a countless, star-filled, expanding galaxy—just one of the countless billions of expanding galaxies that exist in His mystery-abounding Universe? Wow! Wow! Wow! Wouldn't Jesus have considered such awesome knowledge about His amazing "works" as being of great importance to those He wished to impress with His astounding abilities? Certainly, He would: "If you think my walking on water was a mighty and incredible undertaking, let me tell you about black holes and how I was able to make them!" The reason such knowledge isn't found anywhere in the *NT* is because the very knowledgeable Godman who could have and would have relayed such knowledge to His disciples, didn't exist. The *New Testament* was obviously written by script-writers who, in their "inspired" mental state, were convinced the earth was flat, immovable, 4-cornered, and the center of the entire Creation. Could it be that Jesus, the miracle-performing "Showman" who wasn't shy about impressing others with His amazing abilities, had missed a great opportunity to add to His list of superhuman feats by failing to make any mention of the many wonders contained in the curiosity-causing, curiosity-teeming, mind-blowing Cosmos He, supposedly, created with just a few spoken words?

Surely, the miraculous performances of Jesus—water-walking, re-animating the dead, etc., that are spoken of in the Gospels—were a contrivance meant to convince us with what His script-writers promoted as "certain and undoubted" proof of His divinity so that everyone will believe in Him and His superior talents---talents that only a God could possibly possess. Only a fraudulent faith-based religion, one supposedly built on "faith" alone, would have its followers believe in Jesus because of the many miracles He supposedly performed—the abracadabra events meant to "convince" us, the imposed upon, that we should never doubt Him or His Word that is "revealed" to us by unknown reporters. Only a fraudulent religion would have its followers believe the bogus reports about Jesus' ability to raise the dead to life even though such events have gone unwitnessed by our own eyes, events that have only been made known to us by His bogus, late biographers—only a fraudulent religion would find our enchantment with such manufactured events more important than raising our understanding of life and its multitude of mysteries through knowledge and enlightenment! Hmm! Hmm! Hmm!

The subject of "sin" and its remission are the Alpha and Omega of religion and the art and the science of, who else, but the cunningly deceptive, God-making, sin-absolving priests who, despite their apparent ignorance of the world around them when they wrote the *Bible*, knew from experience how to profit from the guilt associated with the sinful trespasses of others—the equally ignorant victims of their parasitic pursuits.

> *And the priest shall make an atonement for him with the ram of the trespass offering before the Lord for his sin which he hath done: and the sin which he had done shall be forgiven him.* (Thanks be to God for the soul-cleansing abilities of His butchering priests, please pass the mint sauce to Aaron! ---kvk)

> ---*Lev.* 19:22

It is truly a "sin" that priests are still profiting from their lucrative scam, especially Catholic priests—still profiting from their "theological trespasses"—still receiving free room and board and not having to pay anything for their gifted, parasitic existence—still eating bread not earned from the sweat of their own labors but, like all priests, from the sweat and labor of others!

Only the ignorant, primitive mentalities of Jesus' script-writing, scam artists would have Him---the most intelligent person ever to have existed and the Knower-of-Everything (except for the Hour or the Day of The Judgment!) ---reveal to us that demons, I repeat, "demons," (evil, unclean spirits) taking up residence within our bodies are responsible, I repeat, "responsible" for making us ill and that casting them out of our bodies (cleaning house) is the only means for making us well again---*Matt.* 8:2-3; *Luke* 11:14-26---a not-so-strange diagnosis coming from the ignorant, uneducated, primitive-minded "makers" of a Semitic deity---a very strange diagnosis, indeed, coming from the All-Knowing Creator who must have forgotten having made the disease-causing microbes that truly make us sick! ---really? I hope I've made enough lemonade for everyone!

It is important to note here that when Jesus ordered evil spirits to leave an insane man's body as stated in *Mark* 5:6-13, the evil spirits, whom Jesus knew with certainty were responsible for causing the man's uber-abnormal behavior and who were not wanting to be left homeless and living on the street, beseeched an obliging Jesus to allow their evil asses to enter the bodies of exactly 2000 pigs---and guess what happened to the poor little piggies as a result of Jesus' divine-doings? You guessed it---they, as Jesus stood by and watched, all died as a result of their jumping off a steep cliff, flying briefly, and then drowning in the waters of Swine Lake! ---is it possible that the evil spirits were all wanting to drown too?---is it possible that these evil spirits were all content to leave the presumed comfy confines of their luxury lunatic condo and commit suicide with the death of the swineherd? ---of course not, for according to divine Semitic justice, it is only the innocent who are always made to pay with their lives, never the evil troublemakers who continue to live quite comfortably among all of us---*"Praise the Lord"!*

Who then was totally responsible for this devastating act imposed upon 2000 hapless piggies? ---you guessed it! Who was it that provided *Bible*-readers with this even-numbered, precise body count done with absolute, inerrant and infallible *Bible*-accuracy---was it the Gentile pig farmer who was trusted to provide an accurate number of his losses? ---was it Jesus who took the time to count each member of the herd? ---or, was it His disciples who entered Swine Lake to count every piece of floating bacon? ---isn't it quite remarkable that there were exactly enough pigs to accommodate each and every one of the crazy man's many demons? By the way, how many educated, medical doctors in today's world do you think regard insanity to be the result of demon possession? ---someone should take a poll in Gospel-land to find out! ---my educated guess is: "not a single one!" ---even though an Almighty, All-Knowing God and His inspired script-writers have ignorantly informed us otherwise! ---why, therefore, does anyone put trust in this God when it is known with certainty from *Bible*-evidence alone that He is an ignorant God-pretender whose every word cannot be believed---cannot be trusted? ---why? ---why? ---why? How many lightbulb moments does one require to come to such a logical conclusion? Wouldn't it be enlightening, too, to hear the Supremes' opinions about the "justice" God dispensed in this mean-spirited, despicable Gospel-tale about demons and swine, and why all nine of them feel so honored to declare their trust in Him! ---why? ---why? ---why?

Since Jesus avoided entering Gentile territories like the plague and demanded of His disciples to do the same---*Matthew* 10:5,6---what the hell was He thinking when He decided to make a long and tiresome, out-of-the-way, lake-crossing trip with all of His disciples in order to make an unplanned visit to Porkland especially since He had no other destination in mind and no stated reason or purpose for making the journey in the first place? It is apparent, after reading this *Bible*-tale, that Jesus was on a sacred mission for no other reason but to impress others with His power and His authority over demons (which He had previously demon-strated several times before!) ---surely, He, for no other reason, was on a sacred mission to harass and destroy a poor, hard-working, Gentile farmer's livelihood for no other reason but to show off His (less-than-sacred) God talents and sail away without even having said: "I'm sorry" to the distraught farmer for being the cause of his losses and his woes---incredible!

Surely, if Jesus was on a sacred mission to impress others that day, which obviously He was, He should have resurrected all of the 2000 dead porkers and delivered them back alive and well to the Gentile farmer---now that truly would have been impressive and it only would have taken Him a mere moment more to accomplish! ---He could have left the Gentile territory with His head held high---He could have left without doing harm to anyone or anything!

Surely, Jesus, being God, must have known, well before crossing the lake, what He was about to find when He arrived onshore---imagine an all-knowing God not knowing what to expect or being taken by surprise! ---Jesus, being God, must have known exactly who and what He would find there: a crazy Gentile man whose wacko behavior Jesus, being God, knew was caused by his being possessed by a large number of evil spirits---He must have known, too, about the large number of harmless, demon-free animals that just happened to be nearby for Mr. Merciful to impose upon, causing their deaths, to show others His mighty God-abilities---animals that all Jews, to this day, continue to avoid like the plague!

Do you think Jesus, with malice aforethought, would have wantonly caused the deaths of 2000 sheep owned by a Jewish farmer? ---I think not! What would be your thoughts about Jesus if the victims of His insentient doings that day happened to be kittens and puppies instead of Jew-detested pigs? Jesus was quite fortunate that day that He was not killed by an angry Gentile farmer or a mob of his farming friends---according to "tolerant, Gentile traditions and principles," He was only asked to leave their territory! ---which He was allowed to do unscathed---Wow! ---what a damn lucky Guy! ---certainly, His absence from their lives and their territories should be seen as quite a blessing!

Where, one wonders, did the evil spirits take up residence after the incident at Piggie's Leap, (the jumping off point for ending belief in God's Word!) and where do they reside now? Did they beseech Jesus again to provide them with new digs? ---where would they have gone that day if Jesus had denied their beseeching request? ---would they have remained in the lunatic's body and perished with his death?

It is important to further note here that inerrant and infallible *Bible*-evidence proves that evil spirits seek God's permission in order to conduct their wicked, evil activities, and that the always spiritually-motivated Jesus was pleased to let them have their way---Jesus was pleased to aid and abet evildoers think about that, folks! ---think about what it was that motivated Jesus to make this, out-of-the-way, pig-destroying trip in the first place! Being a loving, "do-no-evil" God, instead of being a malevolent SOB, you'd think He, Jesus, the uber-paragon of spiritual behavior, would have removed the crazy man's demons without all the drama and without causing the slightest bit of harm to any sentient being---you'd think! ---right? ---wrong! Just think about where we would be without this ignorant, divinity-lacking, demon-assisting "God" directing our lives---just think about how possessed and crazy are the believers in His Word!

If you had to choose between an all-knowing Creator and an ignorant, paleo-minded, witch-doctor-believing, *Bible* script-writer---whose lack of knowledge about the cause of insanity likely caused the creation of evil spirits to explain its bizarre behaviors---who do you believe would have been the author of such an unbelievable, concocted account that would have us believe that demons are the cause of the erratic behavior of a mentally disturbed individual?---there's only one logical, common sense answer---an answer that proves Semitic scripture is not divinely inspired--- an answer that proves the *Bible* is not inerrant and infallible---an answer that proves the *Bible* was written by uber-ignorant men who stood to profit from deceiving others with their lies---an answer that proves the *Bible*-Jesus, by His own *Bible*-words, is a complete and utter fraud---an answer that proves that God's "Word" is little more than a steaming pile of pig droppings that an equally ignorant "Saint" Patrick dumped upon Ireland---a guy who is still honored there for putting the Irish in a kneeling position---intent on making them believe "everything" written in the *Bible* no matter how bizarre, brutal, or unbelievable are the events "revealed" on its pages! Once the true nature of the *Bible* is "revealed" in full to the brainwashed people of Ireland, another uprising against tyranny will surely occur there!

Isn't it a bit strange that we are imposed upon to believe every single word spoken by Jesus but not so much when His discourses deal with the subject of insanity and its inerrant and infallible *Bible*-cause! Ask yourself, folks, who was the more insane that day: the wacko Gentile guy who lived amongst the graves and went around screaming and mutilating his body or was it the megalomaniac Jew who thought He'd prove He is God by attempting to make others believe He conversed with demons and had power over them because they obeyed His orders regardless of the unfair, inhumane outcome? If you are counted among those who believe that Jesus, in this case, had proven His case that He is God---a God with uber-ignorant reckonings about demonic possession being the cause of insanity, you, too, are *Bible*-possessed and completely out of your mind! ---so, too, was the patron saint of Ireland and all who continue to promote his mental illness---all who continue to allow themselves to be imposed upon by a bunch of ignorant, lying SOB's whose intelligence is often exceeded by kindergarteners!

One wonders, too, if evil spirits are visible to the naked eye? ---can they be photographed? ---wouldn't the Gospel-tale writers have told us what they looked like after learning everything there is to know about evil spirits from merely asking their all-knowing Teacher, Jesus, about such things? How are evil spirits able to enter and exit bodies—is it through the mouth, the nose, or in and out of the kazoo---surely, the curious and inquisitive Gospel-tale writers would have asked Jesus about the fine details and important physical processes involved in the acquiring and the transferring of evil spirits---surely, they would not have failed to pass such information along to us had they known it!---surely, they would have told us the gender of evil spirits and how they propagate themselves to accommodate a growing world population---they would have told us if evil spirits come in different shapes and sizes---if they die or if they live on forever---surely, they would have told us the reason why God had created so many of them in the First Place! If the bodies of Adam and Eve contained evil spirits, why didn't God remove them and transfer them to the talking snake where they belonged?---so many unanswered questions! Because of the undeserved treatment Jesus imposed upon those thousands of scapegoats pigs that perished that day, it's no wonder why Jews abstain from eating pork---it's the curse!

One wonders, too, where these uber-evil, demons (boogeymen!) go on Judgment Day to spend their eternity? ---will they all go to Hell residing in the bodies of everyone they had possession of? ---surely, every Televangelist knows the inerrant and infallible answers to these reasonable questions! If, however, evil spirits are not visible to the naked eye, then no one was able to witness Jesus' miraculous removal and relocation of them---why then did the townspeople ask Jesus to leave the area when they could not have known with certainty that He was the cause of the lunatic's recovery and the cause of the flying-pig massacre? ---they could not have known that He had performed a miracle that day because no one would have been able to witness it! ---however, from inerrant and infallible *Bible*-evidence, we know, with certainty and with clarity, exactly what a mean-spirited, self-promoting Jesus had in mind to accomplish on that very revealing day!

Referring back to an All-Knowing Creator's amnesia concerning His creation of disease-causing microbes, ---evidently, divine-dementia is a difficult disease to diagnose in a deity, but, if one truly "believes" the words of Jesus, then His lapse of memory must have a demon-induced dimension as well---His lapse of divinity that supports evildoers confirms it---I believe the correct medical term for His condition is: "Devil-Brain"! Does anyone need further evidence or another light-bulb-moment to prove that Jesus Christ is just as ignorant as the geniuses who created Him? Shouldn't Jesus Christ have been able to tell us something about disease that only He, being God, would know? Instead, Dr. Genius would have us believe that there's a devil in your gall bladder causing all of your pain! ---really? On the other hand, I must admit my knowing it to be true that *Bible*-demons are constantly trying to get into our heads, our hearts, and up our asses (the obvious cause of hemorrhoids!) ---so "BEWARE," folks, "BEWARE"! If, however, you are one of the unfortunate many who are to be counted among the ***"fools and hypocrites"*** professing belief in the words of Jesus, please recommend to me a Christian practitioner, a Televangelist, who is good at performing devil removals (demon-ectomies!) ---one who will gladly accept my measly medical insurance because I have this pain in my be-deviled ass that just won't go away!

All kidding aside, the disease of Christianity and its never-ending obsession with gettin' the Devil outta folks has been the cause of more bodily torture (burnings, impalements, etc.), suffering, and death than anyone can imagine. Shouldn't every Jesus-believing, Jesus-following Televangelist avoid seeking the care of medical doctors who, obviously, are not able to remove demons? ---what uber-hypocrites these uber-Christians be! Isn't it time, we begin removing the very source of these true demonic woes from our bodies? *"Yes, Virginia, all of your monthly-reoccurring miseries are being caused by the comings and goings of IUD's: intra-uterine demons, who, thankfully, will eventually tire of their visits and will, in time, vacate the premises for good (menopause!). Why of course it's true, girl---what else could be causing them? ---read your Bible!"*

Primitive man was not able to understand the phenomenon of nature. Because of that misunderstanding, he filled the world with good and evil spirits. A combination of ignorance and fear led him to his conclusion. These two factors are the basic elements of all religions.

---James Hervey Johnson

It is hoped that Reason's Tribunal will be able to determine why the Pope and Mega-Church Moguls, along with genuflecting Gentiles everywhere—true believers all in the infallible and inerrant Gospels, do not beseech the Centers for Disease Control to implement, worldwide, the "undoubted" truth of the *Bible* and its God-given, God-proven method for removing the unclean spirits that are the singular cause of heart disease, cancer, diabetes, hemorrhoids, Covid 19, etc., etc., especially since exorcisms like those Jesus performed are, without doubt, completely safe, foolproof, and certainly "possible" for all Christians to do *"according to" John* 14:12.

Dispelling dirty demons to bring about a cure, following the example of God's infallible and inerrant Gospel-proven technique, would not require costly health insurance, surgeries, x-rays, MRI's, blood or lab work, medicines, therapies, or even a doctor's examination. Dispelling dirty demons would not require a visit to Vatican City or to the overworked Miracle-Dispensary at Lourdes---LOL! ---would not require Holy Water or religious relics, invocations and prayers to saints, or the lighting of candles in hopes of receiving a curative miracle. Dispelling dirty demons is a totally non-invasive technique that is 100% effective except against the unclean spirits that cause AIDS which, according to many fundamentalist, God-mind-reading Christians, is God's punishment for being a homosexual person—punishment, however, not meant for all homosexuals, but just for some of them! Dispelling dirty demons is a technique that does not require hospitalization, intensive-care recuperation, or any follow-up, and is not subject to any known adverse side effects except for the disbelief of educated and enlightened people: the beneficiaries of Reason's Tribunal!

How strange and interesting it is that folks who supposedly believe every word in the Gospels (including the Pope and the hordes of Holy-Hustlers who, of course, lead by their infallible, exemplary examples!) prefer to "worship and adore" Jesus rather than to "follow" Him---prefer to enlist the care of doctors and hospitals (like Mother Teresa did) and not the care of priests and churches for their demon-dislodging, health care needs. Hmm, Hmm, Hmm! Thomas Jefferson's assertion that Christians are always of two classes: *"fools and hypocrites,"* is well demonstrated by the fact that Christians say they believe (and want others to believe!) the blatantly ignorant and bogus claims of Jesus yet they refuse to rely on His "infallible" remedy for all that ails them—*"fools"* (for saying they believe the instructions of their "inerrant" Instructor) —*"hypocrites"* (for not following them)! Muslims, too, are *"fools"* for believing their hallowed, Koranic instructions, but they, at least, are not *"hypocrites"* when they strive to follow them by attempting to annihilate us—they are truly being devout followers of Allah and His every Word!

How strange and interesting, too, that the leaders of a supposed Christian nation will often credit advances in the medical profession and our knowledge of the cosmos through scientific study as being the work of "genius" while the Christian religion has so often opposed such progressive advances---preferring, instead, to prevent them from ever happening! It does not require genius, however, to ascertain why a functioning brain and Reason's Tribunal are perceived as threats to the accepted beliefs of Semitic religions and their knowledge-lacking Gods! Man help us—to cast out all of the disease-causing, destructive devils that reside within the deeply disturbed minds of all God-worshiping *"fools and hypocrites"* for, it is certain, that such devotees haven't sense enough to be ashamed of their debasing Christian dogmas!

(NOTE TO READER: as you are assuredly aware by now, Gods addiction to alliteration is alarmingly acute—please accept my apologies for all of the abounding literary abuses and assaults He had demanded of me to write down in this book! ---you try reasoning with this Guy! ---kvk)

Wake up, America! . . . Wake up and begin to question in Reason's Tribunal why a so- called, "example-setting-God" ordered us to "love" and "forgive" our enemies, yet He is happily content to mistreat and torture them without end! ---must be His special "loving" way of "doing unto others" . . . Wake up folks and begin to question in Reason's Tribunal why the Golden Rule is associated with the "Law of Moses" ---a guy who, according to the sacred words of the *Bible,* "did unto others" without any justifiable cause whatsoever until he and his God-goons had murdered, raped, and stolen the lands/possessions of countless, inoffensive, unprovoking neighbors---neighbors that Moses' "exemplary" and "adored" God commands us to L-O-V-E . . . Wake up folks and begin to question in Reason's Tribunal why someone in their right mind would be happily content to call themselves an avid believer, a genuflecting worshiper, and a loyal supporter of such a God and His promoters . . . Wake up and begin to question why religion is deemed so necessary and useful in our personal doings, yet, not so for the operations of our government which must take steps (often inadequate steps) to separate its doings from any religious influence . . . Wake up and just say "No!" to religion and stop enriching and rewarding its parasitic pushers and promoters . . . Wake up from your induced Judeo-Christian coma that has put rational thinking to sleep for millennia in order to stifle inquiry into its manufactured "mysteries" and into its manufactured "miracles" . . . Wake up from the mental stupor of religion-imposed ignorance and use the clarity of unencumbered intelligence to discern the realities, the ramifications, and the extrapolations of all Semitic religions . . . Wake up and realize that it is only because of uncontested belief in the Chutzpah Chronicles of Semitic religions that is responsible for generating the greater part of the most wicked human activity ever undertaken in recorded human history . . . Wake up and realize that the *Old Testament* God of the Jews (that is now worshiped and adored by Christians) despised everyone who was not a Jew, but don't take my word for it . . . Wake up and realize that the *Koran*-God of the Muslims despised everyone who was not a Muslim, but, again, don't take my word for it . . . Wake up from the unconscious, mental-default-setting that automatically defends the delusional and irrational tenets of your Semitic religion and dedicate yourself to discovering their deceptions so you can finally delete them from affecting your conscious day to day thinking . . . Wake up and learn, as Christians, that your belief in Jesus being the Son of God is the worst possible sin of all in Allah-Land, a crime known as "shirk" which every shirker must pay for with their lives according to the *Koran.*

Wake up and use your intellect to determine if your kindergarten fantasy about a Magic Kingdom where Adam and Eve encounter a Wizard of Oz-like disembodied voice, a talking, beguiling snake, miraculous trees whose fruit when eaten confers either the knowledge of good and evil or the gift of eternal life---is true or whether we've been imposed upon . . . Wake up and ascertain why none of the four Gospels existed before the latter half of the second century and why (except for a couple of obviously forged accounts) the dozens of Pagan and Jewish writers who lived during and immediately following the time Jesus is said to have existed are curiously silent about Him.

Wake up, America, and take note of the wickedness, cruelty, terror, and torment embedded in the Sunday-school, *Bible*-dogma imposed upon innocent minds, and the hypocrisy of every Christian and every Sunday-school teacher who possesses two shirts ... Wake up and wonder why the Vatican, home to Christ's #1 guy on earth, doesn't welcome or offer asylum, shelter, or comfort, within its vast expanses and its treasure-filled rooms, to the homeless, the diseased, the destitute, or the oppressed people of the world—not one, I repeat, "not one" of the many *"lost sheep"* and "loser dogs" in the world ever shares in the splendor or the security that the Pope is accustomed to living in ... Wake up and begin to cure yourselves of a Semitic disease that demands the adoration and praiseful worship of a Commandment-breaking Commander who seeks to impose eternal, agonized torment upon those who have merely "coveted" a neighbor's possessions or "doubted" the perfect nature of the *Koran* ... Wake up and realize that every religion is a cult---the only difference between the likes of Jim Jones and his faithful---David Koresh and his faithful---the Heaven's Gate guru and his faithful---and the rabid promoters of Judaism, Christianity, and Islam is merely in the number of their scripture-inspired members ... Wake up and realize that mere "imperfect" mortals have more compassion and mercy than the perfect, Hell-creating, torment-seeking Gods of Semitic religions ... Wake up and realize that the cunning God-makers (the script-writers of the *Bible* and the *Koran*) also fabricated the less-than-divine words they chose to have Him speak—words that would understandably favor their homies, God's "chosen," fatuous followers, with perks, privileges, and pretentious promises ... Wake up and admit that Moses the Murderer and Muhammad the Molester, had they lived in these times, would be convicted felons confined to prison cells for their crimes against innocent men, women, children, and animals ... Wake up and determine who the real benefactors and saviors of humanity are.

Wake up, America, and acknowledge the shameful, vengeful behavior of Jesus, the Godman, whom, we are told, in *Matt.* 2:2, was born to be King of the Jews and who supposedly endows everyone: Jews (sheep) and Gentiles (dogs) with the free-will to choose between good and evil but only demands virtuous behavior from His "chosen," not from Gentiles. He instructs His disciples not to minister to the Gentiles but to minister only to *"the lost sheep of the house of Israel."* He then creates a Heaven to reward a person's ethnicity, not their ethics, and a Hell to punish folks who don't believe in Him---*Matt.* 25:32,33,41 ... Wake up and admit that Jesus was a ***"hypocrite"*** for telling His disciples *"Be not afraid of them that kill the body"* ---*Luke* 12:4 when *"He would not walk in Jewry, because the Jews sought to kill him."* ---*John* 7:1 ... Wake up ye who are Gentiles and wonder how your entrance into Heaven will occur when there are only 12 gates there, one for each of the 12 tribes of the house of Israel to enter through---*Rev.* 21:12 ... Wake up ye who are Muslims and acknowledge the insanity of Allah, whom the *Koran* tells us, "wills" people to be disobedient than "wills" their deaths because of their disobedience ... Wake up folks and realize that there is no valid evidence (that would survive Reason's Tribunal) of communication between God and man ever having taken place, no valid evidence for believing in a "Promised Land" except what man has written in his own self-serving Word of God interests.

Wake up, America, to the reality that the bogus, scripture-based, chutzpah-laden traditions and glorified activities of a "God-chosen" people and their reprehensible heroes are steeped in terror and tribulation—David, the exalted and exemplary King of the Jews, was such a "religious" guy that his résumé touted his talents as an adulterer, a lecher, a thief, a murderer, and the first ethnic-cleansing Hitler-type to employ the use of brick ovens in his death-dealing activities which included sawing people apart and driving over them with chariots (it's hard to be more religious than that!) ... Wake up to the reality that the "revealed" and revered "Word" of the God of Jews and Christians is linked to the "revealed" and revered Word of Allah that is responsible for the religion-inspired nightmare of our times ... Wake up and learn why it is so important to challenge the "legitimacy" and the "authority" of the *Bible* and the *Koran* in hopes of insuring a peaceful future for our planet ... Wake up and learn why it is so important to debunk the *Bible* and the *Koran* and their pretentious spiritual claims if we are earnest in ridding the world of the scourge of Semitic theologies and the terror and tribulations that lay embedded in their pious pages that continue to "inspire" their believers to commit atrocity in the name of God ... Wake up and make a solemn, *Bible*-free oath to never again abandon or renounce your rational abilities, your decent, compassionate, justice-seeking nature, and your hard-won *"knowledge of good and evil"* or allow them to become subverted because of creed, cultural bias, coercion, or custom.

Wake up, America, so that we can ensure the ***"Blessings of Liberty"*** shall not perish from the earth even if Allah "wills" it, for Allah's will is not the will of any divine entity, it is but the will of manipulative, tyrannical men—a "human invention" ... Wake up to the certainty that religion is a pathogen—a pernicious virulence capable of destroying mankind---that continues to flare up time and again—a contagious disease for which we must now find a cure or succumb, eventually, to its ravages . . . Wake up so that we can begin to enlighten ourselves via our own personal and/or public court of critical and impartial examination conducted under the unbiased, fearless scrutiny of "Reason" and "Truth,": (Reason's Tribunal) --- so that, figuratively and literally, we can place Semitic religions, their bogus Gods, and their bogus "written words" on trial, at last, to be "revealed" as the frauds that they are and to be held accountable for the bloodshed they have caused in the past and for their present, less-than-sacred activities that continue to impose their dismal, malevolent dogmas, meant only to serve and benefit the selfish interests of a few and impede human progress for the many. Reason's Tribunal will unconditionally investigate all Semitic religions to uncover the ***"facts and evidence"*** that will result in exposing their diabolical, tyrannical doctrines, their ungodly, violent histories of wickedness, their cruel and unusual practices, their constant threat to world peace and to the survival of civilization.

Wake up and realize that Judaism, Christianity, and Islam are only able to survive through compulsion on their parts and compliance on ours, for their Gods are but created, scripted characters and their scriptures are but fabricated works of fiction—only the ignorance, pain, suffering, and death they cause are real . . . Wake up and begin removing the mental shackles of the imposed, contrived beliefs of Semitic religions that enslave us and darken our days.

Wake up, America, so we can begin to free ourselves from the bogus beliefs and diabolical dogmas of Judaism, Christianity, and Islam that require and inspire deadly devotion to their bogus words in the *Bible* and in the *Koran,* so that we can ***"begin the world over again,"*** creating a sane and safe future for mankind, a future free from the intimidating nightmares of burning eternally in a *"furnace of fire"* where the *"wailing and gnashing of teeth,"* of the endlessly tormented is all that is heard—a future free from the ever abusive doom and gloom continuum of Semitic religions and their ungodly endeavors!

We the freedom-blessed citizens of:

> *A new nation conceived in Liberty, and dedicated to the proposition that all men are created equal.*

A nation of men and women who resist being tread upon and who prefer to ***"live free or die"*** must heed and honor the wisdom and warnings of our secular-minded founding fathers dealing with the evils of Abrahamic religions. As Freedom-Lovers and Caretakers of Liberty, we must read *The Age of Reason*: Thomas Paine's profound last offering to his fellow-citizens, and other critical books on the subject of Semitic theology, in hopes of acquiring the skills and the tools that will enable us to begin the long-delayed, long-needed American Revolution *"in the system of religion."*

> *Fix reason firmly in her seat, and call to her tribunal every fact, every opinion. Question with boldness even the existence of a god; because, if there be one, he must more approve the homage of reason, than that of blindfolded fear. ...Do not be frightened from this inquiry by any fear of its consequences. ...we are not afraid to follow truth wherever it may lead, not to tolerate any error so long as reason is left free to combat it.*

---Thomas Jefferson

Success in our efforts to analyze and abolish religious tyranny will allow us to live, at last, in an "Age of Reason" . . . the long-overdue "Age" where the "Word" of all the Gods of Semitic religions, have, at last, been questioned with boldness and convicted of fraud and imposition in Reason's Tribunal . . . an Age where we allow "truth" to *"finally and powerfully prevail"* in such matters thus achieving its sacred, sane, and unfettered destiny to set us free—free, at last, from the murderous mindsets of prayer-mumbling robots and God-worshiping *"fools and hypocrites"* and their scripture-authorized madness . . . an "Age" where:

> *We hurl the truth against falsehood, and it knocks out its brain, and behold, falsehood doth perish!* (a real no-brainer! ---kvk)

---*Koran* 21:18

. . . an Age whose banner will *"finally and powerfully"* proclaim, at last, the enlightened legacy of truth-hurling Infidels:

IN REASON WE TRUST
IN TRUTH WE PREVAIL

Some Final Thoughts

Before I end my labors to complete this book, before I put down my hammer after nailing my last nail, I have some final thoughts to share with you, the readers of *Reason's Tribunal*:

"According to" Matthew 27:3-5, a suicidal Judas repented his betrayal of Jesus, returned the thirty pieces of silver to the chief priests and hung himself---(the official *Bible*-cause of Judas' Death #1). Surely, this death of Judas had to have been witnessed by *Matthew* because hearsay testimony is certainly not *Bible*-worthy---because hearsay testimony cannot possibly be inerrant and infallible! However, in *Acts* 1:18, we learn that an apparently non-suicidal Judas didn't return the money but, instead, he used it to purchase a field where he "fell to his death" (in a field!) causing his gut to burst and his insides to spill out---(the official *Bible*-cause of Judas' Death #2). Surely, the second death of Judas had to have been witnessed by the gushing, unknown author of *Acts* 1:18 because hearsay testimony is certainly not *Bible*-worthy---because hearsay testimony cannot possibly be inerrant and infallible! It is obvious, dear reader, that at least one of these two differing money-use and cause-of-death accounts cannot be true yet both contradictory, non-sensical accounts appear on the pages of the *Bible,* the inerrant and infallible, non-confusing, literal Word of God because it was He, the Perfect Communicator, who, we are made to believe, inspired unknown authors to write both "perfect" eyewitness accounts exactly as He wanted them written down!

Isn't it quite interesting, folks, that the *Bible's* script-writers always seem to be in the right place at the right time with pen in hand to make a *Bible*-worthy record of events even though they often disagree on time, place, and circumstance, and often come up short on revealing relevant details? Be assured folks that Judas neither returned nor spent his tarnished silver, nor did he perish as a result of a hanging or a projectile bowel movement---he passed away from the evidence produced by Reason's Tribunal's autopsy which disemboweled what God and His script-writers had wrought!

One would think that the remaining eleven disciples would have assembled together soon after Christ's ascension into the clouds of heaven in order to write down their eye-witness, ear-witness, first-hand accounts of His life's story for the purpose of having consensus and unity in their recollections about Him in order to *"Gather up the fragments* (of Christ's life: His teachings and His astounding abilities,) *that none be lost."* Wouldn't such an undertaking be the most likely and the most worthwhile endeavor for Jesus' disciples to undertake before embarking on distant journeys to reveal His uber-mighty works and His uber-mighty message to the world? Why did a century and a half pass after Jesus' passing before any of the Gospels made their dubious appearance? ---why were they written *"according to"* only four of Jesus' disciples---why were they not directly written by the very named disciples themselves? Shouldn't there have been eleven individual Gospels or, at least, one Gospel co-written by eleven authors shortly after the resurrection of Jesus?

Is it really believable that each remaining disciple, before meeting their end, would not have chronicled, in written form, their personal experiences with God and His glorious miracles---miracles that they had supposedly witnessed with their very own eyes? In the least, shouldn't they have left written record of their exclusive involvement with Jesus describing, in detail, the means that only they had knowledge of in order to save souls from the ever-impending, ever-expanding fires of Hell? ---what could have held greater importance than that for Jesus' hand-picked missionaries? Could it be possible that the disciples' enigmatic, lifelong silence about their supposed intimacies with God Almighty lies in the distinct possibility that there was nothing in their individual, personal histories with Him (in His Jesus Christ disguise) that was really worth recording for posterity? ---a silence that speaks volumes to us about the need for, and the existence of unknown script-writers to create and reveal the greatest fictional story ever told---a silence that speaks volumes about the unbelievable nature of the contrived Gospels and the non-existence of Jesus, the Miracle-Man!

Events that were worth recording in the Christian Chutzpah Chronicles such as *Matthew, Mark,* and *Luke's* tale about the transfiguration of Christ is, curiously, never mentioned by *John*, the only eyewitness and earwitness to this miracle among the above-named bogus authors. Hmm! Also, the death-defying drama of Lazarus coming *"forth"* from going dead four days earlier was surely witnessed by all of the disciples and, according to Lazarus' sister, his decomposing body was stinking up the sealed cave where he was entombed the day Jesus decided to pay him a lively visit---a stench that, incidentally, can still be detected in the *Bible* to this very day! ---yet, according to *Bible*-evidence, *John* is the only Gospel-tale author who was inspired enough to reveal this uber-spectacular miracle of Jesus! ---somebody certainly has some more "splaining" to do!

Shouldn't some historian have told us what became of stinking ol'

Lazarus or, at least, given us his final obituary? Shouldn't some historian have told us the cause of his second death as was done in the case of Judas? Surely, it is a matter of utmost interest, at least to me, to know how long a restored Lazarus remained amongst the living after God had cured his death and given him renewed life? Shouldn't gratitude for his incredible grave robbery have made Lazarus a devoted, dedicated follower of Almighty Jesus on the spot---a grateful follower who would never ever want to leave Jesus' side? ---a grateful follower who would unhesitantly defend Jesus with all of his might even if it meant losing his own life again? Think about it folks, had you, the reader, been the grateful recipient of Jesus' return-to-life miracle, would you have departed from such a Miracle-Man who had just defeated death for your exclusive benefit? Could it be possible that Lazarus, after having been returned to life, had more important obligations or some other interests that would have taken precedence over his being in the constant presence of someone who had just resurrected his dead ass? ---someone who had power over life and death? Where, therefore, was a grateful Lazarus when Jesus was being arrested? ---where was a grateful Lazarus when Jesus was being crucified? Shouldn't a grateful Lazarus, along with every witness to his miraculous recovery from death and return to life, been pleading with Pontius Pilate to convince him that a life-restoring-Jesus had to be none other than God Almighty Himself? Shouldn't a grateful, formerly deceased Lazarus, at least, have paid a visit to Jesus' tomb? ---really?

The Gospel script-writers who deceive us with guilt, with guile, and with lies so big that even the extension ladders of reason and truth have trouble reaching and toppling them, have used the detail-lacking Lazarus tale to great effect in their Chutzpah Chronicle accounts of Jesus, the Jewish fella they want us to believe is God, the supposed death-defying, Almighty Creator of the Universe! One wonders why Lazarus' world-changing return to life would not have been recorded by frenzied historians or any of the many startled Jews---*John* 11:45 who supposedly witnessed it with their own eyes? ---why such a world-changing event is revealed to us by a single, unknown author penning a couple of verses about it in a book known to be filled with obvious deceivings, hearsay evidence, and outright lies? Hmm! There's that smell again!

Could any fear of the Jewish authorities or even the fear of "dying" have possibly been a deterrent to Lazarus' becoming a martyr in the defense of the God/Man who suspended Nature's laws on his behalf? How long did Lazarus and the other folks revivified by Jesus survive between their return to life and their final deaths? ---was it days, weeks, months, years, lifetimes, or more? Could it be possible that these folks didn't die after all, after their receiving the sacred gift of life a second time from God Almighty Himself---for what power on earth could possibly have taken away the life-force that God, Himself, had restored to them with His miracles? ---or was it God's intention that the families of these folks should be made to grieve again over the second loss of their loved one?

Did any of these reanimated folks live lives of note or had they sprung to life again like many deceased saints supposedly had done upon the day of Jesus' death only to be seen meandering about without any purpose whatsoever days later---only to receive no further script-writers' attention even though the *Bible* tells us that they were seen by many strolling about in Jerusalem? ---really? Unfortunately, for *Bible*-heads, when the saints came marching in to town, there was not a pen-in-hand, *Bible*-witness around to tell us their "precise" number---Hmmmmm!

> *And the graves were opened; and many bodies of the saints which slept arose, and came out of the graves after His resurrection, and went into the holy city, and appeared unto many.*

> ---*Matthew* 27:50-53

> *They were polite enough to sit in their open graves and wait for Christ to rise first.*

> ---Robert G. Ingersoll

What was the reason, in *Matthew's* account, for the decomposing remains of *"many"* dead saints to suddenly spring back to life upon the death of Jesus and tunnel out of their graves to wander about aimlessly like zombies after His supposed resurrection? ---did they look like skeletal creatures in a horror movie? ---did they have any clothes or footwear on? ---if so, where did they acquire them? ---did they scare the hell out of everyone who saw them? ---did they eat or drink anything? ---did they have anything of uber-importance to tell the world? ---did they, sometime after the supposed ascension of Jesus, go back and re-occupy their graves or were they allowed to remain on the loose to this very day? ---miracle after astounding miracle after astounding miracle were seemingly wasted that day in an all-out, no-holds-barred effort to convince gullible folks of Jesus' divinity---miracle after astounding miracle after astounding miracle were seemingly wasted that day only to "impose" upon the lives of others, never to make "improvements" in them! ---but what would you expect from the script-writers of the *Bible* when lies and deception are the only tools in their tool kits---the only tools needed to build Semitic religions?

Why weren't the *Bible*'s script-writers filling in the blanks to the above logical questions with their inspired words and their inspired answers to that day's many puzzling, astounding events? ---why didn't they reveal to us the awesome, world-changing details of the many miracles it must have taken to get a mob of dead folks returned to life---miracles that gave them the ability to exit their graves and then, presumedly, make their gruesome appearances presentable for public viewing---get them de-wormed and maggot-free, deodorized, clothed, and able to walk around and then have them return to their former state of decay and decrepitude allowing them to safely tunnel back to their "final" resting places to resume their dust-to-dust disintegration right where they had left off? ---for surely, every miracle, no matter how seemingly insignificant or unbelievable it may appear to be, is still an astounding world-changing event after all! The *Bible*'s script-writers, it appears, had missed a great opportunity to tell us about the finer details of "all" of these lesser known, wondrous miracles that had to have occurred on the day of Jesus' death and on the day of His supposed resurrection---miracles that, if reported, would surely have added immensely to the glory of God. Hmm! Hmm! Hmm! Apparently, inspired liars know when to stop adding more relevant details that would only subtract from their inspired, conniving endeavors!

Isn't it obvious, folks---that the *Bible's* attempt to make people believe that the rotting remains of dead men actually "arose" from their death-disintegration upon the death of Jesus and thus were able to leave their graves and walk around here and there on the streets of Jerusalem immediately following the supposed resurrection of Jesus three days later---was merely a pious-ploy to convince the gullible that Jesus had to be none other than God Himself. Isn't it quite strange, however, that the *Bible* has nothing further to tell us about the fate of these world-shaking folks and their world-shaking walk-about? ---not a single word! Isn't it strange that *Matthew*, a witness to Lazarus' coming-out party is curiously mute, too, on the particulars of this uber-amazing event but not so when it comes to revealing the "precise" number of baskets of leftovers that were collected with care from meals eaten in the desert! Apparently, again, inspired liars know when to stop adding more relevant details that would only subtract from their inspired, conniving endeavors!

If delivery from death is not a reason for history's attention, what the hell is? Why was it so important for the *Bible's* script-writers to have God expound ad nauseum on the gruesome details and merits of ritual animal sacrifice, as revealed page after page in *Leviticus,* and then silence Him when it comes to expounding on the glorious details and resulting outcomes of religiously restoring life to the dead? Hmm! Hmm! Hmm! And, dear reader, have you ever wondered or concerned yourself about why it was so uber-important for God, in His sacred, *NT* Jesus-disguise, to command His followers to "love their enemies" and "turn the other cheek" to their assaults? ---commands, no doubt, that all Christians are so pleased and eager to comply with! ---LOL!

Evidently, it's not really that important for Christians to "follow" all of Jesus' commands as long as they continue to have "absolute belief" in Him and "unshakeable faith" in His "Word" ---as long as they can pick and choose which parts of the *Bible* are worthy of their belief---as long as they remember to merely call out the name of Jesus with their dying breath in order to gain their well-earned share of sky-pie! Jesus, however, in His sacred, *OT* Jehovah-disguise, uber-tormented (in a sacred, religious manner of course!) all Egyptians, His perceived enemies, and murdered their innocent firstborn! ---sound cheeky to you? At the same time, He even uber-tormented, with plagues and pestilence, all of His chosen people who were supposedly being held in bondage in Egypt---incredible! And, one wonders where, oh where, in the many beloved chapters and verses of the *Old Testament* are we to find just one example of its God ever having loved His enemies or ever having turned the other cheek to them? Where, oh where, in the many beloved chapters and verses of the *New Testament* are we to find just one example of its God ever having loved His enemies or ever having turned the other cheek to them? "Do as I say, not as I do"! Hmm! Hmm! Hmm! It all sounds a bit too cheeky to me!

Never forget, folks, that, according to the revered, chapter and verse perfection of the revered Chutzpah Chronicles, there were no survivors, I repeat, "no survivors" to the holocaust that completely exterminated, I repeat "completely exterminated" the Canaanites---never forget that the Canaanites were all victims of the anti-Canaanite mindset of their God-favored, God-obeying! Semitic neighbors---never forget that the Canaanites were all put to the sword because the holy *Bible* tells us that its holy God *"so loved the world"* ---the Jewish *"world,"* obviously! And, since we are to believe that *Bible*-evidence is completely "valid," it must of necessity be beyond any reproach---the supposed infallibility and inerrancy of the *Bible's* chapters and verses, therefore, is certain proof, at least to the Christian mindset, that the above four-word statement about God's love for everyone is the absolute truth because its supposed author, *John*, a guy who, according to "valid" *Bible*-evidence, lied to God's face and forsook Him (*Matthew* 26:35,56), would never tell us anything but the truth in *John* 3:16! ---LOL again! Never forget, too, that it only requires a very small hole in the right places to sink the infallible and inerrant, unsinkable vessel known as the "*SS Holey Bible*" ---therefore, the order has been given in this book, *Reason's Tribunal,* to abandon the above leaking and foundering ship now or go down with it!

Have you ever wondered or concerned yourself, too, about why God, in His favoring of Jews and Jews only, annihilated, I repeat, "annihilated" entire nations of unoffending, I repeat, "unoffending" Canaanite men, women, children, and animals without cause, but not the one and only, I repeat, "not the one and only" "Jew-persecuting" Egyptian Pharaoh? ---a person whom a sick-minded God had willfully caused, I repeat, "had willfully caused" to act in the sick-minded way the *Bible* reveals his God-imposed pathology---surely, the imposed-upon Pharaoh was a person who could not have behaved in any other way than God had caused him to behave---surely, he was a person who could have been easily exterminated for his mistreatment of Jews if only God's chosen tormentors of "all" Egyptians, Moses and Aaron, had thought to recharge the battery in their magic wand, raise it high into the air, and "VOILA"! ---now what could be more religious (more sick-minded) than that? ---tormenting, killing, and exterminating the innocent in the name of an example-setting, sick-minded deity so that *"Thy will* (tormenting, killing, exterminating the innocent) *be done on earth as it is in Heaven"* ---that should make the Heaven-bound think twice before packing their bags and boarding the bus! ---and for all of God's "willed" terrorist activities conducted here on earth (tormenting, killing, exterminating the innocent) we do so love Him---He that *"so loved the world"*! ---sick stuff, folks, ---really sick stuff!

And, just think about it dear reader, since it was the *Bible*-God who was the *Bible*-confirmed cause of the Pharaoh's cruel stubbornness, wouldn't that make the *Bible*-God the one, the only one, responsible, according to American justice, for the captivity and mistreatment of His very own chosen people? ---yes, it would! ---how sick is this Guy? Surely, God would not have caused the captivity and mistreatment of His favorite people and added to their sufferings and their miseries with a magic wand assault on all who lived in Egypt if they hadn't deserved it---right?---what's wrong with this picture?---a picture that has been produced from "valid" *Bible*-evidence---evidence that reveals just a few of the vile things that are ever the hallmarks of all Semitic religions---religions which, of necessity, required their God to always remain in hiding behind a cloud---religions which must now find a new place in the sky above in order to conceal His dreaded physical appearance---a physical appearance that, according to the *Bible's* script writers, if seen, causes instant death to all who attempt to get a mere glimpse of Him---a slick way for power-lacking, power-seeking, script-writing priests to impose upon the fears of other knowledge-lacking folks in order to intimidate them and prevent their curiosities from wanting to investigate the very existence of their bogus God for they had learned, like all of their kindred deceivers had learned, that whomever is in control of God, is in control of all! ---slick---very slick!

That's the business model of all pious parasites and what success they've achieved with it! However, the ignorant, paleo-minded script-writers of the *Bible,* who had an obvious need to prevent investigation into their bogus claims, could not conceive of or envision the existence of man or machine ever being able to fly above the clouds to see, with absolute certainty, what truly exists behind them---clouds that now, because of religion-stifled, scientific achievements that include satellite imagery, can no longer be used as a place of concealment for the scripted God of scripted Semitic scriptures---a God who, of necessity, will always be obliged to remain out of sight---will always have need for an object to hide behind in order to conceal His bogus, physical identity and allow for Him to continue indulging in His favorite pastimes without having to show His ugly face--- pastimes that "valid" *Bible*-evidence reveals as the tormenting, killing, exterminating the innocent, destroying the planet, playing Hide-n-Seek from behind clouds and bushes, savoring the smell of burnt flesh, and His favorite of favorites---favoring the Jewish world without any concern for the fate and the welfare of anyone or anything else!

Where, oh where, is the God of Judaism (and Christianity!) hiding now? Where has He gone after being so intimately and personally involved with His uber-favorite folks day after day after day after day, being so dedicated as He was, to advancing their racial ambitions and their supremacist agendas? Why has God stopped taking time out of His very busy, Universe-operating-schedule to provide for them and only them with measures and miracles that only He can provide? It appears to me that because of His continuing, inexplicable absence everywhere around the world, God has finally thrown in the towel---how 'bout you? *"Yes, Virginia, as you clearly know from each disciple's behavior, "abandonment" is just another hallmark of Semitic religions"!*

If I were He, I'd surely want to vacate the premises and remain in hiding, too! If I were He who *"so loved the world,"* I would not have wasted miracles impressing certain others with my uber-abilities to turn mere water into moonshine---something that the disciples must have been able to do because Jesus had given them the power (*Matthew* 10:1) to perform miracles (with their magic wands, perhaps?) which, incidentally, might explain the delirium of the (heavy drinking?) disciples who "witnessed" Jesus walk on water, create instant foods, awaken the dead, etc., etc.! (man, that must have been some real fine wine!). I, if given the power of God, would have, instead, eliminated everything that caused the sufferings, the sorrows, and the deaths of every living thing on the planet---but I'm not a sacred, "world-loving," Semitic God who has these abilities and, unfortunately, I don't possess a magic wand! Fortunately, however, because of every Televangelist's close, personal relationship and connection with Him, we are able to learn from them with certainty where God is presently concealing Himself and how He is occupying every minute of His time in absentia---how blessed are we to have such folks in our midst---how blessed are we to be able to support these pious, *"Praise the Lord"* parasites with every penny we have so that they can continue living their carnal-denying---LOL, sin-free---LOL, exemplary---LOL, Christian lives in splendor---so that we can continue to know, with certainty, what God is thinking and wanting us to do day after day after day---how blessed are we!

Personally, I am so thankful that Reason's Tribunal has given me the ability to see this Semitic God-impostor as he really is---a phantom deity whom I now realize is not such a big deal after all---he's not anyone special---in fact, he's nothing at all, I repeat, "he's nothing at all"! May you, the reader, come to a similar realization---may you also think, now and again, about where we would all be without the certainty of vast numbers of people thinking that a Semitic God is always there for believers---always there on their privileged side only, to guide them, protect them, and provide for their personal welfare.

Where would we all be without His constant dedication to running the entire Universe for His believers' exclusive benefit---where would we all be without His divine justice that punishes the innocent instead of the guilty and metes out eternal bliss to the few and never-ending torment to the many---where would we all be without His believers being able to experience the warm fuzzies of knowing they are constantly receiving God's never-ending love, attention, and sacred blessings---where would we all be without half the world having unquestioned belief in His perfect Word, the *Bible* and the *Koran*---books that continue to inspire the unquestioning hearts and minds of terrorists, lunatics, supremacists, and "fair and balanced" Fox News journalists whose conservatism is proud to promote the God of the *Old* and *New Testaments*---where would we all be without having Jehovah to care for Jews, without having Jesus to care for Christians, without having Allah to care for Muslims---where would we all be without this mighty, immutable, three-in-one, Semitic God to rely on to run our individual nations' affairs and to further all of our righteous self-interests with the absolute certainty that all unenlightened Americans continue to boast of: that of America being *"one nation under God"* and that it is only *"in* (this) *God we trust"* ---where would we all be without our beloved Semitic religions that are all firmly rooted in the phobic, barbaric past where superstitious, ignorant, thunder and lightning-cowering paleo-minded people built sacrificial altars to indulge regularly in their "sacred," God-commanded, God-instructed bloody rituals of murder, mutilation, and cremation in order to please Him and receive His uber-generous attention? (While on the subject of paleo-minded folks---why do supposedly educated (but not enlightened!) folks in this day and age such as televangelists and other *Bible*-thumpers still preach that hurricanes, tornadoes, earthquakes, and floods, etc., are often the work of a wrathful God taking revenge on sinners? ---I suppose it might have something to do with the ability to intimidate and manipulate the weaker-minded among us for the purposes of ***"power and revenue"***! ---otherwise, what purpose would it serve?)

These things---the above murder-rituals, the mutilations and cremations---were uber-indulged in by God's "chosen people" for the sole purpose of their wanting to please the obsessive, carnal nature of their beloved *Bible*-God by obeying His "Word" that revealed His surgically-precise instructions for slaughtering and dismembering the bodies of sentient beings, sprinkling their blood in a ritual manner, and roasting their remains for the sheer delight the aroma of their barbecued flesh provides Him---for there is little that God enjoys more than His being able to smell the *"sweet savor"* of butchered, burnt bodies arising to His nostrils and, as everyone knows, making God happy is much, much better than pissing Him off and, oy vey, it only requires the use of a wood-fired grill---such a deal! In dutiful performance of these sacred ceremonies, the *Bible* proudly tells us, that God's favorite people, the founders of all Semitic religions, had uber-succeeded in uber-pleasing and uber-satisfying the lusting, carnal desires of their beloved sin-absolving, brutal-minded, bloodshedding, flesh-burning, smell of roasted-meat-enjoying, multi-personality, trifle-obsessing, world-destroying, uber-pathological Creator of the Universe who always rewards His faithful abundantly for their insentient activities for surely, if one offers the mere pittance of a *"sweet savor"* unto the Lord, shouldn't one expect to get the world in return? ---of course one should! ---such a deal! ---Welcome, folks, to Judaism! ---Welcome to Christianity! ---Welcome to Islam---the Semitic religions whose followers offer mere pittances to God and expect the world in return---the Semitic religions whose followers proudly worship and promote the very same deeply disturbed deity in their very own deeply disturbed, pious ways! Just think, dear reader, where the hell we would all be without Semitic religions and their "sacred," God-endearing, hate-generating endeavors! Just imagine what the world would be like for everyone without such malevolent, parasitic institutions---a world where there is *"no hell below us---above us only sky"* with no clouds to hide behind! Just imagine, folks, what the world would be like!

Thanks to the bold efforts of Thomas Paine, Thomas Jefferson, and many many other Freedom-Loving Infidels and Caretakers of Liberty throughout the religion-oppressed centuries of history, truth now has a chance to ***"finally and powerfully prevail."*** Surely, the time has ***"finally"*** come to give Judas, Lazarus, and all the other foul-smelling, bogus *Bible*-tales a decent burial once and for all time. ***"We the people"*** (every man, woman, and child) should, therefore, all be grateful and give thanks to Reason's Tribunal for revealing the fraudulent foundations of the less-than-sacred Semitic religions: Judaism, Christianity, and Islam so that we, in this more knowledgeable, less paleo-minded, less barbaric age of reason, understanding, and enlightenment can begin to end their tormenting, theistic tyrannies and turn their despicable, dirty deceivings, their despicable, dirty dealings, and their despicable, dirty divinities back into the dirty dust from which they all emerged, so that "everyone" (emphasis on "everyone") can enjoy their ***"Life,"*** their ***"Liberty,"*** and their ***"pursuit of Happiness"*** ---so that "everyone" (emphasis on "everyone") can live *"free at last"* (emphasis on *"free at last"!*)

. . . .

"Yes, Virginia---Semitic Gods do not exist, but don't take my word for it---so remember to always wash your hands after handling the Bible, after handling the Koran, and continue to drink heartily your fill of Liberty's lemonade, the blessed beverage that has the amazing ability to expose God's Word in order to end the nightmare of Semitic religions! ---Cheers!" ---kvk

A FINAL NOTE TO READER: Remember the Canaanites---remember that God-loving people were acting under God's orders and blessings when they, with joy in their hearts, exterminated the Canaanites! Remember the Inquisition---remember that God-loving people were acting under God's orders and blessings when they, with joy in their hearts, tortured and burnt countless others to death! Remember 9/11---remember that God-loving people were acting under God's orders and blessings when they, with joy in their hearts, carried out the atrocities of that day! Remember, too, that there is a way to prevent the recurring horrors and tribulations of "us" and "them" Semitic religions from ever happening again. Man help us! Man help us!

Kevin Vincent Kelly
Puttin' the hammer down!

www.ingramcontent.com/pod-product-compliance
Lightning Source LLC
Chambersburg PA
CBHW032039050726

47590CB00001B/53